MANAGING FRONT OFFICE OPERATIONS

Educational Institute Books

HOSPITALITY FOR SALE
C. DeWitt Coffman

UNIFORM SYSTEM OF ACCOUNTS AND EXPENSE DICTIONARY FOR SMALL HOTELS, MOTELS, AND MOTOR HOTELS
Fourth Edition

RESORT DEVELOPMENT AND MANAGEMENT
Second Edition
Chuck Y. Gee

PLANNING AND CONTROL FOR FOOD AND BEVERAGE OPERATIONS
Second Edition
Jack D. Ninemeier

STRATEGIC MARKETING PLANNING IN THE HOSPITALITY INDUSTRY: A BOOK OF READINGS
Edited by Robert L. Blomstrom

TRAINING FOR THE HOSPITALITY INDUSTRY
Second Edition
Lewis C. Forrest, Jr.

UNDERSTANDING HOSPITALITY LAW
Second Edition
Jack P. Jefferies

SUPERVISION IN THE HOSPITALITY INDUSTRY
John P. Daschler/Jack D. Ninemeier

SANITATION MANAGEMENT: STRATEGIES FOR SUCCESS
Ronald F. Cichy

ENERGY AND WATER RESOURCE MANAGEMENT
Second Edition
Robert E. Aulbach

PRINCIPLES OF FOOD AND BEVERAGE OPERATIONS
Jack D. Ninemeier

MANAGING FRONT OFFICE OPERATIONS
Second Edition
Charles E. Steadmon/Michael L. Kasavana

STRATEGIC HOTEL/MOTEL MARKETING
Revised Edition
Christopher W.L. Hart/David A. Troy

MANAGING SERVICE IN FOOD AND BEVERAGE OPERATIONS
Anthony M. Rey/Ferdinand Wieland

THE LODGING AND FOOD SERVICE INDUSTRY
Second Edition
Gerald W. Lattin

SECURITY AND LOSS PREVENTION MANAGEMENT
Raymond C. Ellis, Jr., & the Security Committee of AH&MA

HOSPITALITY INDUSTRY MANAGERIAL ACCOUNTING
Raymond S. Schmidgall

PURCHASING FOR HOSPITALITY OPERATIONS
William B. Virts

THE ART AND SCIENCE OF HOSPITALITY MANAGEMENT
Jerome J. Vallen/James R. Abbey

MANAGING COMPUTERS IN THE HOSPITALITY INDUSTRY
Michael L. Kasavana/John J. Cahill

MANAGING HOSPITALITY ENGINEERING SYSTEMS
Michael H. Redlin/David M. Stipanuk

UNDERSTANDING HOSPITALITY ACCOUNTING I
Raymond Cote

UNDERSTANDING HOSPITALITY ACCOUNTING II
Raymond Cote

MANAGING QUALITY SERVICES
Stephen J. Shriver

MANAGING CONVENTIONS AND GROUP BUSINESS
Leonard H. Hoyle/David C. Dorf/Thomas J.A. Jones

HOSPITALITY SALES AND ADVERTISING
James R. Abbey

MANAGING HUMAN RESOURCES IN THE HOSPITALITY INDUSTRY
David Wheelhouse

MANAGING HOUSEKEEPING OPERATIONS
Margaret M. Kappa/Aleta Nitschke/Patricia B. Schappert

CONVENTION SALES: A BOOK OF READINGS
Edited by Margaret Shaw

MANAGING FRONT OFFICE OPERATIONS

Second Edition

Charles E. Steadmon, CHA
Michael L. Kasavana, Ph.D.

EDUCATIONAL INSTITUTE
of the American Hotel & Motel Association

Disclaimer

The authors, Charles E. Steadmon and Michael L. Kasavana, are solely responsible for the contents of this publication. All views expressed herein are solely those of the authors and do not necessarily reflect the views of the Educational Institute of the American Hotel & Motel Association (the Institute) or the American Hotel & Motel Association (AH&MA). Nothing contained in this publication shall constitute an endorsement by the Institute or AH&MA of any information, opinion, procedure, or product mentioned, and the Institute and AH&MA disclaim any liability with respect to the use of any such information, procedure, or product, or reliance thereon.

Neither AH&MA nor the Institute makes or recommends industry standards. Nothing in this publication shall be construed as a recommendation by the Institute or AH&MA to be adopted by, or binding upon, any member of the hospitality industry.

© Copyright 1988
By the EDUCATIONAL INSTITUTE of the
AMERICAN HOTEL & MOTEL ASSOCIATION
1407 South Harrison Road
P.O. Box 1240
East Lansing, Michigan 48826

The Educational Institute of the American
Hotel & Motel Association is a nonprofit
educational foundation.

Printed in the United States of America
    5 6 7 8 9 10 93 92 91 90

Library of Congress Cataloging-in-Publication Data
Steadmon, Charles E.
Managing front office operations.

Includes bibliographies and index.
1. Hotel management. 2. Motel management.
I. Kasavana, Michael L., 1947- . II. Title.
TX911.3.M27S7 1988   647'.94'068   88-21514
ISBN 0-86612-041-6

Editors: Timothy J. Eaton
          Matthew O. Rowe

Contents

Preface ix

Part I
The World of Hotels

1 **The Lodging Industry** **3**

The Hospitality Industry 3
Hotel Size 4
Hotel Target Markets 5
Levels of Service 11
Ownership and Affiliation 15
Reasons for Traveling 18
Discussion Questions 22

2 **Hotel Organization and the Front Office** **25**

Organizational Planning 25
Hotel Organization 27
Front Office Operations 35
Front Office Personnel 39
The Importance of Teamwork 43
Discussion Questions 44

3 **Front Office Operations** **45**

The Guest Cycle 45
Front Office Systems 52
Front Office Forms 55
The Front Desk 57
Front Office Equipment 58
Front Office Computer Applications 68
Discussion Questions 72

Part II
The Guest Cycle

4   Reservations **77**

    Types of Reservations 78
    Reservation Inquiry 79
    Reservation Availability 84
    The Reservation Record 88
    Reservation Confirmation 90
    Reservation Maintenance 92
    Reservation Reports 94
    Other Topics 96
    Discussion Questions 101

5   Registration **103**

    Pre-Registration Activity 103
    The Registration Record 104
    Room and Rate Assignment 106
    Method of Payment 113
    Issuing the Key 117
    Creative Options 117
    Selling the Guestroom 119
    When Guests Cannot Be Accommodated 120
    Discussion Questions 123
    Supplemental Reading: Upselling Rooms 125

6   Ongoing Front Office Responsibilities **129**

    Communications within the Front Office 129
    Interdepartmental Communications 130
    Guest Services 133
    Guest Relations 137
    Front Office Security Functions 140
    Discussion Questions 151

7   Front Office Accounting **153**

    Accounting Fundamentals 153
    Creation and Maintenance of Accounts 158
    Tracking Transactions 161
    Internal Control 164
    Settlement of Accounts 169
    Discussion Questions 170

8   The Night Audit **171**

    Functions of the Audit 171
    Operating Modes 174
    The Audit Process 178

Automated System Update 185
Discussion Questions 188

9 Check-Out and Settlement **189**

Functions of Check-Out and Settlement 189
Departure Procedures 191
Late Charges 193
Billing and Collection 194
Front Office Records 197
Discussion Questions 200

Part III

Front Office Management

10 Planning and Evaluating Front Office Operations **203**

Management Functions 203
Establishing Room Rates 206
Forecasting Room Availability 208
Budgeting for Operations 215
Evaluating Front Office Operations 219
Discussion Questions 234

11 Managing Front Office Personnel **235**

Recruiting and Selecting Employees 235
The Orientation Process 243
Training 246
Training to Standards 250
Discussion Questions 258

Conclusion: The Challenge Ahead **259**

Hotels of the Future 259
Front Office Employment 261
Career Paths for Front Office Employees 264
Professional Enrichment 267
Personal Satisfaction 267

Appendix: Anatomy of Computer Systems **271**

Data Processing 271
Electronic Data Processing 272
Types of Computers 273
Computer Hardware 274
Input/Output Units 275
The Central Processing Unit 277
External Storage Devices 277
Hardware Configurations 278

Computer Software 280
Applications Software 280
Word Processing Software 281
Electronic Spreadsheet Software 282
Database Management Software 283
Applications Software and User Concerns 284
Systems Software 285
Information Backup Procedures 286
Human Factors 288

Glossary **291**

Index **309**

The Educational Institute Board of Trustees **315**

Preface

From the time guests make reservations and arrive at a property through the time they depart, front office personnel play a central role in meeting their needs. To guests, the front office frequently *is* the hotel. Guests turn to the front office with questions, requests, comments, and complaints. The front office that effectively meets these challenges helps the hotel satisfy its guests. While poorly trained front office employees can antagonize guests and virtually drive them away, a capable, courteous, and professional front office staff can start each guest's stay off pleasantly and properly and see that it remains pleasant. In so doing, front office personnel not only meet the needs of their guests, they also help to ensure the smooth and profitable operation of the hotel. This is no small task.

This second edition of *Managing Front Office Operations* will help you—whether you are a front office manager or staff member or a hospitality student—to understand, organize, perform, and evaluate the front office functions so critical to the success of a hotel. It details information about virtually all aspects of front office operations and management. In addition to preserving the strengths of the first edition, this new edition incorporates several improvements. It expands on the discussion of front office management. Because of the tremendous growth of computer applications in the hotel industry, front office automation is now discussed throughout the text; also, the Appendix presents an introduction to computers that even those who are confused or terrified by computers should find useful. For the student, discussion questions appear at the end of each chapter and key words are highlighted in bold type. An expanded Glossary places definitions of industry terms at your fingertips.

We have also reorganized the book somewhat and this calls for some explanation. The book is now divided into three parts. **Part I: The World of Hotels** (comprising chapters 1 through 3) introduces the attractions and challenges of the hospitality industry, while putting front office operations within the context of hotel operations and the hospitality industry as a whole.

Part II: The Guest Cycle is an in-depth discussion of front office responsibilities which emphasizes the sequence of front office tasks during the guest stay. Chapters 4, 5, and 6 focus on guest services, including reservations, registration, and ongoing front office responsibilities. Chapters 7, 8, and 9 focus on front office accounting, including charge postings, the night audit, and check-out and settlement. In these chapters, current front office employees and students of the hospitality industry can learn the techniques and skills they need to perform efficiently in front office positions.

Part III: Front Office Management provides managers with the insight and management tools needed to more effectively manage the front office. Chapter 10 emphasizes specific management tasks and tools in relation to the planning and evaluation of front office operations. Chapter 11 focuses on several aspects of personnel management, including recruiting, orientation, and training.

We hope these revisions and improvements will provide every reader of this text with a clear and systematic view of front office operations and management.

Textbooks of this scope are never produced without the help of a great many people. We would like to extend special thanks to several industry professionals: Phil Lange, General Manager, Quality Inn Terrace Club Inn, Grand Rapids, Michigan; Pat McCrea, Manager of Front Office Operations, Westin Hotels and Resorts, Seattle, Washington; Aleta Nitschke, Corporate Director of Rooms, Radisson Hotel Corporation, Minneapolis, Minnesota; Rick Stanfield, Executive Assistant Manager, Opryland Hotel, Nashville, Tennessee; Charles L. Eudy, Vice President, Marketing, I.P.C.S., Phoenix, Arizona; and Susan Lawrence, Front Office Manager, Marriott Hotel Resort, Fort Collins, Colorado. Their years of hospitality industry knowledge and experience provided both additional technical information and the broad overview essential to this book. In addition, we would like to thank Raymond S. Schmidgall, Professor, School of Hotel, Restaurant, and Institutional Management, Michigan State University, for his helpful comments on chapters 7 through 10.

Charles E. Steadmon, CHA
National Hospitality Associates, Inc.
Phoenix, Arizona

Michael L. Kasavana, Ph.D.
Professor
School of Hotel, Restaurant, and Institutional Management
Michigan State University
East Lansing, Michigan

Part I

The World of Hotels

1 The Lodging Industry

Hotels treat their customers as guests and strive to provide a spirit of hospitality that exceeds their guests' expectations. Ellsworth M. Statler is credited with the slogan, "The guest is *always* right," and many would agree wholeheartedly.[1] An anonymous source later countered by saying, "The guest is *not* always right, but he is always the guest." Therein lies the ultimate challenge to the lodging industry professional: providing a level of guest service that meets the ever-changing needs and demands of guests.

Front office staff members are typically the first hotel employees to interact with the guests. Each guest who appears at a front desk has different needs, wants, and expectations, and the front office is where satisfying the guest begins. The front office staff must be able to perform registration functions, maintain guest accounts, facilitate the check-out process, and serve as an information resource for guests and visitors. The variety of talents and skills required make front office work both interesting and rewarding. The work is exciting because no two days, or two hotels, are ever the same.

The attraction and glamour of the hospitality industry can be attributed to various elements. For example, all hotels choose an image they wish to project. This is done in part with architecture and design. Yet, no matter how effective the design may be, the building is really only bricks, mortar, steel, glass, and furnishings. The architecture and style of the property may be important in establishing its theme, but it is the hotel's staff—and its front office staff in particular—that is essential to the creation of its ambience.

Hotels may play an important part in a community. Prominent civic clubs, business groups, and local and national companies may meet in hotels. Organizations are attracted to communities with high-quality lodging facilities. A hotel can serve as a central gathering place for an entire community.

The Hospitality Industry

The hospitality industry is part of a larger enterprise known as the travel and tourism industry. The travel and tourism industry is a vast group of businesses with one thing in common: providing necessary or desired products and services to the traveler. It is one of the largest industries in the world. Travel and tourism includes everything which arises from the interaction of people who travel and the businesses, governments, and people with whom they come in contact.

The travel and tourism industry can be divided into five parts. The hospitality industry comprises the lodging and food and beverage operations highlighted in Exhibit 1.1, along with institutional food and beverage services, which do not cater to the traveling public. Lodging operations are unique in that they offer their guests overnight accommodations. Most properties also provide food and beverage service, recreational activities, and more.

Defining the Term *Hotel*

One frequently raised question concerns the differences between such typical lodging properties as hotels, motels, motor hotels, and inns. The fact is that the distinctions are not always clear. Add to this the fact that the owner of a property may choose any title he or she desires for that establishment and it becomes apparent why universally agreed-upon definitions are hard to create. Still, despite the numerous exceptions, there are some widely accepted general distinctions.

A hotel or inn may be defined as an establishment whose primary business is providing lodging facilities for the general public and which furnishes one or more of the following services: food and beverage service, room attendant service, uniformed service, laundering of linens, and use of furniture and fixtures.

A motel or motor hotel is a lodging facility that caters primarily to guests arriving by automobile; motels often provide automobile parking near the guestrooms. Motels may be located in any setting, but are usually found in suburban or roadside areas. Many motels are two-story or low-rise buildings located near major highways. Motels often have pool areas with shrubbery, trees, and children's playgrounds.

Throughout this text, the term **hotel** should, unless otherwise indicated, be understood as a general term meant to include motels, motor hotels, inns, suite hotels, conference centers, and so forth.

Hotel Classifications

Classifying hotels into categories is not easy. Since the industry is so diverse, many hotels do not fit into any single well-defined category. Nonetheless, there are several general classifications. The categories discussed in this chapter are based on hotel size, target market, levels of service, and ownership/affiliation. It is important to note that a particular property may overlap several categories.

Hotel Size

One common way to categorize hotels is on the basis of size—the number of guestrooms in the property. For example, the accounting firm of Laventhol & Horwath, in its annual report on lodging operations, groups hotel properties into four size categories: under 150 rooms, 150 to 299 rooms, 300 to 600 rooms, and over 600 rooms. These classifications enable hotels of similar size to compare operational and statistical results

Exhibit 1.1 Overview of the Travel and Tourism Industry

Travel and Tourism Industry				
Lodging Operations	**Transportation Services**	**Food and Beverage Operations**	**Retail Stores**	**Activities**
Hotels	Ships	Restaurants	Gift Shops	Recreation
Motels	Airplanes	Lodging Properties	Souvenir Shops	Business
Motor Hotels	Autos	Retail Stores	Arts/Crafts Shops	Entertainment
Resorts	Buses	Vending	Shopping Malls	Meetings
Camps	Trains	Catering	Markets	Study Trips
Parks	Bikes	Snack Bars	Miscellaneous Stores	Sporting Events
Pensions	Limousines	Cruise Ships		Ethnic Festivals
Motor Homes		Bars/Taverns		Art Festivals
				Cultural Events
				Seasonal Festivals

within an industry segment. Unless noted otherwise, hotels in the classifications discussed in the remainder of this chapter may be of any size.

Hotel Target Markets

There are many types of markets targeted by hotels. The most common forms of target market properties include commercial, airport, suite, residential, resort, bed and breakfast, time-share, casinos, and conference center hotels. There are also several alternative entities which compete directly with hotels.

Commercial Hotels

A commercial hotel is a property that caters primarily to business clients. Commercial hotels are usually located in downtown or business districts. Although the primary objective of commercial hotels is to serve business travelers, many tour groups, individual tourists, and small conference groups also find these hotels attractive. In the past, commercial hotels were referred to as transient hotels. This term was used to describe the relatively temporary nature of their guests' stays, in comparison to other hotel types. The commercial hotel category contains the largest number of hotels.

Guest amenities in some properties include free newspapers, morning coffee, local telephone calls, and cable television. In addition, car

Swimming pools are a popular attraction in many types of properties. (Courtesy of Best Western Midway Motor Lodge, Grand Rapids, Michigan.)

rental arrangements, airport pick-up services, coffee shops, and semi-formal dining rooms and cocktail lounges may be provided. Most commercial hotels have a number of conference rooms and guestroom suites available; banquet meal service may also be available. In a commercial hotel, laundry-valet service, uniformed service, concierge service, retail stores, and gift shops may often be found. Swimming pools, health clubs, saunas, and jogging areas may also be located on the premises.

Airport Hotels   Airport hotels are popular because of their proximity to major travel centers. More than any other hotel type, airport hotels vary widely in size and service level. Typical markets for these hotels include business clientele, airline passengers with overnight layovers or canceled flights, and airline personnel. Hotel-owned limousines or courtesy vans are used to transport guests to and from the airport. Signs which announce direct telephone service to nearby hotels for reservations and pick-up service are common in most airports. Many airport hotels offer conference rooms

Suite hotels may appeal to vacationing or relocating families. (Courtesy of Radisson Suite Resort, Marco Island, Florida.)

for guests who wish to arrive at and leave meetings by air with as little travel as possible. The cost savings and convenience which may arise from this arrangement can be significant.

Suite Hotels   Suite hotels are the fastest-growing segment of the lodging industry. Suite hotel accommodations feature guestrooms with separate bedroom and living room or parlor areas. Some guest suites include a compact kitchenette with refrigerator and wet bar. In exchange for more complete living quarters, suite hotels generally offer less public space and fewer guest services than other hotel types in order to remain price competitive.

Suite hotels appeal to several different market segments. They may provide temporary living quarters for people who are relocating, serve as "homes-away-from-home" for frequent travelers, or appeal to families interested in non-standard hotel accommodations. Professionals such as accountants, lawyers, and executives find suite hotels particularly attractive since they can work or entertain in an area which is separate from the bedroom. Some suite hotels invite guests to a complimentary evening reception and/or offer complimentary breakfast service. Such gatherings offer guests an opportunity to socialize, which may be an important dimension for guests who are staying for extended periods.

Residential Hotels

Although residential hotels still exist, they are not nearly as prevalent as they once were. At one time, residential hotels were quite common. The layout of a residential guest unit may closely resemble that of a suite hotel. Guest quarters generally include a sitting room, bedroom, and small kitchenette. People who contract to live in residential hotels may, depending on the case, be considered tenants by law.[2] Residents may choose to contract for some or all of the services provided to guests in a commercial hotel. A residential hotel may provide daily housekeeping service, telephone service, a front desk, and uniformed service. A restaurant and lounge may also be located on the premises.

Many types of hotels directed primarily at other markets also house semi-permanent or permanent guests. Likewise, residential hotels may also offer short-term (transient) guest accommodations along with their other facilities.

Resort Hotels

Unlike several lodging property types, resort hotels are the planned destination of their guests. Guests often vacation at a resort hotel. Resort hotels typically provide scenery and activities unavailable at most other hotel properties. Resort hotel guests normally stay longer than guests at most other types of hotels. Most resort hotels provide food and beverage, valet, room, and recreational services.

A more leisurely, relaxed atmosphere distinguishes most resort hotels from their commercial counterparts. The purpose of the resort hotel is to provide an enjoyable guest experience that will encourage repeat business and recommendations. Group activities such as dancing, golf, tennis, horseback riding, nature hikes, and more are frequently planned for guests. Resort hotels normally employ social directors who plan, organize, and direct a range of guest programs.

Resort hotel communities are an expanding area of resort development. These communities may be developed from existing hotel facilities sold as time-share hotel investments, or as new destination properties developed specifically as resort communities.[3]

Bed and Breakfast Hotels

Bed and breakfast hotel operations, sometimes called B&Bs, are an often forgotten group of lodging properties. B&B hotels vary from houses with a few rooms converted to overnight facilities to small buildings with 20 to 30 guestrooms. The owner of a B&B hotel—the host or hostess—usually lives on the premises, and is responsible for serving a breakfast to the guests. Breakfast service may range from a simple continental breakfast to a full course meal. There are thousands of B&Bs in operation today. The reason for their popularity is their intimate, personal service.

Time-Share Hotels

Another expanding hotel segment is the time-share or condominium hotel. Time-share properties typically involve individual or corporate owners who form an association and hire a management company to operate their units as a hotel. The guest may not know the property is a condominium, since it operates as a hotel or a resort. Normally, the condominium units contain bedrooms, living room, dining area, and kitchen. Guests staying in a time-share hotel have an average stay of

Resorts may carefully attempt to retain desirable aspects of the natural environment. (Courtesy of The Tides Inn, Irvington, Virginia.)

seven nights and may purchase that same time period on an annual basis. Time-share properties are especially popular in resort areas.

Casino Hotels

Hotels with gambling facilities may be categorized as a distinct group—casino hotels. Although casino hotel guestrooms and food and beverage operations may be quite luxurious, the hotel functions primarily in a support role to the casino. Until recently, guestrooms and food and beverage facilities were not expected to earn a profit. Today, most casino hotels expect all aspects of operations to generate profits.

Casino hotels attract guests to their facilities by promoting gaming and headliner entertainment. Casino hotels frequently provide specialty restaurants and extravagant floor shows, and may offer charter flights for guests planning to gamble. Gambling activities at some casino hotels operate 24 hours a day, 365 days a year. This may have a significant impact on the food and beverage operation and the rooms division.

Conference Centers

While many hotels provide meeting space, conference centers are specifically designed to handle group meetings. Most full service conference centers offer overnight accommodations. Because meetings are their focal point, conference centers typically place great emphasis on providing all the services and equipment necessary to ensure a meeting's

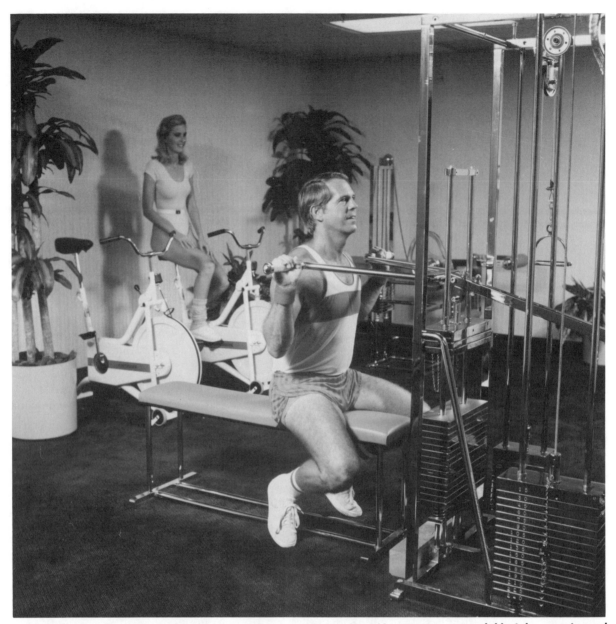

Many guests appreciate the health clubs and fitness centers offered by some commercial hotels, resorts, and conference centers. (Courtesy of Radisson Mart Plaza Hotel, Miami, Florida.)

success—for example, high quality audiovisual and sound equipment, technical assistance, comfortable chairs, flipcharts, and so forth.

Conference centers are often located outside metropolitan areas and may provide extensive leisure facilities: golf courses, indoor and outdoor swimming pools, fitness centers, spas, jogging and hiking trails, and more. Conference center hotels typically charge a single price which includes guestroom, meals, meeting rooms, audiovisual equipment, and other related services. Guest amenities may not be as plentiful at conference centers, since they aim more to meet the needs of meeting planners and organizers than the desires of program attendees.

Alternative Lodging Properties   Somewhat like hotels, because they involve the rental of space, are recreational vehicle parks, campgrounds, and mobile home parks. While there may be some similarity between hotels and alternative lodging possibilities, their chief significance is that they compete with hotels for accommodation revenues. In some resort areas, these alternative properties compete vigorously with traditional lodging entities and may be a competitive factor which hotels cannot ignore.

Levels of Service

Another way of classifying lodging properties is by level of service. Service level is a measure of the benefits provided to the guest. The level of service offered in a hotel varies without regard to hotel size or type. Some hotels offer more than one level of service. The level of service is usually included in the room rate.

Before discussing specific levels of service, we should examine some basic issues surrounding service.

The Intangibility of Service. Hotels are not simply in the business of selling tangible products such as clean beds and good food. In fact, it is the intangible services a hotel provides which contribute most to an experience of hospitality. These services are not physical things, but rather actions, deeds, performances, or efforts. For example, a meal served in a hotel dining room is certainly a tangible element of a guest's experience. However, hospitality means more than just a good meal—it means surrounding the meal with a particular ambience, including the dining room's decor and the attitude of its staff. These intangible elements can be just as important as the tangible elements to the guest during the meal.

The difficulty is that after a service has been delivered, the purchaser generally has nothing tangible to show for it. Services cannot be touched, tasted, or tried on for size, and it is virtually impossible to "return" a service. For the most part, guests leave a hotel with only the memories of their experiences. To counteract this, many hotels try to create an image of their services that is powerful, clear, and precise. The hotel's service becomes an instantly recognizable signature of the hotel, almost like a tangible product. The hotel's employees must then sustain the image through their commitment to the appropriate level of service for the hotel's market.

Every service provided by a hotel must be appropriate to the market the property wishes to attract and satisfy. For example, guests in an economy property probably would be surprised by an attempt to escort them to their rooms. However, in a hotel with an appropriately defined level of service and market, escorting guests to rooms can become a tangible reference to the image of the hotel.

Quality Assurance. The intangible services that a hotel delivers tend to be less standardized than the tangible objects produced by manufacturing equipment. One of the greatest challenges facing the hospitality industry today is controlling service variability. The consistent delivery of services is the result of quality assurance.[4]

The traditional quality control techniques of manufacturing industries may not be appropriate for service industries. In manufacturing industries, consumers are normally isolated from the production processes, and products are tested and inspected before they are sold. In hotels, some quality control techniques of manufacturing industries may apply: rooms are inspected after they are cleaned, and recipes are tested before they appear on the menu. However, in many instances, guests are not isolated from the production processes of a hotel. For example, the interaction that takes place between front office employees and guests at registration is a service that is produced, delivered, and consumed simultaneously.

The key to quality service is consistency. The keys to consistency are the standards that a property develops. But, while standards define quality and make it possible, only the staff can make quality a reality.

For the sake of simplicity, lodging properties can be discussed in terms of three basic levels of service: world-class, mid-range, and economy/limited.

World-Class Service

Hotels offering world-class service target top business executives, entertainment celebrities, high-ranking political figures, and wealthy clientele as their primary market. World-class hotels provide upscale restaurants and lounges, exquisite decor, concierge service, and opulent meeting and private dining facilities. Guests may find oversize bath towels and bars of soap, shampoo, shower caps, clock radios, and more expensive furnishings, decor, and art work in the hotel's guestrooms. Bath linens are typically replaced twice daily, and a nightly turn-down service is usually provided. Daily newspapers and magazines may be delivered to each guestroom.

The public areas of a world-class hotel may be elaborately decorated and furnished. Several food and beverage outlets are frequently available to cater to the tastes of the hotel's guests and visitors. In addition, a variety of shops, such as international newsstands, gift shops, clothing shops, jewelers, and specialty retail shops, may also be found.

World-class hotels stress the personal attention given to guests, and maintain a relatively high ratio of staff members to guests. This ratio enables the hotel to offer a wide variety of guest services and respond quickly to guest requests. World-class hotels frequently employ a concierge who provides extra help for guests, including such services as special registration procedures, ticket office services, secretarial services, and other arrangements.

Executive Floors. In some hotels, only certain floors, usually the top ones, are singled out for world-class attention. Hotels offering the "executive floor" idea or the "tower concept" upgrade the furnishings and decor of the guestrooms on these floors and provide additional guest services. Executive floors normally provide very large, deluxe guestrooms that may contain a number of amenities. The room or suite may be stocked with fresh cut flowers, bathrobes, and fresh fruit.

World-class hotels often provide distinctive guest amenities. (Courtesy of Radisson Mark Plaza Hotel, Alexandria, Virginia.)

The luxury services offered by executive floors are not confined to the guestroom. A concierge may be stationed on each executive floor. Entry to these floors may be restricted by the use of special elevator keys that allow access only to authorized guests. In many cases, the towers or executive floors contain a private lounge area for the exclusive use of registered guests. A special beverage service may be offered in the evening, and a continental breakfast may be available in the morning.

Mid-Range Service

Hotels offering mid-range service appeal to the largest segment of the traveling public. The level of service offered is modest but sufficient. Although the staffing level is adequate, the mid-range property does not try to provide elaborate services. A mid-range property may offer uniformed service, airport limousine service, and food and beverage room service. Like world-class hotels, mid-range properties range in size from small to large, although the typical hotel offering mid-range service is of medium size.

A V.I.P. suite may be located on an executive floor. (Courtesy of Radisson Plaza Hotel at Austin Centre, Austin, Texas.)

The property may house a specialty restaurant, coffee shop, and lounge that cater to visitors as well as hotel guests. The lounge may offer entertainment on the evenings when the hotel is expected to be busy. Guests likely to stay at a mid-range hotel include businesspeople, individual travelers, and families. Mid-range service hotels often offer special reduced rates to frequent guests, groups, and families. These hotels may also provide special rates for military personnel, educators, travel agents, senior citizens, and corporate groups. Since meeting rooms are usually found at mid-range hotels, people planning conferences, training meetings, and small conventions may also be attracted to these hotels.

Economy/ Limited Service

Economy hotels are a growing segment of the hospitality industry. The emphasis is on providing clean, comfortable, inexpensive rooms and meeting the most basic needs of guests. Economy hotels appeal primarily to budget-minded travelers who want rooms with all the amenities required for a comfortable stay, but without the extras they don't really need or want to pay for. The clientele of economy properties may include families with children, bus tour groups, traveling businesspeople, vacationers, retirees, and groups of conventioneers. A large market for economy properties is that portion of the population traveling on limited funds.

In comparison to the early 1970s when the only amenity offered may have been a black-and-white TV, most economy properties now offer color TV (many with cable or satellite reception), swimming pools, limited food and beverage service, playgrounds, small meeting rooms, and other special features. However, economy properties do not usually offer room service, uniformed service, banquet rooms, health clubs, or any of the more elaborate amenities found at mid-range and world-class properties.

Food and beverage service may not be provided, which means guests may need to eat at nearby restaurants. Many economy hotels do, however, provide a free continental breakfast in their lobby area. This service has become quite popular with guests.

In seeking out a more upscale clientele, some companies have dropped the "economy" label in favor of "limited service."

Ownership and Affiliation

Another way to classify hotels is to examine their ownership or affiliation. There are two basic structures—independent hotels and chain hotels. An independent hotel has no affiliation with other properties. Chain hotels may take a number of forms depending on the association that the chain organization has with each property. The distinctions in chain affiliation discussed in this chapter are parent company, management contract, and franchise and referral group hotels. Many chains today include a mix of these relationships.

Independent Hotels

Independent hotels have no ownership or management affiliation with other properties. They have no relationship to other hotels with regard to policies, procedures, or financial obligations. A typical example is a family-owned and operated hotel that is not required to conform to any corporate policy or procedure. While some properties are organized as sole proprietorships or partnerships, many independent hotel owners incorporate their properties to limit their risk and personal liability.

The unique advantage of an independent hotel is its autonomy. Since there is no need to maintain a particular image, the independent operator can offer a level of service that aims to attract a specific target market. Moreover, the flexibility inherent in a limited organization allows the independent hotel to quickly adapt to changing market conditions. An independent hotel, however, may not enjoy the exposure or management insight of an affiliated property.

Parent Company

Properties which are owned and operated by a multiple unit company are referred to as **parent company hotels.** The properties often carry the same name, and their managers report to a central or corporate headquarters. The parent organization typically establishes standard operating procedures for all properties in the chain. Guidelines requiring

The lobby of a world-class hotel may be elaborately furnished and decorated. (Courtesy of Opryland Hotel, Nashville, Tennessee.)

individual hotel managers to seek approval for major decisions, especially those involving large capital expenditures, may also be set.

There are a number of advantages in owning and operating a group of hotels. From a financial standpoint, chains can more readily gain access to cash and credit. This enables them to more easily purchase or negotiate long-term leases on land and buildings. Similarly, chains can usually purchase various operating supplies in larger quantities to obtain volume purchase discounts.

From an operating viewpoint, chains can generally afford staff specialists who are knowledgeable in the areas of finance, construction, operations, personnel, etc. These individuals can develop the necessary standard operating procedures and help identify and resolve problems in the chain's properties.

In contrast to independent properties, chains, especially those which have a highly centralized organizational structure, can become bureaucratic and impose many rules, policies, and procedures. Creative responses to changing markets may not receive the highest priority.

Management Contract

Another type of chain organization operates properties that are owned by other entities ranging from individual businesspeople and partnerships to large insurance companies. An example of this arrangement might occur if a group of local businesspeople decided their city needed a hotel to enhance business conditions. If the group's feasibility study were favorable, the group then might attempt to obtain financing to build the hotel. Many lending institutions, however, would require professional hotel management (and possibly chain affiliation) before they would approve a loan. At this point, the group could contract with a professional hotel management company to operate the proposed property, probably on a long-term basis. Assuming the hotel management company was acceptable to the lenders, a **management contract** would be drawn up between the developers and the operating company.

Under this type of contract, the owner/developer usually retains the financial and legal responsibility for the property. The management company usually pays the operating expenses and, in turn, receives an agreed-upon fee. Any remaining cash after operating expenses and management fees have been paid goes to the owner, who may use this cash to pay debts, insurance, taxes, and so forth.

Management contracts have proven very successful for many major chains (for example, Sheraton and Hilton) as a means of rapidly expanding their operations with far less investment per property than direct ownership requires. In addition, companies are sometimes specifically established to manage hotels for investors. With their expertise in operations, financial management, staffing, marketing and sales, and reservation services, these chain operators appear to have a unique advantage.

Franchise and Referral Groups

Among the best-known hotels today are those belonging to franchise and referral groups. They can be found in most cities and towns, along interstates, and in resort areas. There is, however, an organizational distinction between these two types of chain hotels.

Franchising is simply a method of distribution whereby one entity that has developed a particular pattern or format for doing business—the **franchisor**—grants to other entities—**franchisees**—the right to conduct such a business provided they follow the established pattern.[5] In the lodging industry, most organizations offering franchises have first established the quality of their product and expertise in operations by developing parent company (franchisor-owned) hotels. Franchise organizations typically have set standards for design, decor, equipment, and operating procedures to which all properties must adhere. This standardization is what enables franchise chains to expand while maintaining a consistent, established product and level of service.

Franchises, however, are not necessarily right for all properties. Some operations are so distinct that belonging to a franchise system and conforming to a set of standards is perceived as harmful. For these operations, a referral group might be appropriate. **Referral groups** are composed of independent hotels which have banded together for their common good. While each property in a referral system is not an exact replica of the others, there is sufficient consistency in the quality of service to satisfy guest expectations. Hotels within the group refer their guests to other affiliated properties. This approach may gain an independent hotel a much broader level of exposure. The largest hotel/motel system in the world today, Best Western International, is an example of a referral group.

The most obvious benefits of belonging to a franchise or referral group are guest recognition, a more extensive reservation system, and expanded advertising through pooled resources. These advantages are so important that lending institutions may often be reluctant to loan money to potential investors unless an affiliation with a franchise group or referral organization has been established.

Reasons for Traveling

Several ways to categorize hotel properties have been introduced. It is also possible to categorize hotel guests (or markets) in other ways. These classifications, some quite elaborate, are typically most useful to a property's marketing function.[6] However, one system which classifies guests by their reasons for traveling offers some useful general insights into their differing wants and needs.

The market for the lodging industry can be segmented into three major categories in terms of the purpose for traveling—business, pleasure, and groups and conventions. In a recent year, 30% of U.S. lodging customers traveled for leisure, 42.1% traveled for business or government, 18.9% were conference participants, and 9% had other reasons for staying at a hotel.[7]

The more information a hotel has about its guests, the better it can anticipate and serve their needs. Although industry-wide statistics can provide an overview of the typical hotel guest, the cross-section for a particular hotel can vary tremendously according to hotel location and type. Individual hotels may develop specific profiles of their guests' characteristics through the use of a research questionnaire. A wide variety of guest characteristics and habits can be surveyed to provide a better understanding of specific guest wants and needs.

Business Travel   The business travel market is important to many lodging properties. In the United States, approximately 18 million people—12% of the adult population—take business trips in any given year. They average six trips per year and, because business travelers are less likely to share rooms or stay in the homes of friends or relatives, they account for the bulk of lodging demand. Regular business travel is that segment of the business travel market not related to meetings and conventions.

Regular business travel is an important source of business for many lodging properties. Within the last few years, airlines and hotels have targeted specific products and services toward the traveling business executive. The specific needs of the traveling businesswoman are also receiving increased attention. Frequent business travelers generally provide their travel agent with broad parameters outlining the type of hotel at which they wish to stay. A special segment of business travelers has a predisposition to stay at luxury hotels. The growth of suite hotels and their advertising directed toward the business traveler have affected this market segment.

Pleasure Travel

The segments of the pleasure travel market often overlap. The specific segmentation of the pleasure travel market often depends on the attractions, products, and services offered by the destination area of a lodging property. Typical market segments include specialized resort travel (for example, those seeking health spa facilities or instruction in such sports as tennis and golf), family pleasure travel, travel by the elderly, and travel by singles and couples.

Pleasure travelers are among the more fickle of the travel industry market segments. They are generally price-sensitive. Income is an important factor in shaping the demand for pleasure travel. In contrast to business travel, which is considered a necessary expense, vacations and related lodging accommodations are competing for the traveler's discretionary income, as well as the individual's leisure time. An individual's discretionary income is the amount of income left after taxes and expenditures for basic living needs. This discretionary income directly affects pleasure travel because it is income that can be spent for leisure activities.

There are two hybrids of business and pleasure travel. Incentive travel is financed by a business as an employee incentive, but the traveler's intent is pleasure. Another form of hybrid travel occurs when a business traveler adds vacation travel to the end of a business trip.

Groups and Conventions

Groups and conventions are here classified as separate from business travel because some groups (such as organized tours) travel for pleasure.

Business travel related to meetings and conventions is commonly classified into two markets: institutional and corporate/government. Gatherings held by the institutional market are usually open to the public. Examples of institutional gatherings include the national conventions held by trade associations. Gatherings held by the corporate/government market are usually closed to the public because they often deal with private corporate or government business matters. Examples of corporate gatherings include management meetings, sales meetings, new product introductions, training seminars, professional/technical meetings, and stockholder meetings.

Conventions and smaller meetings are critically important to much of the lodging industry. They result in sales not only of guestrooms, but of banquet and meeting room facilities as well. In addition, they can often be induced to stay at a hotel during off-peak periods. Meetings and conventions can attract hundreds or thousands of people, but the decision of where and when to have a meeting is made by only a few meeting planners. Sales and marketing efforts can be efficiently focused on these meeting planners.

Buying Influences

When a traveler decides where to stay for the night, many buying influences are involved. Buying influences may include satisfactory experience with a hotel, advertisements by a hotel or a chain organization, recommendations by others, hotel locations, and preconceptions of a hotel based on its name or affiliation. To induce prospective guests to choose a particular hotel, the hotel develops a marketing plan that may include billboards, advertisements in newspapers and other publications,

Conventions and smaller meetings often result in banquet sales as well. (Courtesy of Opryland Hotel, Nashville, Tennessee.)

personal and telephone sales efforts, public relations, and direct mailings. Travel agents may be influential in helping the consumer select lodging. Guests often depend on travel agents to assure them that the hotel is appropriate to their needs.

A potential guest's buying decision may also be influenced by the ease of making reservations and the reservations agent's description of the hotel and its rooms. The hotel representative's tone of voice, helpfulness, efficiency, and knowledge are all factors that may contribute to a caller's commitment to stay at a particular hotel. Sometimes the potential guest may call several hotels in the destination area to compare room rates, services, and amenities. Exhibit 1.2 summarizes guests' reasons for staying at a particular hotel for the first time, in order of their importance to the arriving guest. Many of these factors can be emphasized by front office personnel in their conversations with potential guests.

Exhibit 1.3 provides some data on guests' reasons for returning to a hotel or motel. The single most important reason for a traveler to return to a hotel is its cleanliness and appearance. Although this applies primarily to guestrooms, cleanliness is also important in the public areas of the hotel. Good service is second in importance, and front office staff members are among the most visible hotel representatives in this regard.

Exhibit 1.2   Factors Influencing the Selection of a Hotel or Motel for the First Time

Question: What is most important in your selection of a hotel/motel for the first time?

Finding:

Reason for Choosing	By Total Travelers	By Frequent Travelers
Location/Convenience	56%	63%
Appearance	50%	48%
Price/Reasonable Rates	46%	42%
Facilities: Good Food, Beverage, Accommodations	23%	29%
Recommendation/Reputation	22%	25%
Recreation Facilities	10%	8%
Good Service	9%	8%

Source: "Bringing in the Business and Keeping It." Study done for Procter & Gamble by Market Facts.

Exhibit 1.3   Factors Influencing Decision to Return to a Hotel or Motel

Question: What is the most important factor in your decision to return to a hotel/motel?

Finding:

Reason for Returning	By Total Travelers	By Frequent Travelers
Cleanliness/Appearance	63%	63%
Good Service	42%	45%
Facilities	35%	41%
Convenience/Location	32%	38%
Price/Reasonable Rates	39%	35%
Quiet and Private	9%	8%

Source: "Bringing in the Business and Keeping It." Study done for Procter & Gamble by Market Facts.

The challenge to the front office staff, then, is to obtain repeat business by providing the level of service that meets and exceeds guest expectations.

Serving business travelers (no matter what their purposes for traveling) offers a tremendous opportunity for repeat business. Satisfied business travelers may not only return for the same business purposes, but may also bring their spouses or even revisit the property with their families during their next vacation.

Lodging guests may be loyal to particular chains or properties. Chain or brand loyalty can be explained as a matter of habit, maximization of value to price, or past satisfaction with the product or service. Since it is difficult to obtain reliable pre-purchase information about services, consumers may be reluctant to change brands because they are uncertain whether the change will actually increase their satisfaction. In order to "comparison shop" for services, consumers must visit various service establishments in person. Also, consumers often perceive greater risks in purchasing services than they do in purchasing manufactured products. This increases the likelihood of brand loyalty when a lodging property succeeds in satisfying its guests.

Another reason guests may become brand loyal is their own recognition that repeat patronage may lead to greater satisfaction of their needs. This can be an especially important factor in the luxury sector of the lodging industry. The hotel staff and management may learn the tastes and preferences of regular guests and therefore be better able to anticipate and satisfy these guests.

One factor mitigating brand loyalty in the lodging industry is the availability of individual brands in certain locations. If a consumer prefers to stay in hotels belonging to a certain chain, but is unable to locate one in a particular destination, he or she may decide to stay in another chain hotel. In this way, the consumer learns about competing brands. If the competing brand is roughly the same quality level or higher, loyalty to a particular hotel chain may diminish.

Notes

1. Floyd Miller, *Statler—America's Extraordinary Hotelman* (New York: Statler Foundation, 1968), p. 36.

2. See Jack P. Jefferies, *Understanding Hotel/Motel Law* (East Lansing, Mich.: Educational Institute of the American Hotel & Motel Association, 1983), Chapter 4, regarding the distinction between a guest and a tenant.

3. For more information on resort operations, interested readers should consult Chuck Y. Gee, *Resort Development and Management* (East Lansing, Mich.: Educational Institute of the American Hotel & Motel Association, 1988).

4. For a detailed examination of lodging industry quality assurance, see Stephen J. Shriver, *Managing Quality Services* (East Lansing, Mich.: Educational Institute of the American Hotel & Motel Association, 1988).

5. Jefferies, p. 207.

6. For more information on such methods, see Christopher W. L. Hart and David A. Troy, *Strategic Hotel/Motel Marketing*, Revised Edition (East Lansing, Mich.: Educational Institute of the American Hotel & Motel Association, 1986), Chapter 6. Our discussion of why guests travel is adapted from this text.

7. Laventhol & Horwath, *U.S. Lodging Industry—1987* (Philadelphia: Laventhol & Horwath, 1987), p. 20.

Discussion Questions

1. What do all travel and tourism businesses have in common? Discuss how the hospitality industry relates to the travel and tourism industry.

2. Describe four ways of generally classifying hotels. Why can hotels fit into more than one category?

3. Discuss some distinctions between resort hotels and commercial hotels.

4. For what purpose are conference centers specifically designed? Discuss how they serve their target market.

5. Discuss some basic issues surrounding the concept of service. How can a hotel help ensure consistency in an intangible product?

6. Describe world-class service. What personnel are common in a world-class hotel? What is an executive floor?

7. What is a unique advantage of an independent hotel? Discuss how it might be a disadvantage.

8. How might a management contract be involved in the development of a hotel? Discuss the potential advantages of a management contract.

9. What are the differences between a franchise and a referral group?

10. What are the three chief categories of travelers, in terms of the purpose for traveling? Discuss how a hotel can influence a traveler's decision to visit or return to the hotel.

2 Hotel Organization and the Front Office

For a hotel to operate effectively and efficiently, every employee must know, and work to achieve, the overall mission of the property. Each employee must ensure that guests receive the level of service that will make them want to return and recommend the property to others. Essential to this goal is the establishment of sound guest relations. While every hotel department and division should strive to improve guest relations, it is especially important to front office operations. The ability of front office employees to answer questions, offer choices, and satisfy guest requests is critical to the hotel's mission. Guests, visitors, other functional areas, and hotel management all depend on the front office for information about guests and events in the property. Unfortunately, in most hotels the daily flow of guests is not constant. During peak periods, well-trained employees and efficient planning are necessary to keep the front office from becoming hopelessly swamped and incapable of providing adequate guest service.

Organizational Planning

Missions

All organizations—hotels included—must have a reason for existence. A **mission** (or a **mission statement**) defines the unique purpose that sets a hotel apart from other hotels. It expresses and focuses on the underlying philosophy that gives meaning and direction to the hotel's actions. A well-conceived mission statement provides a sense of purpose to hotel employees. A hotel's mission statement addresses the interests of three diverse groups of people: guests, management, and employees.

First, a hotel mission statement should address the basic needs and expectations of the hotel's guests. Regardless of a hotel's size or service level, all guests will arrive with such basic needs as:

- A clean, comfortable guestroom
- Courteous, professional, and friendly service
- Safe, secure accommodations
- Well-maintained facilities and equipment

Guests generally anticipate a particular level of service. If a hotel clearly defines its market and then consistently delivers the level of service that its market expects, it can enhance guest satisfaction and encourage guests to return.

Second, a hotel's mission statement should reflect its management philosophy. Since styles of operation vary, each hotel's mission should be different. In fact, a mission is one of the principal characteristics by which hotels distinguish themselves from one another. It should guide managers so they can act within the framework of the organization's basic values and character.

Third, the mission statement should help the hotel's employees fulfill the expectations of both guests and management. It can serve as a basis for job descriptions and performance standards, and can also be a good introduction to the property for new employees. The property's mission statement should appear in employee handbooks, job descriptions, and training manuals.

Objectives   Once the hotel has defined its mission and formulated it in a written mission statement for future reference, it should set objectives. **Objectives** are those ends an organization must achieve in order to effectively carry out its mission. An objective is more specific than a mission and represents levels of achievement which can be measured. Having measurable objectives encourages hotels to monitor their progress. This provides management with a basis for determining whether or not the objectives have been achieved, and may indicate the need for corrective action. Establishing measurable objectives enables hotel divisions, departments, and employees to focus their efforts on specific goals and strategies that will help the property achieve its objectives.

For example, specific objectives involving front office operations might include the following:

- Increase the hotel's average occupancy level above the previous year's level by 2%

- Increase the amount of repeat guest business by 10%

- Reduce the average time it takes guests to check in and check out by two minutes

- Reduce the number of guest complaints by 20%

Achieving these objectives might involve the participation of other hotel departments and divisions, such as sales and housekeeping. It is for this reason that hotel objectives are generally stated as property-wide formulas, not simple departmental or divisional goals.

Departmental and Divisional Planning   Goals and strategies set at the departmental and divisional levels should correspond to the mission and objectives established property-wide. **Goals** define the purpose of a department or division and direct the actions of employees and the functions of the department or division toward the hotel's mission. To achieve its goals, a department or division establishes **strategies** which describe specific procedures it should follow. Strategies are the methods by which a department or division plans to achieve its goals. In turn, the department's or division's goals enable its actions to contribute to the objectives and overall mission of the organization.

Hotel Organization

All organizations require a formal structure to carry out their mission and objectives.[1] A common method of representing that structure is the organization chart. An **organization chart** is a schematic representation of the relationships between positions within an organization. It shows where each position fits into the overall organization and illustrates the divisions of responsibility and lines of authority. Supervisor-subordinate relations are indicated by solid lines between the positions on the chart. Positions not in a direct-line relationship but requiring a high degree of cooperation and communication are connected by a dotted line.

An organization chart should be flexible. It should be reviewed and revised yearly, or more often if business conditions significantly change. The responsibilities of various employees may change, depending on their qualifications and strengths, as they assume more duties. Some organizations list each employee's name on the chart along with his or her position title. A copy of the property's organization chart should be included in the employee handbook distributed to all employees.

Since no two hotels are exactly alike, organizational structures must be tailored to fit the needs of each individual property. The charts in this chapter show a variety of possible organizational structures.

A full-service lodging property, offering both guestrooms and food and beverage service, will probably have an extensive organizational structure. All staff report ultimately to one person. Exhibit 2.1 is an organization chart for the management level positions in a large full-service property. All but two of the lines on the chart are solid, indicating reporting relationships. The dotted lines connecting the sales director to the catering director and the reservations manager represent the dependence of the catering and reservations functions on the sales function.

Some hotels may lease their food and beverage outlets to another company. The food and beverage operations and the guestroom operations are separately owned and managed. When two managers direct separate enterprises on the same property, there is potential for conflict. Exhibit 2.2 shows a typical organization chart for a hotel with leased food and beverage operations. In this example, there are informal consulting (dotted-line) relationships between the managers and owners of the two businesses.

A possible organization chart for a property with no restaurant is shown in Exhibit 2.3. Note that this sample chart shows an organization of the guestroom operations that differs from that of the two previous organization charts.

Classifying Functional Areas. The divisions and departments of a hotel may be classified according to a variety of methods. According to one method, each operating division and department is classified as either a

Exhibit 2.1   Organization Chart Showing Management Positions in a Large Hotel

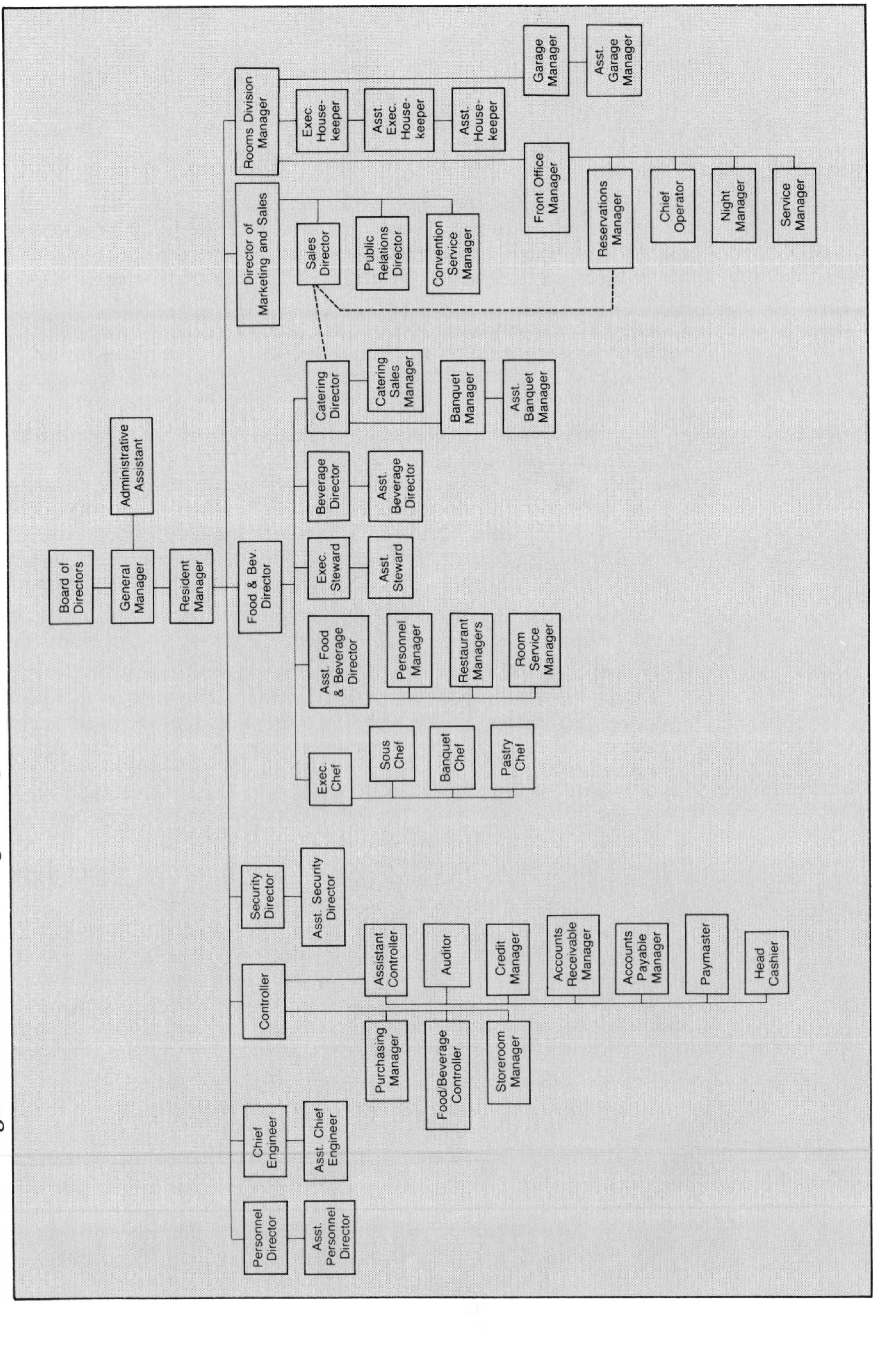

Exhibit 2.2   Organization Chart for a Hotel with a Leased Food and Beverage Operation

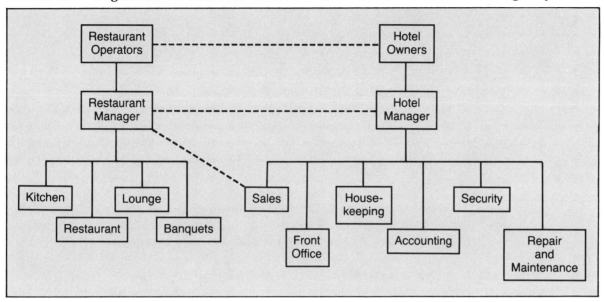

Exhibit 2.3   Organization Chart for a Rooms-Only Hotel

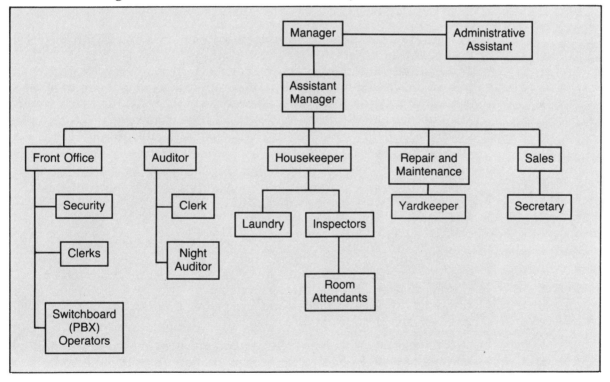

revenue center or a support center. A **revenue center** sells goods or services to guests and thereby generates revenue for the hotel. The front office, food and beverage outlets, room service, and retail stores are examples of typical hotel revenue centers. **Support centers** include the housekeeping, accounting, engineering and maintenance, and personnel functions. These functions do not generate direct revenue, but play a supporting role to the hotel's revenue centers. Hotel segmentation by revenue centers and support centers is especially useful for purposes of accounting and information systems design.

The terms **front of the house** and **back of the house** may also be used to classify hotel departments and divisions and the personnel within them. Front-of-the-house functional areas are those in which employees have extensive guest contact, such as food and beverage facilities and the front office. Back-of-the-house functional areas are those in which personnel have less direct guest contact, such as engineering, accounting, and personnel.

An examination of the typical hotel divisions may provide a better understanding of hotel operations and better enable you to see front office functions in the context of the entire property.

Rooms Division

The rooms division is composed of departments and functions which play essential roles in providing the services guests expect during a hotel stay. In most hotels, the rooms division generates more revenue than other divisions; see Exhibit 2.4 for the distribution of hotel industry revenues. The front office is one of the departments in the rooms division.

The Front Office. The most visible department in a hotel, with the greatest amount of guest contact, is the front office. The front desk, cashier, and mail and information sections of the front office are located in the busiest area of the hotel's lobby. The front desk itself is the focal point of activity within the front office. Guests are registered, assigned rooms, and checked out at the front desk. The organization of the front office department is discussed later in this chapter; front desk design is discussed in Chapter 3.

In some properties, the reservation and switchboard functions are separate departments within the rooms division. Throughout this text, however, reservation and switchboard functions will be considered in the discussion of front office tasks.

Reservations. The reservation function or department is responsible for receiving and processing reservations for accommodations in the future. Reservations agents must maintain accurate reservation records and closely track availabilities to ensure that no date is overbooked. Close coordination with the sales and marketing division is essential when large groups are booked into a hotel.

Telephone switchboard. The telephone switchboard function or department maintains a complex communication network similar to that of any large company. (Telephone switchboard equipment may also be referred to as a **private branch exchange,** or **PBX.**) Hotel switchboard or PBX operators may have responsibilities beyond merely answering calls and connecting them to the appropriate extension. When long-distance calls are routed and priced through the switchboard, charges must be relayed to a front office cashier for posting to the proper guest account.

Exhibit 2.4   Source of the Hotel Industry Dollar

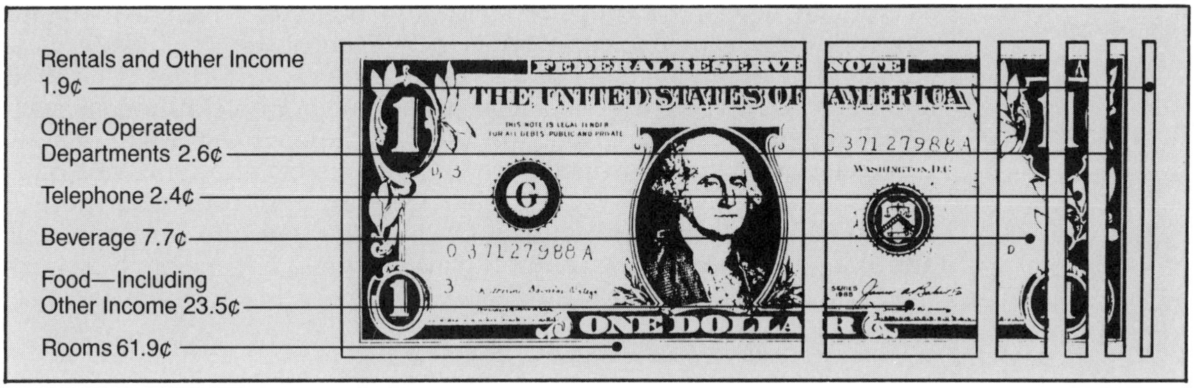

Rentals and Other Income
1.9¢

Other Operated
Departments 2.6¢

Telephone 2.4¢

Beverage 7.7¢

Food—Including
Other Income 23.5¢

Rooms 61.9¢

Reprinted from *Trends in the Hotel Industry, U.S.A. Edition,* ©1987 Pannell Kerr Forster.

Telephone operators may also be required to place wake-up calls, monitor automated systems, and coordinate emergency communication systems.

Housekeeping. Housekeeping is perhaps the most important front office support department. The housekeeping department inspects rooms for sale, cleans occupied and vacated rooms, and coordinates room status with the front office. In some hotels, the housekeeping function is considered an independent hotel division. The housekeeping department often has more personnel than other rooms division departments. Normally, an executive housekeeper is in charge of the department and may be assisted by an assistant housekeeper, inspectors, room attendants, and laundry managers. Room attendants are assigned to specific sections of the hotel, and may be asked to clean from 8 to 18 rooms a day depending on the level of service expected, the room size, and the tasks required. If the hotel has its own laundry, housekeeping department staff take care of the property's linens.

To ensure speedy, efficient rooming of guests in vacant and ready rooms, the housekeeping and front office departments must inform each other promptly of any changes in a room's status or availability. Chapter 5 discusses methods of communication between the front office and housekeeping. Close coordination and cooperation between the two departments help ensure guest satisfaction.

Uniformed Service. Parking attendants, door attendants, porters, limousine drivers, and bellpersons make up the uniformed service staff. Uniformed service personnel have a great degree of contact with guests. They meet, greet, and help guests to the front desk and to their rooms. At the end of the stay, they take guests to the cashier, out the front door, and to their means of transportation.

Food and Beverage Division

The other major revenue center in most hotels is the food and beverage division. Total food and beverage revenues usually amount to less than total rooms division revenues.

There are almost as many varieties of food and beverage operations as there are hotels. Many hotels offer guests more than a single food and beverage outlet. Possible outlet types include quick service, table service, specialty restaurants, coffee shops, bars, lounges, and clubs. The food and beverage division typically also supports other hotel functions such as room service, catering, and banquet planning. Banquets, normally conducted in the hotel's function rooms, can contribute significant revenues to the food and beverage division. Catering performed elsewhere in the hotel or off-premises can also be an active revenue center. Hotels appealing to group and convention markets typically generate high banquet and catering revenues.

Sales and Marketing Division

The sales and marketing staff in a hotel can vary from one part-time person to a dozen or more full-time employees. These personnel typically have four functions: sales, convention services, advertising, and public relations. A primary goal of the division is to manage the sale of products and services offered by the hotel. A close working relationship is needed with other hotel divisions and the front office to effectively communicate guest needs.

The goal of marketing activity is to attract guests to the property; this goal is achieved through research of the marketplace, competing products, guest needs and expectations, and future demand. Sales is oriented toward generating revenue from the hotel's products. The front office plays a central role in the most common hotel sales activity, which is room sales. When a potential guest contacts a hotel to make a reservation, the reservations agent takes on the role of a sales agent. Front desk agents handling walk-in guests also function as sales agents. These personnel must be prepared to influence potential guests to stay, and to interest the guest in the hotel's services.

Accounting Division

A hotel's accounting division is responsible for monitoring the financial activities of the property. Some hotels employ off-premises accounting services to complement the work of their internal accounting division. In this case, the hotel's staff collects and transmits data to a service bureau or to chain headquarters. A hotel that performs all of its accounting work in-house will employ a larger accounting staff with a higher level of responsibility.

Accounting activities include paying invoices owed, distributing statements and collecting payments, processing payroll information, accumulating operating data, and compiling financial statements. In addition, the accounting staff may be responsible for making bank deposits, securing cash, and performing other control and processing functions required by the hotel's management.

Close coordination with the front office is essential to the success of the hotel's accounting division. The front office must safeguard the revenue it produces. The front office cashiering and guest accounting functions are charged with monitoring cash, checks, credit cards, and other methods of guest account settlement. The main financial transactions handled by front office staff members are making change, receiving cash payments, verifying checks, imprinting credit cards, and handling guest statements.

Engineering/ Maintenance Division

A hotel's engineering and maintenance division is responsible for maintaining the appearance of the interior and exterior of the property and keeping its equipment operational. It is typically also responsible for swimming pool sanitation and the landscaping and upkeep of the property's grounds, although some hotels staff a grounds division or an outdoor and recreation division to perform these and other tasks. Not all engineering and maintenance work can be handled by the hotel's staff. Often, problems or projects require outside contracting.

The front office must efficiently exchange information with the engineering and maintenance division to ensure guest satisfaction. Guest complaints may need to be referred to engineering and maintenance personnel. Also, whenever a problem prevents a room from being rented, the front office must know as soon as the problem is corrected.

Security Division

Safety and security for hotel guests, visitors, and employees should be a concern of all hotel employees.[2] Security staff might include in-house personnel, contract security officers, or retired or off-duty police officers. Security responsibilities may include patrolling the property, monitoring surveillance equipment, and, in general, ensuring that guests, visitors, and employees are safe and secure at the hotel. The cooperation and assistance of local law enforcement officials are critical to the security division's effectiveness.

The security program is most effective when employees who have primary responsibilities other than security also participate in security efforts. For example, front desk agents should issue room keys to registered guests only; housekeeping employees should open a guestroom door (if at all) only for guests who can prove that the room is theirs. All employees should be wary of suspicious activities anywhere in the property, and report such activities to an appropriate security authority.

Human Resources Division

In recent years, hotels have increased investment in and dependence on areas of human resources management. The size and budgets of human resources divisions have grown steadily, along with their responsibility and influence. This expanded role is mirrored by the growing preference for the broader term *human resources* over *personnel*. In properties that are not large enough to justify the creation of a separate office or position, the general manager usually handles the human resources function.

The scope of the human resources division has changed in recent years, in response to new legislation, the shrinking labor market, and the growing pressures of competition. The basic functions of the human resources division remain the same: employment (including external recruiting and internal reassignment); training; employee relations (including quality assurance); compensation; benefits; administration (including employee policies); labor relations; and safety.[3]

Other Divisions

Many hotels staff a variety of other departments and divisions to serve the needs of their guests. The range of possibilities is representative of the variety of types and markets of hotels.

Retail Outlets. Lodging properties often establish gift shops, newsstands, or other retail outlets in their lobbies or other public areas. Like the rooms division and the food and beverage division, these outlets generate revenue for the hotel.

Recreation. Some hotels—primarily resorts—staff a division dedicated to providing group and individual recreational activities for guests. Some recreation divisions are also responsible for landscaping and grounds maintenance. Golf, tennis, bowling, tours, day trips, hikes, and other activities may be arranged by the recreation division staff. Activities for children may also be planned and directed. Typically, the recreation staff collects fees for organized activities or posts charges to the guests' accounts.

Casino. In areas where gambling is legal, the staff of a casino property operates games of chance for guests and protects the property's interests in the gambling area. The casino division may offer various forms of entertainment and other attractions to draw customers into the property and its gambling facilities.

Hotel Management

Hotel management is the person or people authorized by ownership to represent its interests. Management is responsible for guiding the operation of the hotel and regularly reporting to ownership the property's overall operating health and any other pertinent facts. The major duties of a hotel management team include planning, organizing, coordinating, staffing, directing, controlling, and evaluating to reach specific objectives and goals. These duties require coordination of the activities of the various divisions and departments.

The top executive of a property is usually called its general manager, managing director, or director of operations. The general manager in an individual hotel reports directly to the owner or to an assigned person in the owner's company. Chain organizations usually have a district, area, or regional executive supervising the properties in a particular group. The hotel general manager supervises all divisions, either through a resident or assistant manager or directly through the division heads.

While the general manager is responsible for supervising all the divisions of a hotel, he or she may assign specific divisions or departments to the resident manager to oversee. Typically, resident managers are assigned departments in the rooms division of the hotel to supervise. When the general manager is absent from the property, the resident manager becomes the acting general manager. A manager-on-duty is often appointed to take responsibility when the general manager and the resident manager are both absent from the property.

To qualify for a department head position, an individual must thoroughly understand the functions, goals, and practices of a particular department. Although there are many variations in management structure, front office managers are usually considered department heads. The front office manager is typically the preferred candidate for manager-on-duty.

Front Office Operations

Traditional front office functions include reservations, registration, room and rate assignment, guest services, room status, maintenance and settlement of guest accounts, and creation of guest history records. The front office is responsible for developing and maintaining a comprehensive database of guest information, coordinating guest services, and ensuring guest satisfaction. These functions are accomplished by personnel in diverse areas of the front office department. While there are no industry standards established for front office staff positions, front office organization charts are normally used to define departmental reporting and working relationships. Front office job descriptions, job specifications, and typical work shifts are designed to provide optimal levels of employee and guest satisfaction.

Front Office Organization

In larger hotels, the front office is often organized along functional lines, with different employees handling separate operational areas. This division provides enhanced internal control over front office operations. If each area is responsible for only a segment of the guest's stay, front office personnel can provide more specialized attention. This separation of duties may not be practical in a small hotel, where it is common for one or two individuals to be responsible for all front desk operations.

The front office in a large hotel supports many positions with a considerable separation of job duties. These typically include:

- A front desk agent who checks people in and maintains the room rack

- A cashier who handles money, posts charges, and checks people out of the hotel

- A mail and information clerk who is responsible for taking messages, giving directions to guests, and filing

- A telephone operator who manages the switchboard and places wake-up calls

- A reservations agent who takes reservations and keeps reservation records in order

If the property is computerized, each employee may be restricted to accessing only those computer records pertinent to his or her function.

The front office in a mid-size hotel performs the same functions, but there are fewer employees, and job duties are typically combined. For example, in the organizational structure shown in Exhibit 2.5, a front desk agent performs the functions of the receptionist, cashier, and mail and information clerk. The front desk agent may also assume the role of

Exhibit 2.5   Organization Chart for the Front Office of a Mid-Size Property

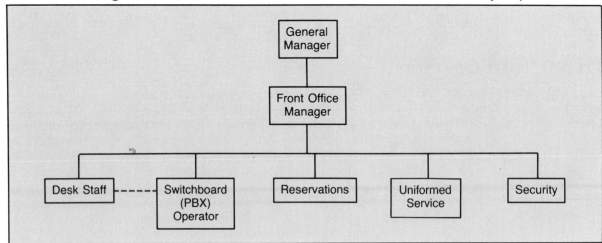

the switchboard operator or the reservations agent in their absence. During busy periods, two or three desk agents may be on duty at the same time. Although each person is generally assigned the same duties, the desk agents may informally decide among themselves that, for example, one person will register guests and handle the switchboard, another will check guests out and post charges, and a third will handle reservations and information requests.

The organization of a front office in a small hotel is similar. One front desk agent often performs nearly all the functions with little assistance. If the front desk agent becomes overburdened, the manager or accountant usually provides assistance. Management may also be more involved with the details of front office operation.

Front Office Goals and Strategies

Goals and strategies at the level of the front office department are subordinate to—but supportive of—the hotel's mission and objectives. For example, to help the hotel meet an objective of increasing its occupancy percentage, one front office goal might be to encourage more walk-ins to stay at the property. A strategy to reach that goal could be for front desk agents to improve their sales presentation by better describing the rooms and services available to guests. Another objective might be to reduce the time taken at registration; a goal might be to eliminate distractions at the front desk; and a strategy might be to ensure that front desk agents talking with guests are never interrupted by phone calls. These sample goals and strategies are related to the hotel's objectives as outlined earlier. The front office department adopts the objectives of the hotel as its own goals and creates consistent strategies to reach those goals.

Front Office Workshifts

In most hotels, a 40-hour week is the typical employee workload. Federal and state wage and hour laws apply to the front office, and some properties are also bound by union contracts and rules. A front office employee may be offered any one of the property's shifts, depending on the needs of the front office at the time. Traditional front office workshifts are:

Day shift:	7:00 a.m.– 3:00 p.m.
Evening shift:	3:00 p.m.–11:00 p.m.
Night shift:	11:00 p.m.– 7:00 a.m.

A recent trend in front office operations is to provide a limited level of guest service during the late night hours, reducing the number of employees required on the night shift. The front office may be partially closed off during these hours.

Front office workshifts may vary with traffic patterns. A program of flexible work hours, or **flextime,** allows employees to vary their times of starting and ending work, although certain hours during a shift may require the presence of most workers. For example, one front desk agent may work from 6:00 a.m. to 2:00 p.m., so that wake-up calls and check-outs can be handled more efficiently through the 7:00 a.m. shift change. On the other hand, scheduling a front desk agent to work from 10:00 a.m. to 6:00 p.m. permits continuity in processing guest arrivals through the meal periods of staff assigned to the evening shift.

Other types of alternative scheduling include arrangements of work hours or staffing which vary from the traditional workweek of five 8-hour days per employee. A program of alternative scheduling requires careful planning. A **compressed work schedule** is a method of working full-time hours in fewer than the traditional five days—for instance, four 10-hour days. Part-time employees are an increasingly important source of labor. Many potential workers—such as students, parents of young children, and retirees—are unable to work full-time. Part-time workers allow the front office flexibility to respond to fluctuating guest demands, and may also reduce overall labor costs. **Job sharing** is an arrangement by which two or more part-time employees share the responsibilities of one full-time position. Each worker may perform all aspects of the position, or duties may be divided among participants.

Job Descriptions

A job description is a listing of all the tasks and related information which make up a work position. A job description may also outline reporting relationships, responsibilities, working conditions, equipment and material to be used, and other important information specific to the requirements of the property. To be most effective, job descriptions must be tailored to the operational procedures of an individual property. Job descriptions should be task oriented; they should be written for a position, not for a particular employee. They may become inappropriate as work assignments change, and should be reviewed at least once a year for possible revision. Employees should be involved in writing and revising job descriptions for their positions. Properly written job descriptions can ease employee anxiety by specifying responsibilities, requirements, and peculiarities.

Well-written job descriptions can also be used:

- In evaluating job performance

- As an aid in training or reorienting employees

- To prevent unnecessary duplication of duties

- To help ensure that each necessary task is performed

- To help determine appropriate staffing levels

Each front office employee should be given a copy of the job description for his or her position. A job description may also be given to all final job candidates before an employment offer is extended. This is preferable to having someone accept the job and then decide it is unsuitable because he or she was unaware of its requirements.

Front office job descriptions are prepared by the front office manager with input from the front office employees. (Job descriptions are discussed further in Chapter 11.)

Job Specifications   Job specifications list the personal qualities, skills, and traits needed to successfully perform the tasks outlined by a job description. Job specifications provide current and prospective employees with an understanding of the front office's expectations. A job specification is usually developed after a job description, since a particular job may require special skills. Factors that might be considered in developing job specifications include formal education, work experience, general knowledge, previous training, physical skills, communication ability, and equipment skills. Job specifications are often the basis for advertising job opportunities and identifying eligible applicants; they may also be used to identify current employees to be considered for promotion.

Although front office job specifications are not standardized across the industry, certain traits and skills can be expected in the job specifications of most hotels. Front office positions, because of their high degree of guest and visitor contact, often require specific interpersonal skills. Traits important to front office work include:

- Professional demeanor

- Congenial personality

- Helpful attitude

- Flexibility

- Spirit of hospitality

- Well-groomed appearance

Maintaining an outgoing personality and exhibiting a willingness to learn are especially important qualities. However, evaluating an applicant on the basis of these traits is a subjective process.

Successful performance in a front office position usually also requires various general skills acquired through education or experience. Practical skills, knowledge, and aptitude can make a valuable employee. Two specific skills often required in front office work are mathematical aptitude (for accounting tasks) and typing skills (for recordkeeping and computer operation).

Front Office Personnel

The jobs described here are typical front office positions found in a mid-size hotel. Many hotels are moving toward more universalized front office positions than those presented here. In a small hotel, for instance, it is typical for one employee to handle reservations, registration, switchboard, and check-out tasks. Also, with the spread of computerized front office recordkeeping systems, which combine information used in several tasks into one common database, the lines of responsibility have become less defined. Whatever its end use, all the information required for most front office tasks can be accessed at identical computer terminals. Many hotels simply refer to all front office employees as **front office agents, guest service representatives,** or something similar. The actual division of duties is decided along with the division of workshifts.

Even in hotels which maintain the traditional division of duties among positions, the titles given to each position may change over time. These changes may reflect a reevaluation of the tasks involved in a position, or may be intended to avoid the negative associations of some old-fashioned titles. The position titles used in this text are representative of new trends in the lodging industry.

The position and responsibilities of front office managers are discussed in Chapters 10 and 11.

Front Desk Agent   The traditional functions of a front desk agent center on the registration process. However, it is the front desk agent who most represents the hotel to the guest throughout *all* stages of the guest stay. Front desk agents should maintain a spirit of hospitality in all interactions with guests. A front desk agent typically:

- Performs pre-registration activities, when appropriate

- Determines guests' reservations status

- Identifies guests' length of stay requirements

- Ensures completion of guest registration cards

- Assigns appropriate guestrooms, accommodating requests whenever possible

- Determines room rates, including packages and discounts

- Determines guests' method of payment and follows established credit-checking procedures

- Distributes guest and room information to appropriate racks and personnel

- Coordinates room status updates with the housekeeping department

- Coordinates maintenance work with the engineering and maintenance division

- Maintains guestroom key storage

- Maintains safe deposit boxes and supervises access

- Handles guest mail, messages, and information requests

The mail and information function was once a prominent area of most hotel front offices, and the position of **mail and information clerk** was common. In recent years, however, the responsibility for distributing mail and messages to guests and answering requests for information has been divided among front desk agents, switchboard operators, and concierges, so that a full-time employee is generally not required for these duties alone.

The front desk agent is often the first contact the guest has with hotel personnel. A guest who has never stayed at the hotel before will not know what the property has to offer; a returning guest may not know about new services or options. It is one task of front desk agents to sell the guest on the hotel's rooms and services. For some employees, the idea of being a salesperson causes anxiety. However, front desk agents should not practice hard-sell techniques. Rather, they should present options and alternatives to guests and offer assistance in making choices.

In the initial encounter, the front desk agent need not try to sell each guest on each hotel revenue outlet. It is appropriate, however, to call attention to special promotions or events as part of the registration process. A directory of other services is usually placed in each guestroom, but the front desk agent must still be knowledgeable about these services. Even if the revenue outlets are not operated by the hotel itself, the leasing of space may provide revenue for the hotel. Each revenue outlet contributes to the hotel's profitability. The more successful they all are, the better off the hotel is.

In order to be effective and successful, the front desk agent must have pride in the hotel in which he or she works. A sales-minded front office staff is also a public relations staff for the hotel.

Reservations Agent

Whether the reservation function is assigned to the front office or is a separate department within the rooms division, reservation personnel are responsible for all aspects of reservations processing. Like front desk agents, reservations agents must also act as sales representatives for the hotel. Close coordination with the sales and marketing division is essential when large groups are booked into a hotel. The reservations agent typically:

- Monitors and responds appropriately to guest, travel agent, and referral network communications concerning reservations arriving by mail, direct telephone, telex, cable, or central reservation system referral

- Creates and maintains reservation records, by date of arrival and alphabetical listing

- Prepares letters of confirmation

- Processes cancellations and modifications promptly, and relays information to the front office

- Tracks future room availabilities on the basis of reservations

- Develops room revenue and occupancy forecasts

- Communicates reservation information to front desk agents

- Prepares expected arrival lists for front office use

- Assists in pre-registration activities, when appropriate

Switchboard Operator   The switchboard operator may seldom be face-to-face with guests of the hotel, but nonetheless plays an important role in representing the hotel to the guest. For this position, a friendly and courteous tone of voice is all-important. The switchboard operator typically:

- Answers incoming calls

- Directs calls to guestrooms through the switchboard or PBX system

- Takes and distributes messages for guests

- Provides information on guest services

- Processes guest wake-up calls

- Answers inquiries about public hotel events

Many properties have a fully automated system to track and place guest wake-up calls. The switchboard operator monitors the operation of such a system, and places wake-up calls personally when the system is not in operation. Despite the advances of technology, hotels often prefer human wake-up calls to electronic ones. While placing each call personally can put a heavy load on switchboard operators during early morning hours, the personal touch may seem friendlier to guests.

Front Office Cashier   The tasks of the front office cashier center on the guest accounting cycle. The front office and the accounting division require efficiency and accuracy in guest accounting tasks. The most crucial duties of the front office cashier occur when guests wish to settle their accounts and check out of the hotel. Departing guests especially appreciate efficient check-out procedures. The front office cashier typically:

- Posts revenue center charges to guest accounts

- Receives payment from guests at check-out

- Coordinates billing of credit card and direct-billed guest accounts with the accounting division

- Balances accounts at the close of each shift

- Assumes responsibility for cash used in processing front desk transactions

In many hotels, the front office cashier is responsible for the management of safe deposit boxes, instead of the front desk agent. Depending on hotel policy, the front office cashier may also perform a variety of banking services for guests, such as check cashing.

The hotel's revenue centers communicate charge purchase information to the front desk for posting. The cashier follows front office posting procedures to ensure collection of monies owed. In hotels equipped with point-of-sale electronic cash registers, charge purchase data can be transmitted directly from revenue centers to electronic guest folios. The posting of charges is minimized.

Night Auditor   The night auditor checks the accuracy of front office accounting records and compiles a daily summary of hotel financial data. Traditionally, this task is conducted at the close of the business day, on the hotel's night shift. For this reason, the auditing process is called the **night audit,** and the employee handling these tasks is called the **night auditor.** The night auditor typically:

- Posts room charges and taxes to guest accounts

- Processes guest charge vouchers and credit cards

- Posts guest charge purchase transactions not posted during the day by the front office cashier

- Verifies all account postings and balances

- Monitors the current status of coupon, discount, and other promotional programs

- Summarizes the results of operations for reporting to management

The auditor tracks room revenues, occupancy percentages, and other front office statistics, and prepares a summary of cash, check, and credit card activities. These data reflect the hotel's financial performance for the day. The hotel's accounting division, using audit data prepared in the front office, determines the property's daily profile and reports its findings to management. In many hotels, the night auditor is actually an employee of the accounting division.

Concierge   Concierge services are common in European hotels and resorts, but their introduction in American hotel front offices is a relatively recent development. The basic task of a concierge is to serve as the guest's liaison with both hotel and non-hotel services. In a sense, the function of a concierge is an extension of the function of a front desk agent. Some hotels find that front desk agents are too busy with other tasks to provide appropriate personal service; a concierge has the time and ability to specialize in a more personal approach to guest services. In some large hotels, the concierge is a fully staffed department.

A concierge must be unusually resourceful and knowledgeable about the hotel and the surrounding community. Regardless of whether inquiries concern in-hotel or off-premises attractions, facilities, services, or activities, a concierge specializes in providing assistance to guests. Typical guest requests handled by a concierge include:

- Providing directions and information

- Making airplane, theater, or other reservations and obtaining tickets

- Organizing special functions, such as VIP cocktail receptions

- Arranging for secretarial services

The concierge may call guests after they have been roomed to ask whether there are any immediate guest service needs. In some hotels, the concierge is designated to handle all guest complaints, whether the guest appears in person or telephones the desk.

In the absence of a concierge, many hotels enlist other front office staff members to provide the same services.

The Importance of Teamwork

Hotels are complex organizations with many facets that are invisible to the casual observer. Teamwork is the key to a smooth operation. All employees and functional areas must cooperate with and assist the other employees and functional areas of the hotel. Although the general manager is responsible for coordinating, instituting, and implementing the teamwork philosophy, every employee can help. Employees should treat one another as they treat guests. Each department as a whole should ensure that guests receive service that will make them want to return and to recommend the property to others. Employees working together as a team will make the hotel a success. That success will reflect on the employees.

Notes

1. For more information on organizational structure, see Jerome J. Vallen and James R. Abbey, *The Art and Science of Hospitality Management* (East Lansing, Mich.: Educational Institute of the American Hotel & Motel Association, 1987), Chapter 6.

2. For further information, see Raymond C. Ellis, Jr., and the Security Committee of AH&MA, *Security and Loss Prevention Management* (East Lansing, Mich.: Educational Institute of the American Hotel & Motel Association, 1986).

3. See David W. Wheelhouse, *Managing Human Resources in the Hospitality Industry* (East Lansing, Mich.: Educational Institute of the American Hotel & Motel Association, forthcoming).

Discussion Questions

1. Discuss the purpose of a hotel's mission statement. What are the three groups of people whose interests a mission statement addresses?

2. How do a hotel's objectives relate to its mission statement and to departmental and divisional goals and strategies?

3. Discuss how an organization chart shows employee reporting and consulting relationships. Why should an organization chart be flexible?

4. Which hotel departments and divisions are typically classified as revenue centers? Why?

5. Discuss the seven main divisions typically found in the organization of a full-service hotel. How does the front office interact with the rest of the rooms division and the other six divisions?

6. Why is it not possible for some front offices to divide employee duties along functional lines?

7. Discuss the three traditional front office workshifts. What variations on the traditional workweek might a hotel adopt?

8. Discuss the uses of job descriptions. How do they differ from job specifications?

9. Describe the typical tasks of a front desk agent. In what way is a front desk agent a salesperson?

10. Discuss the roles of the front office cashier and the front office auditor in handling guest accounting transactions. What guest interaction is possible in these positions?

3 Front Office Operations

The front office is the main point of contact between guests and the hotel. All front office functions and activity areas are oriented toward supporting guest transactions and services. Appropriately designed and used front office desks, equipment, and forms are critical to the success of the department and the hotel. It is also important to accurately plan and monitor the transactions that occur at the front office. Front office functions can be separated into a guest cycle of four phases: pre-arrival, arrival, occupancy, and departure. Within each phase of the cycle, the guest services and guest accounting functions of the front office can be approached in a logical and professional manner.

The Guest Cycle

Guest transactions during a hotel stay determine the flow of business through the property. The flow of business can be divided into a four-stage **guest cycle.** Exhibit 3.1 contains a diagram of these four stages. Within each stage, important tasks related to guest services and guest accounting can be identified and analyzed.

The guest cycle shown in Exhibit 3.1 is not an inflexible standard. Since activities and functions tend to overlap between stages of the guest cycle, some properties have revised this traditional guest cycle into a sequence of pre-sale, point-of-sale, and post-sale events. For computerized properties, this segmentation may allow for improved coordination among hotel operating departments. However, the traditional guest cycle is still widely used in the industry and is the basis for the discussion of guest services and guest accounting tasks in Part II of this book.

Front office employees need to be aware of guest services and guest accounting activities at all stages of the guest stay. A clear understanding of the flow of business through the hotel will enable front office employees to efficiently serve guest needs. Exhibit 3.2 indicates which front office personnel are most likely to serve the guest during each stage of the guest cycle. The guest cycle also suggests a systematic approach to managing front office operations.

Pre-Arrival   During the pre-arrival stage, the guest chooses a hotel to patronize. This choice can be affected by a variety of factors, including previous experiences with the hotel, advertisements, recommendations from oth-

Exhibit 3.1   The Guest Cycle and Related Front Office Functions

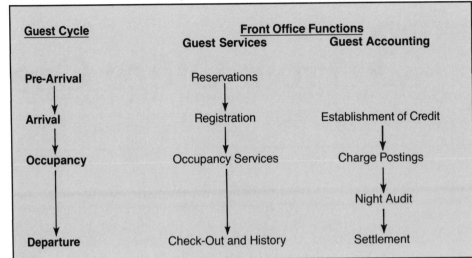

ers, the hotel's location, and preconceptions based upon the hotel's name or chain affiliation. A guest's choice may also be influenced by the ease of making reservations and the reservations agent's description of the hotel and its facilities, room rates, and amenities. The attitude, efficiency, and knowledge of the front office staff may influence a caller's decision to stay at a particular hotel.

A reservations agent must be able to respond quickly and accurately to requests for future accommodations. The proper handling of reservation information can be critical to the success of a lodging property. Efficient procedures will also allow the reservations agent more time for attention to detail and greater opportunity to market hotel services.

If a reservation can be accepted as requested, the reservations agent creates a reservation record. The creation of a reservation record initiates the hotel guest cycle. It enables the hotel to personalize guest service and appropriately schedule needed staff and facilities. Confirmation of a reservation allows the hotel to verify a guest's room request and personal information, and assures the guest that his or her needs will be addressed. Pre-registration activities—such as specific room and rate assignment for guests who have not arrived yet and creation of guest folios—may also be possible based on information collected during the reservations process.

An effective reservation system helps maximize room sales by accurately monitoring room availabilities and forecasting rooms revenue. By analyzing reservation information, front office management can develop an understanding of the hotel's reservation patterns. Data collected during the reservations process become especially useful in subsequent front office functions. Perhaps the most important outcome of a reservation, however, is having the room available when the guest arrives.

Chapter 4 discusses the reservations process in detail.

Arrival   The arrival stage of the guest cycle includes registration and rooming functions. When the guest arrives at the hotel, he or she establishes a

Exhibit 3.2 Guest-Front Office Interaction During the Guest Cycle

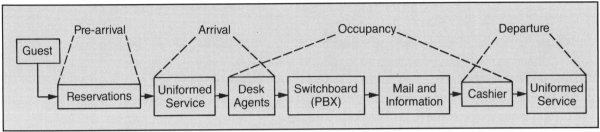

business relationship with the hotel through the front office staff. It is the staff's task to clarify the nature of the guest-hotel relationship and the expectations of the hotel and the guest.

The front desk agent should determine the guest's reservation status before beginning the registration process. Pre-registration activities may have already taken place for guests who have made reservations. Walk-in guests, on the other hand, present an opportunity for front desk agents to sell guestrooms. To do this, the front desk agent must know the hotel's products thoroughly and describe them positively. Registration will not occur if the guest is not convinced of the value of renting a particular hotel room.

A registration record, completed either as part of pre-registration activity or at check-in, is essential to efficient front office operation. A registration record should include information about the guest's intended method of payment, the planned length of stay, and any special guest needs such as a rollaway bed, a child's crib, or a preferred room location. These data enhance the front office's ability to meet special guest needs, forecast room occupancies, and settle guest accounts properly. At check-out, the guest's registration card may also be used as the primary source for creation of a guest history record.

Registration information is used in the assignment of a room and rate for each guest. Room and rate assignment also depends on an effective room status system which allows front desk agents to determine room status and rate availability. The front desk must learn of changes in the housekeeping status of a room as soon as possible to allow maximization of room sales. Exhibit 3.3 defines some common terms for the various statuses of a guestroom.

When assigning guestrooms, the front desk agent must also be aware of the characteristics of the rooms in each room category. Hotel room types can range from a standard single guestroom to a luxurious suite of rooms. Exhibit 3.4 defines some common terms for hotel room types. Differences between rooms within the same category generally lie in their furnishings, amenities, and location within the property. Exhibit 3.5 shows typical floor plans for five types of hotel rooms. The double-double, studio, and king guestrooms each occupy approximately the same amount of floor space. The junior suite shown is twice the size of these rooms, and the suite is the equivalent of a junior suite and two connected single rooms.

Once it has been determined that a guest will be accommodated, the guest's method of payment becomes an important concern. The registra-

Exhibit 3.3   Room Status Definitions

While the guest is in the hotel, the housekeeping status of the guestroom changes several times. The various terms defined here are typical of the terms used in the lodging industry. Not every room status will occur for each guestroom during every stay.

Occupied: A guest is currently registered to the room.

Complimentary: The room is occupied, but the guest is assessed no charge for its use.

Stayover: The guest is not checking out today and will remain at least one more night.

On-change: The guest has departed, but the room has not yet been cleaned and readied for re-sale.

Do not disturb: The guest has requested not to be disturbed.

Sleep-out: A guest is registered to the room, but the bed has not been used.

Skipper: The guest has left the hotel without making arrangements to settle his or her account.

Sleeper: The guest has settled his or her account and left the hotel, but the front office staff has failed to properly update the room's status.

Vacant and ready: The room has been cleaned and inspected, and is ready for an arriving guest.

Out-of-order: The room cannot be assigned to a guest. A room may be out-of-order for a variety of reasons, including the need for maintenance, refurbishing, and extensive cleaning.

Lock-out: The room has been locked so that the guest cannot re-enter until he or she is cleared by a hotel official.*

DNCO (did not check out): The guest made arrangements to settle his or her account (and thus is not a skipper), but has left without informing the front office.

Due out: The room is expected to become vacant after the following day's check-out time.

Check-out: The guest has settled his or her account, returned the room keys, and left the hotel.

Late check-out: The guest has requested and is being allowed to check out later than the hotel's standard check-out time.

*A hotel should not employ a lock-out without consulting legal counsel; relevant laws vary from state to state. See also Jack P. Jefferies, Understanding Hotel/Motel Law (East Lansing, Mich.: Educational Institute of the American Hotel & Motel Association, 1983), Chapter 4, on the hotel's right to evict guests or others.

Exhibit 3.4   Room Types

The following room type definitions are common throughout the lodging industry.

Single: A room assigned to one person. May have one or more beds.

Double: A room assigned to two people. May have one or more beds.

Triple: A room assigned to three people. May have two or more beds.

Quad: A room assigned to four people. May have two or more beds.

Queen: A room with a queen-size bed. May be occupied by one or more people.

King: A room with a king-size bed. May be occupied by one or more people.

Twin: A room with two twin beds. May be occupied by one or more people.

Double-double: A room with two double (or perhaps queen) beds. May be occupied by one or more persons.

Studio: A room with a studio bed—a couch which can be converted into a bed. May also have an additional bed.

Mini-suite or junior suite: A single room with a bed and a sitting area. Sometimes the sleeping area is in a bedroom separate from the parlor or living room.

Suite: A parlor or living room connected to one or more bedrooms.

Connecting rooms: Rooms with individual entrance doors from the outside and a connecting door between. Guests can move between rooms without going through the hallway.

Adjoining rooms: Rooms with a common wall but no connecting door.

Adjacent rooms: Rooms close to each other, perhaps across the hall.

Exhibit 3.5   Room Diagrams

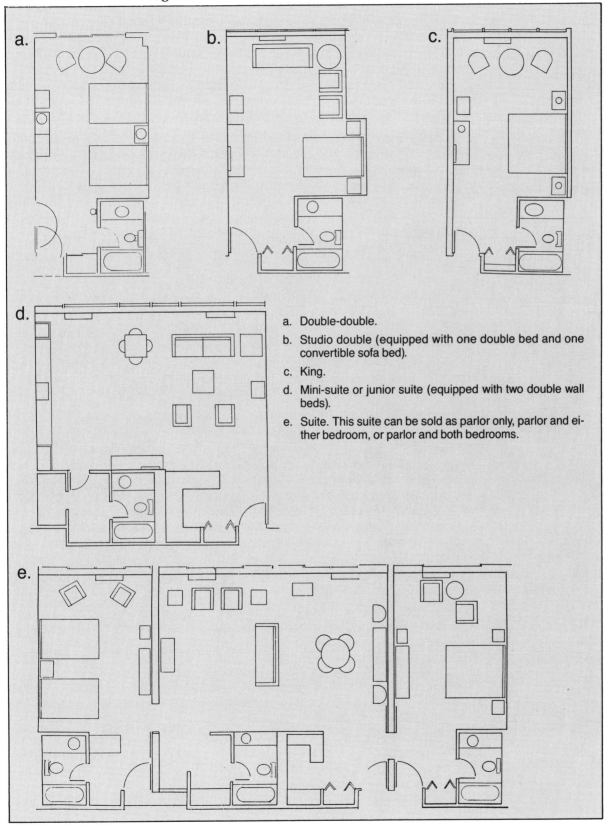

a. Double-double.

b. Studio double (equipped with one double bed and one convertible sofa bed).

c. King.

d. Mini-suite or junior suite (equipped with two double wall beds).

e. Suite. This suite can be sold as parlor only, parlor and either bedroom, or parlor and both bedrooms.

tion process plays an essential role in the guest accounting cycle by gathering information concerning payment for services rendered. Whether the guest will use cash, a check, a credit card, or an alternative method of payment, the front office should take measures to ensure eventual payment. A proper credit check at the outset of a transaction greatly reduces the potential for subsequent settlement problems. If a guest's credit rating is found to be poor, extreme care and tact should be exercised in denying the guest's request for credit.

After the establishment of a method of payment, the registration process is complete, and the guest is issued a key and begins occupancy. The guest may be given a room key and a map of the property and allowed to proceed to the room without assistance, or a uniformed service person may be assigned to show the guest to the room. When the guest arrives at the room and accepts it, the occupancy stage of the guest cycle begins.

Chapter 5 discusses guest registration and rooming procedures in more depth.

Occupancy

Throughout the guest cycle, the front office represents the hotel to the guest. This role is especially important during the occupancy stage. As the center of front office activity, the front desk is responsible for coordinating guest services. Front office guest services may include providing the guest with information, equipment, supplies, or services. The front office's response to requests should be timely and accurate to maximize guest satisfaction. A concierge is often employed to offer special attention to such needs.

A major front office objective—during occupancy and all other phases of the guest cycle—is to satisfy guest needs in a way that will encourage a return visit. Essential to this objective is the establishment of sound guest relations. Guest relations depend on clear, constructive communications between the front office, other hotel departments and divisions, and the guest. If a guest has a complaint, the hotel must know of it in order to resolve it. Front desk agents should be attentive to complaints and try to seek a resolution satisfactory to both the guest and the hotel.

Another primary front office concern during occupancy (and indeed, to some extent, throughout all stages of the guest cycle) is security. Security topics likely to apply to front office employees include the protection of funds and valuables, and key control, surveillance, safe deposit, lost and found, and emergency procedures.

Guest services are discussed in Chapter 6.

The occupancy stage of the guest cycle also produces a variety of transactions affecting guest and hotel financial accounts. Most of these transactions will be processed according to front office account posting and auditing procedures.

The largest single guest account charge is usually for the guestroom itself. Additional expenses can be charged to guest accounts if the guest established acceptable credit at the front desk during the arrival stage. Goods or services purchased from the hotel's restaurant, bar, room service, telephone, garage, valet service, gift shop, and other revenue outlets may be charged to guest accounts. Many hotels limit the amount which guests can charge to their accounts. Guest accounts must be carefully and continually monitored to ensure that this limit is not exceeded.

It is important to periodically review and verify the accuracy and completeness of front office accounting records. The night audit process is intended to fulfill this need. In hotels with computerized front office accounting systems, this phrase may not be strictly accurate, since the audit can be conducted at any time during the day. Some computerized properties choose to call the audit the **front office audit** or **update.** However, even though computerized properties *can* perform the audit at any time, they nonetheless almost invariably follow tradition and do it at night.

Regardless of how or when it is performed, room charges are posted to guest accounts as part of the audit routine. In addition, charges posted to guest accounts are verified, the accounts are balanced and checked against credit limits, discrepancies in room status are resolved, and operating reports are produced.

Guest accounting and auditing activities are discussed in detail in Chapters 7 and 8.

Departure　　The fourth phase of the guest cycle is departure. As Exhibit 3.1 shows, both the guest services and guest accounting aspects of the guest cycle are completed during this phase. The final element of guest service is checking the guest out of the hotel and creating a guest history record. The final element of guest accounting is settlement of the guest's account.

At check-out, the guest receives an accurate statement of account for settlement, returns the room keys, and departs from the hotel. Once the guest has checked out, the room's status is updated and the housekeeping department is advised.

Other primary concerns of the front office during check-out are determining whether the guest was satisfied with the stay and encouraging the guest to return to the hotel (or another property in the chain). Obtaining new customers is generally more expensive than retaining old ones, because of the resources that must be devoted to attracting new guests. A satisfied guest is more likely to return.

The more information the hotel has about its guests, the better it can anticipate and serve their needs and develop marketing strategies to increase business. Hotels often use expired registration cards as a basis for a guest history file. This information allows the hotel to better understand its clientele and provides a solid base for strategic marketing. The hotel can also develop a profile of guest characteristics through the use of a research questionnaire. A wide variety of guest characteristics and habits can be surveyed to provide the hotel with a better understanding of its guests' wants and needs.

The purpose of account settlement is to collect money due the hotel. At departure, depending on the guest's credit arrangements, cash is paid, a credit card voucher is signed, or direct billing instructions are verified. Account balances should be verified and errors corrected before the guest leaves the hotel. A potential problem in guest account settlement is charges which are not posted to the guest's account until after the guest has checked out. These charges are referred to as **late charges.** Even if the charges are eventually collected, the hotel usually incurs additional costs in billing the guest. The billing of departed guest accounts is generally handled by the back office accounting division, not the front office. However, the front office is responsible for providing complete and accurate billing information to the back office accounting division.

Chapter 9 discusses in detail the check-out and settlement process.

Once the guest has checked out, data related to the guest stay can be analyzed by the front office. Front office reports can be used to review operations, isolate problem areas, indicate where corrective action may be needed, and point out trends. Daily reports typically contain information about cash sales, charge sales, accounts receivable, and front office operating statistics. Operational analysis establishes a standard of performance which can be used to reveal the effectiveness of front office operations.

The evaluation of front office operations is presented in depth in Chapter 10.

Front Office Systems

The technology used for front office recordkeeping and equipment has evolved in three stages:

- Non-automated (manual)

- Semi-automated (electro-mechanical)

- Fully automated (computer-based)

During the 1950s, non-automated operations dominated lodging operations. The semi-automated operations of the 1960s laid much of the groundwork for the development of automated operations in the 1970s. The following operational overviews represent the evolution of front office recordkeeping systems. In practice, many properties combine elements of each approach to produce a workable system.

Non-Automated

Non-automated front office recordkeeping systems rely solely on handwritten forms. Some small hotels may still find this method of recordkeeping sufficient to meet their needs. The elements of handwritten systems have determined the structure of many front office processes. Techniques common to non-automated systems can be found in even the most advanced automated facilities.

Pre-arrival activities. Reservations agents enter requests into a loose-leaf notebook or onto index cards. Hotels typically accept reservations for six months into the future (called a six-month **horizon**) and are unlikely to commit space beyond that time. Reservation confirmations, pre-registration activities, and occupancy forecasts are not common in non-automated hotels.

Arrival activities. Upon arrival, guests sign a page in a registration book or complete a formatted registration card. Room assignments are made using a manual card replacement technique involving a room rack and, sometimes, color-coded flags. The room rack is also used to indicate each room's housekeeping status.

Occupancy activities. Carbon-copy registration cards allow copies of the guest's personal data to be distributed to switchboard operators and uniformed service personnel. The original registration card often doubles as a room rack card and guest account folio. Revenue outlets send documentation of guest charges to the front desk for posting to folios, and maintain a sales record so that postings can be cross-checked as part of an audit. Adding machines facilitate accounting procedures, but most of the process is repetitive, cumbersome, and tedious.

Departure activities. At check-out, guests settle their accounts and return their room keys, and the cashier notifies the housekeeping department of departures. Registration cards or rack slips are marked to indicate departure, then filed in a box which serves as the hotel's guest history file.

Semi-Automated

A semi-automated, or electro-mechanical, front office system uses both handwritten and machine-produced forms. Semi-automated systems and equipment are common in small and mid-size hotels today. Advantages of a semi-automated system over a non-automated system include automatically generated audit trails and output which is easier to read. However, semi-automated equipment may be difficult to learn and complex in operation.

Pre-arrival activities. Guests making reservations may call a national reservations network or contact the hotel directly. When reservation requests grow beyond the front desk's ability to handle them efficiently, many hotels create a reservation department. Pre-registration activities include preparation of registration cards, guest folios, and information slips. As in a non-automated system, room assignments are based on room rack status.

Arrival activities. Upon arrival at the hotel, guests with reservations simply verify the prepared registration information and sign in. Walk-in guests generally complete a multiple-copy registration card. Copies are distributed to the room rack, the switchboard operator, and the information rack.

Occupancy activities. The use of semi-automated systems may not significantly reduce the paperwork needed to chart the hotel guest cycle. Vouchers are used to communicate charges to the front desk, and revenue outlets rely on sales record entries to prove transactions. Mechanical cash registers and posting machines are used to process many of the records formerly processed by hand, enabling the front office to handle guest accounting transactions more rapidly. A night audit is used to verify account entries and balances.

Departure activities. A more thorough audit routine leads to faster and smoother guest check-outs. Desk agents experience fewer guest account discrepancies and are able to quickly reconcile accounts and relay room status information to the housekeeping department. Registration cards may be collected for the property's guest history files.

Fully Automated

In fully automated hotels, front office recordkeeping is computer-based. Computer systems designed for use in the hospitality industry were first introduced in the early 1970s. These initial systems tended to be expensive, and were therefore attractive to only the largest hotel properties. During the following decade, computer equipment became less expensive, more compact, and easier to operate. Applications evolved into user-friendly packages which did not require the sophisticated technical training demanded by earlier computer systems. The development of versatile personal computers provided the impetus for system vendors to approach smaller lodging properties. By the 1980s, computer systems appeared cost-effective to hotels of all sizes. Exhibit 3.6 illustrates the degree of property automation within the lodging industry in 1986.

Service bureaus may enable properties to enjoy the benefits of automation without having to support an in-house computer system. However, most service bureaus focus on back office functions, not front office activities.

Pre-arrival activities. The reservations module of an in-house computer system may directly interface with a central reservation network and automatically block rooms according to a pre-determined pattern. The reservations module may also automatically generate letters of confirmation and pre-registration activities. Electronic folios can be established and pre-registration transactions can be processed for guests with confirmed reservations. Reservations modules may also generate lists of expected arrivals, occupancy and revenue forecasts, and a variety of informative reports.

Arrival activities. Guest information is either copied from the computer's reservation record or, for walk-in guests, entered by the front desk agent. The guest may then be presented with a computer-prepared registration card for verification and signature. The installation of on-line credit card authorization terminals enables front desk personnel to receive timely credit card approval. Registration and room rack data are stored electronically in the computer and can be retrieved whenever necessary. Electronic guest folios are also created and maintained in the computer's memory.

Occupancy activities. Room racks and electro-mechanical posting machines are replaced by computer terminals throughout the front office. As guests charge purchases at revenue outlets, the charged amounts are electronically transferred to the front desk and automatically posted to the proper folio. Instantaneous postings, simultaneous guest account and departmental entries, and continuous trial balances free the night auditor to spend time auditing, rather than just balancing guest accounts.

Departure activities. A neatly printed electronic folio assures the guest of accuracy in statement preparation. Depending on the method of settlement, the computer system automatically posts the transactions to appropriate guest and hotel accounts. For a direct-billed account, the system produces a bill to be sent to the guest. Once the guest's account is settled and the postings are complete, guest information is used to create a guest history record.

Exhibit 3.6 Property Automation in the Lodging Industry

CENTRAL RESERVATION SYSTEM	76.4
COMPUTERIZED FRONT OFFICE SYSTEM	57.4
COMPUTERIZED BACK OFFICE SYSTEM	63.9
COMPUTERIZED ENERGY MGMT SYSTEM	22.9
AUTOMATIC CHECKOUT MACHINES	7.3
ELECTRONIC CARD KEY SYSTEM	11.9
POINT OF SALE TERMINALS FOR F&B	48.4
FIRE DETECTOR (HEAT OR SMOKE)	93.9
MICRO-COMPUTERS FOR GUEST USAGE	4.1

PERCENTAGE (0 10 20 30 40 50 60 70 80 90 100)

Source: Laventhol & Horwath, *U.S. Lodging Industry—1987* (Philadelphia: Laventhol & Horwath, 1987), p. 12. Reprinted by permission.

Front Office Forms

The front office relies on various forms in monitoring the hotel guest cycle. This section discusses front office documents employed in the four stages of the guest cycle. The number and nature of documents will vary depending on the degree of automation in a hotel.

Pre-Arrival

Since reservations initiate the guest cycle, capturing and maintaining reservation data is critical to effective front office operations. Reservations are recorded on a **reservation record** or entered into a computer-based **reservation file.** The guest may be sent a **letter of confirmation** to verify that a reservation has been made and that its specifications are accurate. Confirmation permits correction of errors before the arrival stage, and allows the front office to verify that it has a correct address for the guest.

Front offices which use a reservation rack to monitor reservations require **reservation rack slips.** The information contained on a reservation rack slip represents only a portion of a complete reservation record. Reservation rack slips are often color coded to indicate the characteristics of the reservation they represent.

Arrival

The front office may use a **registration card** or a computer-based equivalent to process guest check-in. Registration cards require the guest to furnish personal data in addition to indicating length of stay and method of settlement. In most states, the guest's signature is required for the establishment of a legal guest relationship with the hotel. Registration cards may also be required by law to contain printed statements relating to the storage of guest valuables.

Front offices that use room racks depend on the creation of **room rack slips** during the arrival stage of the guest cycle. A room rack slip may contain guest personal data, room rate, expected departure date, and room number. Room rate data make the preparation of rooms revenue reports possible; an expected departure date helps the front office develop future room availability schedules. Completed room rack slips are placed in the room rack to indicate room status. The presence of a rack slip in an assigned room slot indicates that the room is occupied.

Occupancy

Once the guest is registered, the front office initiates a **guest folio.** A guest folio is a record of the charges incurred and credits acquired by a guest during occupancy. While folio information is comparable across front office recordkeeping systems, folio formats tend to vary. In all recordkeeping systems, information from the guest registration card is transferred to a folio during folio creation. Folios should be pre-numbered for control purposes; the folio number can be entered onto the guest's registration card for cross-indexing. Folios may have several duplicate pages depending on the hotel's needs. One copy is the front office's record of the guest's stay, and one copy is given to the guest during the departure stage of the guest cycle, as documentation of the charges accrued during occupancy. Other copies are used for a variety of purposes, such as direct billing after departure.

In a non-automated system, a folio card contains a series of columns for recording debit entries, credit entries, and a running balance. At the end of the business day, each column is reviewed and the ending balance is carried forward as the opening balance for the following day.

In a semi-automated system, guest transactions are posted sequentially on a folio card. Data recorded include the transaction date, the originating revenue center, the transaction amount, and the resulting account balance.

In a fully automated system, electronic folios simplify transaction posting and handling. For a guest with a reservation, personal data already stored in the computer are verified at registration or as part of pre-registration activities. Walk-in guest accounts require the desk agent to enter guest information during the registration process. Once all needed information is entered, an electronic folio is automatically created and available for immediate transaction posting. Electronic folios are stored internally and can be printed on demand.

A **voucher** is a support document detailing the facts of a transaction. Non-automated and semi-automated properties depend on vouchers to communicate information from remote revenue centers to the front desk area. Common types of vouchers include charge vouchers, allowance vouchers, transfer vouchers, and paid-out vouchers. During a night audit routine, vouchers help ensure that all transactions requiring account posting have been processed correctly. Fully automated properties may require few vouchers (or none), since remote points of sale may be electronically interfaced with a front office computer system, reducing the need for support documentation. (Vouchers are discussed in Chapter 7.)

An **information rack slip** may be prepared to enable switchboard operators and guest services personnel to quickly determine the location of a specific guest in the hotel. When a telephone caller asks to be connected with a guest, the switchboard operator can search the information rack to identify the guest's room number and complete the connection. Automated front office systems replace traditional information racks with a computer terminal, thereby eliminating the need for information racks and rack slips. These terminals can be used to quickly access the guest's record and display the comprehensive information it contains.

Departure   Guest folios should be kept current throughout occupancy to ensure an accurate account balance for settlement at departure. In addition to the guest folio, other forms may be required for account settlement. A **credit card invoice,** for example, will be needed if the guest wishes to settle the account using a credit card. In some hotels, a **cash voucher** is used to document a cash settlement. A **transfer voucher** will be needed if the guest's account is to be direct billed for payment—that is, transferred from a guest receivable to a non-guest receivable account. Even in a fully automated system, several documents may be produced to prove transactions and provide a basis for comprehensive auditing.

Guest history files may require creation of a separate **guest history record** during the departure stage. A guest history record contains information relevant to marketing, sales, and servicing the guest's return. In addition, state law may require retention of certain guest data for some period of time. Most fully automated systems automatically generate an electronic guest history record as part of the check-out process.

The Front Desk

Most front office functions are performed at the front desk. Since guests directly interact with front desk personnel, the front desk represents the hotel to the guest. It is the initial point of contact during the arrival stage, the source for guest service support during the occupancy stage, and the location for account settlement and check-out during the departure stage of the guest cycle. The front desk serves as the sounding board for guest complaints. It is the major source of guest information and services and is responsible for the maintenance of guest records.

Most front desks are prominently located in the hotel lobby, parallel to a lobby wall, with four to six feet of working space between the wall and the desk. The front desk surface is a counter approximately three and a half feet high and two and a half feet deep. Its length may vary according to the number of rooms in the hotel, the duties performed at the front desk, and the configuration of the hotel lobby. Signs may be placed on or above the various activity centers to indicate the functional division of the desk for registration, cashier, check-out, information and mail handling, and other guest services. Partitions may be used to screen front office data (much of which is confidential and proprietary) from guests or visitors standing at the desk.

Functional Organization   The functional efficiency of a front desk depends on the organization of the work stations located at the desk. The design and layout of the desk should provide each front desk employee with easy access to the equipment, forms, and supplies necessary for his or her assigned tasks. Ideally, the front office layout is planned and its furniture and fixtures situated according to the functions performed at designated activity centers along the desk. The current trend of flexibility in the roles of front office staff members, discussed in Chapter 2, often leads to a lack of set positions for front desk functions.

Studies of the interactions of front office personnel with guests and equipment are often used to suggest changes in the design of front desk areas. Efficiency is an important concern in front office design. Whenever front office employees have to turn their backs to guests, leave guests unattended, or take too long to complete a process, front desk design could be improved.

Design Alternatives

Various hotel supply companies have researched industry needs and redesigned front desk areas to make them more aesthetically appealing. For instance, there is general agreement that traditional mail, message, and key racks may be unnecessary at the front desk. Mail, messages, and keys can be stored in drawers or slots located under or away from the front desk. The front desk area may appear more streamlined as a result.

Some hotels have installed circular or semicircular front desk structures. The circular desk is a ring that encloses the desk staff with its counter, as shown in Exhibit 3.7. In a semicircular arrangement, there is normally a straight wall at the back of the desk with a door leading to front office support services. Circular and semicircular desks allow greater service to more guests at the same time; they also tend to appear more modern and innovative than the traditional straight desk. A potential problem is that, although front office work stations and equipment may dictate where functions must be performed, guests can approach these desks from all angles. Therefore, extra care may be necessary to ensure the success of these and other innovative desk designs.

Some hotels have experimented with a lobby arrangement which includes no front desk at all. In a deskless environment, registration and room assignment may be handled at a small table or personal desk in a low-traffic area of the lobby. A concierge, receptionist, or special service employee may serve as guest host. Although a guest host may perform many of the same functions as a front desk agent, the service is intended to be more personal and informal. Guests often enjoy a casual, seated registration instead of a long wait standing at a front desk counter.

Handicapper Access. The traditional standards for front desk design may not satisfy the physical needs of all hotel guests. Accessibility for handicapper guests is an important consideration in the design of a hotel in general, but applies especially to the front office area. Some city governments have legislated construction standards to ensure that handicapper guests are not discriminated against with respect to front desk activities. Recently constructed hotels and remodeled properties both should strive to make the front desk equally accessible to all guests and visitors.

Front Office Equipment

In non-automated and semi-automated properties, the layout of the front desk is centered on a collection of racks and specialty equipment

Exhibit 3.7 Circular Front Desk

Courtesy of the Ramada Inn, Ithaca, New York.

designed to produce, store, or display front office forms. In a semi-automated system, these racks are augmented by posting machines, cash register devices, and other pieces of equipment designed to facilitate front office tasks. Exhibit 3.8 shows one possible layout of front office equipment in a semi-automated hotel.

Most of the machinery described in the following sections will not appear in a hotel which uses a non-automated recordkeeping system. In a fully automated hotel, most of the machinery and other equipment is replaced by a front office computer system. Thus, the following discussion of front office equipment applies chiefly to semi-automated properties.

Room Rack   The room rack has traditionally been considered the most important piece of front office equipment. A **room rack** is an array of metal file pockets designed to hold room rack slips displaying guest and room status information. Exhibit 3.9 shows a typical room rack design. The room rack is normally recessed into the front desk counter, tilted against the desk, or mounted below or behind the desk. When key slots are added to the room rack, it can serve as a combination room and key rack.

The room rack contains a summary of information about the current status of all rooms in the hotel. A room rack slip or, in some hotels, the

Exhibit 3.8 Layout of Front Office Equipment

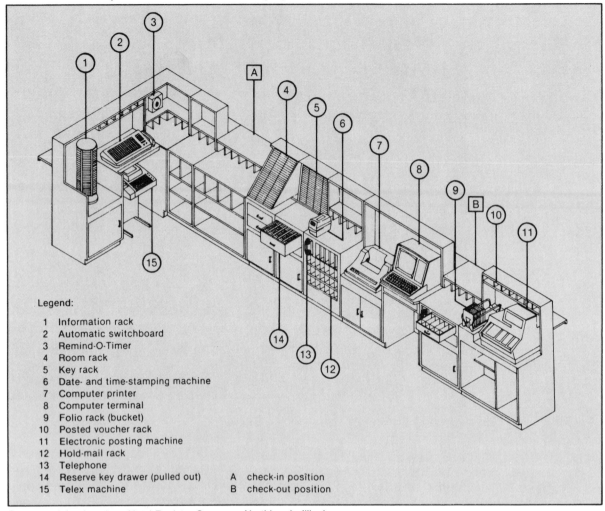

Legend:

1 Information rack
2 Automatic switchboard
3 Remind-O-Timer
4 Room rack
5 Key rack
6 Date- and time-stamping machine
7 Computer printer
8 Computer terminal
9 Folio rack (bucket)
10 Posted voucher rack
11 Electronic posting machine
12 Hold-mail rack
13 Telephone
14 Reserve key drawer (pulled out)   A check-in position
15 Telex machine   B check-out position

Courtesy of the American Hotel Register Company, Northbrook, Illinois.

guest registration card itself can be inserted into the room rack to display summary guest data, room number, and room rate. One glance at the room rack should immediately inform the front desk agent of the occupancy and housekeeping status of all rooms. The room rack may also contain information about room types, features, and rates. Front desk agents use this information to match available rooms with guest needs during the registration process.

In a fully automated property, the need for a room rack may be eliminated. Equivalent information can be stored in a computer system and displayed on a front desk terminal whenever needed.

Mail, Message, and Key Rack

A **key rack** is an array of numbered compartments used to maintain guestroom keys. To minimize the number of racks in the front desk area, most hotels combine the key rack with either the room rack or the **mail and message rack.** A combination **mail, message, and key rack** can be

Exhibit 3.9 Room Rack

either a freestanding wall unit or an under-counter row of compartments. Some front offices use this rack as a room divider by placing it between the front desk and the switchboard areas of the front office. When the mail and message compartments of the rack are open from both sides, telephone operators and front desk agents have equal access to rack contents. Operators who record telephone messages can insert them from the rack's back side; front desk agents can retrieve the messages for guest distribution from the front side.

If guestroom telephones in the hotel are equipped with message lights, they can be used to notify guests of messages awaiting their retrieval. In-room message lights may be activated with a control switch beside each room's slot in the mail, message, and key rack.

In a fully automated lodging property, a mail and message rack may be all that is necessary. The function of a key rack may be performed by the master console of an **electronic locking system.** Features of electronic locking systems and their impact on hotel security are discussed in Chapter 6.

Reservation Racks

Front offices often use both advance reservation racks and current reservation racks. In an **advance reservation rack,** reservation rack slips are arranged by the guests' scheduled dates of arrival and, within each day's grouping, alphabetically by the guests' or groups' names. A **current reservation rack** is a portable subset of the advance reservation rack. Early each morning, the advance reservation rack slips for that day's expected arrivals are loaded into the current reservation rack and taken to the front desk. The current reservation rack is used by front desk agents during registration.

In a fully automated property, both advance and current reservation racks may be eliminated. The equivalent information is internally managed by the computer system.

Information Rack

An **information rack** is an index of in-house guests, by both last name and room number. It is commonly used to assist front office employees with proper routing of telephone calls, mail, messages, and visitor inquiries. The information rack normally consists of aluminum slots designed to hold guest information slips. These slots can be rearranged easily to fit the immediate needs of the hotel. Exhibit 3.10 shows a typical front office information rack design.

Front office computer systems eliminate the need for an information rack since guest name and room number data are easily retrievable through a system computer terminal.

Folio Trays

In non-automated and semi-automated properties, guest folios are stored in a front office **folio tray** (or **folio bucket**) and arranged by guestroom number. Guest folios remain in the tray throughout the occupancy stage of the guest cycle, except when they are used in posting transactions. Both the front office cashier and front desk agent are likely to require access to folios stored in the tray.

A second folio tray is normally located in the hotel's accounting office. This secondary storage location contains the folios of departed guests whom the hotel is direct billing or who settled their account by credit card. Once these accounts are settled, the folios are moved to a permanent storage location.

In a computerized front office, there is little need for a folio tray since folios are stored electronically, not in printed form. However, folios may be printed in advance of check-out for those guests expected to depart; a folio tray may be necessary for temporary storage of these pre-printed folios.

Account Posting Machine

Semi-automated hotels that allow guests to make charge purchases to room accounts use an **account posting machine** to post, monitor, and balance these charges. The posting machine shown in Exhibit 3.11 is

Exhibit 3.10 Rotary Information Rack

Courtesy of the American Hotel Register Company, Northbrook, Illinois.

common in the hospitality industry. A posting machine normally provides:

- A standardized means of recording transactions

- A legible statement of guest account

- A basis for cash and deferred payment management

- An analysis of departmental sales activity

- An audit trail of charge purchase transactions

In a semi-automated operation, the account posting machine should be located near the front office folio tray and voucher rack.

Posting machines have several advantages and disadvantages. Two of the main advantages are that the guest's copy of the folio is printed, not handwritten, and that the machines have built-in tabulation devices that allow management to systematically audit current charge postings. Additionally, posting machines update account balances after each posting.

Exhibit 3.11   Account Posting Machine

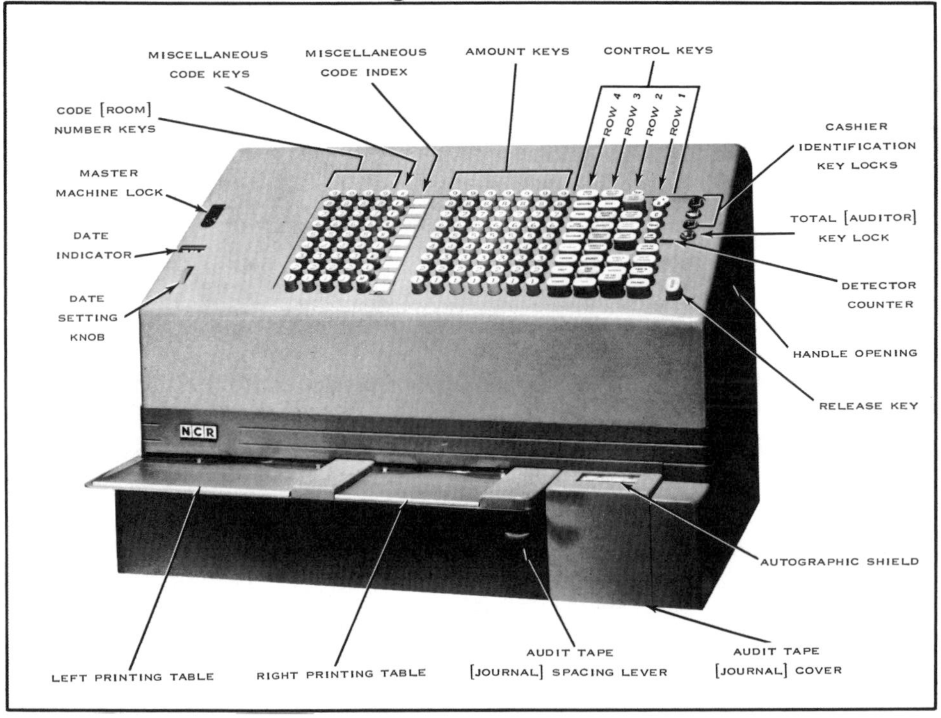

Courtesy of NCR Corporation, Dayton, Ohio.

On the other hand, the operation of posting machines may be difficult to learn, cumbersome, and prone to error. Although a semi-automated posting procedure is more efficient than a manual posting procedure, it still may not be very fast.

There is no need for account posting machines in a fully automated environment since the system relies on electronic folios, not printed copies.

Voucher Rack

After a voucher has been used to support the posting of a transaction, it is stored for verification during the audit. Vouchers are normally filed for future reference in a **voucher rack** located near the account posting machine.

Cash Register

A front desk **cash register** is used to record cash transactions and maintain cash balances. The front office cashier is primarily responsible for its operation and contents. Cash registers can use a mechanical, electro-mechanical, or computer-based mode of operation. A typical electro-mechanical cash register is shown in Exhibit 3.12. Many specialized functions can be built into a cash register to facilitate close monitoring of hotel/guest transactions. An electronic front desk cash register may also be interconnected with a front office computer system to provide more complete control over financial transactions and folio handling.

Cash registers are designed primarily to record sales transactions and to hold cash. Most cash registers also include printing devices for

Exhibit 3.12 Cash Register

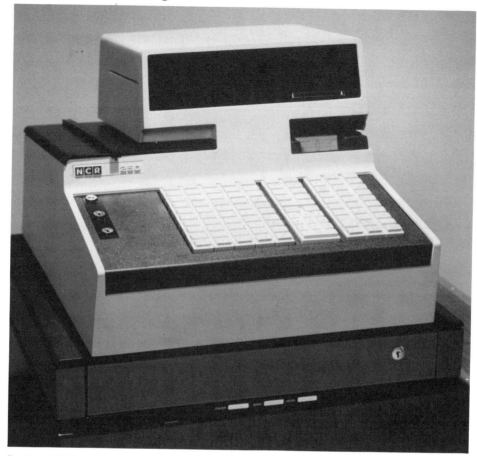

Courtesy of NCR Corporation, Dayton, Ohio.

producing transaction tapes, sales receipts, and inventory and price controls. Keys on a cash register may perform a variety of operations, including:

- Recording the amount of a transaction

- Recording the affected departments

- Recording the type of transaction

- Recording the identity of the cashier

- Correcting, totaling, and computing change for a transaction

An indicator panel allows the guest and the operator to follow the progress of the transaction. The cash drawer may be divided into several money compartments, or may have removable drawers for individual cash banks.

Telephone Equipment   The deregulation and divestiture of the American Telephone & Telegraph Company (AT&T) has had significant impact on the United States hospitality industry. Since deregulation, other telephone companies have been able to market telephone equipment and long-distance carrier services in direct competition with AT&T. Smaller telephone companies provide most local services, while several larger carriers can provide long-distance service between telephone company territories. Hotels are able to choose what equipment to buy and from whom, how to handle guest long-distance calls, how to price those calls, and which long-distance carrier company to use. Regulations affecting the pricing of calls may vary from state to state.

For long-distance interstate calls, hotels may purchase long-distance service from one of several common carriers and resell such service (at a profit) directly to guests. In-state telephone calls, however, fall under the jurisdiction of the state's Public Service Commission. Some states regulate the amount of hotel service surcharges on intrastate and local calls, while others do not.[1] A hotel's telephone call rates must be in accord with applicable regulations.

Call Accounting Equipment. The need to accurately account for guest telephone calls has encouraged the development of specialized telephone **call accounting systems.** A device linked to the telephone system identifies each phone number dialed from guestroom telephones. This eliminates the need for a telephone company operator to intervene and record the details of each guest call. Calls are thus charged at the lower station-to-station rates rather than the more expensive operator-assisted rates. This call placement technique is referred to as **least-cost routing.**

Call accounting systems provide a record of each room's local, in-state, and long-distance phone calls so that appropriate charges may be posted to the guest's folio. If the hotel supports a front office computer system, call information may be directly transferred and posted to electronic guest folios.

New Technology. Often, telephone systems with sophisticated features are installed in hotels for reasons other than just measurable cost efficiency. Examples of this trend include automatic call dispensing systems, telephone/room status systems, and facsimile (fax) machines.

In many cases, automatic call dispensing is limited to wake-up services. The operator enters the room number and time for each wake-up call into the computer, and at the scheduled time, a telephone call is automatically placed to the guest's room. Once the guest answers the call, the computer may activate a synthesized voice that reports the current time, temperature, and weather conditions.

Telephone/room status systems can assist with rooms management and prohibit the unauthorized use of telephones in vacant rooms. Housekeeping or room service employees can use guestroom telephones to enter data concerning room service charges (for example, restocking in-room bar inventories), maintenance information, and current room status information. Ideally, these features will not only lower payroll costs, but ensure a more pleasurable stay for guests while providing the front office with comprehensive communication capabilities.

Hotels catering primarily to business travelers sometimes possess a fax machine. A fax machine makes it possible to transmit full-page documents. The process involves an exchange of information, usually by wire, between two photocopy machines.

Support Devices

In addition to the racks, registers, and machines often found in the front office, numerous pieces of support equipment are also possible. These devices help make cumbersome functions straightforward, facilitate information handling, and provide additional storage for necessary data, files, and reports used in the front office area.

Credit card imprinter. An imprinter is used to press a credit card voucher against a guest's credit card. The impact causes the raised card number, expiration date, and name on the card to be recorded on the voucher for use in credit card billing and collection procedures. Imprinters may be manual or electric.

Magnetic strip reader. A magnetic strip reader, such as the one shown in Exhibit 3.13, reads data magnetically encoded and stored on the magnetic tape strip on the back of a credit card and wires this data to a credit card verification service. On the basis of the credit card data and transaction data, the credit card verification service either approves or disapproves the transaction.

Telewriter. The operator of a telewriter writes with a pen-like stylus on a specially designed surface. The handwritten message written on this surface is displayed on a similar device located elsewhere.

Time stamp. Folios, mail, and other front office paperwork are inserted into a time-stamp device to record the current time and date. This recording can be very important in establishing a chronology of events.

Security monitor. Closed-circuit television monitors allow front office employees or security personnel to monitor security and safety throughout the hotel from a central location. Hotel safety and security topics are discussed in Chapter 6.

Wake-up devices. A non-automated wake-up device is typically a specially designed clock which allows multiple alarm settings to remind front desk agents or telephone operators to place wake-up calls. A wake-up call log kept beside the clock informs the agents or operators which room numbers are to be called at what times.

Telex. International travelers are likely to make reservations by means of a telex network connection. The caller directs a message from a telex machine to the hotel's telex machine. A return telex is used to confirm the reservation. Telex communication is faster than the postal service and more reliable than telephone networking since the hotel receives a written message.

Self-registration/check-out terminals. Fully automated hotels may provide self-registration and check-out terminals for guests. These terminals do not eliminate the need for front desk agents, but can free them to attend to other hotel duties, enhancing guest service. The use of these terminals for guest registration and check-out is described in Chapters 5 and 9.

Exhibit 3.13   Magnetic Strip Reader

Front Office Computer Applications

Front office computer systems do not all operate identically. However, some generalizations about **property management systems (PMS)** may serve to illustrate the nature of front office computer applications.[2] The four most common front office software modules are designed to help front office employees perform functions related to:

- Reservations

- Rooms management

- Guest accounting

- General management

Exhibit 3.14 summarizes front office computer system applications. For a useful introduction to computer functions and terminology, see the Appendix at the back of this text.

Reservations   A **reservations module** enables a hotel to rapidly process room requests and generate timely and accurate rooms, revenue, and forecasting reports. Most lodging chains participate in computer-based central reservation systems. Central reservation systems typically store reservations data, track rooms reserved, control reservations by room type, and monitor the number of reservations received. Reservations received at a

Exhibit 3.14 Front Office Computer Applications

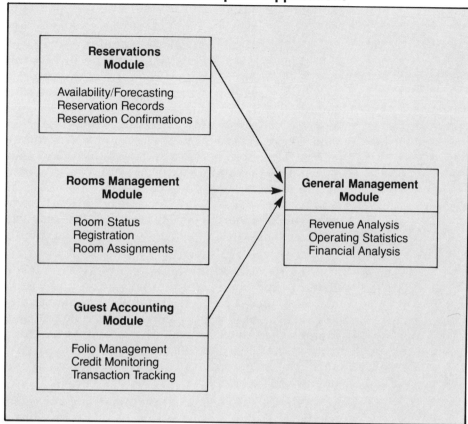

Source: Michael L. Kasavana and John J. Cahill, *Managing Computers in the Hospitality Industry* (East Lansing, Mich.: Educational Institute of the American Hotel & Motel Association, 1987), p. 21.

central system office can be processed, confirmed, and communicated to the destination property before the reservations agent finishes the telephone conversation with the caller.

When the destination property uses a front office computer system, its reservations module can receive data sent directly from the central reservation system. Both advance and current reservation racks are eliminated. As the reservations data are received at the hotel, in-house reservations records, files, and revenue forecasts are immediately updated. This enables the system to remain current and in control of reservations activities. In addition, previously received reservations data can be automatically reformatted into pre-registration materials. An updated expected arrivals list can be produced just prior to the day's registration. Various reservation reports containing a summary of reservation data and guest account status information can also be generated.

Rooms Management   A **rooms management module** maintains current information on the status of rooms, assists in the assignment of rooms during registration, and helps coordinate guest services. A rooms management module can also provide rapid access to room availability data during the reservation process. This information can be especially useful in reservation confirmation and rooms revenue forecasting. Since the rooms management module replaces most traditional front office equipment, it often becomes a major determinant in the selection of one computer system over another.

The module alerts front desk employees of each room's status just as the room rack and information rack do in non-computerized environments. For example, with a room rack, an upside-down card without a folio covering it may signify that the previous night's guest has checked out, but that the room has not yet been cleaned for resale. This status will remain unchanged until housekeeping notifies the front desk that the room is clean and ready for occupancy. In a computerized system, the front desk employee simply enters the room's number at a computer system terminal and the current status of the room appears immediately on the terminal's display screen. Once the room has been cleaned and readied for occupancy, the housekeeping staff changes the room's status by means of a terminal located in the housekeeping work area. Changes in room status are immediately communicated to the front desk.

Guest Accounting

A **guest accounting module** increases the hotel's control over guest accounts and significantly modifies the night audit routine. Guest accounts are maintained electronically, eliminating the need for folio cards, folio trays, and posting machines. The guest accounting module monitors predetermined guest credit limits and provides flexibility through multiple folio formats. At check-out, outstanding account balances can be automatically transferred to an accounts receivable file for billing and collection.

When the hotel's revenue outlets are connected to the front office computer system, remote electronic cash registers can be used to communicate guest charges to the front office. These charges can then be automatically posted to appropriate electronic guest folios.

General Management

A **general management module** cannot operate independently of other front office modules. General management applications tend to be report-generating packages which depend on data collected through reservations, rooms management, and guest accounting modules. For example, the general management module may be able to generate a report showing the day's expected arrivals and the number of rooms available for occupancy—a combination of reservations and rooms management data. In addition to generating reports, the general management module serves as the central link between front and back office computer system applications.

Back Office Interface

A completely computerized installation also involves the hotel's back office. It is possible to implement front and back office software packages independently of each other. However, integrated front and back office systems offer the hotel a full range of control over all operational areas, from room sales and payroll to guest and non-guest account analysis. An integrated system cannot produce complete financial statements unless all the required data are stored somewhere in the system's memory. The back office system's generation of reports depends on the front office system's collection of data. Several back office application modules are available from most vendors. The four most popular applications are:

- An **accounts receivable module** which monitors guest accounts and account billing and collection when integrated with the front office guest accounting module

- An **accounts payable module** which tracks the hotel's purchases and helps the hotel maintain sufficient cash flow to satisfy its debts

- A **payroll accounting module** which processes such data as time and attendance records, pay distribution, and tax withholdings

- A **financial reporting module** which helps the hotel develop a chart of accounts in order to produce balance sheets, income statements, and transactional analysis reports

Other Interface Applications

Other computer applications are available to a fully automated hotel property. It may be possible to interface these systems with a front office management system. Common interfaces include:

- A **point-of-sale system** which allows guest account transactions to be quickly transmitted from remote points of sale to the front desk for account folio posting

- A **call accounting system** which directs, prices, and tracks guestroom telephone use for resale and posting to guest accounts

- An **electronic locking system** which may interface with rooms management modules to provide enhanced guest security

Call accounting systems have been discussed in this chapter. Electronic locking systems are covered in Chapter 6, and point-of-sale systems are covered in Chapter 7.

Guest-Operated Devices

Some hotels have gone beyond basic property management systems by installing a variety of automated guest-operated devices. As the world's traveling public becomes more familiar with using computers, there may be significant growth in this element of lodging services.

Automated information devices in public hotel areas provide guests with the opportunity to inquire about in-house events and local activities. When a printer is connected to a lobby information terminal, guests may receive individually prepared lists of events.

Recent technological advances offer guests the opportunity for in-room folio review and check-out. When in-room computers are interfaced with a guest accounting module, they are able to access folio data and provide guests with a means by which to approve and settle their accounts. Guestroom telephones interfaced with the computer system may also be used for this purpose. When in-room computers can be linked to external computer information services, guests may also access airline schedules, local restaurant guides, entertainment guides, stock market reports, news and sports updates, shopping catalogs, and video games.

An **in-room movie system** can be interfaced to a front office accounting module or can function as an independent, stand-alone system.

When it is interfaced to the accounting module, the system triggers automatic posting of charges to the appropriate guest folio. However, with older systems, a guest may turn on the television set without knowing that it is tuned to a pay channel. Hotels with such systems should instruct the housekeeping staff to select a non-pay channel when cleaning the guestrooms. Incorporating a preview channel can significantly reduce the number of charges disputed by guests. Newer systems do not allow guests to inadvertently tune in a pay channel. Stand-alone in-room movie systems generally require the guest to dial an in-house service and request that the pay channel be turned on. The operator who turns on the program posts the charge to the proper guest folio.

There are two types of **in-room beverage service systems.** Non-automated honor bars are stocks of items in both dry and cold storage areas within a guestroom. The bar's beginning inventory level is recorded, changes in the inventory are noted daily by hotel employees, and appropriate charges are posted to the guest's folio. However, since honor bars are open for use at all times, this system may often result in late charge postings to guest folios. Fully automated guestroom vending machines contain electro-optical sensors that record the removal of stored products from designated compartments. When a sensor is triggered, the room device sends appropriate information to the front office accounting module for folio posting.

Notes

1. For further information, see Jack P. Jefferies, *Understanding Hotel/Motel Law* (East Lansing, Mich.: Educational Institute of the American Hotel & Motel Association, 1983), pp. 125-127.

2. For further information, see Michael L. Kasavana and John J. Cahill, *Managing Computers in the Hospitality Industry* (East Lansing, Mich.: Educational Institute of the American Hotel & Motel Association, 1987).

Discussion Questions

1. Describe the activities involved in the four stages of the traditional guest cycle. Why have some properties replaced the traditional cycle with a three-stage sequence?

2. How does the departure stage of the guest cycle conclude both guest services and guest accounting activities? Describe how data related to the guest stay can be used by the front office.

3. Summarize the technological evolution of front office recordkeeping systems.

4. How does a fully automated front office recordkeeping system enhance front office control over guest accounting data?

5. Discuss the forms and/or equipment used in typical non- and semi-automated hotels during the pre-arrival stage of the guest cycle. Why are there two reservation racks?

6. Discuss the forms and/or equipment used in typical non- and semi-automated hotels during the arrival stage of the guest cycle. How can mail, message, and key racks be adapted to the uses of a particular hotel?

7. Discuss the forms and/or equipment used in typical non- and semi-automated hotels during the occupancy stage of the guest cycle. How do vouchers support front office accounting tasks?

8. Discuss the forms and/or equipment used in typical non- and semi-automated hotels during the departure stage of the guest cycle. What are the uses of a guest history record?

9. Discuss the organizational concerns of front desk design. What criteria determine the appropriateness of a design?

10. What are the four most common front office software modules? Discuss their use in streamlining front office recordkeeping. How does a general management module depend on the other three?

Part II

The Guest Cycle

4 Reservations

The ability of the front office to plan, coordinate, staff, and organize activities can be enhanced by an effective reservations process. Since a majority of hotel guests make reservations in advance of their stay, reservations serve an important front office function. Exhibit 4.1 summarizes the reservation mix in the United States, both for all properties and by property size.

The reservations process often involves the important first contact between the guest and the hotel. A reservations agent must be able to respond quickly and accurately to requests for future accommodations. Thus, the volume of paperwork, filing, and other clerical procedures associated with the reservations process should be held to a minimum. Efficient procedures will allow the reservations agent more time for attention to detail and greater opportunity to market various hotel services when appropriate. An effective reservations process depends on set procedures for handling requests, updating information, and generating confirmations.[1]

Processing reservations involves matching room requests with room availability; recording, confirming, and maintaining reservations; and producing management reports. Regardless of the type of equipment used to support the process, reservation information is especially useful in subsequent front office functions. For example, room and rate assignments, guest accounts, and guest history files can be created from the information obtained during the reservations process. Perhaps the most important outcome of a reservation, however, is having the room available when the guest arrives. The success of the process depends on effective reservations management.

The following sections describe typical activities associated with the reservations process. These activities include:

- Reservation inquiry

- Determination of availability

- Creation of the reservation record

- Confirmation of the reservation

- Maintenance of the reservation record

- Production of reservation reports

Exhibit 4.1 Reservation Mix

	All Establishments	Size of Property			
		Under 150 Rooms	150-299 Rooms	300-600 Rooms	Over 600 Rooms
Advanced Reservation Mix					
Direct Inquiry	41.4%	50.5%	36.4%	32.0%	35.5%
Own Reservation System	23.2	24.4	25.9	21.2	26.6
Independent Reservation System	4.3	2.8	4.3	5.7	3.7
Travel Agents	13.9	10.5	14.2	16.8	20.9
Tour Operators	4.8	4.0	5.3	5.4	6.1
Hotel Representatives	11.3	6.4	13.0	18.1	6.5
Transportation Company	1.1	1.4	0.9	0.8	0.7
Total	**100.0%**	**100.0%**	**100.0%**	**100.0%**	**100.0%**

*All amounts are means.

Source: Laventhol & Horwath, *U.S. Lodging Industry—1987* (Laventhol & Horwath, 1987), p. 17. Reprinted by permission.

Before these activities can be addressed, however, the nature of reservations must be examined.

Types of Reservations

A brief discussion of the major types of reservations will clarify some important distinctions.

Guaranteed Reservations

The hotel assures a guest with a **guaranteed reservation** that a room will be held for him or her until check-out time of the day following the day of arrival. In return, the guest guarantees payment for the room, even if it is not used, unless the reservation is canceled in accordance with the hotel's cancellation procedures. The term **no-show** refers to a guest who made a room reservation but did not use it or cancel it. Guaranteed reservations protect the hotel's revenues even in the case of a no-show. Variations of guaranteed reservations include:

Prepayment. A **prepayment guaranteed reservation** requires a payment in full made before the day of arrival. From the perspective of the front office, this form of reservation guarantee is generally the most desirable.

Credit Card. Major credit card companies have developed systems to guarantee participating properties payment for reserved rooms that remain unoccupied. Unless a **credit card guaranteed reservation** is properly canceled before a stated **cancellation hour,** the lodging property will post the charge to the guest's credit card account and the card company will subsequently bill the card holder. This is the most common method of reservation guarantee.

Advance Deposit. An **advance deposit guaranteed reservation** (or partial prepayment) requires the guest to furnish a specified amount of money in advance of arrival. The deposit is typically large enough to cover one night's lodging plus taxes, but may be larger if the reservation is for a longer stay. Should a guest holding an advance deposit reservation fail to show or cancel, the hotel may choose to retain the deposit and cancel the reservation for the entire stay.

Travel Agent. Although **travel agent guaranteed reservations** were quite popular before the 1980s, they are becoming less common since both travel agents and hotels tend to prefer credit card or deposit guarantees when possible. Under this guarantee method, the hotel generally bills the travel agency after a guaranteed reservation has been classified a no-show.

Corporate. A corporation may sign a contractual agreement with the hotel in which it agrees to accept financial responsibility for any no-show business travelers it sponsors. The use of corporate contracts is often popular in hotels with large transient markets.

Non-Guaranteed Reservations

In the case of a **non-guaranteed reservation,** the hotel agrees to hold a room for the guest until a stated reservation cancellation hour, usually 6:00 p.m., on the day of arrival. The property is not guaranteed payment under this type of reservation. If the guest does not arrive by the cancellation hour, the hotel is free to release the room for other use; it is effectively added to the list of rooms available for sale. If the guest arrives after the cancellation hour and rooms remain available, the hotel will accommodate the guest.

Hotels nearing full occupancy may choose to begin accepting only guaranteed reservations once a specified number of expected arrivals has been achieved. In full occupancy situations, the efficiency of the reservations process is especially critical.

Reservation Inquiry

A reservation request can be received in person, over the telephone, in the mail, through a central reservation system, or through an intersell agency connection. Regardless of its origin, the request is formulated as a **reservation inquiry** by the reservations agent. This inquiry typically collects the following information about the guest's proposed stay:

- Date of arrival
- Date of departure (length of stay)
- Type and number of rooms requested
- Room rate code (standard, special, package, etc.)
- Number of persons in party

The agent enters these data onto a reservation form or computer terminal according to clearly defined procedures. Exhibit 4.2 shows a sample non-automated reservation form, while Exhibit 4.3 shows a computer terminal reservation display screen.

Exhibit 4.2   Sample Reservation Form

EFG MOTOR LODGE GUEST RESERVATION FORM

Date of Res. _____

Res. Clerk _____

Please Print or Type

ARRIVAL DATE	DEPARTURE DATE	NO. NIGHTS	NO. PERSONS	RATE CONFIRMED
_____	_____	_____	_____ Adults	$ _____
_____ a.m.	_____ a.m.		_____ Children	
_____ p.m.	_____ p.m.			

NO. ROOMS	ROOM TYPE:	QUEEN BED (1 Qn. bed)	2 DOUBLE BEDS (2 Dbl. beds)	SUITE (2 bdrms.)

OTHER   Crib   Connecting   Balcony   Other (Specify)
REQUESTS: Rollaway   Adjacent   Pool overlook   _____

NAME RESERVATION WILL BE UNDER   TEL: (   ) _____

Last _____ First _____ Mid. Init. ____ (Title, if one is offered) _____

STREET ADDRESS	CITY	STATE	ZIP

REPRESENTING (WHERE APPLICABLE)   TEL: (   ) _____

STREET ADDRESS	CITY	STATE	ZIP

IS RESERVATION GUARANTEED?*   Yes ____   No ____

RESERVATION GUARANTEED BY

Credit Card No.   No.   Exp. Date   Deposit   Other (Specify)

RESERVATION MADE BY (if other than above) _____

REMARKS _____

- -

CHANGE OF RESERVATION

Original Reservation No. _____ Original Date of Arrival _____ Original Rate _____

Remarks _____

*Reservations may or may not be guaranteed.

Reservations can be made for individuals, groups, tours, or conventions. A guest coming to the hotel as an individual and not part of a group is called a **free independent traveler,** or **FIT.** Persons coming to the hotel as part of a group may be handled according to different procedures than FIT guests. For example, reservations for group members may be filed under the group's name rather than the guests' individual names.

Exhibit 4.3 Computer Reservation Screen

```
RESERVATION #: 002115     CONFIRMED? Y   GUARANTEED? Y

01-ARRIVES:      10/6/XX MONDAY        05-ROOM TYPE:  KING
02-DEPARTS:      10/7/XX TUESDAY       06-ROOM BLOCK:
   NIGHTS:       1                     07-ROOM RATE:  72.00
03-# ROOMS:      1
04-PERSONS:      1
----------------------------------------------------------------
08-NAME:         TRAVELER, JAMES MR    15-PAYMENT:     CREDIT CD
09-COMPANY:      CAPITAL MANUFACTURING 16-CARD TYPE:   VISA
10-ADDRESS:      733 LINCOLN BLVD      17-CARD #:      1234 5678 9098 7654
11-CITY:         HASLETT               18-EXP DATE:    11/XX
12-STATE:        MI   13-ZIP:   48840  19-D/B ACCT:
14-PHONE:        517 555-1234             TOTAL DEP:
----------------------------------------------------------------
20-GROUP:
21-TRVL AGENT:   ARCADIA
22-SPECIAL
   NEEDS:        MODEM
23-VIP:          YES
24-COMMENTS:     MEETING/CONVENTION PLANNER
                 FIRST VISIT
                 CONCERNS: CONFERENCE ROOM SECURITY; FIRE SAFETY SYSTEM
```

Sources of Reservations

There are various reservation market sources within the hospitality industry. The three most common sources of reservation transactions are central reservation systems, intersell agencies, and property direct reservations. Exhibit 4.4 shows the interrelationships among these reservation systems. Hotels may experience large volumes of reservation transactions as a result of supporting a variety of reservation alternatives. The interrelationships depicted in Exhibit 4.4 are especially important to high reservation volume properties.

Central Reservation Systems. More than two-thirds of lodging properties belong to one or more central reservation systems. Industry-wide, over one-quarter of all reservation transactions use central reservation systems.[2] There are two basic types of central reservation systems: affiliate networks and non-affiliate networks.

An **affiliate reservation network** is a hotel chain's reservation system in which all participating properties are contractually related. Chain hotels link their operations to streamline the processing of reservations and reduce overall system costs. Affiliate reservation networks may also allow non-chain properties to join the system as **overflow facilities.** Overflow facilities receive reservation requests only after all room availabilities in chain properties within a geographic area have been exhausted.

A **non-affiliate reservation network** is a subscription system designed to connect independent (non-chain) properties. Non-affiliate res-

Exhibit 4.4 Interrelationships Among Reservation Systems

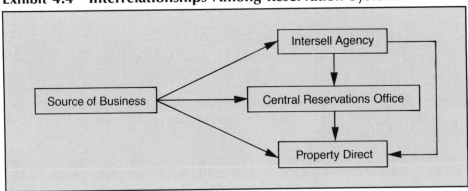

ervation networks enable independent hotel operators to enjoy many of the same benefits as chain-affiliated operators. Like an affiliate reservation network, a non-affiliate network usually assumes responsibility for advertising its service.

A central reservation office typically deals directly with the public by means of a toll-free (800) telephone number. Most large lodging chains actually support two or more reservation centers, with calls being directed to the center nearest the caller. Reservation centers often operate around the clock and at peak times may have as many as several hundred agents on duty at one time.

Central reservation offices typically need to exchange room availability information and process reservation transactions with member properties at regularly scheduled intervals. Many central reservation systems use computers to connect the central system office with member properties. Some reservation systems also place telephone calls directly to destination properties to further ensure successful communication. Central reservation systems normally provide participating properties with necessary communications equipment and bill the properties for reservation transactions the systems handle. In turn, each property must provide accurate and current room availability data to the central reservation office. Without such data, the central reservation office cannot effectively handle the reservations process.

Affiliate and non-affiliate networks often perform a variety of services in addition to managing reservations processing and communications. A central reservation system may also serve as an inter-property communications network, an accounting transfer system, or a destination information center. For instance, a central reservation system is used as an accounting transfer system when a chain hotel communicates operating data to company headquarters for processing. A central reservation system may operate as a destination information center by serving as a communications channel for local weather, special events, and seasonal room rate reports.

Intersell Agencies. An **intersell agency** is a central reservation system that contracts to handle more than one product line. Intersell agencies typically handle reservation services for airline companies, car rental

Radisson 800 reservations agent. Courtesy of Radisson 800 Reservations Center, Omaha, Nebraska.

companies, and hotel properties—a "one call does it all" approach. Although intersell agencies typically channel their room reservation requests to a central reservation system, they may also be able to communicate directly with individual destination properties. The fact that a hotel participates in an intersell arrangement does not preclude its also being a part of a central reservation system.

Property Direct. Exhibit 4.1 shows that, in addition to those reservations received through central reservation systems and intersell agencies, hotels handle over 40% of their reservation transactions directly. Depending on the volume of direct customer contact at a property, the hotel may staff its own reservation department. This department is responsible for handling all direct requests for accommodations, monitoring the communications links with central reservation systems and intersell agencies (if any), and maintaining updated room availability status reports.

There are several possible communication methods for handling property-direct reservation requests:

- **Telephone:** Customers may telephone the hotel directly.

- **Mail:** Written requests for reservations are common for group, tour, and convention business. Mail requests are generally sent directly to the reservation department of the destination property.

- **Property-to-property:** Chain hotel properties typically encourage customers to plan their stays ahead of time by offering direct communications between affiliated properties. This approach can significantly increase the overall number of reservations.

- **Telex, cable, and other:** Telex is often used to communicate international reservation requests. Cable and other methods of communication tend to account for a small proportion of total reservation transactions.

Group Reservations

Group reservations can involve a variety of contacts: meeting planners, housing or convention bureaus, tour operators, and travel agents. Group reservations typically involve intermediary agents and require special care. Usually, when a group selects a hotel, its representative deals with the hotel's sales division. If space is available, an agreed-upon number of rooms, called a **block,** is set aside for the group's members. Group members may be given a special reservation form, such as the one in Exhibit 4.5, with which to reserve rooms within the group's assigned block. As reservations are received from group members, they are applied against the rooms held in the group's block, thereby reducing the number of rooms available within the block. Rooms reserved for specific guests are referred to as **booked;** hence, as group members reserve rooms, their status changes from blocked to booked.

Reservation Availability

Once inquiry data are received, they are compared to previously processed reservations to determine the availability of remaining accommodations. Processing a reservation request results in one of several responses. These responses include:

- Acceptance of the reservation as requested

- Suggestions of alternative room types and/or rates

- Suggestions of alternative hotel properties

In any reservation system, it is necessary to keep a close check on reservations to avoid **overbooking**—that is, accepting reservations that outnumber available rooms. A hotel may certainly try to book for a full house, but avoiding overbooking makes good business sense in several ways. Most important, it helps maintain good customer relations and encourages repeat business. In addition, hotels may be subject to lawsuits when they fail to furnish agreed-upon accommodations. To avoid overbooking, hotels must monitor room availability through reservations coordination. A reservations control book, wall chart, computerized system, or some other control device must be established and maintained.

Control Book

A **reservations control book** is usually a standard three-ring, loose-leaf binder with a tally page for each day of the year. Control books are

Exhibit 4.5   Group Reservation Card

Tear along dotted line. Moisten here, fold here, fold flap down and seal.

Welcome to the Opryland Hotel

Name of Group

Dates of Function

(Please print or type)

Name _____

Address_____

City_____ State_____ Zip_____

Phone (____)_____

Sharing room with _____

Arrival Date _____ Departure Date _____

Room Selection:

ROOM TYPE	SINGLE		DOUBLE	
Standard	$ 82	☐	$ 82	☐
King*	$ 92	☐	$ 92	☐
Conservatory*	$102	☐	$102	☐
Jr. Suite	$150	☐	$150	☐
SUITE TYPE	1 BEDROOM		2 BEDROOM	
Standard Parlor*	$232	☐	N/A	☐
Colonnade*	$400	☐	$482	☐
Parthenon*	$452	☐	$554	☐
Centennial*	$282	☐	N/A	☐
Concierge*	$552	☐	$654	☐

*Subject to availability. If room selected is not available, the next available room will be assigned.

Reservations must be accompanied by one night's room deposit (refunds will be made only when cancellations are received at least 72 hours prior to scheduled arrival date) or by using your American Express. any major credit card.
AMEX ☐☐☐☐ ☐☐☐☐☐☐ ☐☐☐☐☐
Expiration Date ☐☐/☐☐

Reservations received after October 11, 1987 will be confirmed on a space available basis at regular rates.

Check-in
3 p.m.
Check-out
11 a.m.

Approximate Arrival Time _____

Arrival by Auto____ Air____ Flight #_____

If you need additional information, call our Reservations Department at 615/889-1000.

Rates are quoted for single or double occupancy. Children age _12_ and under and sharing room with adult are free. The rate for additional persons over age _12_ is $ _12.00_ per person.

Special Requests:

Rollaway Bed* _____

Crib* _____

Connecting Room* _____

Handicapped Room* _____

Other _____

*Subject to availability

Courtesy of Opryland Hotel, Nashville, Tennessee.

used in non-computerized hotels. Exhibit 4.6 shows two sample tally pages from a reservations control book. On each page, the hotel's rooms and/or suites of rooms are divided into categories and each room is assigned a number. For instance, if a hotel has 20 kings (that is, 20 rooms with king-size beds), the numbers 1 through 20 will be listed under that room category. When a reservation is received, an X is placed over the highest unmarked number for the requested room category on the expected arrival date. If the reservation is for more than one night, subsequent days are circled rather than X'd on the following pages. The circles are used to denote stayover guests, rather than guests expected to register.

Exhibit 4.6 shows that, within the category of 20 kings, 2 individual arrivals, 3 stayovers, and 15 available rooms are expected for the date in question. For the 60 double-bed rooms, 2 individual arrivals, 3 group

Exhibit 4.6 Sample Tally Sheets

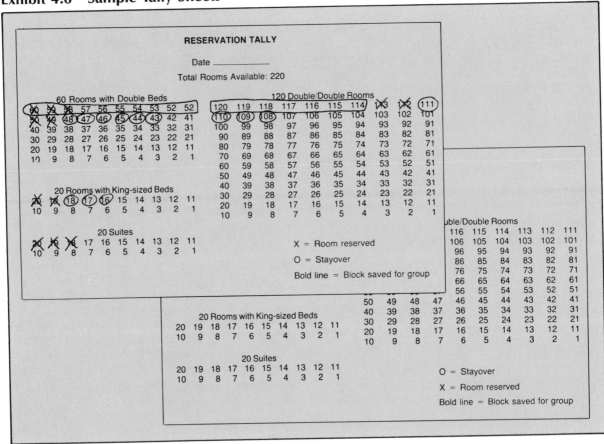

arrivals out of 10 blocked, 6 stayovers, and 42 available rooms are expected. Some reservation tally sheets may also track the number of guests expected as well as the number of rooms, allowing for the production of **multiple occupancy statistics.** Multiple occupancy statistics are important sales mix data which can be useful in planning and forecasting.

The reservations control book must be updated as the hotel receives notification of cancellations or changes in reservations. A property may choose to make initial control book entries in pencil so they can be changed as needed; if initial entries are made in pen, a different color pen should be used to record cancellations or changes. The use of a second color helps the hotel maintain a history of changes in control book transactions.

Wall Chart   Another control technique uses a procedure developed and copyrighted by Dallett Jones.[3] A specially designed **reservations wall chart,** shown in Exhibit 4.7, displays hotel rooms vertically and days of the month horizontally. Non-computerized hotels build customized wall charts by entering appropriate room numbers, rates, and codes. Different colors of ink are often used to differentiate room types. When accommodations are requested, the chart is checked for availability based on the guest's date of arrival, length of stay, and type of room. If space is

Exhibit 4.7　Wall Chart

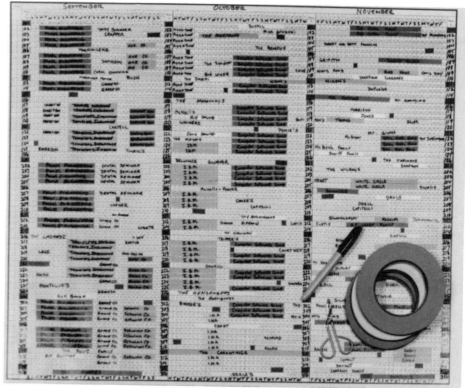

Courtesy of American Hotel Register Company, Northbrook, Illinois.

available, the reservations agent can assign the guest a specific room by taping over the line that represents that room. The tape extends from the day of arrival to the day of departure. Hotels may also record the guest's name on the tape.

Once all reservations are charted, vacant spaces represent the exact dates when specific rooms are available. The wall chart technique allows available space to be determined at a glance, and eliminates the need for erasures and rewriting associated with control book monitoring. When a reservation change is necessary, the reservations agent simply moves the tape to another space. In the case of a cancellation, the tape is removed entirely. Reservations wall charts are also called **reservations density charts.**

Computerized Systems

An in-house computerized reservation system can keep close track of reservations. In addition to tightly controlling room availability data, computer systems are capable of automatically generating many reservation-related reports. Exhibit 4.8, for example, presents a daily expected arrival, stayover, and departure report. It shows that for January 19, there are 19 arrivals, 83 stayovers, and 4 departures expected. This report also projects estimated revenue based on reported reservation information. Reports summarizing reservations by room type, guest profile, and many other characteristics are also available.

Exhibit 4.8 Daily Arrival and Departure Report

```
ARRIVALS, STAYOVERS, DEPARTURES FOR KELLOGG CENTER
PAGE 001
01/19/XX   15:03
```

DATE	ARRIVE	STAYON	DEPART	GUESTS	SOLD	UNSOLD	REVENUE
01/19	19	83	4	135	102	43	5,185.00
01/20	34	57	45	131	91	54	4,604.00
01/21	37	55	36	130	92	53	4,495.50
01/22	15	6	86	29	21	124	1,116.00
01/23	12	14	7	36	26	127	1,252.00

Courtesy of Kellogg Center, Michigan State University.

Once all rooms in a specific category are sold, the computer can be programmed to refuse to accept any further reservations in that category. The computer screen may display an informative message such as: *The category of rooms requested is not available.* Some systems are designed to suggest alternative room types or rates, or even other nearby hotel properties. Computers can be programmed to itemize room availability for future periods, or display open, closed, and special event dates for an extended period of time. The computer can store reservations made for the distant future until the reservations agent requests them, and is also capable of automatically creating waiting lists for high-demand periods and effectively processing group reservations. Recall from Chapter 3 that the time frame for which a property tracks reservations is referred to as its horizon. Most computer-based systems have horizons of two to five years into the future.

The Reservation Record

The reservations agent creates a **reservation record** as a result of guest interaction, an act that initiates the hotel guest cycle. Reservation records identify guests and their anticipated occupancy needs before arrival at the property. In addition, they enable the hotel to personalize guest service and appropriately schedule needed staff. Data contained in a reservation record can also be instrumental in generating several important management reports.

Only after a reservation request has been matched with room availability data does the reservations agent create a reservation record. The agent collects and enters such necessary guest data as:

- Guest name (and group name)
- Home address
- Telephone number, including area code

- Name, address, and telephone number of the guest's employer, if appropriate

- Name of and pertinent information about the person making the reservation, if not the guest

- Number of people in the party, perhaps with ages of any children

- Expected time of arrival

- Reservation type (guaranteed, non-guaranteed)

- Special requirements (infant, handicapper, or no-smoking accommodations)

- Additional information as needed (method of transportation, flight number, room preference, etc.)

If the guest plans to arrive after the hotel's normal reservation cancellation hour, the reservations agent can recite the property's policy on non-guaranteed reservations. Once the agent has recorded the necessary information, some hotels immediately assign the guest a **reservation confirmation number,** which provides a unique reference to the reservation record.

Reservations agents will need to obtain additional information for guaranteed reservations. Depending on the method of guarantee, an agent may be required to obtain one of the following:

- **Credit card information:** The credit card type, number, and expiration date, and the cardholder's name. A cancellation bulletin—listing numbers of invalid and expired cards—or a computer verification service should be consulted to make certain the credit card is valid. Some computerized reservation systems perform credit card verification automatically.

- **Prepayment or deposit information:** An agreement from the client that a required deposit will be received at the hotel before a specified date. A proposed advance deposit or prepayment guarantee should be closely monitored to make certain the correct amount is paid by the designated date; if it is not, the reservation may need to be canceled or reclassified as non-guaranteed.

- **Corporate or travel agency account information:** The name and address of the booking company, the name of the person making the reservation, and the client's corporate or travel agency account number as assigned by the hotel. To facilitate a more efficient process, the hotel may provide reservations agents with a list of approved corporate and travel agency account numbers for verification during the reservation transaction.

Reservations agents should review with the guest the important aspects of guaranteeing a reservation. Guests must be aware that their accommodations will be held until check-out time the day following their scheduled arrival, and that failure to cancel before a specified time could lead to forfeiture of the deposit or a charge against the guarantee.

Individual properties and chains may differ in their policies on quoting and confirming room rates during the creation of a reservation record. Although published rates may be subject to change without notice, a rate quoted and confirmed during the reservations process should be honored. Reservations agents should be aware of several considerations when quoting rates during the reservation record process, including:

- Supplementary charges for extra services or amenities

- Minimum stay requirements in effect for the dates requested, if any

- Special promotions in effect for the dates requested, if any

- Applicable foreign currency exchange rates, if quoting rates to a foreign traveler[4]

- Applicable room tax percentages

Reservation Confirmation

A **reservation confirmation** allows the hotel to verify a guest's room request and personal information by telephoning or mailing a letter of confirmation. A written confirmation, which the guest is expected to produce at registration, states the intent of both parties and confirms important points of agreement: dates, rate, type of accommodation, and number of guests. *Confirmed reservations may be either guaranteed or non-guaranteed.*

Reservation departments normally generate letters of confirmation on the day the reservation request is received. Information can be retrieved from the reservation record and manually or electronically entered onto a specially designed form, such as the one shown in Exhibit 4.9. While there are probably as many confirmation letter formats as there are hotels, confirmation generally includes:

- Date and time of arrival

- Room type and rate

- Length of stay

- Number of persons in party

- Reservation classification: guaranteed or non-guaranteed

- Confirmation number

Depending on the nature of the reservation, a confirmation notice may also include a request for deposit or prepayment, or an update of the original reservation detailing reconfirmation, modification, or cancella-

Exhibit 4.9   Letter of Confirmation

```
                    THE  KELLOGG  CENTER
    MICHIGAN STATE UNIVERSITY,  E. LANSING,  MICHIGAN 48824    (517) 332-6571
```

Q Name	Arrival Date	Arrival Time	Departure Date	No. Guest	No. Rooms	Preferred Accommodations
	01/26/88		01/30/88	1	1	LUXURY DOUBLE

Remarks   THANK YOU FOR YOUR PATRONAGE.   ALL SPECIAL REQUESTS ARE SUBJECT TO AVAILABILITY.   REQUEST RIVERSIDE ROOM.   NON-SMOKING

JOHN DONOVAN
ATLAS INC.
1299 MICHIGAN BLVD
FLINT, MICHIGAN 48458

We will not knowingly rent a guest room on which we already have an advance deposit or guaranteed payment reservation from a customer. If, for any reason beyond our control, a room should not be available for a customer who has either an ADVANCE DEPOSIT RESERVATION, CREDIT CARD GUARANTEED RESERVATION, or COMPANY GUARANTEED RESERVATION, we shall arrange for accommodations at another hotel or motel, pay for such room, provide complimentary transportation to that property (and back to this property if for more than one night), and honor the payment of one long distance phone call to notify business or family contact of these arrangements.
If your plans change, please notify us. Thank you.

MODIFICATION   01/19/88

CHECK IN TIME AFTER 1 P.M.

Courtesy of Kellogg Center, Michigan State University.

tion. For instance, the confirmation in Exhibit 4.9 shows the word "modification" and the corresponding date below the guest's personal data.

**Confirmation/
Cancellation
Numbers**

As part of confirmation, central reservation systems and individual properties may assign a **reservation confirmation number.** A confirmation number assures the guest that a reservation record exists and can be especially useful to the hotel in referencing the appropriate reservation record for modification or cancellation, if needed. Similarly, hotels may issue a **cancellation number** to guests properly canceling a reservation. The issuance of such a number protects both the guest and the hotel. In the event of any future misunderstanding, a cancellation number can provide proof that a cancellation was received. In the case of cancellation of a guaranteed reservation, having a cancellation number may well relieve the guest of responsibility for charges posted against the guarantee. For instance, without a cancellation number a guest may have trouble refuting a no-show billing made to his or her credit card account. Cancellation numbers are not normally assigned to guests who cancel their reservation after the hotel's stated cancellation hour.

Reservation systems typically devise unique methods of generating cancellation and confirmation numbers. These numbers can include the guest's arrival date, the reservations agent's initials, a property code, and other relevant information. For example, under one system, the cancellation number 36014MR563 is devised from these data:

360 = guest's scheduled date of arrival (from consecutively numbered days of the year)
14 = property code number
MR = initials of the reservations agent issuing the cancellation number
563 = consecutive numbering of all cancellation numbers issued in the current year

Calendar dates can be expressed in three digits when the days of the year are numbered consecutively from 001 through 365 (366 in a leap year). For example, the number 360 above might correspond to December 26. Many office desk calendars indicate these sequential numbers in a corner of each day's page.

Cancellation and confirmation numbers should be recorded in a log such as the one shown in Exhibit 4.10. Cross-referencing all cancellation numbers by scheduled date of arrival can also help facilitate subsequent front office functions. Procedures for issuing cancellation numbers may be part of an established agreement between the hotel and a credit card company relative to no-show billing.

Reservation Maintenance

Even when care is taken during the reservations process, sometimes changes or cancellations in a reservation record are necessary. Efficient methods of file organization and file retrieval are critical. If a caller requests a reservation modification, for example, the reservations agent must be able to quickly access the correct record, verify its contents, and process the modification. Subsequent re-filing of the reservation record and updating of pertinent reservation reports should also be promptly handled.

Modifying Non-Guaranteed Reservations

Guests often make non-guaranteed rather than guaranteed reservations because they expect to arrive at the property before the reservation cancellation hour. Then a flight is delayed, a conference takes longer than expected, weather slows traffic, or some other unforeseen situation arises that makes an on-time arrival impossible. Since experienced travelers know that non-guaranteed reservations may be canceled at the hotel's reservation cancellation hour, they often change their reservations to guaranteed status when it becomes apparent that arrival will be delayed. Reservations agents processing these status changes must take care to adhere to hotel policies. Typical steps include the following:

1. Obtaining the guest's name and accessing the correct non-guaranteed reservation record

2. Obtaining the guest's credit card type, number, and expiration date and the cardholder's name, and verifying the validity of the credit card

3. Assigning the guest a new reservation confirmation number

4. Completing the change from non-guaranteed to guaranteed reservation status according to additional property procedures, if any

The bottom of the sample reservation form in Exhibit 4.2 presents a simple format for recording reservation changes.

Reservation Cancellation

A prospective guest who takes the time to cancel a reservation is doing the hotel a service. Reservation cancellation informs the hotel that a

Exhibit 4.10 Cancellation Number Log

Date Cancellation Received	Source of Cancellation	Scheduled Date of Arrival	Guest Name	Cancellation Number Issued

previously reserved room has become available to others, and helps the front office update its planning. Hotels should make cancellation easy and efficient. Cancellation, like any guest service, requires front office staff to be as polite, courteous, and effective as possible.

Non-Guaranteed. To cancel a non-guaranteed reservation, the reservations agent should obtain the guest's name and address, number of reserved rooms, and proposed arrival and departure dates. This information will ensure that the correct reservation is accessed and canceled. After the cancellation is recorded, the caller may be asked whether he or she would like to make an alternate reservation.

Credit Card Guaranteed. Most credit card companies will support no-show billings only if the hotel issues cancellation numbers for properly canceled reservations. Reservations agents may follow a credit card guarantee cancellation procedure involving the following steps:

1. Obtain pertinent information—guest's name and address, number of rooms, proposed arrival and departure dates—and assign the guest a reservation cancellation number. Explain that the cancellation number should be retained as proof of cancellation in case an erroneous credit card billing occurs.

2. Access the proper reservation record, mark it canceled, properly initial and date it, and add the cancellation number to the reservation record. If the cancellation is made by someone other than the guest, add the caller's name to the canceled reservation record.

3. Log the reservation cancellation number.

4. File canceled reservation documentation for future reference.

Advance Deposit. Policies related to the cancellation of advance deposit reservations vary greatly among hotels. The reservations agent should treat advance deposit cancellations with as much care as any other cancellation. The deposit will need to be returned to the guest who cancels a reservation properly.

Other Guaranteed Reservations. The person contacting the hotel to cancel a corporate account or travel agency guaranteed reservation is likely to be a representative of the corporation or travel agency, and not the traveler. The name of the person canceling the reservation is important and should be noted on the reservation record. A reservation cancellation number should be issued and logged according to guidelines similar to those for canceling a credit card guaranteed reservation.

Reservation Reports

An effective reservation system helps maximize room sales by accurately monitoring room availabilities and forecasting rooms revenue. Regardless of the degree of automation, the number and type of management reports available through a reservation system are functions of the hotel's needs and the system's capability and contents. Common management reports include:

- **Reservation transactions report:** This report summarizes daily reservations activity in terms of record creation, modification, and cancellation. Specialized summaries such as cancellation reports, blocked room reports, and no-show reports are also possible.

- **Commission agent report:** Agents with contractual agreements may be owed commissions for business they have booked at the property. This report tracks the amounts owed each.

- **Turnaway report (or refusal report):** This report tracks the number of guests refused because rooms were not available as requested. It is especially helpful to hotels operating near full occupancy or hotels considering expansion.

- **Revenue forecast report:** This report projects future revenue by multiplying predicted occupancies by current room rates. This information can be especially important for long-range planning and cash management strategies.

Some of these topics are considered more fully in Chapter 10. Two of the more important reservations-related reports are discussed in the following sections.

Expected Arrival and Departure Lists

Expected arrival and departure lists are prepared daily to indicate the number and names of guests expected to arrive and depart as well as the number of stayover guests. In a non-automated or semi-automated system, the reservation department manually develops expected arrival data from a control book, wall chart, or reservation rack. Hotels with high reservation volume often load the reservation rack with information for the next several days. Each evening, the data for the next day's expected

Exhibit 4.11   Expected Arrivals List

```
EXPECTED ARRIVALS 01/26/88 KELLOGG CENTER
01/19/88  15:04
PAGE      1


RN#  NAME                    CONVEN   R  T        D  $  P TIME  SPCL SERV
                                               ADD RES

     ADAMS, PROFESSOR               1 TB49   1 G  1       BT TA
     ALAN, MR. ROBERT       VETS    1 SD56   1 N  1
     BAES, THOMAS           VETS    0 TB26   1 N  1
                                            SLATIN
     BAKER, STEVEN          VETS    1 TB52   1 N  2
     BAULAY, ELDEN          VETS    1 DB52   1 N  2
     BEAUFAIT, HENRIETTA    VETS    1 TB44   1 N  1
     BLOGG, CHARLES         VETS    1 TB44   1 N  1
     BOHM, DR. HERBERT              1 TB49   2 G  1       BT TA
     BOYD                   VETS       14    2 N  1
```

Courtesy of Kellogg Center, Michigan State University.

check-in guests are reviewed. Once verified, reservations are assembled alphabetically and either held in the reservation department overnight or brought to the front desk for the night. In a computerized system, a list of expected arrivals may be displayed or printed at the front desk upon demand (see Exhibit 4.11). The presence of this information at the front desk facilitates the registration process.

Computers can also produce preprinted registration cards for guests arriving with reservations. Some hotels pre-register special guests, such as VIPs or those staying in special room categories. Based on information collected during the reservations process, a registration form may be produced requiring only the guest's signature. This procedure further facilitates a rapid check-in process.

Reservations Histories

By analyzing reservation information, front office management can develop an understanding of the hotel's reservation patterns. The hotel's sales and marketing division can use these data to identify new trends, review product mixes, and assess the impact of its marketing strategies. Reservations histories include statistics on all aspects of the reservations process, including the number of guests, occupied rooms, reservations (by source), no-shows, walk-ins, overstays (people staying after their stated departure date), and understays (people who checked out before their stated departure date).

Exhibit 4.12 shows one possible format for recording reservations and occupancy information on a daily basis. Trends can be revealed by grouping occupancy statistics on a daily, weekly, monthly, or yearly basis. Chapter 10 introduces formulas and procedures for developing occupancy forecasts. Knowing overstay and understay percentages at various times of the year can help a hotel devise a plan for handling walk-ins or last-minute reservation requests.

Exhibit 4.12   Sample Format for Recording Daily Occupancy Data

OCCUPANCY HISTORY

Month of December, 19XX

Day/ Date	No. of Guests	No. of Occ. Rooms	No. of Adv. Res.	Res. Systems	Travel Agents	Corp. Accts.	Indiv. Traveler	Other	No. of No-shows	No. of Check-outs	No. of Walk-ins	No. of Over-stays	No. of Under-stays	Remarks
1	93	47	45	22	6	3	13	—	—	37	2	2	1	—
2	114	56	53	25	7	4	18	—	1	10	3	1	—	—
3	117	58	55	24	8	4	19	—	1	15	4	—	—	—
4	73	32	34	10	2	1	21	—	2	41	—	3	4	—
5														
6														
7														
8														
9														
10														

Other Topics

The topics covered in this section are not part of the typical reservations process. Nonetheless, it is important for the reservations agent to understand the legal implications of a reservation and be familiar with waiting lists, group reservations, and errors in the reservations process.

Legal Implications

The reservation agreement between the hotel and the guest begins at the time of guest contact. The agreement may be oral or written. Confirming a reservation to a prospective guest in language which states definitely that the guest will be accommodated on a particular date may constitute a contract binding the hotel to provide accommodations on that date. If the confirmation is made in response to a request from the prospective guest for this reservation, it may also be binding on the prospective guest.[5]

Waiting Lists

Occasionally, a reservation request must be denied because the hotel is fully booked. However, if there is enough lead time before the proposed date of arrival, interested guests may be put on a **waiting list.** This technique is often used by hotels located in high-volume areas. A waiting list might be developed and used according to guidelines similar to the following:

- Advise the guest that no rooms are currently available for the requested dates.

- Offer to take the guest's name and telephone number.

- Accommodate the guest immediately if a room becomes available due to a cancellation.

- Help the guest find alternative dates or accommodations should nothing become available.

Developing waiting lists is good business practice and helps create an atmosphere of good service.

Reservation Phone Techniques

Since this chapter examines the reservations process, it may be helpful to review how a typical reservation request might be handled over the telephone. A sample dialogue between a guest and a reservations agent is presented here. Note how the agent leads the conversation and collects necessary information, recording it on a reservation record or entering it into a computer system.

Agent: "Thank you for calling the Sherwood Inn. This is the reservation office, Gregory speaking."

Guest: "This is Wallace Stevens in Kansas City. I'm going to Dallas and I need a room at your hotel."

Agent: "How many are in your party, sir?"

Guest: "Just me."

Agent: "Are you part of a group or convention at the Inn?"

Guest: "No, I'm not, but I do have an Air Attic Frequent Flyer discount card."

Agent: "Great. What date will you be arriving and how many nights do you plan to stay?"

Guest: "On December 11, for two nights."

Agent: "Would you care to reserve a suite in our special service tower, Mr. Stevens?"

Guest: "Yes, I stayed there last time; that'll be fine."

The agent now checks the control book, wall chart, or computer file for rooms available on the dates requested. Knowing that Mr. Stevens has been a guest at the Sherwood Inn before might also suggest a quick check of the hotel's guest history records.

Agent: "A suite is available, sir. Do you have any other special requests that the Inn can provide, such as a no-smoking room?"

Guest: "Yes, I think I'd like that."

Agent: "May I have the spelling of your first and last names and your area code, phone number, and home address?"

Guest: "W-a-l-l-a-c-e S-t-e-v-e-n-s. My phone number is area code 816-555-1990, and my home address is 4729 Pleasant View Road, Kansas City, Missouri 66041."

Agent: "May I have your Air Attic Frequent Flyer certificate number?"

Guest: "That's A37-P4088."

Agent: "What time do you expect to arrive on the 11th, Mr. Stevens?"

Guest: "I expect to be there around 9 o'clock that evening."

Agent: "Since you'll be arriving after 6 p.m., you might wish to make a guaranteed reservation with a check or a credit card. This ensures that your room will be held after our 6 p.m. cancellation hour. You can arrive any time that evening and a room will be waiting for you. If your plans change, simply call us before 6 p.m. Dallas time on the 11th to cancel. Would you like to make a guaranteed reservation, Mr. Stevens?"

Guest: "Yes. Do you take American Express?"

Agent: "Yes, we do; may I have your card number and expiration date?"

Guest: "It's card number 1234-567890-12345, and it expires 12/94."

Agent: "Fine; your guaranteed reservation is confirmed for a no-smoking suite of rooms at the Sherwood Inn in Dallas, arriving the night of December 11th, and departing on the morning of December 13th. Your reservation confirmation number is 293GG566. My name is Gregory. We'll send you a letter of confirmation, which you should present at the front desk when you arrive. If your plans change and you should have to cancel or change your reservation, please call the hotel before 6:00 p.m. Central Standard Time on the 11th. Do you have any questions?"

Guest: "No, that's it."

Agent: "Thank you, Mr. Stevens. Have a good day."

Group Reservations

Although group reservation procedures are usually relatively simple, a number of problems may develop. The following sections consider possible solutions to some of these awkward situations.[6]

Conventions and Conferences. A close working relationship between the hotel's sales staff and the group's meeting planner is one of the critical elements of hosting a successful convention or conference. If good communication and a spirit of cooperation are established early on, many problems can be avoided. Exhibit 4.13 lists some suggestions that hotels may wish to use in dealing with convention groups.

Housing/Convention Bureaus. Large conventions sometimes require the use of rooms at more than one hotel to accommodate all the convention attendees. Often, room requirements at several hotels may be coordinated by a separate housing or convention bureau. Each hotel must determine the number and type of available rooms it is willing to commit for convention use. The objective of the bureau is to accommodate all attendees by coordinating hotel availabilities with reservation requests. On a daily basis, the housing/convention bureau will communicate reservation requests to the hotels involved. In return, each hotel informs the bureau of any requests or cancellations communicated directly to the property. Through such exchange of information, the bureau should be able to help each hotel manage its convention block.

Tour Groups. Tour groups typically are groups of people who have had their accommodations, transportation, and related travel activities arranged for them. Hotels should be especially careful to research the reliability and past performance of tour operators and travel agents. Once acquainted with a tour operator's history, reservations agents can feel

Exhibit 4.13 Considerations for Dealing with Convention Groups

1. Know the convention group's profile, including its cancellation, no-show, and last-minute reservation history.

2. Review all relevant hotel reservation policies with the convention planner.

3. Be sure reservation agents are aware the convention has been scheduled.

4. Produce regularly scheduled reports to update the status of the convention block.

5. Generate an up-to-date list of registrants at regular intervals.

6. *Immediately* correct any errors found by the convention planner.

7. Confirm reservations from attendees as soon as possible.

8. When group members cancel reservations properly, return the rooms to the group's block and inform the convention planner.

9. Distribute the final rooming list to the convention planner and all hotel staff involved with the convention.

more secure when blocking and booking reservations for a tour group. Exhibit 4.14 suggests some important points related to tour group reservations handling.

Potential Reservation Problems

Some steps of the reservations process are more susceptible to error than others. If reservations agents are aware of these trouble spots and know how to avoid them, mistakes will be less likely. Some common problems are listed here.

Errors in the Reservation Record. For example:

- A reservations agent records the wrong arrival or departure date, misspells the guest's name, or mistakenly reverses first and last names (e.g., Troy Thomas might be recorded as Thomas Troy).

- A caller making a reservation for another person is mistaken for the guest and the caller's name is entered on the reservation record, or the caller inadvertently gives his or her own name.

To avoid such problems, after recording information obtained during a telephone call, the reservations agent should read it back to the caller for confirmation. Taking this basic care can be especially important to hotels catering to international travelers. Not being able to access a reservation record can prove disastrous to a hotel-guest relationship.

Misunderstandings Due to Industry Jargon. For example:

- A family with a confirmed reservation arrives two hours after the cancellation hour only to find that the hotel has no rooms available; the family thought a confirmed reservation was the same as a guaranteed reservation.

- Two business travelers book a double room, expecting two beds; they find their room has only one double bed.

Exhibit 4.14   Considerations for Dealing with Tour Groups

1.   Specify the number and types of rooms to be held in a group block, including rooms for drivers and guides.

2.   Clearly state a cut-off date, after which unused rooms in the block will be released for other hotel use.

3.   Also state a date by which the organizer will provide a rooming list.

4.   Monitor the amount and due date of advance deposits required.

5.   Note on the reservation record any services and amenities the property will provide as part of the group package.

6.   Include the name and telephone number of the tour group's representative or agent.

- A family wishing to have the children stay in a connecting room mistakenly requests an adjacent room instead. Upon arrival, the family finds that the children's room is across the hall.

To avoid such problems, reservations agents should make every effort to understand what the guest needs and to explain what various terms mean at their particular property. After accepting a reservation, agents should repeat and confirm the exact nature of reserved accommodations, in addition to stating the hotel's general reservation policies and procedures.

Miscommunications with External Reservation Systems. For example:

- A central reservation system serving several hotels in the same city books the guest into the wrong hotel; for instance, an airport rather than a mid-city property.

- A system that handles hotels in similarly-named cities books the guest into a hotel in the wrong city (e.g., New York City instead of New City, New York; Pasadena, California, instead of Pasadena, Texas).

To avoid such problems, the reservations agent should furnish the guest with the name and address of the property at which a reservation has been made. When a reservation center books rooms in more than one hotel in the same city, a thorough description of the hotel's location can be helpful.

Central Reservation System Failures. For example:

- The hotel fails to update the system on room availability and rate changes in a timely fashion.

- The reservation system is slow in informing the property of reservations accepted.

- Communications equipment, at either the reservation system or the hotel, suffers mechanical problems.

- The hotel closes communications with the system too early or too late.

To avoid such problems, reservations agents must be aware of the need for accurate and timely communication between the hotel and the central reservation system. When notifying the central system to close reservations for a certain date, the hotel must try to identify any reservations accepted by the central system but not yet delivered. Faulty equipment at either end of the communication channel may cripple the entire reservations process. Attention must be given to ensuring a sound working relationship with the central reservation system.

Notes

1. Some of the information in this chapter is adapted from *Selling Out: A How-to Manual on Managing Reservations* (East Lansing, Mich.: Educational Institute of the American Hotel & Motel Association, 1985).

2. Laventhol & Horwath, *U.S. Lodging Industry—1986* (Philadelphia: Laventhol & Horwath, 1986), p. 54.

3. This discussion is adapted from "'The System'—How It Works," in *Hotel and Motel Front Office Planning* (New York: Whitney Duplicating Check Co., 1975), p. 44.

4. For further discussion of front desk responsibilities to the visitor from abroad, see *The Care and Feeding of Guests from Abroad* (East Lansing, Mich.: Educational Institute of the American Hotel & Motel Association, 1980).

5. For further discussion of a hotel's legal responsibilities in the reservations process, see Jack P. Jefferies, *Understanding Hotel/Motel Law* (East Lansing, Mich.: Educational Institute of the American Hotel & Motel Association, 1983), p. 9.

6. For further discussion of reservations handling for conventions, see David C. Dorf, Buck Hoyle, and Tom Jones, *Convention Management* (East Lansing, Mich.: Educational Institute of the American Hotel & Motel Association, 1988).

Discussion Questions

1. What are the major types of reservations? Discuss the responsibilities of the guest and the hotel in each case.

2. What information does a reservations agent need in order to formulate a reservation inquiry?

3. How do non-affiliate reservation networks differ from affiliate reservation networks? How do central reservation systems differ from intersell agencies?

4. What are three common reservation control devices used by hotels? Discuss how each is used to monitor room availabilities.

5. What guest information is necessary for a reservations agent to guarantee a reservation?

6. What is the main purpose of a confirmation letter or telephone call?

7. How does proper cancellation of a reservation benefit the hotel? Discuss how the hotel can make cancellations as easy as possible for guests.

8. What is the purpose of a cancellation number? How might a cancellation number be generated?

9. What management reports can be generated from reservations data? Discuss the uses of expected arrival lists and reservations histories.

10. How can reservation procedures for conferences, conventions, and tour groups be made more efficient?

5 Registration

The first step in the registration process is giving the guest a sincere welcome. A warm greeting sets the stage for everything that follows. After greeting the guest, the front desk agent should determine the guest's reservation status and begin the registration process. A reservation record can provide much of the information upon which the registration process relies. Registration is simpler and smoother when front office personnel have accurate and complete information at their disposal.

From a front desk agent's perspective, the registration process can be divided into five steps:

- Pre-registration activity

- Creation of registration record

- Room and rate assignment

- Establishment of method of payment

- Issuing the room key

In addition to examining these five steps, this chapter discusses creative registration options, the sales role of the front office staff, and procedures for turning away guests who cannot be accommodated.

Pre-Registration Activity

When a guest makes a reservation, he or she provides nearly all the information required to complete the registration process. For this reason, guests arriving with reservations may not be required to complete all the sections of a registration card or its equivalent. The front desk can facilitate a more effective registration process by means of pre-registration activities performed before the guest's arrival at the property. Pre-registration is possible when necessary guest information is obtained during the reservations process. The guest who has been pre-registered often needs only to verify the information already entered onto a registration card by front office personnel. Typically, the guest signs the registration card as proof that the information it contains is accurate and complete.

Pre-registration normally involves more than producing a registration card. Pre-arrival room and rate assignment, creation of a guest folio, and other functions may also be part of pre-registration activity. Some front office managers may be reluctant to assign a specific room in advance of check-in, because of the likelihood of canceled or modified reservations. Hotels tend to develop their own policies based on experience.

In non-automated and semi-automated front office systems, pre-registration tasks are performed manually. Hence, pre-registration services may be limited to specially designated guests or groups. In a computerized system, pre-registration can be an automatic process. A sample computer-generated pre-registration card is shown in Exhibit 5.1. Although a hotel might risk having to void some pre-arrival room assignments, the registration time saved for those who do arrive usually compensates for the work associated with cancellations.

Pre-registration also provides the opportunity for innovative registration options. For instance, a guest arriving by airplane who has a hotel reservation might be picked up at the airport by the hotel's courtesy van. The driver of the van, provided with appropriate information and forms, could request the guest's signature on a prepared registration card, imprint the guest's credit card, and present the room key even before arrival at the hotel. A less sophisticated approach to pre-registration is for guests designated for VIP service to be registered at a location away from the front desk—for example, at a concierge desk. Some hotels arrange for VIP guests to be taken directly to their rooms, bypassing the front desk altogether.

The Registration Record

Following the guest's arrival, the front desk agent creates the **registration record,** a collection of important guest information. For guests who have made reservations, the registration record may confirm information collected during the reservations process.

Non-automated hotel front offices typically use a **registration card** to facilitate the registration process. The registration card requires guests to provide such personal information as name, address, telephone number, company affiliation (if appropriate), and other relevant data. A sample registration card is shown in Exhibit 5.2. The registration card usually provides a space for the guest's signature. In most states, a signature is a legal prerequisite to establishing a guest relationship with a hotel.

Even in automated front desk operations where registration cards can be pre-printed, a signature may still be a legal requirement. Thus front desk agents in an automated hotel would still present a registration card to the guest. However, the computer's information record, not the registration card, becomes the main registration record. Desk agents may input data from a registration card into the computer, or question the guest directly and input his or her spoken answers.

Registration cards or their computer equivalent also ask for information about the guest's intended method of payment for the room rate and other charges. In addition, the guest should be asked to reconfirm his or her date of departure. This is a critical variable in effective rooms management. Some registration cards, such as the one shown in Exhibit 5.2, include a printed statement about the hotel's responsibility for the storage of guest valuables, as required by state laws.

Exhibit 5.1 Pre-Printed Registration Card

Card 1 (left):

NAME BUCKNER, LORIN ROOM
FIRM TYPE TB
ADD 777 RED CEDAR RD • PTY 1
CITY PLYMOUTH, MICHIGAN 48995 DEP 05/24
RATE 47.00 ARR 05/23
TELE CLERK 19

MY ACCOUNT WILL BE SETTLED BY
☐ AMEX
☐ VISA/M. CHG
☐ CASH
☐ CB ☐ OTHER

SPECIFY

IF ABOVE INFORMATION IS NOT CORRECT,
PLEASE SPECIFY IN AREA BELOW.

PLEASE PRINT
(LAST) (FIRST) (INITIAL)
NAME
☐ HOME
STREET ☐ BUSINESS
CITY STATE ZIP
COMPANY
SIGNATURE

SS CODES: RESV#: 38923

BC4423000015692435

** MSU IS AN AFFIRMATIVE ACTION/EQUAL OPPORTUNITY INSTITUTION **
BUCKNER, LORIN 05/23
47.00
777 RED CEDAR RD 05/24
PLYMOUTH, MICHIGAN 48995 #G 1

BC4423000015692435

ROOM: RATE: 47.00
NAME: BUCKNER, LORIN
DEPARTING: 05/24
SS CODES:
GNAME:

Card 2 (right):

NAME DONOVAN, JOHN ROOM 727
FIRM ATLAS INC. TYPE LD
ADD 1299 MICHIGAN BLVD. • PTY 2
CITY FLINT, MICHIGAN 48458 DEP 05/24
RATE 75.00 ARR 05/23
TELE 313-686-0099 CLERK 19

MY ACCOUNT WILL BE SETTLED BY
☐ AMEX
☐ VISA/M. CHG
☐ CASH
☐ CB ☐ OTHER

SPECIFY

IF ABOVE INFORMATION IS NOT CORRECT,
PLEASE SPECIFY IN AREA BELOW

PLEASE PRINT
(LAST) (FIRST) (INITIAL)
NAME
☐ HOME
STREET ☐ BUSINESS
CITY STATE ZIP
COMPANY
SIGNATURE

SS CODES: UF SS RESV#: 38921

NGUAR

** MSU IS AN AFFIRMATIVE ACTION/EQUAL OPPORTUNITY INSTITUTION **
727 DONOVAN, JOHN 05/23
ATLAS INC. 75.00
1299 MICHIGAN BLVD. 05/24
FLINT, MICHIGAN 48458 #G 2

UF SS

NGUAR

ROOM: 727 RATE: 75.00
NAME: DONOVAN, JOHN
DEPARTING: 05/24
SS CODES: UF SS
GNAME:

Courtesy of Kellogg Center, Michigan State University.

Exhibit 5.2 Guest Registration Card

ROOM
NAME
RATE
RESV. ID
ADDRESS
ARRIVAL | ETA | FLIGHT
GROUP
DEPARTURE | RATE | PERS.
CLERK INITIALS
ADULT | CHDRN. | RESV. CLERK | RESV. DATE

REGISTRATION
FOR SAFE KEEPING OF MONEY, JEWELRY AND OTHER VALUABLES INDIVIDUAL SAFE DEPOSIT BOXES ARE PROVIDED AT THE FRONT DESK AT NO CHARGE. THE SHERATON INN-LANSING WILL NOT BE LIABLE FOR ANY ITEMS NOT SECURED IN THIS MANNER.

HOTEL | TYPE | NR-ROOM | NIGHTS
ROOM DESCRIPTION

GUEST'S SIGNATURE X

HOME ADDRESS
DEPOSIT
CITY | STATE | ZIP
SPECIAL SERVICES
DR. LIC. # | STATE
D.O.B.

METHOD OF PAYMENT

☐ AMERICAN EXPRESS ☐ CASH ☐ DINERS CLUB ☐ CHECK
☐ VISA ☐ CARTE BLANCHE ☐ MASTER CARD

Sheraton Inn Lansing ®
S. Creyts Rd. at I-496
Lansing, MI 48917

95093 (4-82)

Courtesy of The Sheraton Inn—Lansing, Lansing, Michigan.

During occupancy, the guest's registration record is either filed in the room rack, attached to the guest folio and placed in the folio tray, or electronically stored in a computer file.

Exhibit 5.3 is a diagram of the flow of guest registration information to other areas and functions. For example, the guest's method of payment may be used to determine his or her point-of-sale charge privileges. A guest paying cash at registration is likely to have a no-post status in the hotel's sales outlets (that is, he or she may not be allowed to charge expenses to his or her room account), while a guest presenting a credit card at registration may be allowed point-of-sale charge privileges. Similarly, at the time of check-out, the guest's registration card may be used as the primary source for creation of a guest history record. This record may then become part of the hotel's sales and marketing data base. This data base can be analyzed to develop marketing strategies, targeted marketing lists, and other detailed reports.

Room and Rate Assignment

Room assignment is the identification and allocation to a guest of an available room in a specific room category. When this assignment is not possible, or when the guest's request is not specific, a survey of all room categories may be necessary to identify a match.

Exhibit 5.3   Destinations of Registration Information

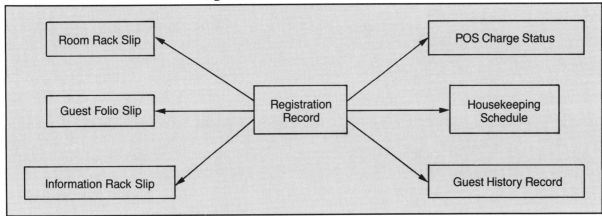

Specific rooms and rates may be assigned before the guest's arrival at the property based on reservation information. Of course, the assignment of a specific room depends on its current availability status and its appropriateness to the guest's needs. Regardless of when it is first determined, this assignment is finalized as part of the registration process.

Hotels may offer a number of rates for rooms of the same type. Rates for similarly bedded rooms may vary based on room size, quality of furnishings, location, amenities, and other factors. Thus, determining the guest's needs by room type alone is often insufficient. Both room type and rate category must be considered. This process requires that each front desk agent be aware of each room's current occupancy status, furnishings, location, and amenities in order to best satisfy the guest's request. Future reservation commitments may also need to be considered during room assignment so that rooms previously committed for use in the near future are not misassigned.

Front desk agents must be able to determine room status and appropriate rates in order to efficiently complete this step of the registration process. Each of these important topics is addressed separately.

Room Status   Effective room and rate assignment depends on accurate and timely room status information. Room status information is usually discussed along two time lines. In the long term (beyond the present night), a room's readiness is described by its **reservation status.** In the short term, a room's readiness is described by its **housekeeping status,** which refers to its availability for immediate assignment. Knowing whether the room is occupied, vacant, on-change, out-of-order, or in some other condition is important to rooms management.

Changes in the housekeeping status of a room should be promptly communicated to the front desk to allow maximization of room sales. Keeping housekeeping status information up-to-date requires close coordination and cooperation between the front desk and the housekeeping department. A **room status discrepancy** is a situation in which the housekeeping department's description of a room's housekeeping status differs from the room status information being used by front desk employees in room assignment. Room status discrepancies can seriously affect a property's ability to satisfy guests and maximize rooms revenue.

Promptly notifying the front desk of the housekeeping status of rooms is a tremendous aid in getting early-arriving guests registered, especially during high-occupancy or sold-out periods. The more rapid the registration process, the less exasperated the incoming guest is likely to become. At most properties, the front desk agent is not allowed to assign guestrooms until the rooms have been cleaned, inspected, and released by the housekeeping department. Even though guests may be forced to wait for their room assignments, this is usually a better procedure than simply issuing a key to a room as soon as the previous guest checks out.

The two commonest systems for tracking room status are mechanical room racks and computerized status systems.

Room Rack. The front desk may use a room rack to track the current housekeeping status of all rooms. A **room rack slip** containing the guest's name and other relevant information is normally completed during the registration process and placed in the room rack slot corresponding to the room number assigned to the guest. The presence of a room rack slip indicates that the room is occupied. When the guest checks out, the rack slip is removed and the room's status is changed to on-change. An **on-change status** indicates that the room is in need of housekeeping services before it can be recycled for availability. As unoccupied rooms are cleaned and inspected, the housekeeping department notifies the front desk, which updates the room's status to **available for sale.**

Non-automated properties may experience room status discrepancies for at least two common reasons. The cumbersome nature of tracking and comparing housekeeping and front desk room status information often leads to mistakes. For example, if a room rack slip is mistakenly left in the rack even though the guest has departed, front desk agents may falsely assume that a vacant room is still occupied. This is an example of a room status discrepancy called a **sleeper:** the rack slip is "asleep" in the rack, and the potential revenues from sale of the room are lost.

Room status discrepancies may also arise from delays in communicating housekeeping status changes from the housekeeping department to the front desk. Communication between the front desk and the housekeeping department may be spoken, written, or conveyed by means of a telewriter. Spoken communication—over the telephone—relays information quickly, but without supporting documentation. A written report has the advantage of documenting the information, but it is time-consuming because it must be hand-delivered. A telewriter communicates and documents information quickly without requiring anyone to be on its receiving end. Telewriters are especially helpful when front desk agents or housekeepers are busy with other responsibilities and do not have time to place a call or answer the telephone.

Each night, a front desk agent typically produces an **occupancy report.** The occupancy report lists rooms occupied that night and indicates those guests expected to check out the following day. The executive housekeeper picks up this list early the next morning and schedules the occupied rooms for cleaning. The rooms occupied by guests expected to check out are usually cleaned last, since the check-out hour generally takes place near the end of the housekeeping shift and since these rooms are likely to require more time. If a guest checks out before the stated departure date, the front desk must notify the housekeeping department that the room is no longer a stayover. A special housekeeping routine will be needed for cleaning and inspecting early check-out rooms.

At the end of the shift, the housekeeping department prepares a **housekeeping status report** (see Exhibit 5.4) based on a physical check of each room in the property. This report indicates the current housekeeping status of each room. It is compared to the front desk occupancy report, and any discrepancies are brought to the attention of the front office manager. This process helps ensure that front desk agents work with a room rack that contains accurate information. This is especially important in preparation for late check-ins.

Computerized System. In a computerized room status system, housekeeping and the front desk often have instantaneous access to room status information. When a guest checks out, a front desk agent enters the departure into a computer terminal, and housekeeping, through a remote terminal located in the housekeeping department, is alerted to the fact that the room needs cleaning. Housekeeping attendants then clean the room and notify the housekeeping department when it is ready for inspection. Once the room is inspected, housekeeping enters this information into its departmental terminal. This informs the front office computer that the room is available for sale.

While room occupancy status within a computerized system is almost always current, reporting of housekeeping status may lag behind. The housekeeping supervisor may inspect several rooms at once, but may not update the computer's room status files until the end of an extended inspection round. Calling the housekeeping department after each room is inspected is generally inefficient in a large operation, since answering the phone can be a constant interruption. A delay may also occur when a list of clean, inspected rooms is furnished to the housekeeping office but not immediately entered into the computer system.

The problems in promptly reporting housekeeping status to the front office can be eliminated when the computer system is directly connected to the guestroom telephone system. With such a network, supervisors can inspect rooms, determine their readiness for sale, and then enter a designated code on the room telephone to change the room's status in the hotel's computer system. No one needs to answer the phone, since the computer automatically receives the relay, and there is little chance for error. Within seconds, the room's updated status can be displayed on the screen of a front desk computer terminal. This interface can significantly reduce not only the number of guests forced to wait for room assignment, but also the length of their wait.

Room Rates

A **room rate** is the price a hotel charges for overnight accommodations. The cost structure of the hotel dictates the minimum rate for a room, and competition helps the hotel establish its maximum rate. The **room rate range** is the range of values between these two limits. A hotel

Exhibit 5.4   Housekeeper's Report

Housekeeper's Report						A.M. P.M.	
Date _____, 19_____							
ROOM NUMBER	STATUS	ROOM NUMBER	STATUS	ROOM NUMBER	STATUS	ROOM NUMBER	STATUS
101		126		151		176	
102		127		152		177	
103		128		153		178	
104		129		154		179	
105		130		155		180	
106		131		156		181	
107		132		157		182	
108				158			
		145		170		195	
121		146		171		196	
122		147		172		197	
123		148		173		198	
124		149		174		199	
125		150		175		200	

Remarks:

_____

_____

_____

_____

Housekeeper's Signature

Legend:
- ✔ - Occupied
- 000 - Out-of-Order
- — - Vacant
- B - Slept Out (Baggage Still in Room)
- X - Occupied, No Baggage
- C.O. - Slept In but Checked Out Early A.M.
- E.A. - Early Arrival

will usually designate a standard rate for each room, typically called the **rack rate** because, traditionally, the standard rate was posted on or near the room rack. Front desk agents may sometimes be allowed to sell a room at a price other than its rack rate. Normally, this occurs only when the hotel's occupancy level is exceptionally high or low. Some hotels establish seasonal rate schedules in order to anticipate business fluctuations and limit misjudgment on the part of front desk agents.

Other room rate schedules may reflect variations in the number of occupants assigned to the room, service level, and room location. For example, room rates may cover a variety of billing arrangements for meals. Under the **American Plan,** room charges include the guestroom and three meals. Under the **Modified American Plan (MAP),** the daily rate includes charges for the guestroom and two meals—typically breakfast and dinner. According to the **European Plan,** meals are priced separately from rooms. Resorts frequently use either the American Plan or the Modified American Plan, while most non-resort hotels in the United States determine their rates according to the European Plan.

Room rates may also vary based on the guest's status rather than the characteristics of the guestroom. If authorized, front desk agents should know how and when to apply these special rates during the registration process. Special room rates may include:

- **Commercial rate** for frequent guests

- **Complimentary rate** (zero rate) for business promotion

- **Group rate** for a number of affiliated guests

- **Family rate** for parents and children in the same room

- **Day rate** for less than an overnight stay

- **Package plan rate** for a room as part of a combination of events or activities

Management policy and the guest's profile usually indicate eligibility for special rate application.

The determination of room rates is addressed in Chapter 10.

Room Locations   When assigning guestrooms, the front desk agent must be aware of the characteristics of the rooms in each room category. In most hotels, even older properties, guestrooms within each category tend to be approximately the same size. Differences between rooms generally lie in their furnishings, amenities, and location within the property. Front desk agents should be familiar with the hotel floor plan in order to satisfy guest rooming requests. Exhibit 5.5 contains an example of a simplified hotel floor plan.

The room rack or its computer equivalent should contain specific data about each room, such as its type, cost, and other pertinent information. Although the room rack is designed primarily as a rooming control technique, it can also function as a source of room location information if its layout reflects the hotel's floor plan. Computer systems can be programmed to provide similar types of information.

Individual guests or groups of guests may specify certain room locations in the hotel as part of their reservation requests. In the case of a group request, the sales or catering department may, after checking room availabilities with the reservation office, assure a group that its preferred rooming needs will be met. The reservation department then blocks the rooms, and on the day of the group's arrival a front desk agent assigns the guests to the desired block of rooms. If the guests are not given the rooms they requested, they will undoubtedly be dissatisfied.

Future Blocks   One of the primary concerns in the rooming process is awareness of the near-future availability of rooms based on reservations blocks. Usually, a reservations agent or the front office supervisor blocks reserved rooms on a calendar, wall chart, control book, or computer reservations file. If for any reason reserved rooms are not blocked, or if a block is inadvertently overlooked, rooming conflicts may result. For instance, suppose a walk-in guest is assigned a room for a two-night stay. If this

Exhibit 5.5   Hotel Floor Plan

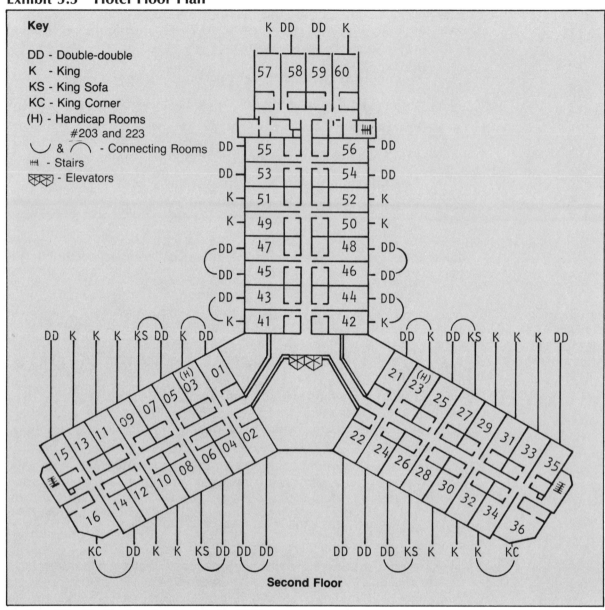

Courtesy of The Sheraton Inn—Lansing, Lansing, Michigan.

specific room has been blocked for a guest arriving the next day, but the desk agent is unaware of this commitment, rooming problems will arise when the second guest registers. Computer systems help reduce the number of errors related to future blocking by disallowing registration for a room that has a conflicting block. The system will not allow the front desk agent to select a pre-assigned, reserved room for a guest checking in.

Many guests believe that once they occupy a room, they can stay as long as they wish. Any attempt to move a guest to another room is often resisted; bad feelings may arise even if the guest agrees to move. The incoming guest, who was promised a room, will probably also be inconvenienced and may be concerned about the front desk's control over its registration process. For all these reasons, awareness of future blocks is an important front office concern.

Method of Payment

The registration process plays an essential role in front office accounting by gathering data concerning payment for services rendered. An important part of ensuring account collection is following appropriate guidelines during the registration process for establishing a method of payment. Regardless of whether the guest will use cash, a check, a credit card, or an alternative method of payment, the hotel should take precautionary measures to ensure eventual payment. A proper credit check at the outset of a transaction greatly reduces the potential for subsequent settlement problems. Each hotel is different, and guidelines for establishing a method of payment may vary. Common methods of payment are discussed in the following sections.

Cash

Guests may wish to pay their room charges during registration, in advance of occupancy. As stated earlier, guests who pay cash in advance face a potential drawback because they may not be extended in-house credit. Revenue outlets are usually given **PIA** (paid-in-advance) **lists** of cash-paying guests who are not authorized to make charge purchases to their room accounts. A computerized system that interfaces with devices in sales outlets replaces PIA lists by disallowing posting to guest accounts not authorized for in-house charges. These guests must settle their charges at the point of sale. At check-in, front desk agents may require a credit card for imprinting to allow the cash-paying guest charge privileges in the hotel's revenue outlets.

Forms of Tender

Cashier's checks, traveler's checks, and money orders are considered by banks to be equivalent to cash. A hotel which accepts such tender should require proper guest identification. Front desk agents should compare the picture and signature on the guest's identification to the appearance and signature of the person presenting the check. When there is doubt, the check may be verified with the issuing bank or agency.

Personal Checks

Guests may also pay in advance of occupancy with a personal check.[1] Some lodging properties allow transactions by personal check, while others have a strict policy against payment by check. Although a hotel has no obligation to accept personal checks, regardless of the checks' validity, it cannot practice illegal discrimination in refusing to accept a check (for example, on the basis of sex or race). Each individual property must establish its own policies for accepting checks. Among the decisions to be made are whether to accept checks written on foreign bank accounts, payroll checks, government checks, traveler's checks, money orders, or second- and third-party checks.

Some hotels allow guests to cash checks as long as they are accompanied by a credit card that provides a check-cashing guarantee, and the amount of the check is within the card's established credit limits. Front desk agents should imprint the credit card onto the check as required. Some hotels accept personal checks only during standard banking hours; this allows the front office to obtain bank verification if it is desired. In some hotels, guests may be allowed to write personal checks for room and room tax charges only; cash or credit card payment may be required for all other purchases.

Hotels that choose to accept personal checks should require proper identification. The guest's driver's license number, address, and telephone number should be recorded on the face of the check (since bank stamps and clearing house imprints will often cover the back of the check). In some hotels, the amounts and dates of cashed checks are recorded on the back of the guest's registration card. This procedure helps ensure that guests do not exceed the established check-cashing limits of the property. If cashiers are not generally allowed to accept checks, they must know to whom they should refer guests who want to cash checks.

Other methods which help protect the property from losses due to accepting bad checks include the following:

- Do not refund cash if the original transaction was settled by check. If possible, return the guest's original check and, when appropriate, ask for another check for the actual amount of the bill. Some properties do not write a refund check until the bank verifies that the guest's check has cleared.

- Do not accept undated or post-dated checks—that is, checks carrying no date or a future date instead of the current date.

- Require that personal checks written to settle an account be made payable to the hotel, not to "Cash." When a guest is allowed to write a check to obtain cash, not to pay a bill, that check should be made out to "Cash." This practice may prevent a non-paying guest (skipper) from later claiming that a check made out to "Cash" was used to pay for room charges.

Second- and Third-Party Checks. In general, hotels do not choose to cash second- and third-party checks. A second-party check is one made out to the guest presenting the check. A third-party check is one made out to someone who has then signed the check over to the guest presenting the check. Hotels accepting such checks may experience collection problems if the maker of the check stops payment. If the hotel accepts a second-party check, the front desk agent should require the guest to endorse the check at the desk, even if it has been previously endorsed. The agent can then compare the signatures on the check to each other (if it was previously endorsed) and to that on the identification offered by the guest.

Check Guarantee Services. Check guarantee services can be a valuable aid to the hospitality industry. A front desk agent usually telephones a check guarantee service and provides check-related data and the amount of the transaction. The service, in turn, determines the check writer's credit history and guarantees or refuses to support payment. Since the hotel must pay a fee per check for this service, its use is normally restricted to checks written to settle hotel accounts.

Credit Cards

Careful checking and verification of credit cards are as important to the hotel's financial security as the precautions taken with any other method of payment. Individual hotel properties usually define explicit steps for processing credit card transactions. Credit card companies often require various procedures to ensure proper settlement. Hotels should have an attorney review their credit card procedures to be sure the hotel adheres to state and federal laws and the specifications contained in credit card company contracts. Local banks may also be able to provide procedural guidelines. The following points might be considered in establishing a front desk policy for handling credit cards.

Expiration Date. When a guest presents a credit card, the desk agent responsible for handling the transaction should immediately check the card's expiration date. If the card has expired, this should be pointed out to the guest so that another method of payment can be provided. Credit card companies are not required to honor transactions settled through the use of an expired card. If an expired card is inadvertently accepted, the hotel may not be able to receive payment for the amount of the charged purchase.

On-Line Verification. After checking a credit card's expiration date, the desk agent should make certain the credit card in question isn't stolen or otherwise invalid. Many hotels use on-line computer services for credit card validation over telephone lines. Required credit card and transaction data may be spoken, entered on a touch-tone key pad, or automatically input through a magnetic strip reader. On the basis of credit card and transaction data, the credit card verification service consults its credit records and generates an **authorization code** or a **denial code** for the transaction.

On-line verification services have the advantage of allowing the desk agent to proceed to other tasks while the service verifies the transaction; the front desk agent later checks the authorization terminal to obtain and record the authorization or denial code number.

Cancellation Bulletins. In properties without on-line verification, the desk agent should validate the card by consulting credit card cancellation bulletins. Expired cancellation bulletins should be retained and filed in case a dispute later arises between a credit card company and the hotel. These bulletins can be used to prove that a card number did not appear in the bulletin at the time the hotel accepted it as a method of payment. An attorney can advise the hotel on how long such documentation should be retained.

Invalid Card. If a credit card proves invalid after being double-checked, employees should follow established hotel and credit card company procedures. Normally, an alternate form of payment is requested. If none is available, front desk agents typically alert the front office credit manager or hotel general manager, who handles the situation. In case a stolen card is discovered, security personnel might also be asked to be available.

Although the federal government has made credit card fraud a criminal offense, lodging properties should be wary of detaining guests they suspect of theft or fraudulently avoiding payment of their bills. Such detention, especially if unjustified or improperly instituted, might expose the property to suits for false imprisonment and slander. The hotel's attorney should advise the hotel concerning its vulnerability to such suits.[2]

Imprinting the Voucher. Once a valid credit card is approved, an imprint of the card is made onto a **credit card voucher.** Some hotel front offices require desk agents to circle the card's expiration date and initial the validation number on the imprinted voucher as proof that they have followed procedures. Normally, the guest is not requested to sign the voucher until account settlement, at the time of check-out.

Floor Limits. Credit card companies may assign hotels a **floor limit:** the maximum amount in credit card charges the hotel is permitted to accept on behalf of a card member without special authorization. If the amount to be charged approaches or exceeds the hotel's floor limit, the front office should contact the credit card company to request approval for any additional transactions. In some cases, the penalty for not obtaining additional authorization is forfeiture of the entire amount charged, not just the amount in excess of the floor limit. A computerized system capable of monitoring guest account balances may be able to identify guest accounts approaching a credit card company's floor limit. Some properties request higher floor limits so they will not have to annoy guests with last-minute authorizations or requests for alternate payment methods.

Reserving Credit. Hotels may consider reserving a specified amount of credit in a guest's credit card account to ensure payment for services rendered, but they must be aware of local laws regarding such procedures. Thus, if a guest comes to a hotel planning to stay several days and the hotel knows that the anticipated charges will exceed the authorized floor limit, it may wish to reserve the amount of the anticipated charges in the guest's credit card account. But if the guest then decides to leave earlier than planned, his or her credit is now tied up. Laws vary from state to state, but in some states, the hotel is obligated to notify the credit card company to release the unused credit that had been authorized. Also, in some states, a hotel can only request such a reserve of credit if it informs the guest beforehand of the amount it wishes to reserve and obtains the guest's consent. This is another area in which a hotel's policy should be approved by local counsel.

Direct Billing   Some hotels extend credit to guests by agreeing to bill the guest or the guest's company for charges incurred. This credit arrangement, called **direct billing,** is normally established through correspondence between the guest or company and the hotel. A guest or company representative may be asked to complete the hotel's application for credit. A list of approved direct billing accounts is usually maintained at the front desk for desk agents to refer to during registration. At check-out, the guest simply signs his or her folio after approving its contents, and a statement is direct-billed for collection. In a direct billing arrangement, the hotel, not a credit card company or third party, becomes its own collection agent.

Special Programs   During registration, guests may present vouchers, coupons, or special incentive awards received from businesses, airlines, or other authorized agencies. Front desk agents must be aware of all hotel agreements to honor such vouchers and to give proper credit to the bearer. Care must be taken when handling vouchers, since they may differ in value, conditions, and/or terms. Since such vouchers may be the actual documents the hotel will use to bill the issuing company for payment, they should be handled as carefully as other forms of payment.

Denying a Credit Request   If a guest's credit rating is found to be poor, extreme care and tact should be exercised in denying the request for credit. A person's credit involves more than money. His or her sense of self-esteem may be at stake. In discussing problematic credit issues, it is important to remember to be as diplomatic as possible. Front desk staff should keep their voices friendly and subdued, no matter how belligerent the guest may become. While the property has certain rights to credit information, the customer also has the right to know why the hotel will not accept his or her personal check, credit card, or direct-bill arrangement. Exhibit 5.6 lists some approaches to common situations. These suggestions should be modified to fit the problem, the guest, and the property's philosophy.

Issuing the Key

The issuance of a room key completes the registration process. In some hotels, a newly registered guest is simply handed a map of the hotel and a key. For the security of both the guest and the property, room keys must be very carefully controlled. Key theft and loss and the unauthorized duplication and use of keys present a threat to hotel security. Hotels should have written policies governing key control. There should be policies stating to whom keys are to be issued and how they are to be stored at the front desk. The topic of key control and locks is addressed in detail in Chapter 6.

If the property provides bell service, the desk agent should first ask the guest whether the assistance of a bellperson is desired. If it is, the desk agent should hand the bellperson the room key and ask him or her to show the guest to the room. On the way to and at the room, the bellperson might explain the special features of the room and such things as restaurant locations, hours of outlet operations, locations of ice and vending machines, and other appropriate information. The bellperson should make the guest comfortable, answer any questions, and hand the room key to the guest. If the guest expresses dissatisfaction with the room, the bellperson should listen attentively and promise to bring the matter to a desk agent's attention for immediate action.

Creative Options

The registration process described in this chapter is typical of most hotels. Some hotels experiment to make their registration process more efficient and satisfying to their guests. Techniques tried, with varying degrees of success, include:

Exhibit 5.6   Suggestions for Denying Credit

When a credit card issuer refuses to authorize a charge:

- Discuss the matter out of the earshot of others.

- Don't refer to the guest's card as "bad" or "worthless."

- Offer the use of a telephone to clear up the matter with a credit card company representative.

- Allow the guest a chance to explain or to provide another means of payment.

When a guest's personal check cannot be accepted:

- Explain the hotel policy.

- Remain friendly and cooperative.

- Discuss alternatives with the guest.

- If banks are open, direct the guest to a nearby branch, or offer the use of a telephone.

Adapted from *Successful Credit and Collection Techniques* (East Lansing, Mich.: Educational Institute of the American Hotel & Motel Association, 1981), pp. 8-9.

- Eliminating the front desk. Instead, a host or hostess waits in a reception area with a list of expected guests and pre-assigned rooms, identifies guests, and escorts them to their rooms.

- Placing a hotel greeter at a special desk in the lobby, and rooming all guests from that desk. The regular front desk is screened off and used only for sorting and filing records and, with the screen temporarily removed, for settlement at check-out.

- Directing VIP guests in their reservation confirmations to an exclusive registration area apart from that for other hotel guests.

The challenge is to make the hotel registration process innovative, while still treating guests with expediency and care and satisfying their needs.

In the case of corporate gatherings, tour groups, and even some convention groups, the rooming process can be simplified. A rooming list with the names of all the members of an expected group can be obtained from the group's coordinator. Rooms can then be assigned before the group arrives, keys placed in envelopes with a welcoming note from the manager, and a separate desk set up in the lobby, away from the front desk, from which to distribute envelopes to incoming guests. The front desk agents are still responsible for registration, but group representatives are often present to welcome the members of their group and to give them information or gifts as they arrive.

In some hotels, to ease the discomfort of arriving guests when check-outs are running late, the front office provides luggage storage until rooms are ready. In addition, front desk agents may have the authority to offer free drinks or coffee to inconvenienced guests. Guests are directed to the lounge or restaurant to wait, perhaps less impatiently, until their rooms are ready.

Self-Registration   A relatively new concept in front office registration is **self-registration.** Self-registration terminals are usually located in the lobbies of fully automated hotels. These terminals vary in design: some resemble automatic bank teller machines, while others possess both video and audio capability. Exhibit 5.7 shows one self-registration terminal design. Recent technological advances allow hotels to place self-registration terminals at remote locations such as airports and car rental agencies. Regardless of which kind of guest-operated device is used, self-registration terminals can significantly reduce time spent on the registration process.

To use a self-registration terminal, a guest generally must arrive at the hotel holding a reservation and a valid credit card. The guest initiates the self-registration process by inserting the credit card into the terminal. The terminal accesses the reservation record and prompts the guest to enter additional registration data using a keypad. Since most terminals are interfaced with a computerized rooms management system, automatic room and rate assignment is then possible. Once the room and rate have been determined, the terminal automatically dispenses a room key or instructs the guest how to obtain one. As electronic locking systems become more prevalent, they may interconnect with self-registration devices as the mechanism for key dispensing.

Selling the Guestroom

Registration itself is not possible if the guest is not convinced of the value of renting a particular hotel room. Part of the front desk agent's job is to create consumer acceptance of his or her product: the hotel's guestrooms and other facilities. There are several approaches to convincing guests of the value of the hotel's products and services and creating acceptance of them. The supplemental reading for this chapter describes three effective tactics for "upselling" at the front desk. Properly trained front desk agents can substantially improve sales.

Even professional salespeople are sometimes called "order-takers," and at times the label may be deserved. The hotel registration process must move through certain stages to ensure that the guest is registered quickly and carefully. However, within these steps front office staff may have the freedom to develop an individual sales presentation. Exhibit 5.8 lists some general suggestions for registering guests and selling guestrooms.

Offering room options is the key to the registration sales process, and it requires thought, planning, and practice. To create guest acceptance, the front desk agent must know the product thoroughly and describe it positively. The guest will probably give several clues about what will be acceptable for the stay; some information may already be available from a reservation record. Along with the physical features of rooms, their benefits to the guests should be mentioned. After each room option is described, the guest may nod approval or indicate that another option is desired. Some hotels, as a matter of policy, offer registering guests more than one option and then ask their preference.

After the guest has selected a room option, he or she is asked to complete a registration card. The desk agent may indicate approval of the

Exhibit 5.7   Self-Registration Terminal

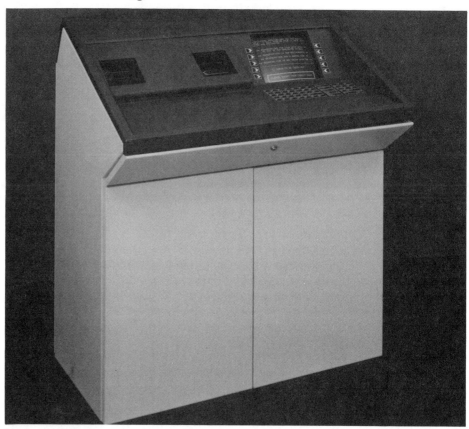

Courtesy of NCR Corporation, Dayton, Ohio.

guest's choice of room. At the close of registration, the desk agent should make the guest aware of the hotel's sales outlets and other facilities. Guests usually appreciate this information.

Before the guest leaves the desk, the desk agent should thank the guest for choosing the hotel and express a personal interest in making the stay as pleasant as possible. Some hotels add a personal follow-up by calling the guest's room shortly after the guest begins occupancy to ensure that everything is to the guest's liking. Front office staff may then review and analyze the registration process to make it even more efficient for the next guest.

When Guests Cannot Be Accommodated

In general, a hotel is obligated to accommodate those persons who arrive as guests.[3] Discrimination in places of public accommodation on the basis of race, color, religion, or national origin is prohibited. Legitimate reasons for refusing to accommodate a guest may include, for example, lack of available rooms, drunk or disorderly behavior, or unwillingness to pay for hotel services. State laws may set forth other reasons a hotel may deny accommodations. However, *this subject must be reviewed by*

Exhibit 5.8   Suggestions for Selling Guestrooms

1.	Smile.
2.	Establish and maintain eye contact.
3.	Use the guest's name whenever possible.
4.	Be pleasant, friendly, efficient, and businesslike.
5.	Suggest good room locations and try to sell up.
6.	Keep accurate, neat records.
7.	Maintain a neat, well-groomed appearance.
8.	Remain calm, and give each guest undivided attention.
9.	Follow up on all promises.

management before a room is refused to anyone. Management, with the advice of legal counsel and the state hotel association, should instruct the front office staff on policies and procedures concerning the acceptance or rejection of potential guests.

On occasion, a hotel may not be able to accommodate a guest because of a shortage of available rooms. This happens most frequently to walk-in guests. Seldom, if ever, should a hotel be unable to accommodate a guest with a reservation, especially a guaranteed reservation. However, circumstances beyond the property's control may result in the demand for rooms exceeding the available supply. It is imperative that the hotel set policies that inform the front office staff how to handle the occasions when the property cannot accommodate a guest.[4]

Walk-In Guests

Walk-in guests who cannot be accommodated should be informed that there are no available rooms. Front desk agents may suggest alternative nearby hotels where rooms may be available.

In the case of a walk-in guest who believes he or she has made a reservation, the situation may be more difficult. The following steps, modified to fit a particular property, might be taken to clarify the situation:

- If the guest presents a letter of confirmation, verify the date and the name of the hotel; the guest may have arrived on a different date or at the wrong property.

- Ask whether another person made the reservation for the guest; the reservation may be at another property, or it may be misfiled under the caller's name.

- Double-check the reservations file in view of the guest; perhaps the reservation was for another date.

- Double-check the reservations file for another spelling of the last name. For instance, B, P, and T are often confused in a telephone conversation. Could the first and last names have been reversed?

- If the reservation was made through a travel agency or representative, allow the guest to call for clarification.

If there seems to be no alternative to **walking**—turning away—the guest, explain the matter in a private office. Registering one guest in view of another who cannot be accommodated can be extremely awkward.

It is logical to assume that a guest who cannot be accommodated at the hotel he or she has first chosen would like lodgings similar to that hotel. A list, with phone numbers, of similar properties in the area should be kept for the use of guests in case the hotel is unable to provide accommodations. While there may be future advantages to the hotel for providing such services, they should be viewed mainly as steps to promote good guest relations. Taking extra care of walk-in guests may help create an industry-wide atmosphere of concern and good will.

Guests with Non-Guaranteed Reservations

As suggested in the previous chapter, guests may be delayed in arriving at a hotel for a variety of reasons. Often a guest may not have a chance to guarantee a non-guaranteed reservation when it becomes apparent that he or she will arrive past the hotel's reservation cancellation hour. As a result, the hotel will not have held a room for the guest and may not be able to provide accommodations upon arrival. If the hotel cannot provide a room, front desk agents must take great care when informing the guest. It must be remembered that the guest had no way to avoid the situation and that the lack of accommodations is neither the guest's nor the hotel's fault.

Guests with Guaranteed Reservations

If reservations are carefully handled and good forecasting procedures are followed, the property should never have to deny accommodations to a guest with a guaranteed reservation. It is nonetheless wise to have a policy for front desk staff members to follow should this situation arise. The following guidelines may be helpful in developing such a policy.

The property should appoint someone to take charge and make necessary decisions when it appears the property will not have sufficient accommodations. This person would:

1. Review all front desk transactions.

2. Take an accurate count of rooms available, using all relevant data; double-check for sleepers.

3. Compare the room rack, housekeeper's report, and guest folios for discrepancies.

4. Telephone **due-outs**—guests expected to check out—who have not yet checked out. If they answer, confirm their check-out time. If they do not answer, physically check the rooms. Perhaps the guest has left without stopping at the front desk. Perhaps he or she expected to be billed, or paid in advance and forgot to check out at the desk. If the guest appears to have been a **skipper**—that is, a guest who leaves with no intention of paying for

the room—an early discovery of this fact will allow the room to be used by another guest.

5. Personally check all out-of-order rooms. Could they be readied for sale if necessary? If a guest would be willing to occupy the room as is, should the room rate be adjusted?

All front desk staff should be consistent when discussing the lack of accommodations with arriving guests. Some helpful suggestions include:

- Guests may be encouraged to return to the hotel at the earliest date of availability. Upon their return, they may be placed on a VIP list and presented with a small gift to compensate them for their trouble.

- A follow-up letter may be sent to all guests with reservations who could not be accommodated, apologizing again for the inconvenience and encouraging the guests to return to the hotel at some future time.

- If a member of a convention block cannot be accommodated, the group's meeting planner should be notified. The planner may be able to solve the problem by asking attendees to double up. In such situations, it pays for the front office to have a good working relationship with meeting planners.

- If a member of a tour group cannot be accommodated, notifying the tour organizer immediately to explain the situation may better enable the organizer to deal with any customer complaints.

Notes

1. This discussion is adapted from Raymond C. Ellis and the Security Committee of AH&MA, *Security and Loss Prevention Management* (East Lansing, Mich.: Educational Institute of the American Hotel & Motel Association, 1986), 114-117.

2. For further discussion of possible dangers involved with invalid credit cards, see Jack P. Jefferies, *Understanding Hotel/Motel Law* (East Lansing, Mich.: Educational Institute of the American Hotel & Motel Association, 1983), Chapter 9.

3. Jefferies, Chapter 1.

4. This discussion is adapted from *Selling Out: A How-to Manual on Reservations Management* (East Lansing, Mich.: Educational Institute of the American Hotel & Motel Association, 1985).

Discussion Questions

1. Describe the five steps of the registration process as it is seen by front desk agents.

2. What are the advantages of pre-registering guests? What might limit the front office's ability to pre-register guests?

3. What information is usually requested on a guest registration card? How is this information useful to the front office?

4. How is current room status information essential to an effective guest registration process?

5. What are the advantages of a computerized room status system?

6. What are some examples of special room rates?

7. Discuss the major methods of payment used by guests. What forms of tender are generally considered equivalent to cash?

8. Discuss front desk agent procedures for accepting credit cards as a method of payment during the registration process.

9. How can front desk agents create acceptance of the hotel's rooms and facilities during the registration process?

10. What procedures should the front office consider when a guest with a guaranteed reservation cannot be accommodated?

SUPPLEMENTAL READING
Upselling Rooms: 3 Effective Techniques

by Marc Gordon, CHA

One of the most effective marketing tools available to a hotel is the upselling of guestrooms by the front office staff. Upselling, in this context, refers to the effort by reservationists and desk agents to induce guests to buy medium-priced or deluxe rooms rather than standard accommodations.

Since hotels normally have several rate categories, based on such factors as decor, size, location, view, and type of beds, the rack-rate difference between two given rooms can be substantial. With such a disparity of rates, a great opportunity for upselling exists.

The impact of upselling on total rooms revenue, average rate, and operating profit can be tremendous. Remember, the cost of selling a deluxe room varies little if at all from that of selling a minimum-rate room. A deluxe room may have extra amenities that slightly increase the cost of occupancy compared to that of a standard room. But more often, *100% of the difference in rates is profit.* Assume that you could upsell half the rooms you are selling to the extent of $10 or $20 per room per day. Compute for yourself what this could mean to your hotel. At hotels where I have worked, the dollar advantage has sometimes been dramatic.

To upsell rooms, front office personnel must be trained to be professional salespeople rather than order-takers. The reservationist and desk agent must realize that they can upsell rooms in much the same way that a food server can sell extra food items by making suggestions to the customer.

So what does the so-called order-taker in the hotel front office need to learn to become a professional salesperson?

- First, how to control encounters with the guest

- Second, how to overcome natural inhibitions in dealing with the guest

- Third, how to be enthusiastic in asking for the sale

Controlling the encounter. The hotel reservationist or desk agent should avoid such open-ended questions to the guest as, "What type of room do you wish?" This allows the guest to take control—to direct the negotiation from that point on. The hotel agent should instead ask specific questions (more later) that move the guest in the direction of selecting medium-priced or luxury rooms.

Getting rid of natural inhibitions. The hotel agent often earns far less money than the guest who stays at his or her property. It can be difficult for such a person, making a modest salary, to recommend a deluxe room rated at $100 a night. In looking at rates from their own perspective, front office personnel may be inhibited from selling rooms at a rate higher than the minimum. They have to overcome such inhibitions before they can upsell effectively.

Asking for the sale. Once the reservationist or desk agent has learned to control the encounter and overcome inhibitions to suggest better accommodations, he or she must learn to ask for the sale. Few guests will buy a better room—even if they would enjoy it—unless the hotel representative suggests it.

After front office personnel are trained and encouraged to be professional salespeople, they are ready to learn special compliance techniques for upselling. Compliance techniques are either pressure or non-pressure.

High-pressure upselling is totally inappropriate for the sale of guestrooms. Hotel guests truly *are* guests and must be treated as such at all times. It is inconsistent to offer gracious services and then imply that only a fool would reserve a standard room. No—hospitality doesn't work that way. Only non-pressure compliance techniques are appropriate in upselling at hotels.

Non-pressure compliance techniques exert little or no perceived pressure on the buyer to induce compliance. There are three non-pressure compliance techniques that are effective in inducing guests to reserve medium-priced and deluxe rooms instead of minimum-rate rooms. I call them:

- The choice-of-doors technique

- The door-in-the-face technique

- The foot-in-the-door technique

Choice-of-Doors

In applying this technique, the desk agent or reservationist gives the guest a choice of rate-category alternatives. He or she then asks: "Which would you prefer?" No pressure is put on the guest. The guest tends to put pressure on himself to choose a room in the middle of the range.

You see, people tend to avoid extremes. They think that a choice of the least expensive room would make them look cheap, whereas the choice of the most expensive room would make them appear extravagant. Thus, internal pressure is created to move to the middle rate to demonstrate to themselves and to others that they are reasonable and compromising.

The choice of alternatives or choice-of-doors technique is an easy and effective way to upsell guests to the middle rate when they might otherwise have chosen the minimum rate and were very unlikely to be susceptible to the deluxe accommodations.

Door-in-the-Face

The door-in-the-face technique has proved effective in various market areas. It begins with a large or unreasonable request from the salesperson—a request so unreasonable that compliance is unlikely. After the original request is refused by the buyer, the seller makes a more moderate offer, which represents the intended compliance request.

Consider this example: A man needs $2 and the only person available is a chance acquaintance who he knows is not likely to lend him any money at all. So he asks the acquaintance for $10, and receives a prompt refusal. He now asks if he could at least have $2. Research shows that his chances of getting the $2 are significantly enhanced because he has used the door-in-the-face technique. The acquaintance feels that $2 is a reasonable compromise.

The door-in-the-face technique can be applied easily in selling hotel reservations or selling rooms to walk-ins. The application could be termed top-down suggestive upselling. The hotel salesperson starts with a strong, enthusiastic recommendation of the highest room-rate category that fits the guest's situation; for example, a deluxe room with king-size beds for a married couple or a deluxe room with two double beds for two commercial travelers. One of two guest responses is likely from the hotel agent's suggestion.

One, the guest might comply and take the room in the highest-rate category. After all, some guests are on liberal expense accounts with their own or client companies. Further, there are also guests who simply want the best room available.

Two, in a more typical situation, the highest room rate will be rejected. The desk agent or reservationist will then go to the next highest rate with an enthusiastic recommendation of its merits. The hotel staff member will continue down in the same manner until the guest makes a decision.

This technique for upselling is used to get more guests to reserve middle and high-rate rooms than would otherwise have done so. Economy-minded guests on restricted budgets will still opt for minimum-rate rooms, but the majority will choose accommodations in the middle range.

Foot-in-the-Door

This technique, by contrast, is applied by obtaining compliance for a moderate request initially, setting the stage for more likely compliance with larger, more substantial requests.

The technique can be illustrated by asking a homeowner to sign a petition requesting the local government to keep his city beautiful. If the homeowner signs the petition, he will be far more likely to comply with a second request, a week later, asking him to contribute $10 to the "keep the city clean" campaign than if he had been asked at the outset to contribute $10.

In the foot-in-the-door technique, people who comply with an initial request imply from their compliance that they are the sort of people who comply with such requests and are therefore more likely to comply with larger requests in the future.

Consider how the foot-in-the-door technique can be applied to the upselling of guestrooms. A desk agent is registering a guest who has a reservation confirming a minimum or low-rate category. The clerk might say, "For $10 more, you can have a king-size bed." Or, "For $20 more you could have a deluxe room with a view of the lake." Or, "For only $35 more, you could have our entire package, including a dinner and a breakfast for two."

Because the guest has already demonstrated a level of compliance (by making the room reservation), the larger request during registration represents not a total outlay but a small increase over the anticipated charge. Often, the guest will comply.

The choice of doors, foot-in-the-door, and door-in-the-face techniques represent powerful, non-pressure upselling tools that every hotel can use to significantly increase total room revenues, average room revenues, average rates, and operating profits. Hotels that train all front office personnel to be professional salespeople will enjoy much greater financial success.

Marc Gordon, CHA, is director of marketing for the Educational Institute of the American Hotel & Motel Association and on the School of Hotel, Restaurant and Institutional Management faculty at Michigan State University. He has nine years' experience with Westin Hotels and Holiday Inns as front office manager, general manager, and regional training director.

Condensed from *Lodging*, January 1986, pp. 64–5.

6 Ongoing Front Office Responsibilities

Ongoing front office functions include rooms management, guest accounting, guest services, guest relations, and security. All these functions rely in part on clear communications. Front office employees must communicate efficiently with one another, with other functional areas, and with the guests. Rooms management was discussed in Chapter 5, and guest accounting and auditing activities are detailed in Chapters 7, 8, and 9. This chapter focuses on guest services, guest relations, security, and the importance of communications to these functions.

Communications within the Front Office

Nearly everything that happens in a hotel affects the front office. Front office employees—front desk agents, uniformed service staff, switchboard operators, front desk cashiers, and reservations agents—communicate with guests and visitors. Other departments and divisions rely on the front office to provide information, satisfy guest requests, coordinate guest services, and collect guest receivables. For example, clear communication between the front office and the housekeeping department is critical to an effective room status system. Likewise, guests' charge purchases at remote points of sale must be communicated to the front desk to ensure collection. Effective front office communications may involve the use of information books, log books, and mail and telephone procedures. The complexity of front office communications tends to be directly related to the number of guestrooms and the extent of public function space in the hotel.

Log Book

To ensure that all front office employees are aware of important events and decisions that have occurred during previous workshifts, a log book may be kept at the front desk. A front office **log book** is typically a journal in which notes of unusual events, guest complaints or requests, and other relevant information are recorded for reference during subsequent shifts. Before beginning their shifts, front desk agents should review the log book to become aware of any current activity—for example, a guest request for maintenance or housekeeping services—as well as potential problems.

Mail Handling

A registered guest relies on the front office to deliver mail quickly and efficiently. The United States Postal Service provides policies and regulations that offer direction for front office mail handling. In general, hotels time-stamp all guest mail upon arrival. Mail for a registered guest is usually held in the appropriate slot in a mail and message rack at the front desk. The guest should be notified of its arrival as soon as possible. If mail arrives for a guest who has not yet registered, a notation should be made on the guest's reservation card and the mail held for the guest's arrival. Mail that is not picked up during occupancy should be time-stamped a second time and returned to its sender.

Guests may also receive registered letters, express packages, or other mail requiring a signature upon delivery. Front office policy may allow a front desk agent to sign for such mail, record its delivery in a log, and require the guest's signature when the mail is picked up or delivered. If the authorized recipients of such mail have been restricted by the sender, other front office procedures may be necessary.[1]

Telephone Services   Most hotels provide in-room local and long-distance telephone service 24 hours a day. Regardless of whether front desk agents answer incoming calls or the hotel employs telephone system operators, all employees answering calls should be courteous and helpful. Issues relating to guest privacy and security may lead a hotel's management to restrict the type of information the front office may furnish to callers.

Telephone messages recorded by front office personnel should be time-stamped and held in the guest's mail and message rack slot until retrieved. Facsimiles (graphic matter transmitted by wire and typically called faxes) received for guests may be treated similarly. If guestroom telephones are equipped with a message indicator light, the in-room message light may be switched on to indicate that a message or a fax is being held for the guest to pick up at the front desk.

Since a guest may well miss an important appointment if he or she oversleeps, wake-up calls require special front office attention. Front office computer systems can be used to remind front desk agents to place wake-up calls, or may be programmed to dial the call and automatically play a recorded wake-up message. Despite technological advances, many hotels still choose to offer personalized wake-up calls for their guests, because some guests prefer to hear a live human voice when they have just awakened.

Interdepartmental Communications

Guest services involve the coordination of activities between the front office and the hotel's other functional areas. Housekeeping and maintenance require the greatest exchange of information with the front office. Front desk agents should also be aware of their marketing and public relations functions and their potential influence on the performance of the hotel's revenue centers.

Housekeeping Department   To ensure efficient rooming of guests, the housekeeping and front office departments must inform each other of changes in a room's status. The more familiar front office personnel are with housekeeping pro-

Guestroom telephone service is valuable to many travelers. (Courtesy of Radisson Mart Plaza Hotel, Miami, Florida.)

cedures (and vice versa), the smoother the relationship between the two departments is likely to be. The nature of communications between the housekeeping and front office departments was detailed in Chapter 5.

Maintenance Division

The front office and the maintenance division must exchange information efficiently. In many hotels, maintenance personnel begin each shift by examining the front desk log book for repair work orders. Front desk agents use the log book to track maintenance problems, such as poor heating or cooling, faulty plumbing, noisy equipment, or broken furniture. The log book can serve as an excellent reference for the hotel's maintenance staff.

Many hotels use a multiple-part work order form to report maintenance problems. Exhibit 6.1 shows a sample work order form. When the work is completed, the maintenance division informs the originating department. If a problem prevents a room from being available for sale, the front office must know immediately when the problem has been corrected. This will minimize the loss of rooms revenue due to out-of-order guestrooms and will enhance guest satisfaction. To speed the maintenance process, some hotels employ maintenance staff around the clock.

Revenue Centers

Although guestroom sales are a major contributor to a hotel's profitability, a hotel may support a variety of additional sources of revenue. In addition to the rooms division, hotels may include such revenue centers as:

- Coffee shops, snack bars, and specialty restaurants
- Bars, lounges, and nightclubs
- Room service
- Laundry/valet service
- Vending machines
- Gift shops, barber shops, and newsstands
- Banquet, meeting, and catering facilities
- Local and long-distance telephone service
- Health clubs, golf courses, and exercise rooms
- Car rentals, limousine services, and tours
- Casinos and gaming activities
- Pay-to-view television movies

To inform guests of these facilities, a directory of hotel services is often placed in each guestroom. Front desk agents must also be familiar with these services to respond knowledgeably to guest inquiries.

Marketing and Public Relations

If a hotel is scheduling an event to gain publicity, the front office staff should be among the first informed. The participation of the front office is crucial to a hotel's overall marketing and public relations effort. Social activities such as guest receptions, health and fitness programs, family events, and even complimentary coffee in a hotel's lobby may provide an environment that stimulates guest interaction and repeat business. Front office personnel may also play a role in hotel newsletters, guest history

Exhibit 6.1   Sample Maintenance Work Order

DELTA FORMS - MILWAUKEE U S A

(414) 461-0086

HYATT HOTELS ®

MAINTENANCE REQUEST

1345239

TIME _____

BY _____ DATE _____

LOCATION _____

PROBLEM _____

_____

_____

_____

_____

_____

ASSIGNED TO _____

DATE COMPL. _____ TIME SPENT _____

COMPLETED BY _____

REMARKS _____

_____

_____

_____

_____

RPHK-04

HYATT HOTELS MAI.. ENANCE CHECK LIST
Check (☒) Indicates Unsatisfactory Condition
Explain Check In Remarks Section

BEDROOM - FOYER - CLOSET

☐ WALLS   ☐ WOODWORK   ☐ DOORS
☐ CEILING   ☐ TELEVISION   ☐ LIGHTS
☐ FLOORS   ☐ A.C. UNIT   ☐ BLINDS
☐ WINDOWS   ☐ DRAPES

REMARKS : _____

_____

_____

BATHROOM

☐ TRIM   ☐ SHOWER
☐ DRAINS   ☐ LIGHTS
☐ WALL PAPER   ☐ PAINT
☐ TILE OR GLASS   ☐ DOOR
☐ ACCESSORIES   ☐ WINDOW

REMARKS : _____

_____

_____

_____

Courtesy of Hyatt Corporation.

systems, and customized registration and check-out processes which help personalize hotel services for frequent guests.

Guest Services

As the center of front office activity, the front desk is responsible for coordinating guest services. Typical guest services involve providing the guest with information and special equipment and supplies. Guests may also request special procedures. An ability to respond to guest requests is critical to guest satisfaction. When a request falls outside the responsibility of front office personnel, they should communicate it to the appropriate person or department.

At a growing number of hotels, a concierge or other designated staff member is responsible for satisfying guest requests. The concierge embodies a hotel's spirit of hospitality. As more hotel functions become automated, the concierge may become even more important for reinforcing the hotel's personal touch in guest services.

Guests dining in a hotel restaurant, one of the primary revenue centers. (Courtesy of Resorts International Hotel, Inc.)

Information Book

Front office personnel need to respond knowledgeably to guest requests for information. Common guest questions may include:

- Can you recommend a nearby restaurant?

- Can you call a taxi for me?

- Where's the nearest shopping center? drugstore? gas station?

- Where's the nearest church? synagogue? temple?

- How do I get to the nearest bank?

- Where is the theater from here? the stadium? Where can I buy tickets?

- When is check-out time?

- How do I get to the university? the library? the museum?

- Where's the federal building? the capitol? the district court? city hall?

- Where's a public restroom?

- What recreational facilities are available in the hotel? near the hotel?

Answers to some guest questions may require access to rather obscure information. Some properties accumulate such information in a bound guide called an **information book.** The front office information book may include simplified maps of the area, taxi and airline company telephone numbers, bank, theater, church, and store locations, and special event schedules. Front desk agents should be familiar with the information book and know how to use it. It can be an excellent reference.

Some hotels have installed computer information terminals in public areas. These terminals can provide guests with the equivalent of the front desk information book while freeing front desk agents to attend to other guest needs.

Equipment and Supplies

Guests may request special equipment and supplies during the reservations process, at registration, or during their stays. Reservations agents should have a reliable method of recording such requests to ensure that they are satisfied. When a guest requests special equipment or supplies at registration or during occupancy, he or she will almost always ask a front desk agent. The agent then relays the request to the appropriate service center or hotel department for processing. Equipment and supplies commonly requested by guests include:

- Roll-away beds
- Additional linens/pillows
- Irons and ironing boards
- Additional clothes hangers
- Audio-visual equipment
- Special equipment for blind, handicapped, or hearing-impaired guests

When other departments (such as housekeeping) are closed or otherwise inaccessible, front desk agents should have an alternative method of satisfying requests. In some hotels, the front office staff may have access to linen rooms during late night hours. In others, the housekeeping department may stock a centrally located linen closet to which appropriate front office personnel have a key. In any case, equipment and supplies should be available to maximize guest satisfaction.

Special Procedures

Guests may request exceptions to standard front office procedures at any time during reservation, registration, occupancy, or check-out. For example, procedural requests affecting the guest accounting process during occupancy (such as split folios) will usually be made during the reservations process. Reservations agents should have a reliable method of recording such requests and communicating them to appropriate front office personnel. Other procedural requests may be handled directly by front desk agents. Procedural requests may require more time and effort to fulfill than equipment and supplies requests. Typical procedural requests include:

- Split account folios

- Master account folios

- Wake-up calls

- Transportation arrangements

- Entertainment reservations

- Newspaper delivery

- Secretarial services

Folio requests can be easily fulfilled if attended to conscientiously. **Split folios** are most often requested by business travelers. In essence, the guest's charges are separated into two or more folios. One folio account may be set up to receive room and tax charges, to be billed to the guest's company. Another folio account may be set up to track incidental charges, such as telephone calls, food, and beverages, to be paid directly by the guest. A convention group meeting in the hotel may request that another type of folio—a **master folio**—be established. Only the charges incurred by the group as a whole are normally posted to the master account folio, for billing to the sponsoring agent. All other charges are the responsibility of the individual members of the group and are posted to their respective folio accounts. The purpose of a master folio is to collect charges not appropriately posted elsewhere.

Other procedural requests may be handled by a concierge, if the hotel employs one. If the hotel has no concierge staff, the front office becomes more dependent on the information book maintained at the front desk.

Guest Relations

No matter how efficient a hotel operation is, at some point a guest may register disappointment or find fault with something or someone. Hotels should try to anticipate guest complaints and plan strategies to deal with them as they arise.

The high visibility of the front office means front desk agents are frequently the first to learn of guest complaints. Front desk agents should be attentive to guests with complaints and seek a satisfactory resolution. Perhaps nothing annoys guests more than having their complaints apparently ignored or discounted. While front office staff generally will not enjoy receiving complaints, they should understand that few guests enjoy complaining. They should also realize that guests who find no opportunity to tell the hotel of their complaints often tell their friends, relatives, and business associates instead.

When it is easy for guests to express their opinions, both the hotel and the guests benefit. The hotel learns of potential or actual problem areas and is given the opportunity to resolve guest complaints, thereby increasing guest satisfaction. The guests have more problems resolved and feel that the hotel cares about their needs. From this perspective,

Handling guest complaints professionally and efficiently increases guest satisfaction.

every complaint is welcome. Remember that guests who leave a hotel dissatisfied may never return.

Complaints   Guest complaints can be divided into four categories of problems: mechanical, attitudinal, service-related, and unusual.

Most guest complaints are related to hotel equipment malfunctions. **Mechanical complaints** usually concern problems with climate control, lighting, electricity, room furnishings, ice machines, vending machines, door keys, plumbing, television sets, elevators, and so forth. Even an excellent preventive maintenance program cannot completely eliminate all potential equipment problems. Effective use of a front desk log book and maintenance work orders may help reduce the frequency of mechanical complaints.

Attitudinal complaints may be lodged by guests who feel they have been insulted by rude or tactless staff members, who have overheard arguing among the staff members, or who have had staff members complain directly to them. The hotel should take precautions to ensure that guests do not overhear staff arguing or complaints. Internal hotel problems which result in dissension should be brought to a supervisor's attention, not the guests'. This is especially critical to maintaining sound guest relations.

Service-related complaints may concern long waiting times for guests, a lack of assistance with luggage, untidy rooms, telephone difficulties, wake-up call errors, food or beverage quality problems, or ignored requests for additional supplies. More service complaints are likely to arise when a hotel is operating at or near full occupancy.

Unusual complaints may involve, for example, the absence of a swimming pool, a lack of public transportation, early lounge closing times, the harshness of the weather, and so on. Many such unusual complaints involve circumstances over which the hotel has little or no control. Nonetheless, guests typically seek hotel resolution of such problems. Difficult situations may arise if the front office has not anticipated receiving such complaints.

Identifying Complaints

All guest complaints deserve attention, even though they differ in nature and importance. An excited guest who loudly demands immediate attention at the front desk will appreciate a quick resolution, while a guest who comments in an offhand manner may invite a different type of response.

Hotels that systematically identify their most frequent guest complaints may well be able to improve guest relations. If the hotel is able to isolate frequent problems, then corrective action can contribute to improving overall guest satisfaction. A review of the front desk log book—if it has been properly used—will enable management to identify recurring complaints.

Another identification approach involves the evaluation of guest comment cards or questionnaires. Exhibit 6.2 shows a guest questionnaire designed to collect information about the hotel's mechanical systems, overall property ratings, and relevant marketing data. Guest questionnaires may be distributed at the front desk, placed conspicuously in the guestroom, or mailed to guests following departure.

By examining the number and type of complaints received, hotel management may gain insight into common and less common problems. Front office staff members may be better able to handle frequent complaints courteously and effectively, especially if they know the problem cannot be corrected immediately.

Handling Complaints

Ignoring a guest complaint is usually counterproductive. In many hotels, front desk agents are instructed to refer complaints to supervisors or managers. This may not always be possible, especially if the situation warrants immediate attention. The hotel may wish to develop a contingency plan in case such a situation arises.

The front desk may receive complaints about food and beverage operations in the hotel, regardless of whether those operations are under the same management as the hotel. Unless procedures for complaint referral are established between the hotel and the food and beverage operators, guests may continue to be upset and the hotel will receive the blame. The hotel and its revenue outlets should maintain close communications and develop procedures designed to satisfactorily resolve guest complaints.

The following general cautions should be considered in handling guest complaints:

- Guests may be quite angry. Staff members should never go alone to a guestroom to investigate a problem or otherwise risk potential danger.

- Staff members should never make a promise that exceeds their authority.

Exhibit 6.2   Guest Questionnaire

Immediate Attention Please

⬇

Room #

Date: _____

Time: _____

Room # _____ Needs:

Maid Service, i.e. _____

_____

_____

Extra Towels _____

T.V. Repair _____

_____

Misc. Repair _____

_____

A/C and/or Heating Unit
Checked _____

Other Services: _____

_____

_____

_____

_____

How Can We Serve You Better?

Your stay at Rodeway is important to us. Satisfying your hospitality needs is our livelihood, and we think we're pretty good at it. But we're not perfect. Let us know if we can make your next stay more pleasant. We want to see you again.

President
Rodeway Inns International

Location of Inn _____ Date _____

How often do you visit this city? _____

Is this trip for business? _____ pleasure? _____ both? _____

How did you arrive? car _____ plane _____ bus _____ other _____

Why did you choose this Inn?
☐ advertising: radio ☐ magazine ☐ billboard ☐ newspaper ☐ TV ☐ other _____
☐ convenience of location
☐ appearance   ☐ stayed at other Rodeway Inns
☐ Rodeway directory   ☐ friend's recommendation
☐ stayed here before   ☐ travel agent's recommendation

Did you make an advance reservation? yes ☐ no ☐

How did you make your advance reservation?
☐ Rodeway Reservations System (toll free)
☐ called this Inn direct
☐ through another Rodeway Inn
☐ through Professional Travel Planner
☐ by local person

Dates of stay _____ Room No. _____

How do we rate?
Please rate us on a scale of 1 to 10 (10 being excellent).
_____ friendly, courteous & efficient front desk personnel
_____ room decor & comfort
_____ room neatness & cleanliness
_____ convenience of location
_____ quality of food in restaurant
_____ service in restaurant
_____ service in lounge
_____ entertainment in lounge

How can we make your next stay more enjoyable? _____

_____

_____

_____

_____

Thank you for taking the time to help us serve you better. Our owners and managers are sincerely interested in your comments. This form will reach them if you give it to the front desk clerk or drop it in the mail. We would also appreciate your name and address.

Name _____

Address _____

City _____

State _____ Zip _____

RODEWAY INNS INTERNATIONAL

We're Out to Win You Over!

Courtesy of Rodeway Inns International.

- If a problem cannot be solved, staff members should admit this early on. Honesty is the best policy.

- Some guests complain as part of their nature, and may never be satisfied. The front office should develop an approach for dealing with such guests.

Suggestions for responding to guest complaints in a professional manner are outlined in Exhibit 6.3. Learning to deal effectively with complaints requires experience. Front office staff members can practice by thinking about how they might resolve some of the hotel's most common complaints. Role playing can also be an effective method in learning to deal with complaints. By anticipating complaints, planning and practicing responses, and receiving constructive feedback, staff members should be better prepared to deal effectively with guest complaints as they arise.

Exhibit 6.3   Complaint Handling Guidelines

1. Listen with concern and empathy.

2. Isolate the guest if possible, so that other guests won't overhear.

3. Stay calm. Avoid responding with hostility or defensiveness. Don't argue with the guest.

4. Be aware of the guest's self-esteem. Show a personal interest in the problem. Use the guest's name frequently. Take the complaint seriously.

5. Give the guest your undivided attention. Concentrate on the problem, not on placing blame. Do NOT insult the guest.

6. Take notes. Writing down the key facts saves time if someone else must get involved. Also, guests will slow down when they are speaking faster than you can write. More important, the fact that a hotel staff member is concerned enough to write down what they're saying is reassuring to guests.

7. Tell the guest what can be done. Offer choices. Don't promise the impossible, and don't exceed your authority.

8. Set an approximate time for the hotel's actions. Be specific, but do not underestimate the amount of time it will take to solve the problem.

9. Monitor the progress of the corrective action.

10. Follow up. Even if the complaint was resolved by someone else, contact the guest to see if the problem was satisfactorily solved. Report the entire event, the actions taken, and the conclusion of the incident.

Follow-Up Procedures

The front desk log book may allow management to initiate corrective action, verify that complaints have been resolved, and identify recurring problems. This comprehensive written record may also enable management to contact guests who are still dissatisfied at check-out. A letter from the front office manager expressing regret about the incident is usually sufficient to promote good will and demonstrate concern for guest satisfaction. Some managers may telephone departed guests to gain a fuller understanding of the incident, depending on its significance. Chain hotels may also receive guest complaints channeled through chain headquarters. Cumulative records of complaints about each hotel in the chain may be compiled and sent to managers on a regular basis. This method of feedback allows the chain's corporate headquarters to evaluate each hotel's guest relations performance on a comparative basis.

Front Office Security Functions

Providing security in a hotel is the broad task of protecting people—guests, employees, and others—and assets.[2] Because the diversity of the lodging industry makes national security standards infeasible, security programs must be developed individually. Each hotel's security program should reflect its own particular needs. The responsibility for developing and maintaining a property's security program lies with its management. The information presented here is intended only as an introduction to this topic, and only those elements relevant to the front office are included. Hotel management should consult legal counsel to ensure that the property is in compliance with applicable laws.

The Role of the Front Office

A security program is most effective when *all* employees participate in the hotel's security efforts. Front office personnel play a particularly important role. Front desk agents, door attendants, bellpersons, and parking attendants have the opportunity to continuously observe whoever arrives at or departs from the premises. Suspicious activities or circumstances involving a guest or a visitor can be reported to the hotel's security function or a designated staff member.

Some procedures that front desk agents may use to protect guests and property have already been introduced. For example, front desk agents should never give keys, messages, or mail to anyone asking for them without first seeing appropriate identification. The front desk agent should not announce an arriving guest's room number in a voice that might be overheard.

Guests may be further protected if the hotel has a policy that prohibits staff members from providing guest information to callers or visitors. Generally, front desk agents should not give out guestroom numbers. People calling guests at the hotel may be directly connected to the appropriate guestroom without being told the room number. Those inquiring in person about a guest may be asked to use the house phone to call the guestroom.

Front office employees may also inform guests of precautions they themselves may take. For example, front desk agents may suggest that a guest arriving by car hide and secure any valuable articles in the car. If a bellperson accompanies the guest to a room, he or she generally provides instructions on the operation of room equipment. The bellperson may also take this opportunity to review the use of access control devices on the guestroom doors and windows, familiarize the guest with pertinent security information, and point out any decals or notices in the room relating to guest security.

A hotel also helps protect its guests' personal property. The front office may develop a method for ensuring the safety and security of the luggage of arriving guests. Often, luggage and other articles received by a door attendant are receipted and moved to a secured area; guests later recover their belongings by presenting the receipt at registration. Other hotel employees can be of assistance in protecting the guests' property. A valet parking attendant, for example, should secure all parked vehicle keys so that they cannot be removed by anyone except authorized employees. Procedures for handling guest's valuables and providing space for their storage are addressed later in this chapter.

Front office personnel also play an important role in asset protection. Failure to collect payment from guests is usually a more significant source of loss than, for instance, the theft of towels or ashtrays. The establishment of a method of payment at registration was discussed in Chapter 5, and other concerns in avoiding losses from unpaid accounts are addressed in Chapter 9.

Key Control

Most lodging properties use at least three levels of guestroom key security: emergency keys, master keys, and individual guestroom keys. An **emergency key** opens all guestroom doors, even when they are double-locked (that is, locked with both a standard door lock and a device operable only from within the guestroom). Emergency keys should be highly protected. Their use should be strictly controlled and recorded. An emergency key should never be taken from the hotel property.

A **master key** opens all guestrooms that are not double-locked. When it is not in use on the property, it should be secured in a designated place of safe-keeping. It should be issued to authorized personnel only, based on their need to use the key, not simply on their status at the hotel. A written record should be maintained of which employees have received a master key.

A **guestroom key** opens a single guestroom if the door is not double-locked. As stated earlier, front desk agents should never simply give a guestroom key to anyone who requests it; appropriate identification should be checked to ensure that the person requesting the key is the guest registered to that room. In addition, front desk agents should remind guests to return keys at check-out. Well-secured key return boxes in the lobby, at hotel exits, and in courtesy vehicles can serve as additional reminders. Some properties have reduced key loss by requiring a key deposit from each guest at registration. The use of a key deposit has the additional benefit of bringing the guest back to the front desk before departure, thus helping to ensure settlement of all guest account charges.

Some properties do not list their name, address, or room numbers on guestroom keys. Then, if a key is lost and falls into the wrong hands, it cannot be traced to the property for criminal use. A code number is typically stamped on the key in place of the room number; a master code list is maintained at the front desk.

Hotel keys should not be taken from the property by employees, regardless of their responsibilities or position on staff. Many organizations require that all keys be returned to security and placed in a locked cabinet in a secured area of the property. Keys issued on a temporary basis should be recorded in a log. The log should indicate the reason for issue, issue date, time out, time in, recipient's name, and issuer's name. Whenever there is any known or suspected compromise of a key, an unauthorized entry by key, or any loss or theft, every lock affected should be changed or rotated to another part of the property.

Electronic Locking Systems. An electronic locking system replaces traditional mechanical locks with sophisticated computer-based guestroom access devices. **Centralized electronic locking systems** operate through a master control console at the front desk which is wired to every guestroom door. At registration, a front desk agent inserts a key/card into the appropriate room slot on the console to transmit its code to the guestroom door lock. The key/card, issued to the guest, is the only working guestroom key. Exhibit 6.4 shows a typical card-operated electronic lock installed in a guestroom door.

Micro-fitted electronic locking systems operate as individual units. Each door has its own microprocessor which contains a predetermined sequence of codes. A master console at the front desk contains a record of all code sequences for each door. At registration, the front desk agent encodes a key/card with the next code in the sequence for the assigned room. The console and each microprocessor must agree on which code in the sequence is currently valid.

Exhibit 6.4 Electronic Guestroom Door Lock

Courtesy of Uniqey.

Most electronic locking systems provide several distinct levels of security, parallel to the levels of keying in traditional systems. Systems may include various other guest safety and convenience features, such as a "do not disturb" signal. One form of electronic locking system does not require keys or cards at all; guests set the locking mechanism by programming their own four-digit code numbers.

Centralized electronic locking systems present an additional opportunity for improved security. Many of these systems keep track of which keys or cards opened which doors, by date and time. If the hotel staff knows of this aspect of the system's capability, employee theft (an unfortunate but sometimes all too real problem) is likely to be reduced, because employees who are tempted to steal know the entry record may incriminate them. Report creation and other system functions should be controlled by operator identification and password security codes.

Surveillance and Access Control

A lodging facility, although open to the public, is private property. An innkeeper has the responsibility to monitor and, when appropriate, to control the activities of persons on the premises. All employees should be trained to watch for suspicious persons and situations. Surveillance plays a role in most aspects of guest and property protection. Effective access control relies in part on procedures for responding to the observations of employees.

In the lobby, if possible, the front desk agent should be able to observe the property's entrances, elevators, escalators, and stairways. Properly placed mirrors may be helpful. The observation of escalators involves both security and safety considerations, and personnel should be instructed in procedures for stopping the escalators in an emergency. In many hotels, there is someone stationed at the front desk at all times. In a small property, a front desk agent may be the only staff member on the premises during late night hours. Under such circumstances, some properties limit access to the lobby and reception area, and the decision to admit someone is assigned to the front desk agent.

Surveillance typically relies on personnel, but it may potentially be enhanced by the use of various types of equipment. Closed-circuit television can sometimes be used effectively as a surveillance tool in multiple-entry properties. Usually, monitors are located in a control center and employees are assigned to respond promptly and appropriately when an incident is noted on the monitors.

It must be realized, however, that surveillance equipment is intended to help employees, not replace them. Equipment may allow an elevator to be programmed to stop at a certain floor for observation, but it is still up to personnel to actually observe it. Likewise, a closed-circuit television system is virtually pointless without personnel monitoring it.

Protection of Funds

The protection of funds is primarily the responsibility of the accounting division. However, other departments, particularly the front office, play important contributing roles in protecting certain financial assets.

The front desk cashiering function is a critical aspect of the protection of funds. The amount of cash in a cash register should be limited through the establishment of a **cash bank** for each front desk cashier. Under a cash bank system, at the start of each workshift each cashier is given the smallest amount of cash that will allow him or her to transact business normally. The cashier becomes responsible for this cash bank and for all cash added to it during the workshift. Ideally, only one person should have access to each cash drawer. (Cash banks are further discussed in Chapter 7.)

All transactions should be recorded immediately. The cashier should close the cash register drawer after each transaction. A cashier working with an open cash register drawer may fail to record a transaction, either accidentally or deliberately. Cashiers should complete any transaction in process before changing currency into different denominations for guests; each change request should be handled as a new transaction to avoid confusion. A supervisor or a member of the accounting division should occasionally conduct an unscheduled audit of the register.

Policy should be established for the placement of currency during a transaction. Generally, the employee should not place currency on the register ledge because this may make it easier for a thief to grab the money and run. Some organizations recommend that the money be placed in the cash drawer, but above the clip until the transaction is completed, to avoid any disputes over what denomination was tendered.

Safe Deposit Boxes

Laws in most states limit a property's liability for the loss of a guest's valuables if the property has safe deposit boxes or a safe for the storage of the guest's valuables and the guest is notified of their availability. The required notice usually takes the form of public postings, often within the guestroom itself; an example is shown in Exhibit 6.5. Employees with safe deposit responsibilities should be trained in proper procedures, and should be aware of the reasons for every rule. Safe deposit attendants should realize the importance and seriousness of this responsibility.

Safe deposit boxes should be located in an area to which there is limited access. Unauthorized persons, whether guests or employees, should not be permitted in the area. Such a location may be in the vicinity of the front desk, where the boxes may be secured while still visible to guests.

Keys and Key Control. Strict control should apply to the storage, issue, and receipt of safe deposit box keys. There should be no access to unissued keys except by employees responsible for this function. When such employees receive the key to a surrendered box, they should immediately secure the key. Spare locks and locks out for repair should also be carefully controlled.

Two keys should be required to open any safe deposit box. The control key, which must be used in conjunction with the guest's key to open the box, should always be secured. Only those persons authorized to grant access to boxes should ever have possession of this key. It should be accounted for at each change of shift.

Under no circumstances should there be more than one guest key for each safe deposit box, even when more than one guest is using the same box. If a guest key is lost, the box should be drilled open in the presence of a witness, the guest or the guest's legally authorized agent, and someone from the property. The safe deposit agreement signed by the guest should make it clear that the guest will be responsible for all costs related to the loss of the key.

Access. Access control is the most critical of all safe deposit responsibilities. The identity of the guest must be established before access is granted. The guest is usually required to sign a form requesting access; the attendant then compares the signature with that on the initial agreement signed by the guest when the box was issued. Some properties ask guests to include a piece of personal information (for example, mother's maiden name) on the initial agreement as an additional safeguard; in such cases, if there is some doubt about the identity of the person requesting access, the attendant can ask for the personal information, which an imposter would be unlikely to know. Whatever the procedure used, it should be followed for every access, regardless of the familiarity of the guest. *No one* should be granted access to the box unless that person's signature appears on the initial agreement.

After identity has been verified, the attendant should accompany the guest to the safe deposit area and use the control key and the guest's key to open the box in view of the guest. Property policies may vary on how the guest's privacy with regard to the contents of the box is to be maintained. Only the guest should place items into or remove items from a box. The attendant should never be alone with a guest's valuables. When

Exhibit 6.5 Michigan Hotel Liability Notice

Hotel Liability Law

AN ACT

To define the duties and liabilities of hotel keepers and innkeepers with relation to the personal property of their guests, and to provide for the protection of inn and hotel keepers, and to repeal act number two hundred twenty-seven (227) of the Public Acts of eighteen hundred ninety-seven (1897), and act number fifteen (15) of the Public Acts of eighteen hundred seventy-five (1875).

The People of the State of Michigan enact:

SECTION 1. The liability of the innkeeper of any inn, whether individual, partnership or corporation, for loss of or injury to personal property of his guest, shall be that of a depository for hire: Provided, however, That in no case shall such liability exceed the sum of two hundred fifty ($250.00) dollars; and in case of the loss of a trunk or chest, and its contents, it shall not exceed the sum of one hundred fifty ($150.00) dollars; in case of the loss of a valise, portmanteau, grip, telescope or dress suit case, and contents, it shall not exceed the sum of fifty ($50.00) dollars; and in case of the loss of a box, bundle or package, and contents, it shall not exceed the sum of ten ($10.00) dollars: And provided further, That nothing in this act shall prohibit an innkeeper from assuming a greater liability than the sum of two hundred fifty ($250.00) dollars for the personal effects of his guest: Provided, Said undertaking and agreement shall be in writing, stating the kind of personal property received and the value thereof, the kind and extent of the liability of said innkeeper, which said agreement shall be signed by said guests and said innkeeper or his clerk: And provided further, That nothing contained in this section shall preclude any remedy now existing for the enforcement of the hotel keeper's or inkeeper's lien.

SECTION 2. No innkeeper, whether individual, partnership, or corporation, who constantly has in his inn a metal safe or suitable vault in good order, and fit for the custody of money, bank notes, jewelry, articles of gold and silver manufacture, precious stones, personal ornaments, railroad mileage books or tickets, negotiable or valuable papers and bullion, and who keeps on the doors of the sleeping rooms used by his guests suitable locks and bolts, and on the transoms and windows of said rooms suitable fastenings, and who keeps a copy of this section printed in distinct type constantly and conspicuously suspended in the office and in the ladies' parlor or sitting room, barroom, wash-room and in five (5) other conspicuous places in said inn, or in not less than ten (10) conspicuous places in all in said inn, shall be liable for the loss of or injury to any such property belonging to any guest, unless such guest has offered to deliver the same to such innkeeper for custody in such metal safe or vault, and such innkeeper has refused or omitted to take it and deposit it in such safe or vault for custody, and to give such guest a receipt therefor: Provided, however, That the keeper of any inn shall not be obliged to receive from any one guest for deposit in such safe or vault any property hereinbefore described exceeding a total value of two hundred fifty ($250.00) dollars, except under special agreement as hereinbefore provided, and shall not be liable for any excess of such property whether received or not, but every innkeeper shall be liable for any loss of the above enumerated articles of a guest in his inn, caused by the theft or negligence of the innkeeper or any of his servants.

SECTION 292. Any person who shall put up at any hotel, motel, inn, restaurant or cafe as a guest and shall procure any food, entertainment or accommodation without paying therefor, except when credit is given therefor by express agreement, with intent to defraud such keeper thereof out of the pay for the same, or, who, with intent to defraud such keeper out of the pay therefor, shall obtain credit at any hotel, motel, inn, restaurant or cafe for such food, entertainment or accommodation, by means of any false show of baggage or effects brought thereto, is guilty of a misdemeanor. No conviction shall be had under the provisions of this section unless complaint is made within 60 days of the time of the violation hereof.

SECTION 293. Obtaining such food, lodging or accommodation by false pretense, or by false or fictitious show of baggage or other property, or refusal or neglect to pay therefor on demand, or payment thereof with check, draft or order upon a bank or other depository on which payment was refused, or absconding without paying or offering to pay therefor, or surreptitiously removing or attempting to remove baggage, shall be prima facie evidence of such intent to defraud mentioned in the next preceding section of this chapter.

FIRE LAWS

Sec. 496 of Act 328 of Public Acts of 1931. Any person who shall carelessly, recklessly or negligently set fire to any hotel, rooming house, lodging house or any place of public abode, or to any bedding, furniture, curtains, drapes, or other furnishings therein so as to endanger life or property in any way, shall be guilty of a misdemeanor.

Courtesy of Michigan Lodging Association. *Note:* Each state law is different, and posting requirements may vary.

the guest is finished, the attendant should lock the box in view of the guest and return the guest's key. When the guest relinquishes the box and returns the key, the guest and the attendant should both sign a release notice.

Space limitations often make it impossible to provide a separate safe deposit box for each guest. If guests choose to share a box, each guest's property must be sealed in a container (such as an envelope) to keep it separate from the other guests' property. The guest key to the safe deposit box used to hold the sealed envelopes should be maintained in a secure place, and its use should be recorded.

Unusual Access. If a guest fails to surrender a box upon check-out, the property should send the guest a registered letter requesting surrender of the box. If the guest does not respond within the appropriate legal time limit, the hotel should dispose of the contents of the box in accordance with state law and the advice of counsel. If a guest who failed to surrender a box mails the key to the property, the property should secure the key and ask the guest to sign a release. If the box is found to contain property, the guest should be requested to personally remove the contents and surrender the box, or forward a power of attorney for the guest's representative to do so. Under no circumstances should access to a safe deposit box be allowed based solely on telephone or telegram authorization.

Any court orders concerning safe deposit boxes should be referred to the property's management. All access should be suspended until the property's rights and obligations are determined.

Lost and Found

The lost and found function may be assigned to any of several departments. Nevertheless, most guests contact the front office to find their belongings. Clear procedures should be developed to deal with inquiries concerning lost and found items. All telephone calls about lost or found items should be directed to the lost and found function. To avoid giving conflicting information to the caller, no one else at the hotel should discuss the matter with the guest. The lost and found employee should request and record a description of the item, estimates of where and when it was lost, and the guest's name and address. A sample form for recording this information is shown in Exhibit 6.6.

Effective procedures for responding to guest inquiries depend, of course, on effective lost and found procedures. When a hotel employee discovers a mislaid article, he or she should immediately bring it to the attention of the lost and found personnel. Some properties require the completion of a form describing the item and stating where it was found, the date, and the employee's name. Lost and found personnel store the item for the length of time designated by law or until it is claimed by the owner, securing it if it is valuable.

Under no circumstances should an article be mailed to the address on a registration card without the guest's explicit permission. A letter should be sent requesting the guest to contact the hotel to identify the item. After identification, lost and found personnel generally mail the item and record the action. In some states, it is legal for a hotel to sell

Exhibit 6.6   Guest Loss Report Form

The **BRO**ᴬ**DMOOR**
Colorado Springs. Colorado 80901

LOSS REPORT

DATE OF REPORT: _____

DATE OF LOSS: _____

NAME: _____

ADDRESS: _____

CITY: _____   STATE: _____

ZIP: _____   DATE OF DEPARTURE: _____

ROOM NUMBER: _____   HOME PHONE: _____

LOCATION (WHERE LOST): _____

DESCRIPTION: _____

REMARKS: _____

SECURITY OFFICER: _____

Courtesy of The Broadmoor, Colorado Springs, Colorado.

unclaimed property if appropriate attempts to contact the owner have elicited no response for a stipulated length of time.[3] This license has been questioned in courts of law. The simplest course of action may be to turn over all such property to law enforcement authorities.

Emergency Procedures

It is the responsibility of management to develop procedures for responding to emergencies such as fires, floods, earthquakes, tornadoes, hurricanes, and so forth, as they apply to a particular property. Medical emergencies and crimes, including robbery of the property itself, should also be considered. Emergency procedures should be regularly reviewed with hotel employees so that they can respond properly to any emergency situation. Staff members who react to an emergency quickly and efficiently may help to avert panic and prevent needless damage, injury, or loss of life.

The front desk may serve as the command center in the event of an emergency, summoning on-premises security staff and/or the local police, as determined by management. Some properties have designated a special telephone extension number for guests and staff members to use in an emergency. This number is monitored by the operator and possibly also by the security function. A means of immediate communication among employees with emergency duties may also be required.

Medical Emergencies. Lodging properties need to face the possibility of a serious illness, injury, or even death among guests or employees. The security function, according to management policy, should be ready to deal appropriately with any of these unfortunate incidents. Front office personnel chiefly serve a communications function in case of such an emergency. Many hotels keep lists obtained from local associations of physicians, dentists, and medical facilities to allow guests freedom of choice; these lists may be held at the front desk. A property should also consider developing procedures for advising callers of a guest's illness, hospitalization, or death.

Robbery. Because lodging properties typically have at least some cash on the premises, cashiers may be confronted by armed robbers. They should try to respond as reasonably as possible under the circumstances. Cashiers should comply with a robber's demands and make no sudden movements that might be seen by the robber as an attempt to thwart the crime. They should not do anything to jeopardize their lives or the lives of other persons. Unexpected actions or a lack of cooperation might prompt the use of a weapon. Other prudent behavior includes remaining quiet unless directed to talk, keeping hands in sight, and not attempting to disarm the robber or use a weapon.

Management may install a silent alarm in the cash drawer that is activated when a certain packet of bills is removed. When complying with a robber's demand for money, the cashier removes this packet with the rest of the money. No comment should be made, and the cashier should avoid the appearance of setting off an alarm.

A property's management may develop a robbery description form to meet its needs. Whether a form is used or not, the cashier and other employees should observe the robber carefully, noting physical characteristics such as height, weight, build, dress, color and style of hair, color of eyes, facial hair, complexion, scars, tattoos, and anything unusual. Attention should also be given to the voice and mannerisms of the robber and to the type of weapon he or she is using. If it can be done without danger, employees should observe the robber's direction of escape and the type and license number of the escape vehicle. If the robber leaves any evidence such as a note, the cashier should not handle it unnecessarily before giving it to the police. Employees should refrain from touching places the robber may have touched or evidence from which fingerprints may be taken.

Following the incident, the property should notify the police.

Fire. The front office is often assigned the responsibility of monitoring fire alarms and alert systems. The Occupational Safety and Health Administration requires that written plans be formulated for possible fire emergencies. These plans are required to include:

- Emergency escape procedures and route assignments

- Procedures to be followed by employees who remain to operate critical hotel operations before they evacuate

- Procedures to account for all employees after evacuation

- Rescue and first aid duties for those employees who are to perform them

- The preferred means of reporting fire and other emergencies

- Names or regular job titles of persons or departments who can be contacted for further information or explanation of duties under the plan

Many cities require a smoke detector in every hotel guestroom.[4] Some communities require the local fire authority to review and approve emergency fire programs for the property. The local fire department may also be able to assist in training employees in fire procedures.

Notes

1. For further discussion of the handling of guest mail, see Jack P. Jefferies, *Understanding Hotel/Motel Law* (East Lansing, Mich.: Educational Institute of the American Hotel & Motel Association, 1983), pp. 35-36.

2. This discussion (through the end of the chapter) is adapted from Raymond C. Ellis, Jr., and the Security Committee of AH&MA, *Security and Loss Prevention Management* (East Lansing, Mich.: Educational Institute of the American Hotel & Motel Association, 1986). The information provided is in no way to be construed as a recommendation by the Educational Institute of the American Hotel & Motel Association or the AH&MA of any industry standard, or as a recommendation of any kind, to be adopted by or binding upon any member of the hospitality industry.

3. For further discussion of a hotel's disposal of unclaimed property, see Jefferies, p. 35.

4. For further discussion of fire protection and smoke control systems, see Michael H. Redlin and David M. Stipanuk, *Managing Hospitality Engineering Systems* (East Lansing, Mich.: Educational Institute of the American Hotel & Motel Association, 1987), Chapter 12.

Discussion Questions

1. What front desk procedures help ensure the proper delivery of mail and messages to guests?

2. How are communications between the front office and the maintenance division handled? Discuss the functions of the front desk log book and maintenance work orders.

3. What are the three main types of requests guests may make at the front desk? Give examples of each.

4. Discuss the purpose of a front desk information book. What sort of information might such a book contain?

5. Why should guest complaints be welcomed by front office staff? How may a property benefit from analyzing the complaints it receives?

6. Discuss the four major types of complaints. Which is most common? Describe general approaches to handling complaints.

7. What role do front desk agents play in ensuring the safety and security of the hotel, guests, employees, and assets?

8. Discuss typical key control systems. What are three common levels of key security? How is key control affected by electronic locking systems?

9. Discuss procedures and guidelines related to front office safes and safe deposit boxes.

10. What emergencies at a property might involve front office personnel? Discuss the provisions of fire protection guidelines.

7 Front Office Accounting

A front office accounting system is an essential process designed to monitor and chart the financial transactions of guests and non-guests at the hotel. An effective guest accounting system includes tasks performed during each stage of the guest cycle. During the pre-arrival stage of the guest cycle, a guest accounting system captures data related to the form of guarantee for a reservation, and tracks pre-payments and advance deposits. When the guest arrives at the hotel, a guest accounting system documents the application of room rate and tax at registration. During occupancy, a guest accounting system is responsible for tracking guest charge purchases. During guest check-out, a guest accounting system ensures payment for goods and services provided.

The financial transactions of non-guests may also be processed within the parameters of front office accounting. Hotels may allow transactions involving non-guests in order to promote the hotel to local businesses, to track the unsettled bills of former guests, or to track transactions related to conference business at the hotel. If a guest's bill is not fully paid at check-out, the balance is transferred from guest to non-guest records. When this occurs, collection becomes the responsibility of the back office accounting division.

The specific functions of a front office accounting system are:

- Create and maintain an accurate accounting file for each guest or non-guest account

- Track financial transactions throughout the guest cycle

- Ensure internal control over cash and non-cash transactions

- Obtain settlement for all goods and services provided

The front office's ability to monitor and chart guest and non-guest transactions will directly affect its ability to collect outstanding balances. Incomplete or inaccurate monitoring may lead to difficulties in settlement.

Accounting Fundamentals

A complete course in bookkeeping is not necessary for an understanding of the purposes of front office accounting tasks. The design of a front office accounting system is unique to hotel operations. Both terminology and report formats often differ from those of other accounting systems. A brief review of some of the basic concepts of front office accounting follows.[1]

Accounts   An **account** is a form on which financial data are accumulated and summarized. An account may be imagined as a bin or container in which the results of various business transactions are stored. The increases and decreases in an account are summarized and the resulting monetary amount is the **account balance.** All financial transactions that occur in a hotel affect accounts. Front office accounts are recordkeeping devices to store information about guest and non-guest financial transactions.

In its simplest written form, an account resembles the letter T:

Account Name
Charges   Payments

This form of recording is called a **T-account.** T-accounts are not generally popular today because of the use of computers in business applications. However, T-accounts remain useful as a tool for teaching bookkeeping principles. For a front office account, charges are increases in the account balance and are entered on the left side of the T, while payments are decreases in the account balance and are entered on the right side of the T. The account balance is the difference between the totals of the entries on the left side and the right side of the T-account.

Journal form is typically used for front office accounting documents. In a non-automated or semi-automated recordkeeping system, journal form might look like this:

Description of Account	Charges	Payments	Balance

Similar to a T-account, increases in the account balance are entered under charges, while decreases in the account balance are entered under payments. In a fully automated system, charges and payments may be listed in a single column with the amounts of payments placed within parentheses to indicate their effect (a decrease) on the account balance.

In accounting terminology, the left side of an account is called the **debit** side (abbreviated **dr**) and the right side is called the **credit** side (abbreviated **cr**). Despite their prominence in other branches of hospitality accounting, debits and credits play a relatively small role in front office accounting. Debits and credits do not imply anything good or bad about an account. The value of debits and credits results from the use of **double-entry bookkeeping,** which is the basis for accounting in all modern businesses. In double-entry bookkeeping, every transaction creates entries that affect at least two accounts. The sum of the debit entries created by a transaction must equal the sum of the credit entries created by that transaction. This fact forms the basis of the night audit.

Guest Accounts. A guest account is a record of financial transactions which occur between a guest and the hotel. Guest accounts are created when guests guarantee their reservations or at the time of their registration. During occupancy, the front office records all transactions affecting the balance of a guest account. The hotel usually seeks payment for any outstanding guest account balance during the settlement stage of the guest cycle, although circumstances may require partial or full payment at other times during the guest cycle.

Non-Guest Accounts. A hotel may choose to extend in-house charge privileges to local businesses or agencies as a means of promotion, or to groups sponsoring meetings at the hotel. The front office creates non-guest accounts to track these transactions. These accounts may also be called **house accounts** or **city accounts**. Non-guest accounts also include accounts of former guests which were not satisfactorily settled at the time of their departures. Unlike guest accounts, non-guest accounts are normally billed on a monthly basis by the hotel's back office accounting division.

Folios

Front office transactions are typically charted on **folios**. A folio is a statement of all transactions affecting the balance of a single account. When an account is created, it is assigned a folio with a balance of zero. The front office records on the folio all transactions which increase or decrease the balance of the account. At settlement, the folio's record of a guest account is returned to a zero balance by cash payment or by transfer to an approved credit card or direct billing account.

The process of recording transactions on a guest folio is called **posting.** A transaction is said to be **posted** when it has been recorded on the proper folio and a new balance has been determined. When posting transactions, the front office may rely on handwritten folios (non-automated system), machine-posted folios (semi-automated system), or computer-based electronic folios (fully automated system). Regardless of the posting technique used, the basic accounting information recorded on a folio remains the same. In a non-automated or semi-automated recordkeeping system, guest folios are maintained at the front desk. In a fully automated recordkeeping system, electronic folios are stored in the memory of a computer and can be retrieved or printed on request.

Four types of folios are in common use in hotel front offices. These folios are used to chart account transactions as follows:

- **Guest folio:** an account assigned to an individual person or guestroom

- **Master folio:** an account assigned to more than one person or guestroom, usually reserved for group accounts

- **Non-guest** or **semi-permanent folio:** an account assigned to a non-guest business or agency with hotel charge purchase privileges

- **Employee folio:** an account assigned to an employee with charge purchase privileges

Often, special circumstances may lead to unusual folio assignments. For example, a business guest may request that his or her charges and payments be split between two folios: one to record expenses to be paid by the business, and one to record personal expenses to be paid by the guest. In this situation, two folios may be created for one guest.

Vouchers

A **voucher** is a document detailing a transaction to be posted to a front office account. A voucher is used to transmit transaction information from the source of the transaction to the front office. A common use of vouchers is to notify the front office of guest charge purchases at the hotel's revenue outlets which need posting. Several types of vouchers are used in front office accounting, including cash vouchers, charge vouchers, transfer vouchers, allowance vouchers, and paid-out vouchers. Most computer systems require few vouchers, since terminals interfaced with the front office computer electronically transmit transaction information directly to front office accounts.

Points of Sale

A **point of sale** is the time and location at which goods or services are purchased. Any hotel department that collects revenues for its goods or services is considered a revenue center and thus a point of sale. Large hotels typically support a wide variety of points of sale, including restaurants, lounges, room service, valet service, parking garages, and telephone service. The front office accounting system must be designed to ensure that all charge purchases at these points of sale are posted to the proper guest and/or non-guest accounts. Some hotels offer a variety of guest-operated devices which may also function as points of sale, resulting in charges to be posted to guest folios (for example, the in-room movie systems and beverage service systems discussed in Chapter 3).

The volume of goods and services purchased at scattered points of sale requires a complex internal accounting system to ensure proper posting and documentation of sales activities. For example, Exhibit 7.1 presents the flow of information that results when a guest charges a restaurant purchase to his or her guest account. A computerized **point-of-sale (POS) system** may allow remote terminals at the points of sale to communicate directly with a front office computer system. Automated POS systems may significantly reduce the amount of time required to post charge purchases to guest folios, the number of times each piece of data must be handled, and the number of posting errors and after-departure (late) charges which may arise.

Ledgers

A **ledger** is a grouping of accounts. A front office ledger is a collection of account folios. The folios used in the front office form part of the front office **accounts receivable ledger.** An **account receivable** represents money owed to the hotel. Front office accounting commonly separates accounts receivable into two subsidiary groups: the guest ledger (for guest receivables) and the city ledger (for non-guest receivables).

Guest Ledger. The guest ledger is the set of all guest accounts currently registered in the hotel. Guests who make appropriate credit arrange-

Exhibit 7.1 Restaurant Bill Charged to a Room Account

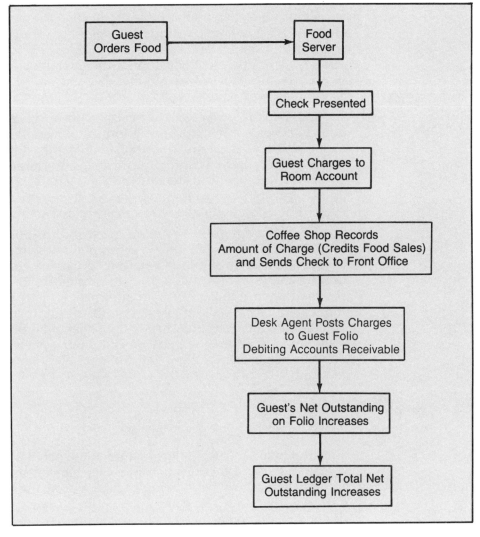

ments at registration may be extended privileges to charge purchases to their individual account folios. Guests may also pay on their accounts at any time during occupancy. Guest financial transactions are recorded onto guest ledger accounts to track receivable balances. The guest ledger may also be called the **transient ledger, front office ledger,** or **rooms ledger.**

City Ledger. The city ledger, also called the **non-guest ledger,** is the collection of all non-guest accounts (house accounts and unsettled departed guest accounts). If a guest account is not settled in full by cash payment at check-out, the guest's folio balance is transferred from the guest ledger to the city ledger for collection. At the time of transfer, account collection becomes the responsibility of the back office accounting division.

Creation and Maintenance of Accounts

Front office operations typically involve the tracking of both guest and non-guest accounts within the front office. The front office is responsible for the accurate and complete recording of all transactions affecting the balance of guest ledger accounts and all transactions except collection (which is the accounting division's responsibility) for city ledger accounts.

Guest folios are created during the reservations process or at registration. To prepare a folio for use, information from the guest's reservation or registration record must be transferred to the folio. If folios are pre-numbered for internal control purposes (as is common in non-automated and semi-automated systems), the folio number is entered onto the guest's registration card for cross-indexing. The printed guest folio cards used in non-computerized systems are stored in a front desk folio tray.

In a fully automated system, guest information is transferred and folios are cross-indexed within the computer system. A preliminary electronic folio may be automatically created when a guest makes a reservation. At check-in, reservation data are verified and may be combined with assigned room number and rate information to create an in-house electronic folio. For a walk-in guest, equivalent information is obtained and entered into the computer during the registration process. Since an electronic folio is created within the computer system, guest information does not require rehandling and the possibility for error is significantly reduced.

Recordkeeping Systems

The format of the information recorded on a folio may differ according to the front office recordkeeping system.

Non-Automated. Guest folios in a non-automated (handwritten) system contain a series of columns to list debits (charges) and credits (payments) accumulated by a guest during occupancy. At the end of the business day, each column is totaled and the ending balance is carried forward as the opening folio balance for the following day.

Semi-Automated. Exhibit 7.2 shows one type of folio used in a semi-automated (posting machine) recordkeeping system. Guest transactions appear sequentially on a machine-posted folio. For each transaction, data recorded includes the date, department, amount of transaction, and new balance of the account. The folio's outstanding balance is the amount the guest owes the hotel, or the amount the hotel owes the guest in the event of a credit balance at settlement. The column labeled *previous balance pickup* provides an audit trail within the posting machine framework.

Fully Automated. Transactions may be automatically posted to an electronic folio. When a printed copy of the folio is needed, debits (charges) and credits (payments) may appear in a single column, with payments distinguished by a minus sign, or in traditional multiple column format.

Charge Privileges

To establish an in-house line of credit, the guest may be required to present an acceptable credit card or a direct billing authorization as part of the registration process. Once a line of credit has been approved, guests

Exhibit 7.2   Sample Guest Folio

ROOM	(LAST)	NAME	(FIRST)	(INITIAL)	RATE	FOLIO NUMBER	**403131**

STREET ADDRESS		OUT			PHONE READING	OUT	
CITY, STATE & ZIP		IN				IN	
NO. PARTY	CREDIT CARD		CLERK	FROM FOLIO			
				TO FOLIO			

DATE	REFERENCE		CHARGES	CREDITS	BALANCE	PREVIOUS BALANCE PICKUP
Jul 27 A	RESTR	103	** 14.25		* 14.25	A* 14.25
Jul 27 A	ROOM	103	** 60.00		* 74.25	A* 74.25
Jul 27 A	LDIST	103	** 6.38		* 80.63	A* 80.63
Jul 27 A	MISCCR	103		** 18.38	* 62.25	A* 62.25
Jul 27 A	PAID	103		** 62.25	* .00	

Last
Balance
Amount Due

are able to make charge purchases. These transactions are communicated electronically or by vouchers from remote POS locations to the front office for proper account posting.

Guests who pay cash for accommodations at registration (known as paid-in-advance or PIA guests) are typically not extended charge purchase privileges. In a fully automated front office accounting system, PIA accounts may be set to a **no-post status.** Point-of-sale terminals throughout the hotel will have access to this information, and revenue outlet cashiers will know instantly if a guest has not been extended charge privileges. In non-automated and semi-automated properties, a physical PIA list is manually distributed to all revenue centers. While this list has the same effect as the computer access list, it may not be as useful or current.

Local businesses or residents may qualify for and establish house accounts. Charge purchases for house accounts, like those for guest accounts, move from the hotel's revenue centers to the front office for posting. Since all POS transactional vouchers are processed by the front office, a thorough audit and comparison of guest and non-guest activities is possible.

Credit Monitoring

The front office must monitor guest and non-guest accounts to ensure they remain within acceptable credit limits. Typically, a line of credit is set for guests who establish charge privileges during the reservations or registration process. Guests who present an acceptable credit card at registration may be extended a line of credit equal to the floor limit authorized by the issuing credit card company. Guest and non-guest accounts with other approved credit arrangements are subject to limitations established by the hotel called **house limits.**

As a front office account approaches its credit limit, management may need to be notified, according to hotel policy. Such accounts are called **high risk** or **high balance** accounts. Management may choose to request additional credit authorization from the credit card company, or request a partial payment from the guest to reduce the account balance. The night auditor is primarily responsible for identifying accounts which have reached or exceeded predetermined credit limits. The front office may deny charge purchase privileges to guests with high balance accounts until the situation is resolved.

Account Maintenance

A folio is used to record transactions which affect a front office account balance. Since guests may inquire about their outstanding account balance or check out of the hotel with little or no advance notice, it is imperative that guest folios be accurate, current, and properly filed. Transaction postings conform to a basic front office accounting formula. The formula is:

$$\text{Previous Balance} + \text{Debits} - \text{Credits} = \text{Net Outstanding Balance}$$
$$\text{PB} + \text{DR} - \text{CR} = \text{NOB}$$

Recall that debits increase the balance of an account, while credits decrease the balance.

This formula can be applied to the folio shown in Exhibit 7.2. The guest registered on July 27 and the first debit, a charge purchase of $14.25, occurred in the hotel's restaurant that evening. Since the front office received no cash payment or credit, the first net outstanding balance on the account was $14.25.

$$\text{PB} + \text{DR} - \text{CR} = \text{NOB}$$
$$0.00 + 14.25 - 0.00 = 14.25$$

Or, stated another way:

Previous Balance:	0.00
+ Debits:	+ 14.25
− Credits:	− 0.00
= Net Outstanding Balance:	= 14.25

The guest's room charge was posted to the account by the night auditor later that evening. This transaction appears on the second line of the folio, producing a new net outstanding balance:

$$
\begin{array}{ccccccccc}
PB & + & DR & - & CR & = & NOB \\
14.25 & + & 60.00 & - & 0.00 & = & 74.25
\end{array}
$$

Next, a long-distance telephone call resulted in a $6.38 debit posting, a credit (account allowance) of $18.38 was recorded, and cash was received in the amount of $62.25. Applied to each of these transactions in turn, the front office posting formula yields a zero net outstanding balance for the account:

$$
\begin{array}{ccccccccc}
PB & + & DR & - & CR & = & NOB \\
74.25 & + & 6.38 & - & 0.00 & = & 80.63 \\
80.63 & + & 0.00 & - & 18.38 & = & 62.25 \\
62.25 & + & 0.00 & - & 62.25 & = & 0.00
\end{array}
$$

At this point, the guest checks out of the hotel and the account is properly closed.

Tracking Transactions

Charge purchase transactions must be properly documented (typically on vouchers) for appropriate postings to be made. Communication to the front office and subsequent posting of transactional information from remote points of sale is a major concern of the front office accounting process. The night audit verifies transactional data to ensure that the hotel collects accounts receivable balances for all goods and services rendered.

The occurrence of a transaction initiates activity within the front office accounting system. Nothing happens without a transaction. For this reason, the front office accounting system is called a **transactional accounting system.** Both the nature of the transaction and its monetary value are required for proper posting procedures. A transaction can be one of several types:

- Cash payment
- Charge purchase
- Account correction
- Account allowance
- Account transfer
- Cash advance

Each type of transaction has a different effect on the front office accounting system. Each transaction type may be communicated to the front office through the use of a different type of voucher, which simplifies auditing procedures.

Cash Payment. Cash payments made at the front desk are posted as credits to a guest or non-guest account, and decrease the balance of the account. The front office may use a **cash voucher** to support such transactions. Only cash payment transactions which take place at the front desk create entries on an account folio. Cash payments to settle an account or pre-pay accommodations also affect front office account balances. A guest who registers and pays cash in advance for accommodations may be provided a copy of his or her folio as proof of payment.

When cash is paid for goods or services at a location other than the front desk, no entry appears on the account folio. The "account" for this transaction is created, increased, settled, and closed at the point of sale, thereby eliminating the need for front office documentation or posting. For example, a cash payment for lunch in the hotel's restaurant would not appear on the guest's folio.

Charge Purchase. Charge purchases represent deferred payment transactions. In a deferred payment transaction, the buyer receives goods and services but does not pay for them at the time they are provided. A charge purchase transaction increases the outstanding balance of a folio. If the transaction occurs somewhere other than the front desk, it must be communicated to the front desk for proper folio posting. In non-automated and semi-automated properties, this communication is normally accomplished by means of a **charge voucher,** also referred to as an **account receivable voucher.**

Account Correction. An account correction resolves a posting error on a folio which is rectified on the same day the error is made, before the close of business. An account correction can either increase or decrease an account balance depending on the nature of the error. For instance, suppose a front desk agent mistakenly applied a lower room rate than was appropriate for a particular guestroom. It would be necessary to adjust the balance of the account. In this instance, the account correction would increase the guest's folio balance. If a higher room rate had been wrongly posted, then the account correction would decrease the account's balance. A **correction voucher** is used to document this type of transaction.

Account Allowance. Account allowances involve two types of transactions. One type of allowance is a decrease in a folio balance for such purposes as compensation for poor service and rebates for coupon discounts. Another type of allowance is used to correct a posting error detected after the close of business. The error will thus be separately entered into the accounting records of the various departments. An account allowance is documented by the use of an **allowance voucher.** The use of allowance vouchers should be approved by management. Note the difference between account allowances and account corrections. Exhibit 7.3 shows sample correction and allowance voucher slips.

Account Transfer. When one guest offers to pay a charge for another guest, the charge must be transferred from one account to another ac-

Exhibit 7.3 Sample Correction and Allowance Vouchers

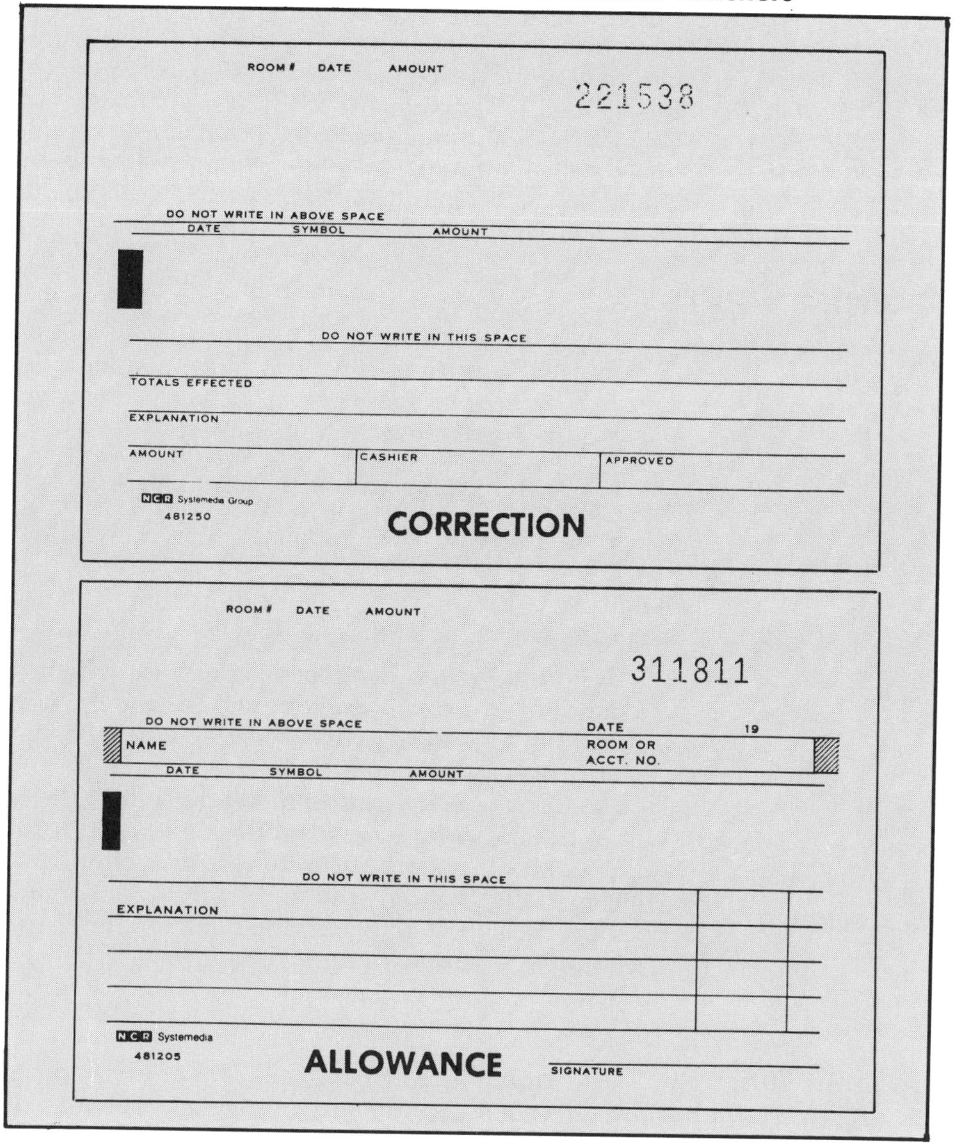

ROOM # DATE AMOUNT

221538

DO NOT WRITE IN ABOVE SPACE

DATE SYMBOL AMOUNT

DO NOT WRITE IN THIS SPACE

TOTALS EFFECTED

EXPLANATION

AMOUNT CASHIER APPROVED

NCR Systemedia Group

481250

CORRECTION

ROOM # DATE AMOUNT

311811

DO NOT WRITE IN ABOVE SPACE

DATE 19

NAME

ROOM OR ACCT. NO.

DATE SYMBOL AMOUNT

DO NOT WRITE IN THIS SPACE

EXPLANATION

NCR Systemedia

481205

ALLOWANCE

SIGNATURE

count. The reduction in balance on the originating folio and the increase in balance on the destination folio will be supported by a **transfer voucher.** An account transfer may also occur when a departing guest uses a credit card to settle his or her account. The guest's account balance is transferred from a guest account to a non-guest account through the use of a transfer voucher.

Cash Advance. Cash advances differ from other transactions in that they reflect cash flow out of the hotel, either directly to or on behalf of a guest. Cash advance transactions are similar to debit transactions and increase a folio balance. Cash advances are supported by **cash advance vouchers.** Cash disbursed by the hotel on behalf of the guest and charged to the guest's account as a cash advance is typically called a **paid-out.**

In the past, front office staff often allowed guests to sign a paid-out slip and receive cash on account; this is no longer common in the hospitality industry. However, a guest who orders a floral delivery, for example, may request that the front desk agent accept the order and pay for the flowers. This payment for flowers is a cash advance on the guest's behalf. The front office pays for the delivery on the assumption that the guest will reimburse the hotel. Hotel policy will dictate how cash advances are to be handled.

Internal Control

Internal control in the front office involves:

- Tracking transaction documents

- Verifying account entries and balances

- Identifying vulnerabilities in an accounting system

Auditing is the process of verifying front office accounting records for accuracy and completeness.

Each transaction produces paperwork which documents the nature and amount of the activity. For example, the transaction that occurs when a guest charges a meal to his or her account folio may be supported by the restaurant's guest check, cash register tape, and charge purchase voucher. The voucher is prepared and sent to the front office as notification of the transaction. A front desk agent, in turn, retrieves the guest's folio, posts the charge purchase transaction, and files the folio and voucher. Later that day, the night auditor ensures that all vouchers have been properly posted to accounts. Discrepancies may be easier to resolve if complete documentation is readily available to substantiate account entries.

Front Office Cash Sheet

The front office is responsible for a variety of cash transactions which may affect both guest and non-guest accounts. Proper cash handling procedures and controls must be established, implemented, and enforced.

Most operations require front office cashiers to complete a **front office cash sheet**, similar to the one shown in Exhibit 7.4, listing each receipt or disbursement of cash. The information on this sheet is used to reconcile actual cash on hand at the end of a cashier shift with the transactions which occurred during the shift. The cash sheet provides separate columns to record transactions affecting guest accounts, transactions affecting non-guest accounts, and miscellaneous transactions. Front office policy may also require the completion of a cash voucher to document each cash transaction affecting a front office account.

Money collected from a departing guest during settlement is the most common entry on a front office cash sheet. When guests pay on their accounts, the cashier typically records the amount paid, the room number, and the folio number. If a guest pays for his or her accommoda-

Exhibit 7.4   Front Office Cash Sheet

FRONT OFFICE CASH SHEET

HOTEL _____

CASHIER _____   FROM _____ A.M. P.M.   TO _____ A.M. P.M.   WATCH _____ 19 ___

CASH RECEIPTS				ROOM NUMBER		FOLIO NO.	NAME	EXPLANATION	ROOM NO.	CASH DISBURSEMENTS	
MISC'L	CITY LEDGER	GUEST LEDGER	PAID ON ACCOUNT	PAID IN ADVANCE	DEPARTURE					GUEST LEDGER	CITY OR MISC'L

tions in advance, the front desk agent records this payment to offset subsequent room and tax charges and to render a zero folio balance.

The front office cash sheet also provides space for itemization of cash disbursements or paid-outs. When a guest charges a room service purchase to his or her account, for example, he or she may include the server's tip in that charge. If the front office cashier pays the server's tip, it is recorded on the front office cash sheet as a paid out transaction. Similar action is followed if the front office accepts and pays for collect mail, telegrams, or other items. Payment for cash advances is generally collected from guests at check-out as part of folio settlement.

Cash Banks   A second set of front office accounting control procedures involves the use of cashier banks. A **bank** is an amount of cash assigned to a cashier so that he or she can handle the various transactions that occur during a particular workshift. Control procedures typically require that cashiers sign for their banks and that a limited number of people have access to any one bank. At the end of a workshift, each front office cashier is responsible for depositing all cash, checks, and other negotiable instruments received during the workshift.

At shift end, after removing the initial bank, the cashier typically places the cash and checks he or she has received in a specially designed cash voucher or cash deposit envelope. The cashier itemizes the contents of the deposit envelope on its outside before dropping it into the hotel's vault. Sound internal control suggests that this procedure be witnessed by at least one other employee. Differences between the money placed in the deposit envelope and the cashier's net cash receipts should be noted on the envelope as overages, shortages, or due backs. Net cash receipts are determined by subtracting the paid-outs disbursed from the payments received. The amount of cash and checks in the cashier's drawer, minus the amount of the initial cash bank, should equal the cashier's net cash receipts.

An **overage** occurs when, after the initial bank is removed, the total of the cash and checks in the drawer is greater than the net cash receipts. A **shortage** occurs when the total of the cash and checks in the drawer is less than the net cash receipts. Neither an overage nor a shortage is typically considered "good" by front office management when evaluating the job performance of front desk cashiers.

A **due back** occurs when a cashier pays out more than he or she receives; in other words, there is not enough cash in the drawer to restore the initial bank. This is unusual in the front office. However, a special kind of due back may occur in the front office if a cashier accepts many checks and large bills during a shift, such that he or she cannot restore the initial bank without including the checks or large bills. Checks and large bills are not very useful for processing transactions, and are usually deposited with other receipts. Consequently, the deposit is greater than the cashier's net cash receipts, with the excess due back to the cashier's bank. Front office due backs are normally replaced with small bills and coins before the cashier's next workshift, restoring the bank to its full and correct amount. Due backs do not reflect positively or negatively on the cashier's job performance, and may occur when the cashier is in or out of balance.

Audit Controls   A number of audit control measures are used to ensure that the front office staff properly handle cash, guest accounts, and non-guest accounts. Publicly held lodging companies are required to have their accounting records audited yearly by independent certified public accountants. In addition, companies with several lodging properties often employ internal auditors to make unannounced visits to individual hotels to audit their accounting records. In both instances, a report is completed for management and ownership review. Exhibit 7.5 presents one firm's internal inspection report. The checklist includes items related to standard hotel procedures designed to protect the integrity of front office operations.

Exhibit 7.5   Internal Control Inspection Checklist

			Sat.	Unsat.
(A)	**GUEST ACCOUNTS**			
1.	Accounts Receivable per audit:			
	a. _____ Sleepers	$_____		
	b. _____ After departure charges	_____		
	c. _____ Prepaid accts. with charges	_____		
	d. _____ Disputed accounts	_____		
	e. _____ Delinquent accounts (over 60 days)	_____		
	f. _____ Skips	_____		
	g. _____ Tour vouchers	_____		
	h. _____ Employee accounts	_____		
	i. _____ Intercompany accounts	_____		
	j. _____	_____		
	k. _____	_____		
	l. _____	_____		
	SUBTOTAL m. Other direct billing accounts	$_____		
	TOTAL DIRECT BILLING n. Total guest accounts	$_____		
	TOTAL ACCOUNTS RECEIVABLE o. Less advance deposits	$_____		
	BALANCE ACCOUNTS RECEIVABLE	$_____		
	p. Variance			
	_____ Direct billing accounts			
	_____ Accounts confirmed by letter	$_____		
	Reset control number per report	_____		
	Reset control number per machine	_____		
2.	Direct billing accounts signed by guest.		_____	_____
3.	Follow-up on accounts receivable in accordance with company policy.		_____	_____
4.	Only authorized individuals permitted to sign direct billing accounts.		_____	_____
5.	Direct billing accounts have copies of all correspondence and supporting charges pertaining thereto.		_____	_____
6.	Direct billing checks deposited promptly.		_____	_____
7.	Monthly listing of accounts receivable prepared properly.		_____	_____
8.	Direct billing payments, posting, billing, separated and supervised.		_____	_____
9.	Corporate credit authorization on file for direct billings.		_____	_____

(continued)

Exhibit 7.5 *(continued)*

			Sat.	Unsat.
(B)		ADVANCE DEPOSITS		
	1.	Folios are complete (date of arrival shown on folios, etc.).	_____	_____
	2.	Advance deposit folios are secured.	_____	_____
	3.	Revenues or refunds processed promptly on stale dated credit balance accounts.	_____	_____
	4.	Advance deposit checks deposited promptly.	_____	_____
(C)		CREDIT CARD PROCEDURES		
	1.	Credit card imprinters are dated correctly.	_____	_____
	2.	An examination of all completed credit card vouchers shows:		
		a. Approval where required.	_____	_____
		b. All cards current (not expired).	_____	_____
		c. All imprints are legible.	_____	_____
		d. Clerk's initials and folio number.	_____	_____
	3.	Credit card transmittals completed correctly (totals correct, non-national credit card charges itemized, adding machine tape included).	_____	_____
(D)		CHECKS		
	1.	Clerk's initials, folio number, endorsement and payee portion completed properly.	_____	_____
	2.	Deposit daily.	_____	_____
	3.	Correct check cashing policies in force.	_____	_____
	4.	Check register maintained correctly.	_____	_____
(E)		FRONT OFFICE		
	1.	Reset control number controlled properly.	_____	_____
	2.	Revenues balanced to D card: (check 3 days)		
		a. Room	_____	_____
		b. Restaurant	_____	_____
		c. Long Distance	_____	_____
		d. Laundry	_____	_____
		e. Miscellaneous	_____	_____
	3.	Paid-outs and allowances are completed and approved by management.	_____	_____
	4.	Corrections controlled and balanced.	_____	_____
	5.	Copies of all vouchers kept on property.	_____	_____
	6.	Long-distance calls taxed properly.	_____	_____
	7.	Long-distance service charges only as permitted by law.	_____	_____
	8.	Room tax charged correctly.	_____	_____
(F)		GUEST FOLIOS AND REGISTRATION CARDS		
	1.	Registration cards and folios filled out completely.	_____	_____
	2.	Folios and registration cards are time stamped in and out.	_____	_____
	3.	Continuation folios marked to and from.	_____	_____
	4.	Alphabetical and numerical filing current and in good order.	_____	_____
	5.	Numerical sequence of unused folios in order.	_____	_____
	6.	Void folios handled correctly.	_____	_____
(G)		SECURITY AND SAFETY		
	1.	Drop facilities constructed properly.	_____	_____
	2.	Deposit witness log used properly.	_____	_____
	3.	House banks stored properly when not in use.	_____	_____

Exhibit 7.5   (*continued*)

4. Night Auditor's clearance key secured.   _____ _____
5. Safe deposit boxes   _____ _____
   a. log maintained correctly
   b. keys available for unused boxes   _____ _____
6. Vehicle drivers properly licensed.   _____ _____
7. Cash drawers locked when not in use.   _____ _____
8. Hotel Safe   _____ _____
   a. Safe combinations last changed: _____.
   b. No terminated employees have safe combinations.   _____ _____
9. Proper security over keys when not in use.   _____ _____
10. Adequate security over storerooms.   _____ _____
11. TV log up to date.   _____ _____
12. Adequate linen inventory control.   _____ _____

(H)   FOLIO ACCOUNTABILITY

1. Unused folios (unopened boxes only):

   Total on hand _____ from number _____ to number _____
   Where are unused folios stored: _____
   How long will supply last: _____
   Per attached check sheets, the following folios were not accounted for: _____
   Total folios checked: _____ Period covered from _____ to _____
   Total number of folios missing: _____

COMMENTS: _____

_____

_____

I acknowledge receipt of this inspection and concur that the ratings given my property are factual and accurate (list any exceptions above).

_____   _____   Same Manager present at last audit?
        Manager   Date   Yes _____   No _____

I hereby certify that on the above date I performed an audit of the above property.

_____
Field Auditor, Audit Services Division

Settlement of Accounts

The collection of payment for outstanding account balances is referred to as account **settlement.** Settlement means bringing the account balance to zero, as a result of a cash payment in full or transfer to an approved direct billing or credit card account. All guest accounts must be settled at the time of check-out. Transfers to approved deferred payment plans move outstanding folio balances from the guest ledger to the city ledger.

Although guest account settlement normally occurs at check-out, guests may make payments against outstanding folio balances at any time. Non-guest folio balances are usually billed on the day the transaction occurred, with settlement due in fifteen to thirty days, depending on hotel policy. For example, consider the case of a guaranteed reservation no-show. The account cannot be settled at check-out, since the guest never registered. Instead, the hotel bills the guest for the amount of the guarantee, hoping to collect the account balance in 15 days.

Notes

1. For further discussion of basic hospitality industry accounting principles, see Raymond Cote, *Understanding Hospitality Accounting I* (East Lansing, Mich.: Educational Institute of the American Hotel & Motel Association, 1987) and *Understanding Hospitality Accounting II* (East Lansing, Mich.: Educational Institute of the American Hotel & Motel Association, 1988). The Educational Institute also offers courses based on these texts. For further information, contact the Institute at Box 1240, East Lansing, MI, 48826.

Discussion Questions

1. What are the specific functions of a front office accounting system? What tasks are performed during each stage of the guest cycle?

2. What is the purpose of an account? How are transactions recorded in an account? How are guest accounts and non-guest accounts different?

3. What are the four types of folios in common use in hotel front offices? How is a folio related to an account?

4. What is a point of sale? How can fully automated point-of-sale systems and guest-operated devices streamline the flow of accounting information to the front office?

5. What information is necessary to create a folio? How does the process differ in non-automated, semi-automated, and fully automated front office recordkeeping systems?

6. What is the basic front office accounting formula? How is it used in posting transactions?

7. What are some common front office accounting transactions? Why is the front office accounting system called a transactional system?

8. How does accounting differ for a cash payment and a cash advance at the front desk?

9. What items are recorded on a front office cash sheet? How does a cash sheet help ensure internal control in the front office?

10. What are *overages, shortages,* and *due backs?* How might these conditions reflect on a front office cashier's job performance?

8 The Night Audit

A major objective of front office accounting is to chart financial transactions and to summarize net outstanding balances on a continual basis. The night audit is a daily review of guest accounts (and non-guest accounts having activity) against revenue center transaction information which helps guarantee accuracy in front office accounting. A successful audit will result in balanced accounts, accurate statements, appropriate credit monitoring, and timely reports to management. The audit also ensures the hotel a higher probability of account settlement.

Since hotels operate 24 hours a day, seven days a week, it is important for the front office to regularly review and verify the accuracy and completeness of its accounting records. An audit process is intended to fulfill this need. While a night audit may be performed using non-automated, semi-automated, or fully automated procedures, the functions of the audit routine remain relatively unchanged.

As mentioned in Chapter 3, the audit is called the night audit because hotels generally perform it at night. A fully automated audit routine may also be called a **system update,** since computer files are updated as part of the audit routine.

Functions of the Audit

The chief purpose of the night audit is to prove the accuracy and completeness of front office guest and non-guest accounts in comparison with departmental activity reports. Specifically, the audit is concerned with:

- Verifying posted entries

- Balancing accounts

- Resolving room status discrepancies

- Monitoring credit limitations

- Producing operational reports

The Role of the Night Auditor

The role of night auditor requires attention to accounting detail, procedural controls, and guest credit restrictions. The auditor should also be familiar with the nature of cash transactions affecting the front office accounting system. The auditor tracks room revenues, occupancy percentages, and other front office statistics, and prepares a summary of cash, check, and credit card activities. These data reflect the hotel's financial performance for the day. The night auditor summarizes the results of operations for reporting to management. The hotel's accounting division may also use audit data prepared in the front office in preparing longer-range statistics to report to management.

Establishing an End of Day

The night auditor generally works on the night workshift, from 11:00 p.m. to 7:00 a.m., compiling and balancing the transactions from the previous day. Each front office must decide what time will be considered the end of its accounting day. An **end of day** is simply an arbitrary stopping point for the business day. The front office must establish an end of day so that the audit can be considered complete through that time.

For example, if a night audit is begun at 1:30 a.m., this marks the end of the business day. The period from 1:30 a.m. until the audit is completed may be called the **audit work time.** Usually, transactions affecting front office accounts received during the audit work time are not posted until the audit is completed. These transactions are considered part of the next business day.

Cross-Referencing

Hotels are notorious for generating volumes of paperwork documenting transactions. **Transactional documentation** identifies the nature and amount of a transaction, and is the basis for data input to a front office accounting system. For each transaction, the original revenue center documents the transaction type (cash, charge, or paid-out) and its monetary value. The front office staff posts an entry to the appropriate folio based on the documentation received.

For internal control purposes, an accounting system should provide some additional, independent documentation to verify each transaction. In a non-automated or semi-automated operation, supporting documents produced by different individuals serve as cross-reference sources. Although the auditor receives information on room revenues from the room rack or its equivalent, room rate postings should be checked against the housekeeping department's report on occupied rooms. This process ensures that rates have been posted for all occupied rooms. Similarly, food and beverage postings are usually performed on the basis of vouchers or guest checks received at the front desk. The restaurant's register tape and/or sales journal can be used to prove front desk postings.

The night auditor relies on transactional documentation to prove that proper accounting procedures were followed. The auditor's review of a day's postings leads to a reconciliation of front office accounts against revenue center and other departmental records.

Account Integrity

Front office accounting systems rely on sound internal control techniques to help ensure the accuracy, completeness, and integrity of the accounting process. In addition to the cash controls introduced in the last chapter, internal control involves the separation of job functions in such a manner that no single individual is wholly responsible for all phases of a sale.

Internal control suggests that different people post, verify, and collect for sales transactions. For example, if a front desk agent were allowed to sell a guestroom, post the charge, verify the posting, and collect for the room, no one else would be able to detect mistakes or embezzlement. Instead, a front desk agent may perform the posting, an auditor the verification, and a cashier the settlement.

The function of the night auditor is essential to ensure that the hotel receives payment for goods and services rendered. The auditor proves account integrity by cross-referencing account postings with departmental source documentation. The audit process is complete when front office and departmental account totals have been proven correct. So long as the audit process presents an out-of-balance position, the audit is not considered complete.

Guest Credit Monitoring   Related to the maintenance of front office account integrity is the supervision of guest and non-guest credit limitations. Credit limits are set depending on a variety of factors, such as credit card company floor limits, the hotel's house limit, or another figure based on the guest's reputation as a good or poor credit risk. The night auditor should be aware of these limits. High account balances may be noticed during the posting process. At the close of each front office business period, an auditor is responsible for identifying to management which accounts have reached or exceeded their credit limits. A report of high balance accounts should be prepared for appropriate management action.

Audit Posting Formula   The steps followed in the audit routine are based on the basic posting formula introduced in the last chapter. Regardless of how the night audit is conducted, the basic posting formula remains constant:

$$\text{Previous Balance} + \text{Debits} - \text{Credits} = \text{Net Outstanding Balance}$$
$$\text{PB} + \text{DR} - \text{CR} = \text{NOB}$$

To understand the use of this formula and its role in the audit, consider the following example. Assume an account has a previous balance of $28,000, departmental charges (debits) equal to $6,000, and payments received (credits) equal to $12,800. During the audit, the auditor picks up a balance of $28,000, totals all departmental charge transactions for the period, and adds these charges to the opening balance for a total of $34,000. Then all credits (cash payments, checks, and credit card payments), totaling $12,800, are subtracted from $34,000 for a result of $21,200. The result of these calculations is a net outstanding balance which becomes the previous balance for the next transaction. Using the formula, these transactions are:

$$\begin{array}{ccccccc} \text{PB} & + & \text{DR} & - & \text{CR} & = & \text{NOB} \\ \$28,000 & + & \$6,000 & - & \$12,800 & = & \$21,200 \end{array}$$

Daily and Supplemental Transcripts

A daily transcript, as shown in Exhibit 8.1, is a detailed report of all guest accounts that indicates each charge transaction that affected a guest account that day. A supplemental transcript may be used to accomplish the same analysis for non-guest accounts.

A daily transcript is typically segmented by revenue center, type of transaction, and overall total. The daily transcript and the supplemental transcript are the basis for a consolidated report of accounting data against which department totals can be matched. The total of charged purchases reported by the hotel's coffee shop, for example, should equal the amount of coffee shop charge purchases posted to guest and non-guest folios. The equality of these totals is an important concern in the audit process.

Daily and supplemental transcripts are simply worksheets designed to detect posting errors. They are preliminary screenings of account totals to find department-level errors. Transcripts facilitate the full audit routine by identifying out-of-balance figures in advance of a detailed review.

Operating Modes

The functions of the night audit may be performed manually, mechanically, or electronically. The following sections briefly discuss each of these three operating modes in relation to the audit routine.

Non-Automated

In a non-automated (manual) system, four major forms are used in addition to vouchers produced by the hotel's revenue centers:

- Folios
- Cash sheets
- Daily and supplemental transcripts
- Audit recapitulation sheets

In a non-automated system, the night auditor prepares daily and supplemental transcripts by copying the day's activities from each account folio to the appropriate line on the transcript. The transcript columns are then summarized to determine the total charges for each day. Information from the transcripts and cash sheets is transferred to a recapitulation sheet, shown in Exhibit 8.2, to provide a summary of the day's activity.

Few large hotel properties rely on a manual audit process. The night audit routines followed in non-automated and semi-automated properties are tedious and often involve more bookkeeping procedures than actual auditing. Given the abundance of relatively inexpensive front office accounting machinery, it appears inefficient and expensive to hand-post and verify all account entries and to compile transcripts and recapitulation sheets. Moreover, manual audit forms tend to be cumbersome and lend themselves to error because of the amount of manual copying and

Exhibit 8.1 Manual Daily Transcript

TRANSCRIPT OF GUEST LEDGER

NUMBER OF				ROOM NO.	BALANCE BROUGHT FORWARD	REG. NUMBER	ROOMS		TELEPHONE		VALET	LAUNDRY	CAFE	SALES TAX		CASH DISC.	TRANSFERS	CHANGES		CASH RECEIPTS	TRANSFERS	CHANGES	REBATES AND/OR ALLOWANCES	BALANCE CARRIED FORWARD	ROOM NO.
TRANSIENT		PERMANENT					TRANSIENT	PERMANENT	LOCAL	LONG DISTANCE															
ROOMS	GUESTS	ROOMS	GUESTS																						
1	2			201	7 50	176 50	14 00				2 00	1 50	27		73				20 00				6 00	
1	1			202		183 21	10 00			1 80		1 00	21						10 01					
2	3			203	8 00	177 63	16 00		36			3 00	36		2 00				29 66				3 00	
1	2			328		183 24	14 00		20	3 10		2 50	30						20 10					
1	2			329	19 00	17 863	15 00		60		2 00		30		1 10							2 00	36 00	
1	1			330		183 27	10 00			1 50		1 50	21						13 21					
43	49			TOTAL	270 17		249 50		3 75	43 59	5 76	2 39	18 75	8 04		3 75				151 82	19 58		9 79	421 98	

A Transcript of Guest Ledger Form with figures from folios entered on it.

computation required. Manual audits are, however, an excellent tool for learning posting and auditing concepts.

Semi-Automated   One of the most important developments in the history of front office procedures was the introduction of posting machines. Posting machines record guest charges on folios and simultaneously perform a number of other activities which simplify the work of the front desk agent and the auditor.

Posting machines may be either electro-mechanical or electronic; the electronic systems are enhanced versions of the older electro-mechanical machines. While some electronic systems serve basically the same functions as their forerunners, others may be linked to point-of-sale devices in the hotel's revenue centers to offer more efficient charge posting procedures.

It is beyond the scope of this book to describe how the several different types of posting machines function. In general, however, front desk agents post charges to account folios based on vouchers received from the hotel's revenue outlets. Physical posting to folios involves locating the folio, removing it from the folio bucket, entering the account's previous balance into the posting machine, posting the charge, balancing the folio, and refiling it in the folio bucket. If the front desk agent enters an incorrect previous balance (referred to as a **pick-up error**) in the process of posting, it will cause the folio to be in error and the audit to be out of balance.

Exhibit 8.2 Manual Recapitulation Sheet

RECAPITULATION OF GUEST LEDGER TRANSCRIPT

HOTEL ______________________ DATE ______________________

Number of Transient Rooms	Number of Transient Guests	Number of Permanent Rooms	Number of Permanent Guests	Sheet No.	Balance Brought Forward		Rooms Transient	Rooms Permanent	Telephone Local	Telephone Long Distance	Valet	Laundry	Cafe	Sales Tax		Cash Disb.	Transfers	Changes		Cash Receipts	Transfers	Changes	Rebate and/or Allowances	Balance Carried Forward	
43	49			1	270 17		247 50		3 75	43 59	5 20	2 39	18 75	8 04		3 75				151 82	19 58		4 74	421 95	
41	46			2	421 72		233 -		2 40	29 11	5 90	2 06	10 05	7 38		15 50				99 55	8 24			614 33	
38	55			3	463 67		283 75		3 60	46 93	2 60	3 05	32 05	9 68		6 62				142 75	116 55			592 65	
				4																					
				5																					
				6																					
				7																					
				8																					
				9																					
				10																					
122	150				1155 56		764 25		9 75	119 63	13 70	7 50	60 85	25 10		25 87				394 12	144 37		9 79	1633 93	
City					8444 03								8 30	8			144 37			30 51				8566 27	
Totals					9594 59		764 25		9 75	119 63	13 70	7 50	69 15	25 18		25 87	144 37			424 63	144 37		9 79	10200 20	

1,026.65 Dr. Accts Receivable Guests
152.75 Dr. Accts. Receivable City
10,278.99 Total

Credit Accts. Rec. Guest 548.28
Credit Accts. Rec. City 30.51
Total 10,278.99

DETAILS OF TODAY'S LEDGER ENTRIES

Name	Detail	Debit	Credit
CITY LEDGER			
A. H. Drake	Food	2 30	
	Tax	8	
J. B. Smith Jr.	Food	6 00	
Harry Golden			5 30
Jack Marshall			25 21
TOTALS		8 38	30 51
GENERAL LEDGER			
TOTALS			

RECAPITULATION OF FRONT OFFICE CASH SHEETS

Clerk	Guest	City	Total	Misc'l and/or Gen'l Ledger	Grand Total
RECEIPTS					
Cave	333 78	30 51	364 29	92	365 21
Coate	41 42		41 42	over 5	41 47
Hansen	19 02		19 02		19 02
Dining Room				391 42	391 42
TOTALS	394 22	30 51	424 73	392 39	817 12
DISBURSEMENTS					
Cave	4 45		4 45		4 45
Coate	21 42		21 42		21 42
TOTALS	25 87		25 87		25 87
NET	368 35	30 51	398 86	392 39	791 25

TURN-INS

Name		For'd	Amount
Cave	360 76		
Coate	20 05		
Hansen	19 02		
Dining Room	391 42		
SUB-TOTAL	791 25	TOTAL	

TRANSFERS

Name	Folio No.	Room No.	Guest Ledger Debit	Guest Ledger Credit	City Ledger Debit	City Ledger Credit
C. A. Smith	18421	706		17 66	17 66	
Walter de Urso	18345	722		66 29	66 29	
James Scofield	18434	523		14 58	14 58	
Mr. and Mrs. H. Jamos	18520	316		8 24	8 24	
Richard Bradford	18514	411		9 28	9 28	
Robert Stern	18451	610		23 32	23 32	
				144 37	144 37	

TURN-INS TO FRONT OFFICE

Name	Detail		Name	Detail	Amount
					391 42
Dining Rm.	Food	366 58	Laundry		92
	Tax	11 79		overage (Coate)	05
	Bar	12 05			
	[illegible]	1 00			
SUB-TOTAL		391 42	TOTAL		392 39

The Recapitulation of Guest Ledger Transcript indicates how information from the transcript is transferred to this summary form for management's information.

As an account folio is posted, several other actions take place at the same time:

- The voucher used to initiate the posting is imprinted with the same information posted to the guest folio, providing machine-printed verification that the voucher has been posted.
- The same information is printed onto a paper tape to provide the machine with an audit trail and to serve as a journal record. (An **audit trail** is an organized flow of source documents detailing each event in the processing of a transaction.)

Exhibit 8.3   Night Auditor's Report

	DATE	TRANS SYMBOLS	NET TOTALS	CORRECTIONS	MACH TOTALS
ROOM	Oct 26	ROOM	15.00		* 15.00
RESTAURANT	Oct 26	RESTR	25.10	2.85	* 27.95
TELEPHONE	Oct 26	PHONE	.30	.55	* .85
LONG DISTANCE	Oct 26	LDIST	2.21		* 2.21
LAUN. & DRY CLEAN	Oct 26	LNDRY	2.00		* 2.00
MISCELLANEOUS	Oct 26	MISC	———		* .00
PAID OUT	Oct 26	PDOUT	.50		* .50
TOTAL DEBITS			45.11	3.40	* 48.51
MISCELLANEOUS CR	Oct 26	MISC CR	10.15		* 10.15
PAID	Oct 26	PAID	13.79		* 13.79
TOTAL CREDITS			23.94		* 23.94CR
NET DIFFERENCE			21.17		
OPENING DR. BALANCE			7209.96		
NET OUTSTANDING			7231.13		
TOTAL MCH. DR. BALANCE	Oct 26				*7231.13
LESS CR. BALANCE					
NET OUTSTANDING					*7231.13

D— NIGHT AUDITOR'S MACHINE BALANCE NO._____ DATE Oct. 26

DETECTOR COUNTER READINGS   ☒ DATE CHANGED

AUDITOR'S CONTROL 960   ☒ CONTROL TOTALS AT ZERO   **AUDITOR**

MACH. NUMBER 1   ☒ MASTER TAPE LOCKED

B-6759—K28YY   ☒ AUDIT CONTROL LOCKED   *John Colvin*

The night auditor's report (D Card) used in a front office posting machine.

- The amount of the posted charge is added to the running total for the department originating the posting; departmental totals are helpful in end-of-workshift and end-of-day reporting.

Forms used in a semi-automated system include cash reports— equivalent to the front office cash sheets of the non-automated audit— and an auditor's report, sometimes referred to as a **D card.** Exhibit 8.3 shows a sample completed report.

Fully Automated

Of the three operating modes, a fully automated night audit is by far the simplest to perform. Fully automated systems can be interfaced with point-of-sale equipment, call accounting systems, and other revenue center devices for quick and accurate automatic postings directly to electronic account folios. These and many more tasks can be performed in a fraction of the time needed in either of the other operating modes. Computerized systems enable the auditor to spend more time auditing transactions and analyzing front office activities. Critical steps involved in checking account balances and posting errors become simple procedures of comparing the guest ledger audit to the final daily report for balancing. If they do not balance, this may indicate a computer system problem or an unusual data handling error.

In a computerized system, the previous balance for each account, along with appropriate detail, is retained in the system. Users are guided through a series of steps to input the data required for posting. Input area specifications define the types of data which the computer will expect. The computer performs various checks to ensure that postings are correct—for example, a range check will recognize postings of unusual size, such as a $15 charge posted as $1,500. Since the computer keeps track of each posting by time, shift, employee, folio number, and department, it maintains a detailed audit trail for all accounting activity. Exhibit 8.4 shows a sample page (listing local telephone calls) from a daily transaction report.

Computer systems can also organize, compile, and print records faster than can be done manually. In the case of the audit, the computer can process a large quantity of data, perform numerous computations, and generate accurate account totals. A system update performs many of the same functions. System updates are run daily to allow for report production, system file reorganization, and system maintenance, and to establish an end of day.

Computerized systems also offer instant access to information, allowing management to keep a constant check on operations. Reports detailing revenue data, occupancy statistics, advance deposits, arrivals, no-shows, room status, and other operational information can be easily generated on request, or as part of the regular audit routine. Exhibit 8.5 shows a computer-generated revenue report.

The Audit Process

A front office accounting system depends on transactional documentation to establish accurate records and to maintain effective operational controls. The discovery and correction of errors is what the audit process is about. It is designed to ensure the integrity of accounts through cross-referencing. Ledger accounts are compared to source documents to prove individual entries and account totals. Discrepancies found during an audit must be corrected.

Due to the transient nature of hotel business, an audit is conducted on a daily basis. Despite tradition, the night audit is not necessarily a nighttime activity. Many computer-based front office systems are capable of performing a nearly continuous system update and providing summary reports upon demand.

The degree of scrutiny required during the audit process is a function of the frequency of errors and the volume of transactions to be checked. While the first of these factors depends on the quality of front office work, the second tends to be closely correlated with the size and complexity of the hotel. Large, complex hotels typically require closer account scrutiny due to the volume of transactions posted.

The following steps are common to the sequence of a night audit:

1. Complete Outstanding Postings

2. Reconcile Room Status Discrepancies

3. Balance All Departments

Exhibit 8.4 Daily Transaction Report—Local Telephone Department

```
LODGISTIX RESORT & CONFERENCE CENTER (90003)              PAGE   1
                                                          JUL12,87
Department Audit Report - JUL12 - All Employees  - LO LOCAL   14:25:03

Folio Room Time Dept  Refer   Chrg/Pymt     Correct       Adjust    Comm Ded    ID

00241  210 0811  LO            .50+                                            PS
00127  105 0813  LO            .50+                                            PS
00152  112 0813  LO            .50+                                            PS
00152  112 0813  LO            .50+                                            PS
00127  105 0814  LO            .50+                                            PS
00171  201 0814  LO            .50+                                            PS
00234  207 0815  LO            .50+                                            PS
00234  207 0816  LO            .50+                                            PS
00243  223 0816  LO            .50+T                                           PS
00243  223 0816  LO            .50+                                            PS
00002  126 0817  LO            .50+                                            PS
00002  126 0817  LO            .50+                                            PS
00226 1000 0817  LO            .50+                                            PS
00226 1000 0818  LO            .50+                                            PS
00237  215 0818  LO            .50+                                            PS
00237  215 0818  LO            .50+                                            PS
00253  240 0819  LO            .50+                                            PS
00234  223 0823  LO            .50+                                            PS
00243  223 0823  LO            .50-T                                           PS
00085  230 0825  LO  2334                                .50-A               PS
00012  107 0826  LO  34455                               .50-A               PS
00022  109 0827  LO            .50-T                                           PS
00023  109 0827  LO            .50+                                            PS
00001  111 0851  LO                        50.00-C                            JS
00001  111 0851  LO                        50.00+C                            JS
00001  111 0852  LO            .50+                                            JS
00022  109 0852  LO            .50+T                                           JS
00166  106 0852  LO            .50+                                            JS
00253  102 1814  LO           6.00+                                            MD

Total LOCAL                  16.00+          .00          1.00-        .00

End of report
```

Courtesy of Lodgistix.

4. Verify Room Rates

5. Verify No-Show Reservations

6. Post Room Rates and Tax

7. Prepare Reports

8. Deposit Cash

9. Back Up the System

10. Distribute Reports

In a computer system update, several of these steps may be condensed or combined. The rest of this chapter examines these audit procedures in some detail.

Exhibit 8.5   Revenue Report

```
LODGISTIX RESORT & CONFERENCE CENTER (90003)

Daily Report - JUL12 - Charges

Dept           Net        Gross       Adjust

ROOM         2301.00+    2301.00+        .00
CITY TAX       42.68+      42.68+        .00
OCC TAX        85.50+      85.50+        .00
TAX           116.60+     116.60+        .00
GIFT SHP         .00         .00         .00
HLTH CLB         .00         .00         .00
LONG DIS       38.36+      38.36+        .00
LOCAL          15.00+      16.00+       1.00-
PARKING         5.00+       5.00+        .00
PAIDOUT          .00         .00         .00
DELIFOOD       10.00+      10.00+        .00
LNG FOOD         .00         .00         .00
POOLFOOD         .00         .00         .00
RESTFOOD      301.31+     301.31+        .00
DELI BEV         .00         .00         .00
LOUNGE         21.62+      21.62+        .00
POOL BEV         .00         .00         .00
REST BEV         .00         .00         .00

Gr Total     2937.07+    2938.07+       1.00-
```

Courtesy of Lodgistix.

Complete Outstanding Postings

One of the chief functions of the audit is to ensure that all transactions affecting front office accounts are posted to appropriate folios before the end of the day. The first step of the night audit is to complete all outstanding postings. Although most front offices attempt to post transactions to the proper accounts as they are communicated, a night auditor must confirm that all transactions have been posted prior to starting the audit. Incomplete postings will lead to errors in account balancing and summary reporting.

The auditor verifies that all voucher postings for revenue center transactions have been completed. If the hotel does not use a computerized telephone call accounting system, outstanding telephone charges may need to be posted. If the hotel has point-of-sale and/or call accounting systems interfaced with a front office accounting system, then the totals from earlier shifts can be verified to ensure that all outlet charges have already been posted.

The night auditor may also need to post previously unposted front office cash transactions. The auditor will often discover some postings remaining from previous workshifts.

Reconcile Room Status Discrepancies

Room status discrepancies must be resolved in a timely manner. Errors in room status can lead to lost and uncollectible room revenues and omissions in postings. For example, if a guest checks out but the front desk agent forgets to properly complete the check-out procedure, the guest's room will appear occupied when in reality it has been vacated. The front office must keep room status current and accurate to effectively monitor the number of rooms available for sale.

The night auditor is responsible for ensuring that discrepancies between the daily housekeeper's report and the front office room status system are reconciled before the end of the day. In order to minimize errors, housekeeping departments are required to report the perceived status of rooms they service. The auditor must review front office and housekeeping department reports to reconcile the occupancy status of all rooms.

If the front office believes a guestroom is occupied, but is reported as vacant on the housekeeping report, the auditor should look for an active folio. If the folio has a balance, there are several possibilities:

- The guest may have departed but forgotten to check out.

- The guest may be a skipper, who left with no intention of paying.

- The front desk agent or cashier may not have closed the folio.

After verifying that the guest has in fact departed, the auditor should process the check-out and set the folio aside for management review and follow-up. If the folio has been settled, the front office room status system should be updated to show that the room is vacant.

In a computerized system, the check-out process automatically changes the room's status. Few, if any, discrepancies with the housekeeping report should result.

Balance All Departments

The night auditor balances all departments using source documents. The auditor seeks to balance all front office accounts against departmental transaction information. Vouchers received at the front desk and other source documents are totaled and compared to revenue center summaries. Even fully automated hotels generally maintain source documents to resolve potential discrepancies as they arise.

The postings to guest and non-guest accounts must equal the amounts charged at revenue outlets for the front office accounting system to be considered **in balance.** An **out of balance** condition indicates a need to investigate the correctness and thoroughness of postings. A detailed department audit (by shift or by cashier) may be produced and individual postings reviewed until the error is discovered. The audit process can become quite complicated at this point. It is generally considered more efficient to balance all departments initially before looking for individual posting errors within an out-of-balance department.

However, a balance in account and departmental totals does not necessarily mean that the proper accounts were selected for posting. Posting the correct amount to an incorrect account would still present an

Exhibit 8.6 Departmental Balancing Sequence

1. Sort the vouchers according to their departments.

2. Consider each department's vouchers.

   a) Separate the correction vouchers according to the departments they are to be applied against.

   b) Total the corrections for each department.

3. After verifying each of the corrections with the departments affected, total the correction vouchers on an adding machine. The corrections tape must coincide with the correction figures on the shift report.

4. Consider the vouchers again.

   a) Run adding machine tapes on the rest of the vouchers.

   b) While running tapes on the vouchers, check the written figure at the bottom of the voucher against the printed figure on the department detail report, as well as against the validated figure if the hotel uses a validating printer.

5. The vouchers should agree with the corrected figures of the departments. If the tapes do not agree with either figure, check to find the error before proceeding.

   a) Check to see that the date on the voucher is the current day's date.

   b) Check off each individual posting against the source document (vouchers) until the error is found. This can be tedious if there are several errors. However, if the hotel uses validating printers, a quick check of the source document validations will help pinpoint errors.

   c) Post any corrections or adjustments.

6. In a computerized system, revised individual shift reports can be printed after the corrections and adjustments have been made. In any operations mode, all of the backup data should be packaged for the accounting office.

in-balance total. This type of error usually goes unnoticed until problems with guest bills arise.

Exhibit 8.6 shows a representative sequence of departmental balancing procedures.

Verify Room Rates

The night auditor may be required to complete a room revenue and count report, as shown in Exhibit 8.7. This report shows the rack rate for each room and the actual rate at which the room was sold, providing an opportunity to analyze room revenues. If a room's rack and actual rates do not agree, there are several factors for the auditor to consider:

- If the room is occupied by a member of a group or by a corporate rate customer, is the discounted rate correct?

- If there is only one guest in a room and the actual rate is approximately half the rack rate, is the guest part of a shared reservation? If he or she is, did the second guest register?

The proper use of room revenue and count information can form a solid basis for room revenue analysis. A copy of this report may be prepared for the front office manager once all room rates have been verified.

Exhibit 8.7 Room Revenue and Count Report

ROOM	CONV.	PERSONS	ROOM RATE	MEALS RATE	ROOM	CONV.	PERSONS	ROOM RATE	MEALS RATE	ROOM	CONV.	PERSONS	ROOM RATE	MEALS RATE	ROOM	CONV.	PERSONS	ROOM RATE	MEALS RATE	ROOM	CONV.	PERSONS	ROOM RATE	MEALS RATE
500 F					600 F					700 G					800 G					900 G				
501 D					601 D					701 E					801 E					901 E				
502 D					602 D					702 E					802 E					902 E				
503 D					603 D					703 E					803 E					903 E				
504 E					604 F					704 F					804 F					904 F				
506 B					606 B					706 D					806 D					906 D				
508 B					608 B					708 D					808 D					908 D				
510 B					610 B					710 D					810 D					910 D				
512 B					612 B					712 D					812 D					912 D				
514 B					614 B					714 D					814 D					914 D				
516 B					616 B					716 D					816 D					916 D				
518 B					618 B					718 D					818 D					918 D				
520 B					620 B					720 D					820 D					920 D				
522 B					622 B					722 D					822 D					922 D				
524 B					624 B					724 D					824 D					924 D				
526 B					626 B					726 D					826 D					926 D				
528 B					628 B					728 D					828 D					928 D				
530 B					630 B					730 D					830 D					930 D				
505 F					605 F					705 G					805 G					905 G				
507 A					607 A					707 C					807 C					907 C				
509 A					609 A					709 C					809 C					909 C				
511 H					611 H					711 I					811 I					911 I				
515 C					615 C					715 D					815 D					915 D				
517 A					617 A					717 C					817 C					917 C				
519 A					619 A					719 C					819 C					919 C				
521 A					621 A					721 C					821 C					921 C				
523 A					623 A					723 C					823 C					923 C				
525 A					625 A					725 B					825 B					925 B				
527 C					627 C					727 D					827 D					927 D				
529 A					629 A					729 B					829 B					929 B				
531 A					631 A					731 B					831 B					931 B				
533 A					633 A					733 B					833 B					933 B ·				
532 D					632 D					732 E					832 E					932 E				
SOCIAL EP	R	P			SOCIAL EP	R	P			SOCIAL EP	R	P			SOCIAL EP	R	P			SOCIAL EP	R	P		
MAP					MAP					MAP					MAP					MAP				
SOCIAL TOTAL					SOCIAL TOTAL					SOCIAL TOTAL					SOCIAL TOTAL					SOCIAL TOTAL				
CONV.					CONV.					CONV.					CONV.					CONV.				
CONV. TOTAL					CONV. TOTAL					CONV. TOTAL					CONV. TOTAL					CONV. TOTAL				
VACANT					VACANT					VACANT					VACANT					VACANT				
TOTAL	33				TOTAL	33				TOTAL	33				TOTAL	33				TOTAL	33			

DATE   FD - 100

**Verify
No-Show
Reservations**

It may be the responsibility of the night auditor to clear the reservation rack or file and post charges to no-show accounts. In posting no-show charges, caution must be taken to verify that the reservation was guaranteed and the guest never arrived.

No-show billings must be handled with extreme care. A hotel that neglects to record cancellations properly and bills clients incorrectly risks having its legal agreements and relationships with credit card companies re-evaluated. It may also risk losing the guest's future business or the business of any travel agency which may have guaranteed the reservation. It is essential for all front office staff to closely follow established hotel procedures when handling reservation cancellations or changes.

**Post Room
Rate and Tax**

The posting of room rates and tax to all guest folios is typically begun at the end of day. Direct posting of room rate and tax at any time is one of the great advantages of a computerized system. Once room rates and taxes are posted, a room rate and tax report may be generated for the front office manager.

**Prepare
Reports**

The auditor is typically responsible for preparation of reports which indicate the status of front office activities. Final department detail and summary reports, a high balance report, the daily report, and specialty reports can be prepared for management review.

Final **department detail and summary reports** are produced and filed with the source documents for the accounting division.

The **daily report of operations** summarizes the day's business and provides insight into revenues, receivables, operating statistics, and cash transactions related to the front office.

The **high balance report,** as shown in Exhibit 8.8, identifies guests who are approaching an account credit limit. In a computerized system, the computer may be programmed to produce a high balance report upon demand.

Deposit Cash

Often the night auditor is responsible for preparing a cash deposit as part of the audit process. Since account and departmental balancing often involves cash transactions, cash depositing may depend on a successful audit. If front office cash receipts have not yet been deposited, the auditor compares the postings of cash payments and paid outs (net cash receipts) with actual cash on hand. A copy of the shift report may be included in the cash deposit envelope to support any overage, shortage, or due back.

**Back Up
the System**

This step applies only to computerized front office systems. Since a computer system eliminates the need for a room rack, reservation cards, and a variety of other traditional front office forms and devices, the front office becomes very dependent on the proper functioning of the computer system. Back-up reports must be run in a timely manner to enable smooth operation of the hotel in the event of a computer system failure.

End-of-day reports are developed and printed by the computer. Normally, at least two guest lists are printed, one copy for the front desk and

Exhibit 8.8   High Balance Report

GUEST LEDGER HIGH BALANCE REPORT			
Auditor *Bonnie Clark*		Date *September 8, 198X*	
		Reviewed by *M. Harless*	
Room No.	**Guest Name**	**Amount**	**Action Taken**
103	Green, Leonard	498.72	contacted - paid $200. Address & credit verified w/confirmed reservation
122	Beck, Patricia	465.32	Owns Beck, Inc. Direct billing OK'd
169	Lateer, William	452.14	Convention VIP Valid Diners Club card
247	Jones, Ray	559.11	Am Ex - approved
260	Hamilton, Joel	659.23	Left 3 messages, did not contact me; — ACTION NECESSARY
295	West, Deanna	355.03	Wants to pay by check — Left message for guest to see me

Source: *Successful Credit and Collection Techniques* (East Lansing, Mich.: Educational Institute of the American Hotel & Motel Association, 1981), p. 15.

one for the switchboard. A room status report allows front desk agents to identify vacant and ready rooms. A guest ledger report, as shown in Exhibit 8.9, carries the ending account balances of all registered guests. An activity report, as shown in Exhibit 8.10, contains expected arrival and departure information for the next several days.

Computer output should also be recorded onto magnetic tape or disk, depending on the system configuration. A system back-up is made after each audit and stored in a safe place.

Distribute Reports   Due to the sensitive nature of front office transactions, the night auditor must take care to deliver appropriate reports in a meaningful format and a timely manner. The distribution of reports is the final step in the audit routine, and it is an important step in overall hotel operations. If all of the reports are completed accurately and delivered in a timely manner, more informed operational decisions can be made.

Automated System Update

A system update in a computerized system accomplishes many of the same functions as a non-computerized night audit routine and more.

Exhibit 8.9   Guest Ledger Report

```
LODGISTIX RESORT & CONFERENCE CENTER (90003)

Preliminary Audit Report - JUL12 - Guest Ledger Balances

        Status          Open Bal   Room/Tax   Incdntl    Food     Bevg    Payment  Close Bal


        Canceled-Keep       .00        .00       .00       .00      .00   220.00-   220.00-
        Canceled-Return     .00        .00       .00       .00      .00   165.00-   165.00-
        No Show          480.00-       .00       .00       .00      .00       .00   480.00-
        Checked-out      312.31+    104.55+      .00       .00      .00   104.55-   312.31+
        Registered      5485.36+   2441.23+    58.36+    311.31+   21.62+ 1440.00-  6877.88+
        House Accounts      .00        .00      8.40+      .00      .00       .00     8.40+
        Group Master Accounts .00      .00     15.00+    14.00+    21.00+     .00    50.00+


        Total Guest Ledger 5317.67+  2545.78+   81.76+   325.31+   42.62+ 1929.55-  6383.59+
```

Courtesy of Lodgistix.

Exhibit 8.10   Activity Report

```
LODGISTIX RESORT & CONFERENCE CENTER (90003)                              PAGE   1
                                                                         JUL12,87
Arrival/Stayover/Departure Activity Report                               13:14:23

               ---Arrivals---  ---Stayovers--  --Departures-- Rem
Date   Avl  Sold   Gtd  6/4  Shr  Gtd  6/4  Shr  Gtd  6/4  Shr  Blk  Adlts  Kids

JUL12  24    49 Trn  28    5    0   12    0    1   14    0    0            71    16
       67.1% Grp      2    0    0    0    0    0    0    0    0     3       2     0

JUL13  36    37 Trn   1    0    0   31    5    1    8    0    0            61    14
       50.6% Grp      0    0    0    0    0    0    2    0    0     0       0     0

JUL14  48    25 Trn   1    0    0   19    5    0   13    0    1            41     8
       34.2% Grp      0    0    0    0    0    0    0    0    0     0       0     0

JUL15  59    14 Trn   3    0    0   11    0    0    9    5    0            21     4
       19.1% Grp      0    0    0    0    0    0    0    0    0     0       0     0

JUL16  68     5 Trn   1    0    0    4    0    0   10    0    0             7     2
        6.8% Grp      0    0    0    0    0    0    0    0    0     0       0     0

JUL17  68     5 Trn   1    1    0    3    0    0    2    0    0             9     2
        6.8% Grp      0    0    0    0    0    0    0    0    0     0       0     0

JUL18  71     2 Trn   1    0    0    1    0    0    3    1    0             3     0
        2.7% Grp      0    0    0    0    0    0    0    0    0     0       0     0


              Total  Transient  Group  Rem Blk
Room Nights    511
   Available   374
        Sold   137      132        2       3
Occupancy %  26.8%    96.3%     1.4%    2.1%

End of report
```

Courtesy of Lodgistix.

System updates are run daily to enable system file reorganization, system maintenance, and report production, and to provide an end-of-day time frame.

Since computer systems perform continuous audits on transactional postings as they occur, there may be little need for an auditor to actually post account entries. A front office accounting system may interface with revenue outlet devices for automatic postings from call accounting systems, point-of-sale systems, in-room movies and bars, and the like. The auditor should review interface procedures to be sure that automatically posted outlet transactions are properly handled. In the case of guaranteed reservation no-shows, postings may be programmed to flow automatically to a billing file. If a transaction needs to be independently posted, the electronic folio may be displayed on a computer terminal screen for processing.

Room status discrepancies are unusual in a fully automated environment, since the room rack is eliminated and registration and check-out functions are internally connected to room status functions. Housekeepers typically report the current occupancy status of a room through the room's telephone before they leave the room. This rapid updating from the housekeeping department is automatically reconciled with a room's electronic room status and a **room variance report** is automatically printed. Even in the event of a skipper, a computer system may help identify the problem quickly enough to enable the hotel to ready the room for resale with minimal loss of income.

Audit balancing is maintained continuously. As a charge purchase is entered at a point-of-sale register, it is instantaneously posted to a guest folio and a departmental control folio. A **control folio** is an accounting document used internally to support all account postings by department. To balance departments, the computer tests all non-control folio entries against the control folio under scrutiny. An imbalance is just as likely to identify a problem in automatic posting techniques as a shortcoming in accounting procedures. Detailed departmental reports can be generated and checked against postings to prove account entries at any time during the day.

Computer systems can be programmed to produce a variety of reports of various length and content. Since a system update involves computer file reorganization as well as accounting detail, most of the output of an update differs from that of its non-computerized counterpart. Reservation confirmations, revenue center summaries, expected arrival and departure lists, folios for guests expected to depart, a daily report of operations, and invoices for non-guest accounts are common products of an automated system update routine. Properties may also produce printed copies of file contents as a hedge against system failure. Activity reports, guest lists, room status reports, and account statements may also be printed.

Since the computer deals with information and not physical inventories, the cash deposit procedures of a non-computerized property are still likely to apply. However, since a computer-based system can also support point-of-sale interfaces, cashier control at revenue outlets may also fall under update control. The degree of specification of these procedures is usually subject to management policy.

Discussion Questions

1. What is the purpose of the night audit? Why is it generally performed at night? Define the term *end of day*.

2. What are the five elements of the night audit process? How does each contribute to the efficiency of the front office accounting system?

3. How do the concepts of cross-referencing and account integrity govern the audit process? What are the usual source documents for guest account transactions?

4. What information does a daily transcript report? What related purpose does a supplemental transcript achieve?

5. What differences exist between the night audit processes in the three front office recordkeeping systems? How has the structure of a non-automated audit governed the historical development of the audit process?

6. How does the night auditor reconcile room status discrepancies? Why is it important that these reconciliations occur as early as possible?

7. Why does the night auditor verify room rates and no-shows before posting room and tax? Why is it important that these postings occur as late as possible?

8. What reports are typically generated during the night audit process?

9. What is the purpose of a system back-up for a fully automated system? What are common elements of a back-up?

10. What are the differences between a fully automated system update and the traditional night audit? What tasks must still be performed separately in a fully automated property?

9 Check-Out and Settlement

The occupancy stage of the guest cycle is followed by check-out and account settlement. At the time of departure, the guest receives an accurate statement of account and is requested to pay any outstanding balance and return the guestroom key before leaving the hotel. Departure activities involve account settlement and the updating of front office records.

Account settlement includes both guest account and non-guest account reconciliation and receipt of payment. Guest accounts are settled at check-out in the presence of the guest. Guest account payments which are deferred to a credit card or an approved billing party are transferred to the back office accounting division for collection. Non-guest accounts are similarly transferred from the front office accounting system to the accounting division for collection.

Functions of Check-Out and Settlement

The check-out and settlement process is designed to accomplish three important functions:

- Settle guest account balances

- Update room status information

- Create guest history records

Guest account settlement is most effectively achieved while the guest is in the hotel. A guest can settle an account by paying cash, charging the balance to a credit card, deferring payment to a direct billing, or using some combination of these payment methods. In most hotels, front office staff are required to ask the guest to specify an eventual method of settlement at registration. Thus, credit card or direct billing information should be known in advance of check-out. This advance notification allows the front office to obtain verification and authorization of a credit card account or confirmation by a direct billing party. These verification activities tend to reduce the guest's actual check-out time while enhancing the hotel's ability to collect outstanding account balances.

Accurate room status information is essential to effective front office operations. Upon settlement of the guest's account, the front office cashier typically notifies the front desk agent that the guest has checked out.

The front desk agent then changes the guest's room status to "on-change" and notifies the housekeeping department of the departure. A housekeeper cleans and readies the room for inspection and resale. In order to maximize room sales, the front office must maintain current occupancy and housekeeping statuses on all rooms, and communicate status information in an accurate and expedient way.

A guest history file is a collection of personal and financial data about guests who have stayed in the hotel. An individual record within the file normally contains personal and transactional information relevant to the guest's stay. Having this information enables the hotel to better understand its clientele and determine relative guest trends, and provides a powerful base for strategic marketing. Guest history files may be constructed from expired registration cards or created through sophisticated computer-based systems which automatically direct check-outs into a guest history database file. Proper analysis of guest history data may provide the hotel with a valuable competitive edge in the hospitality marketplace.

Departure Procedures

During the check-out and settlement process, a well-prepared, well-organized front office staff can provide a smooth, efficient, and pleasant experience for all concerned. The settlement process depends on an effective front office accounting system for maintaining accurate folios, verifying and authorizing a method of settlement, and resolving charge discrepancies through source documentation and audit review.

At check-out, the front office gives the guest a final copy of his or her account folio. At this point in the guest cycle, the guest's account balance should be brought to zero. Thus, guest account settlement is typically referred to as "zeroing out" the account. In order to zero out a folio account, its balance must be settled in full. Guest accounts which are not zeroed out at the departure stage are transferred to the city ledger for billing and collection.

There are several means by which a guest account may be zeroed out. When a guest approaches the front desk to check out, the front office cashier should verify exactly how the account is to be settled, regardless of which method of settlement was specified by the guest at registration. Methods of settlement include:

Cash payment in full. A cash payment in full at check-out will bring an account balance to zero. The folio is zeroed out and marked paid. Since a cash payment in full made at registration may not earn the guest charge purchase privileges in the hotel's revenue outlets, a guest may present a credit card at check-in to receive charge privileges, even though he or she intends to settle the account at check-out with cash. In this situation, the credit card voucher imprinted at registration should be destroyed at check-out.

Credit card transfer. Credit card settlement creates a transfer credit on the guest's folio and moves the account balance from the guest ledger to the city ledger. The front office cashier should imprint the credit card onto a voucher if it was not imprinted during check-in. The cashier should then enter the amount due onto the credit card voucher before presenting it to the guest for signature.

Direct billing transfer. Like a credit card settlement, a direct billing arrangement transfers the account balance from the guest ledger to the city ledger. However, unlike credit card settlement, a direct billing causes the hotel's back office accounting division to become responsible for account billing and collection rather than an outside agency. Direct billings are not normally an acceptable method of settlement unless the billing has been previously arranged and approved by the hotel. To complete a direct billing settlement, the front office cashier should obtain the guest's signature on the folio as an acceptance of all charges listed on the folio.

Combined settlement methods. A guest may choose to use more than one settlement method to zero out a folio account. For example, the guest may make a partial cash payment and charge the remainder of his or her account balance to a credit card. Front office cashiers must accurately record the combined settlement methods and ensure that all required paperwork is properly completed.

Once the guest has checked out, the room's status must be updated. Failure to do this can result in eventual room status discrepancies and lost room revenues. Comparisons with the housekeeper's report may reveal early discrepancies.

Similar precautions should be taken to ensure that the front office does not continue to take messages or accept charges for departed guests. Before the guest leaves the front desk, the front office cashier should check for any messages or mail awaiting guest pick-up. Often front office staff and departing guests are primarily concerned about check-out procedures and forget to inquire about unclaimed messages or mail.

Express Check-Out

Some front offices perform pre-departure activities. Most front offices experience many guest departures between 7:30 and 9:30 a.m. A common pre-departure activity involves the production and early morning distribution of guest folios for guests expected to check out that morning. The folios may be quietly slipped under the guestroom doors between 2:00 and 4:00 a.m. so that no one outside the room can tamper with them. Included with a pre-departure folio, the front office normally distributes an express check-out form such as that in Exhibit 9.1. A guest selecting the express check-out option completes the form and approves transferring the outstanding account balance to an already imprinted credit card voucher (created at registration). The guest then leaves the express check-out form at the front desk on his or her way out.

Express check-out forms may also include a note requesting the guest to notify the front desk if there has been a change in departure plans; otherwise the front office will assume the guest is departing by the hotel's posted check-out time. This procedure usually encourages guests who have changed their departure plans to quickly notify the front desk before check-out time.

Although the guest leaves the hotel after depositing the express check-out form, the front office must complete the guest's check-out by transferring the outstanding folio balance to a previously accepted

Exhibit 9.1 Express Check-Out Form

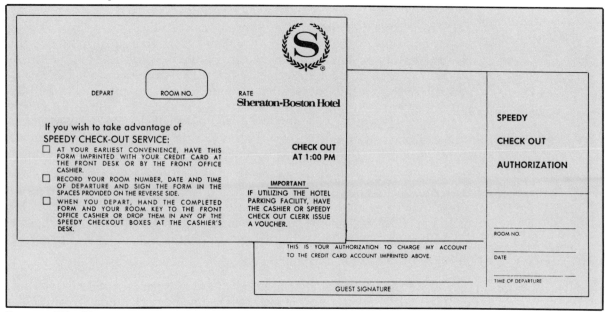

DEPART ROOM NO. RATE
Sheraton-Boston Hotel

If you wish to take advantage of
SPEEDY CHECK-OUT SERVICE:
☐ AT YOUR EARLIEST CONVENIENCE, HAVE THIS FORM IMPRINTED WITH YOUR CREDIT CARD AT THE FRONT DESK OR BY THE FRONT OFFICE CASHIER.
☐ RECORD YOUR ROOM NUMBER, DATE AND TIME OF DEPARTURE AND SIGN THE FORM IN THE SPACES PROVIDED ON THE REVERSE SIDE.
☐ WHEN YOU DEPART, HAND THE COMPLETED FORM AND YOUR ROOM KEY TO THE FRONT OFFICE CASHIER OR DROP THEM IN ANY OF THE SPEEDY CHECKOUT BOXES AT THE CASHIER'S DESK.

**CHECK OUT
AT 1:00 PM**

IMPORTANT
IF UTILIZING THE HOTEL PARKING FACILITY, HAVE THE CASHIER OR SPEEDY CHECK OUT CLERK ISSUE A VOUCHER.

THIS IS YOUR AUTHORIZATION TO CHARGE MY ACCOUNT TO THE CREDIT CARD ACCOUNT IMPRINTED ABOVE.

GUEST SIGNATURE

SPEEDY

CHECK OUT

AUTHORIZATION

ROOM NO.

DATE

TIME OF DEPARTURE

Courtesy of The Sheraton-Boston Hotel, Boston, Massachusetts.

method of settlement. In order to use an express check-out system effectively, the front office must be well-organized and obtain appropriate guest settlement information during registration. The front office must also take extra care to update room status as soon as the guest departs and the express check-out form is received. When guest departure is expedited, both the hurrying guest and the busy front office benefit.

Self Check-Out

Self check-out lobby terminals and in-room computers interfaced with a front office computer system can reduce the time it takes to process guest check-outs and significantly reduce front office traffic. Like self-registration terminals, self check-out terminals vary in design. Some resemble an automatic bank teller machine, while others may possess both video and audio capability.

To use a self check-out system, the guest accesses the proper folio and reviews its contents. Settlement can be automatically assigned to a credit card so long as the guest presented one at registration. The check-out procedure is completed when the guest's balance is posted to a credit card and an itemized statement of account is printed and dispensed to the guest. The system then takes responsibility for automatically updating room status and creating a guest history file.

In-room folio review and check-out functions may rely on in-room computer terminals or guestroom telephones to access and display guest folio data on the guestroom television screen. An interface to a front office accounting system allows the guest to access folio data and approve a method of settlement for his or her account. Newer technology may provide computer-synthesized voice responses through the guestroom telephone. Each method provides guests with folio totals and details and directs a self check-out procedure. Printed folio copies are typically available for guests to pick up at the front desk. Similar to other self check-out technologies, in-room computer applications automatically update room status and create a guest history file entry.

Late Check-Outs At some point, the front office will encounter guests who do not check out by the hotel's posted check-out time. To minimize late check-outs, hotels should be sure to post check-out time notices in conspicuous places, such as on the back of guestroom doors and at the front desk. A reminder of the check-out time can also be included in express check-out materials distributed to guests.

Some hotels charge guests late check-out fees when they depart after the hotel's stated check-out time. When a guest requests permission for a late check-out, the front office should inform him or her if any additional charges will be applied. If no request is made, the extra charges appearing on a folio will probably surprise the departing guest.

Regardless of how the guest is informed about additional expenses, he or she may feel resentment and may refuse to pay. A cool, businesslike demeanor and a reasoned explanation from the front office cashier may help calm an irate guest. A front office manager may have to negotiate the matter with the guest.

Front office staff should not feel defensive about late check-out fees. Check-out time is carefully selected and is not arbitrarily set to inconvenience guests. It is established by management to provide housekeeping with sufficient time to prepare the rooms for newly arriving guests. Rooms must be cleaned and readied for arriving guests before the housekeeping staff completes its shift.

Late Charges

Late charges are a major problem in guest account settlement. A **late charge** is a transaction requiring posting to a guest account that does not reach the front office until the guest has checked out and left the hotel. Restaurant, telephone, and room service charges are common examples. If payment for these charges is not collected before the guest leaves, it may be difficult to ever collect. Even if late charges are eventually paid, the hotel incurs additional costs from account billings—expenses such as department labor, postage, envelopes, and special statement forms—which may total more than the amount of the late charge. Obviously, few hotels can afford a large volume of late charges. Reducing late charges is essential to maximizing profitability.

There are several steps that front office cashiers can take to help reduce costly late charges:

- Post transactional vouchers as soon as they arrive at the front desk to minimize unposted charges during a busy check-out period.

- Before checking a guest out, survey front office equipment (such as the telephone traffic monitors and in-room movie charge meters) for unposted charges.

- Ask departing guests whether they have incurred any recent charges or recently placed telephone calls from their in-room telephones.

While guests tend to respond honestly to direct questions, many guests feel no obligation to voluntarily inform the front office cashier of charges not posted to the folio. Some guests will simply pay the outstanding balance on the folio and disregard unposted charges.

Hotel management may consider establishing a system to ensure that revenue outlet charges are delivered quickly to the front desk for posting, especially during peak morning check-out periods. The front desk may employ runners to pick up transaction vouchers, telephone relays, pneumatic tube networks (similar to those at a drive-through bank), or computer interfacing. A property management computer system that interfaces with revenue center outlets is often the most effective means of reducing or eliminating late charges. With a POS interface, restaurant charge vouchers, for example, can be instantly verified for room account validity, checked for credit authorization, and posted to the guest's folio—before the guest leaves the restaurant. Similarly, an interface with call accounting equipment reduces telephone late charges. Guests who make in-room telephone calls and then go directly to the front desk to check out should find all telephone charges automatically posted.

Billing and Collection

Guest accounts settled to a credit card or direct billing arrangement are transferred to the city ledger for billing and collection. Guests may also have to be billed after departure for late charges or if the guest's method of payment failed to settle the account. Generally, account billing is handled by the hotel's back office accounting division, not the front office. However, the front office is responsible for providing complete and accurate billing information to the accounting division.

Unpaid Account Balances

No matter how carefully the front office performs its functions throughout the guest cycle, there is always the possibility that a guest will leave without settling his or her account. A skipper may leave with no intention of settling the account. Guests may also honestly forget to check out when leaving. The front office may also discover late charges after a guest has checked out. Regardless of the reason, after-departure charges represent unpaid account balances.

A policy which may help reduce unpaid account balances is requiring a key deposit during registration. Guests are usually eager to retrieve their deposits, and are more likely to return to the front desk before they leave the hotel if there is a direct benefit to them. When the front office cashier returns a deposit to a guest, he or she also has an opportunity to retrieve the guest's folio, search for any late charges, and complete the settlement process.

Late charges that are billed should not be assumed to be uncollectible until the front office has followed established billing and collection procedures. A properly completed registration card contains the guest's signature, home and business addresses, and perhaps telephone numbers. If the guest paid cash at check-out, the guest is billed according to the hotel's policies. If the guest used a credit card, specific credit card company procedures for late charges should be followed. Likewise, direct billing late charge procedures must be adhered to.

Sometimes guests do not mean to leave the hotel without paying. A guest may be hurried and actually forget to settle his or her account. Guests may assume that, since they presented a credit card at check-in, all charges will automatically be transferred to their credit card account for billing. Depending on the credit card company's agreement with the hotel, simply writing "signature on file" on the signature line of the credit card voucher may allow the hotel to receive payment for the guest's outstanding balance. (Of course, if front office staff suspect a guest has left without paying, they should be sure the guest has left before they change the room status information to indicate this fact.)

Collection of Accounts

Guest accounts not settled at check-out by cash payment in full—regardless of the credit established or pre-payments made during registration—are transferred from the guest ledger to the city ledger for collection. At that time, the account leaves the control of the front office and becomes the responsibility of the hotel's back office accounting division.

Typical city ledger accounts include:

- **Credit card billings** to authorized credit card companies

- **Direct billings** to approved companies and individuals

- **Travel agency accounts** for authorized tours and groups

- **Bad check accounts** resulting from guests whose personal checks were returned unpaid

- **Skipper accounts** for guests who left the hotel without paying

- **Disputed bills** for guests who refused to settle their accounts (in part or in full)

- **Guaranteed reservations** for no-show guests

- **Late charges** for guests who left before charges were posted to their accounts

- **House accounts** for non-guest business and promotional accounts

To be successful, a hotel must establish a billing policy with specific guidelines. Typically, management determines the procedures and billing cycle appropriate for the hotel and its clientele. Considerations include determining:

- When account balances are payable

- How to contact guests whose accounts are overdue

- The number of days between billings

Exhibit 9.2 Billing Scheduling Chart

Schedule	Method	Timing
1st billing	___ Statement with back-up invoice	Mailed no later than ___ hours after the guest's account is transferred to the city ledger.
2nd billing	___ Statement ___ Telephone call ___ Letter	___ Days later
3rd billing	___ Statement ___ Telephone call ___ Letter	___ Days later
4th billing	___ Statement ___ Telephone call ___ Letter	___ Days later
5th billing and so on.	___ Statement ___ Telephone call ___ Letter	___ Days later

The sooner the collection process is started, the sooner the hotel is likely to be paid. Timing is often the key to success in preparing guest and non-guest accounts for collection. Each property will have its own collection schedule. Collection schedules can range from aggressive to lenient depending on the property's needs, clientele, former collection problems, and so forth. A scheduling chart which may be used to outline the methods and timing cycles for account receivable billings is shown in Exhibit 9.2.

Being polite but firm with those who owe the hotel money often pays off; it is typically more effective than becoming angry. It is important to keep in mind that collection activities that violate a consumer's rights can be more costly than the original debt. The Federal Fair Debt Collection Practices Act and the Fair Credit Billing Act clearly state the responsibilities and rights of those involved in collection activities.[1] The hotel's attorney may also be able to provide advice in setting up an accounts receivable collection system.

Regardless of the procedures followed, problems in approving credit or in billing may develop. The hotel should have a procedure for collecting overdue accounts. If a property has a credit committee, it typically is responsible for examining overdue accounts and deciding among collection options (when appropriate).

Some properties track uncollectible accounts back to the originating department (the department responsible for accepting them). For instance, if a front desk agent does not ask the guest to clarify illegible writing on a registration card, and as a result a wrongly addressed billing is returned by the post office, the front office may be charged the uncollectible amount. This method of tracking receivables to particular departments may help identify which departments are regularly responsible for uncollectible account balances. The credit committee, credit manager, or general manager may be able to analyze a problem departments' procedures (or lack of them) and strengthen them as necessary. Problems often indicate the need for retraining or closer supervision.

Account Aging   Credit card billings are normally paid according to the hotel's contractual agreement with the credit card company. Most other city ledger accounts are usually settled within 30 days of billing, which is generally considered satisfactory. Since some city ledger accounts may take longer than 30 days to collect, the hotel should establish methods for tracking past due accounts. This principle is referred to as **account aging.**

Account aging analysis may differ from property to property depending upon the variety of hotel credit terms in effect. Account aging is typically monitored by the back office accounting division in larger properties, or the night auditor in smaller properties. An account age analysis sheet identifies which accounts receivable are 30, 60, 90, or more days old. Exhibit 9.3 shows a typical aged accounts receivable report.

Front Office Records

The front office usually makes at least two copies of each guest account folio. One serves as a receipt for the guest, and the other is kept as the hotel's permanent record. Hotels that use a three-part folio usually file the third copy with the guest's credit card voucher or direct billing statement for reference in case of guest disputes or refusal of payment by a credit card or sponsoring company.

In non-automated and semi-automated operations, registration cards and folio copies are often maintained in physical storage files. Registration cards are filed alphabetically, while folios are filed numerically by serial number. In a fully automated operation, computer system records may be stored on disks or in printed form. These records back up the original billing.

Promotional Materials. A number of marketing programs may depend on the front office's performance and follow-through at check-out. For example, if the hotel offers a promotion which rewards guests with a free stay after a certain number of visits, the front desk agent may have to validate a coupon or somehow record the number of stays for the guest. If the guest needs a reservation for the next stop on his or her trip, the front office may be able to perform this service. A reservation for a return stay at the hotel can be made at this time as well. Front desk agents should keep in mind that this is their last opportunity to sell on behalf of the hotel. The offer to make reservations for guests in transit, or to make reservations for their next trip to the hotel, will often pay off in repeat

Exhibit 9.3   Aged Accounts Receivable Report

Name	Balance	Current	Outstanding			
			30–60	60–90	90–120	120+
Elizabeth Penny	$125					$125
Mimi Hendricks	$235			$235		
M/M Phil Damon	$486	$100	$386			
Harrison Taylor	$999			$999		
TOTALS	$1,845	$100	$386	$1,234		$125

Title of form: AGED ACCOUNTS RECEIVABLE — As of _____, 19___

Source: *Successful Credit and Collection Techniques* (East Lansing, Mich.: Educational Institute of the American Hotel & Motel Association, 1981), p. 29.

business regardless of whether the guest makes a reservation at this time or not.

Guest Histories

The last step in the settlement process is the creation of a **guest history record.** Many hotels simply use expired registration cards as the basis for their guest history files. Others develop a special form for guest history construction. Exhibit 9.4 shows a typical guest history card. The information on a guest history record can be obtained from the guest's registration card and account folio.

Resort hotels in particular often have extensive forms requesting specific information to help them cater to their guests' needs. Names of spouses and children, birthdays, hotel room preferences, favorite foods, and so on may be placed on file for special guests or all guests.

Exhibit 9.4   Guest History Card

	ARRIVED	ROOM	RATE	DEPARTED	AMOUNT		REMARKS
NAME							
ADDRESS							
FIRM							
POSITION				CREDIT		/	/F/P

		ARRIVED	ROOM	RATE	DEPARTED	AMOUNT		REMARKS
1								
2	12							
3	13							
4	14							
5	15							
6	16							
7	17							
8	18							
9	19							
10	20							
11	21							
	22							
	23							
	24							
	25							

A guest history record can be used by the hotel's sales and marketing division as a source for mailing lists or, in combination with other guest history records, can help identify guest characteristics important for strategic marketing. This information may help in the placement of advertisements, indicate the need for supplementary services, or identify potential guest service enhancements. Software for a computerized guest history system may allow the hotel to excerpt data for use in its marketing efforts, and to measure the effects of past efforts. For instance, a computerized guest history package may enable the hotel to determine the geographic distribution of its guests' home and business addresses. With this kind of data, hotel advertising may be placed more effectively.

It is important to remember that guest history files are confidential and proprietary hotel records. The hotel owes its guests protection from an invasion of their privacy.

Notes

1. For a complete guide to federal and state statutes relating to credit and collection, consult *Credit Manual of Commercial Laws* (New York: National Association of Credit Management, 1981).

Discussion Questions

1. What are the three functions of the check-out and settlement process? Discuss how these functions are essential to the hotel's accounting, housekeeping, and marketing functions.

2. Define *zero out*. What happens to a guest account which is not settled at check-out?

3. What are three methods of guest account settlement at check-out? How is each method processed?

4. How does a typical express check-out procedure work? How does a typical self check-out terminal work?

5. What difficulties arise from late check-outs? How might these problems be reduced by the use of late check-out fees?

6. What are late charges? What steps can the front office take to reduce late charges?

7. What types of guest information are useful in collecting payment for late charges and unpaid account balances?

8. What are some elements of an effective billing and collection process? How can tracking uncollectible accounts to the departments responsible improve internal control?

9. What is account aging? Why is it important? Who might be responsible for account age analysis?

10. What are the uses of guest histories? How can the front office construct a guest history file?

Part III

Front Office Management

10 Planning and Evaluating Front Office Operations

A manager uses available resources to attain an organization's objectives. Resources available to managers include people, money, time, work methods, materials, energy, and equipment. All of these resources are in limited supply. Most front office managers will readily admit that they rarely have all the resources they would like. Therefore, an important part of a front office manager's job is planning how to use the limited resources available to attain the organization's objectives. An equally important part of a front office manager's job is evaluating the success of front office activities in meeting the organization's objectives.

Management Functions

The process of management can be divided into specific management functions. Exhibit 10.1 shows how management functions fit into the overall process of management. Although specific front office management tasks vary from one hotel to another, similar fundamental management functions are carried out. The front office manager's job description in Exhibit 10.2 presents an example of how these general management principles may be more specifically applied.

Planning. Top management executives must initially plan what the hotel is to accomplish by defining its objectives. The front office manager uses these general objectives as a guide to planning more specific, measurable goals for the front office. Planning also includes determining the strategies that will be used to attain the goals. Planning is probably the most important management function performed in any type of business. Without competent planning, every day may present one crisis after another and productivity may be extremely low. Without the direction and focus planning provides, the front office manager can easily become involved with tasks which are unimportant or unrelated to accomplishing the hotel's objectives.

Organizing. Using the planned goals as a guide, a front office manager performs an organizing function when dividing the work to be performed among the front office staff. Work should be distributed so that everyone gets a fair assignment and all work can be finished on time. Organizing includes determining the order in which tasks are to be performed and when each group of tasks should be completed.

Exhibit 10.1   Overview of the Management Process

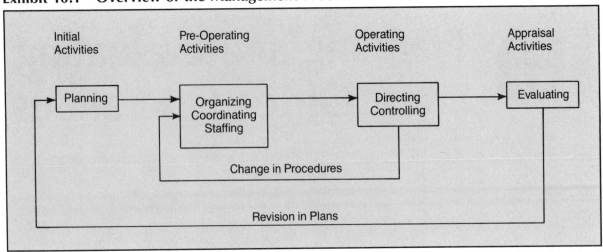

Source: Jack D. Ninemeier, *Planning and Control for Food and Beverage Operations,* Second Ed. (East Lansing, Mich.: Educational Institute of the American Hotel & Motel Association, 1986), p. 17.

Coordinating. The management function of coordinating involves using resources to attain planned goals. A front office manager must be able to coordinate the efforts of many individuals who are all doing different sets of tasks at the same time. A front office manager's ability to coordinate is closely related to other management skills, such as planning and organizing. It involves planning the overall work of the group and assigning duties so that the work is performed efficiently, effectively, and on time.

Staffing. The management function of staffing involves recruiting applicants and selecting those best qualified for positions to be filled. Staffing also involves scheduling employees. Most hotel operations use some type of staffing guidelines. These guidelines are usually based on formulas for calculating the number of employees required to meet guest and operational needs under specified conditions.

Directing. Directing is a complicated management skill which is exercised in a wide variety of situations, and is closely related to other management skills such as organizing, coordinating, and staffing. For a front office manager, directing involves overseeing, motivating, training, and disciplining people who work in the department. For example, in order to direct the work of other people, a front office manager must first analyze the work to be done, arrange the tasks in a logical order, and consider the environment in which the tasks are to be performed.

Controlling. Every hotel has a system of internal controls for protecting the assets of the business. However, internal control systems work only when managers believe in their importance and follow the established procedures for their use. The control process ensures that the actual results of operations closely match planned results. The front office manager also exercises a control function when keeping front office operations on course in attaining planned goals.

Exhibit 10.2   Front Office Manager's Job Description

Basic Functions

The front office manager is responsible for the immediate supervision of all front office personnel and for ensuring proper completion of all front office duties.

Specific Duties and Responsibilities

1.   Train, cross-train, and retrain (when necessary) all front office personnel.

2.   Be knowledgeable about all front office standard operating procedures.

3.   Develop a working knowledge of every front office position. Be prepared to answer any employee's questions concerning his or her job.

4.   Schedule the front office staff.

5.   Supervise workloads during shifts.

6.   Maintain working relationships and communication with all other departments.

7.   Monitor master key control.

8.   Verify that accurate room status information is maintained and properly communicated to ensure maximum revenue.

9.   Resolve guest problems quickly, efficiently, and courteously.

10.   Uphold the hotel's commitment to hospitality.

11.   Ensure that all VIP's and executive floor guests are pre-registered. Process the VIP list and distribute it to staff members.

12.   Update group information; maintain, monitor, and prepare group requirements. Relay information to all concerned.

13.   Review completed credit limit report.

14.   Work within the allotted budget.

15.   Receive information from the previous shift manager and pass on pertinent information to the oncoming manager.

16.   Check cashiers in and out and verify banks and deposits at the end of each workshift.

17.   Ensure that all check-cashing and credit policies are followed.

18.   Conduct monthly meetings of front office personnel.

19.   Wear proper uniform at all times, and require all employees to wear proper uniforms at all times.

Relationships

Report to: Assistant manager

Supervise: All front office personnel

Evaluating. The management function of evaluating determines the extent to which planned goals are, in fact, attained. This task is frequently overlooked in many properties, or it is done haphazardly. Evaluating also involves reviewing and, when necessary, helping to modify front office goals.

This chapter focuses on elements of two front office management functions—planning and evaluating front office operations. It begins by examining three important front office planning functions:

- Establishing room rates

- Forecasting room availability

- Budgeting for operations

It concludes by examining various methods by which a front office manager may evaluate the effectiveness of front office operations.

Establishing Room Rates

Hotels always have more than one room rate category. Room rate categories generally correspond to types of rooms (suites, doubles, singles, etc.) that are comparable in square footage and furnishings. Differences are based on criteria such as room size, location, view, furnishings, and amenities. Based on the number of persons occupying a room, each room rate category is assigned a rack (standard) rate. The rack rate is the "list price" determined by front office management. The rack rate is listed on the room rate schedule to inform front desk agents of the selling price of each guestroom in the hotel. In a fully automated property, front office employees can use a computer terminal to access rack rate data during the reservations or registration process.

Front office employees are expected to sell rooms at the rack rate unless a guest qualifies for an alternate room rate. Special rates are often quoted to groups and certain guests for promotional purposes or to increase occupancies during slack periods. Special room rates typically include:

- Corporate or commercial rates offered to large companies that provide frequent business for the hotel or its chain

- Promotional rates offered to promote future business, often given to group leaders, meeting planners, tour operators, and others capable of providing the hotel with significant revenue

- Incentive rates offered to guests in affiliated organizations such as travel agencies and airlines because of the potential referral business they can generate for the hotel

- Family rates for families with children

- Package plan rates that include a room and a combination of events or activities

- Complimentary rates provided to special guests and/or important industry leaders

The use of special rates must be rigidly controlled. The front office manager should examine the circumstances under which special rates are granted to ensure that front office employees are following hotel policies. All policies should be clearly explained to front office personnel and proper approval should be obtained when applying a special room rate.

Establishing rack rates for room types and determining discount categories and special rates are major management decisions. To set rates that will ensure the hotel's profitability, management should carefully consider such factors as cost, inflation, and competition. The following sections examine two well-known cost approaches to pricing rooms: the rule-of-thumb approach and the Hubbart Formula.

The Rule-of-Thumb Approach

The rule-of-thumb approach sets the rate of a room at $1 for each $1,000 of construction cost per room. For example, assume that the average construction cost of a hotel room was $80,000. Using the $1 per $1,000 approach results in an average price of $80 per room. Singles, doubles, suites, and other room types would be priced differently, but the average room rate would be $80.

The emphasis that this approach places on the hotel's construction cost fails to consider the effects of inflation. For example, a well-maintained hotel worth $100,000 per room today may have been constructed at $20,000 per room forty years ago. The $1 per $1,000 approach would suggest a price of $20 per room; however, a much higher rate would appear to be appropriate.

This approach to pricing rooms also fails to consider the contribution of other facilities and services toward the hotel's desired profitability. In many hotels, guests pay for services such as food, beverages, telephone, laundry, and others. If a hotel is able to earn a positive contribution from these services, there may be less need for higher room rates.

Hubbart Formula

The Hubbart Formula is a more recently developed cost approach to pricing rooms. It is called a **bottom-up** approach because the first item it considers, profit, is at the bottom of the hotel's income statement; the second item, income taxes, is the next item up from the bottom of the income statement; and so on. In establishing the desired average room rate, the Hubbart Formula starts with desired profit, adds income taxes, fixed charges, and operating expenses, and then considers the expected number of rooms sold. Establishing room rates with the Hubbart Formula basically involves eight steps:

1. Calculate the **desired profit** by multiplying the desired rate of return by the owners' investment.

2. Calculate **pretax profits** by dividing the desired profit by the complement of the hotel's tax rate. (This complement is obtained by subtracting the tax rate—for example, 35%—from 100%.)

3. Calculate **fixed charges and management fees** by estimating depreciation, interest expense, property taxes, insurance, amortization, rent, and management fees.

4. Calculate **undistributed operating expenses** by estimating expenses for administrative and general, data processing, human

resources, transportation, marketing, property operation and maintenance, and energy costs.

5. Estimate **non-room operating department income** or **loss.**

6. Calculate the **required rooms division income** by adding pretax profits, fixed charges and management fees, undistributed operating expenses, and non-room operating department loss, then subtracting non-room operating department income.

7. Calculate the **rooms division revenue** by adding required rooms division income, rooms division payroll and related expenses, and other direct expenses.

8. Calculate the **average room rate** by dividing rooms division revenue by the number of rooms expected to be sold.[1]

Even given this comprehensive method of establishing room rates, one fact remains—competition sets the limit that a hotel can charge for its rooms. An appropriate room rate is one that is large enough to cover costs, offers a fair return on invested capital, and is reasonable enough to attract and retain the operation's targeted guest markets.

Forecasting Room Availability

The most important short-term planning performed by front office managers is forecasting the number of rooms available for sale on any given date. Room availability forecasts are used to manage the reservations process and to guide front office staff in selling rooms on busy nights when a full house is possible.

A room availability forecast can also be used as an occupancy forecast. Since there is a fixed number of rooms in the hotel, forecasting the number of rooms available for sale also forecasts the number of rooms expected to be occupied on a given date. Therefore, forecasts are used by the front office manager (and other managers in the hotel) to schedule the necessary number of employees in order to meet an expected volume of business.

Obviously, a forecast is only as reliable as the information on which it is based. Since forecasts serve as a guide in determining staffing levels throughout the hotel, every effort should be made to ensure their accuracy.

Forecasting is a difficult skill to develop. The skill is acquired through experience, effective recordkeeping, and accurate counting methods. Experienced front office managers have found the following types of information to be helpful in forecasting:[2]

-   A thorough knowledge of the hotel and the surrounding area

-   Profiles of the markets the property serves

-   Plans for remodeling or renovating which would place otherwise available rooms out of order

- The occupancy history of the hotel for the past several months, and for the corresponding period of the previous year

- Knowledge of reservation trends, such as the history of lead time for reservations received

- A listing of events scheduled in the area for a particular day

- Profiles of specific groups booked for the day in question

- The number of non-guaranteed and guaranteed reservations booked for a specific day

- The percentage of rooms reserved to date and the cut-off date for any room blocks held for the day in question

Useful Forecasting Data

Forecasting generally relies on historical data. To facilitate forecasting, the following daily occupancy data should be recorded:

- The number of arrivals

- The number of walk-ins

- The number of reservations

- The number of no-shows

- The number of understays

- The number of check-outs

- The number of overstays

These are important forecasting data because they are used in calculating various ratios that help determine the availability of rooms for sale. Most statistical ratios that apply to front office operations are expressed as percentages. The ratios examined in the following sections are percentage of no-shows, percentage of walk-ins, percentage of understays, and percentage of overstays. Occupancy history data of the fictitious Holly Hotel, shown in Exhibit 10.3, are used to illustrate how each front office ratio may be calculated.

Percentage of No-Shows. The percentage of no-shows indicates the proportion of guests with reservations who failed to register on their arrival date. This ratio helps the front office manager decide when to sell rooms to early walk-ins. It also indicates a potential "bail-out" factor for those nights when the hotel has mistakenly overbooked. Hotels with high no-show ratios will have significantly more difficulty in forecasting available rooms.

The percentage of no-shows is calculated by dividing the number of no-shows for a specific period of time (day, week, month, or year) by the total number of reservations for the same period. Using figures from Exhibit 10.3, the percentage of no-shows for the Holly Hotel during the first week of March can be calculated as follows:

Exhibit 10.3   Occupancy History of the Holly Hotel

Occupancy History
First Week of March

Day	Date	Guests	Arrivals	Walk-Ins	Reservations	No-Shows
Mon	3/1	118	70	13	63	6
Tues	3/2	145	55	15	48	8
Wed	3/3	176	68	16	56	4
Thur	3/4	117	53	22	48	17
Fri	3/5	75	35	8	35	8
Sat	3/6	86	28	6	26	4
Sun	3/7	49	17	10	12	5
Totals		766	326	90	288	52

Occ. Rooms	Overstays	Understays	Check-Outs
90	6	0	30
115	10	3	30
120	12	6	63
95	3	18	78
50	7	0	80
58	6	3	20
30	3	3	45
558	47	33	346

$$\text{Percentage of No-Shows} = \frac{\text{Number of No-Shows}}{\text{Number of Reservations}}$$

$$= \frac{52}{288}$$

$$= .1806 \text{ or } 18.06\%$$

Percentage of Walk-Ins. The percentage of walk-ins is calculated by dividing the number of walk-ins for a specific period of time by the total number of arrivals for the same period. The higher the percentage of walk-ins, the more difficulty a hotel may experience in forecasting. Using figures from Exhibit 10.3, the percentage of walk-ins for the Holly Hotel during the first week of March can be calculated as follows:

$$\text{Percentage of Walk-Ins} = \frac{\text{Number of Walk-Ins}}{\text{Total Number of Arrivals}}$$

$$= \frac{90}{326}$$

$$= .2761 \text{ or } 27.61\%$$

Percentage of Overstays. Overstays represent rooms occupied by guests who continue their stays beyond their scheduled departure dates. Overstays may have arrived with guaranteed or non-guaranteed reservations, or as walk-ins. Overstays should not be confused with **stayovers,** who are guests who arrived at the property before the day in question and whose scheduled departure dates are after the day in question.

The percentage of overstays is calculated by dividing the number of overstays for a specific period of time by the total number of check-outs for the same period. The higher the percentage of overstays, the more difficulty a hotel may experience in forecasting. Using figures from Exhibit 10.3, the percentage of overstays for the Holly Hotel during the first week of March can be calculated as follows:

$$\text{Percentage of Overstays} = \frac{\text{Number of Overstays}}{\text{Total Number of Check-Outs}}$$

$$= \frac{47}{346}$$

$$= .1358 \text{ or } 13.58\%$$

Percentage of Understays. Understays represent rooms occupied by guests who check out before their scheduled departure dates. Understays may have arrived at a property with guaranteed or non-guaranteed reservations, or as walk-ins.

The percentage of understays is calculated by dividing the number of understays for a specific period of time by the total number of check-outs for the same period. The higher the percentage of understays, the more difficulty a hotel may experience in forecasting. Using figures from Exhibit 10.3, the percentage of understays for the Holly Hotel during the first week of March can be calculated as follows:

$$\text{Percentage of Understays} = \frac{\text{Number of Understays}}{\text{Total Number of Check-Outs}}$$

$$= \frac{33}{346}$$

$$= .0954 \text{ or } 9.54\%$$

Guests leaving before their stated departure date create empty rooms that typically remain unfilled. Thus, understays tend to represent permanently lost room revenue. Overstays, on the other hand, are guests staying additional nights beyond their stated departure date, and when the hotel is not operating at capacity, overstays result in additional room revenues. However, a problem may arise if the room occupied by an overstay has been reserved for an arriving guest. In an attempt to control understays and overstays, front office employees should:

• Confirm each guest's departure date at registration. Some guests may already know of a change in plans, or a mistake may have been made in processing the reservation.

- Present a card to the guest explaining that an arriving guest holds a reservation for his or her room. A card such as the one shown in Exhibit 10.4 may be placed in the guest's room the day before or the morning of the scheduled day of departure as a subtle reminder.

- Contact potential overstays on their stated departure date to confirm check-out. Each day room occupancies should be examined and rooms with guests expected to check out should be flagged. Guests who have not left by check-out time should be contacted and asked their intentions. This procedure will permit an early count of overstays and allow sufficient time to update previous front office planning (if necessary).

Room Availability Forecast Formula

Once relevant occupancy statistics have been gathered, the number of rooms available for sale on any given date can be determined by the following formula:

Total Number of Rooms
− Number of Out-of-Order Rooms
− Number of Stayovers
− Number of Reservations
+ Number of Reservations × Percentage of No-Shows
+ Number of Understays
− Number of Overstays
_____
= Rooms Available for Sale

For example, the Holly Hotel is a 120-room property: On April 1, there are 3 out-of-order rooms and 55 stayovers. There are 42 guests with reservations scheduled to arrive. Since the percentage of no-shows has been recently calculated at 18.06%, the front office manager calculates that as many as 8 guests with reservations may not arrive ($42 \times .1806 = 7.59$, rounded to 8). Based on historical data, 6 understays and 15 overstays are also expected. The number of rooms projected to be available for sale on April 1 can be determined as follows:

	Total Number of Rooms	120
−	Number of Out-of-Order Rooms	− 3
−	Number of Stayovers	− 55
−	Number of Reservations	− 42
+	Number of Reservations × Percentage of No-Shows +	8
+	Number of Understays +	6
−	Number of Overstays	− 15
=	Rooms Available for Sale	19

Therefore, the Holly Hotel is considered to have 19 rooms available for sale on April 1. Once this figure is determined, management can decide whether or not to accept more reservations and can determine a level of staffing. These decisions must remain flexible, however, and are subject to change as the front office is advised of reservation cancellations

Exhibit 10.4   Sample Notice of Prior Room Reservation

This room has been reserved for a guest arriving on _____ , 19_____. If circumstances cause you to need this room for a longer period of time than that reserved, please contact someone at the front desk. We will gladly attempt to secure alternate accommodations for you.

Check-out time is 12 noon.

and modifications. It should also be noted that room availability forecasts are based on assumptions which may vary in validity on any given day.

Sample Forecast Forms

A hotel may prepare several different forecasts depending on its needs. Occupancy forecasts are typically developed on a monthly basis and reviewed by food and beverage and rooms division management to forecast revenues, project expenses, and develop labor schedules. A 10-day forecast, for example, may be used to update labor scheduling and cost projections and may later be supplemented by a more current 3-day forecast. Together, these forecasts help the hotel maintain appropriate staff levels for expected business volume and thereby help contain costs in proper proportion to expected revenue.

10-Day Forecast. The 10-day forecast at most lodging properties is made by the front office manager and the reservations manager, possibly in conjunction with a forecast committee. This forecast usually consists of:

- Daily forecasted occupancy figures, including arrivals, departures, rooms sold, and number of guests

- The number of group commitments, with a listing of each group's name, arrival and departure dates, number of guests, and, perhaps, quoted room rates

- A comparison of the previous period's forecasted and actual room counts and occupancy percentages

A special 10-day forecast may also be prepared for food and beverage, banquet, and catering operations.

In order to assist various hotel departments, especially housekeeping, in planning their staffing and payroll levels for the upcoming period, the 10-day forecast should be completed and distributed to all department offices by mid-week for the coming period. A 10-day forecast form, as shown in Exhibit 10.5, is developed from data collected through several front office sources.

First, the current number of occupied rooms is reviewed. The number of overstays and expected departures are noted. Next, relevant reservation information is evaluated for each room (and guest) by date of arrival, length of stay, and date of departure. These counts are then

Exhibit 10.5   Sample 10-Day Forecast Form

10-Day Occupancy Forecast

Location _____ # _____ Week Ending _____

Date Prepared: _____ Prepared By: _____

To be submitted to all department heads at least one week prior to first day listed on forecast.

	Fri.	Sat.	Sun.	Mon.	Tues.	Wed.	Thur.	Fri.	Sat.	Sun.
1. Date and Day (start week and end week the same as the payroll schedule).										
2. Estimated Departures										
3. Reservation Arrivals — Group (taken from log book)										
4. Reservation Arrivals — Individual (taken from log book)										
5. Future Reservations (estimate resv. received after forecast is completed)										
6. Expected Walk-ins (% of walk-ins based on resv. received & actual occupancy for past two weeks)										
7. Total Arrivals										
8. Stayovers										
9. TOTAL FORECASTED ROOMS										
10. Occupancy Multiplier (based on # of guests per occ. room for average of the same day for last three weeks)										
11. FORECASTED NUMBER OF GUESTS										
12. Actual Rooms Occupied (taken from daily report for actual date to be completed by front office supervisor)										
13. Forecasted Variance (dif. between forecast & rms. occ. on daily report)										
14. Explanation (to be completed by front office supervisor & submitted to general manager; attach additional memo if necessary)										

APPROVED: _____ DATE: _____

General Manager's Signature

reconciled against reservations control data. Then, the actual counts are adjusted to reflect the percentage of no-shows, anticipated understays, and expected walk-ins. These projections are based on the hotel's recent history, the seasonality of business, and the known history of specific groups scheduled to arrive. Finally, conventions and other groups are listed on the forecast to alert various departments to possible periods of heavy check-ins and check-outs. The number of rooms assigned each day to each group may also be noted on the sheet.

3-Day Forecast. The 3-day forecast is an updated report which reflects the most current estimate of the availability of rooms. It details any significant changes for the 3-day period from the corresponding 10-day forecast. The 3-day forecast is intended to guide management in adjusting labor schedules and modifying room availability information. Exhibit 10.6 presents a sample 3-day forecast form.

Room Count Considerations. Control books, charts, computer applications, projections, ratios, and formulas can be essential in short-and long-range room count planning. Each day, the front office performs several physical counts of rooms occupied, vacant, reserved, due to check-out, and so on in order to finalize expected occupancy for that day. A computerized system may reduce the need for most final counts, since it continually updates room availability information.

It is important for front desk agents to know *exactly* how many rooms are available, especially if the hotel expects full occupancy. Once procedures for gathering room count information are mastered, these skills can be extended to longer periods of time and can provide a more reliable basis for revenue, expense, and labor forecasting. The checklist in Exhibit 10.7 may be applicable to non-automated and semi-automated operations alike.

Budgeting for Operations

The most important long-term planning function performed by front office managers is budgeting front office operations. The annual operations budget is a profit plan for the hotel which addresses all revenue sources and expense items. Annual budgets are commonly divided into monthly plans. These monthly plans become standards against which management can evaluate the actual results of operations.

The budget planning process requires a closely coordinated effort of all management personnel. The hotel's accounting division normally supplies department managers with statistical information which is essential to the budget preparation process. The accounting division is also responsible for coordinating the budget plans of individual department managers into a comprehensive operations budget for top management's review. The general manager and controller typically review departmental budget plans and prepare a budget report for approval by the property's owners. If the budget is not satisfactory, elements requiring change are returned to the appropriate managers for review and revision.

The primary responsibilities of the front office manager in budget planning are forecasting rooms revenue and estimating expenses.

Forecasting Rooms Revenue

Historical financial information often serves as the foundation on which managers build revenue forecasts. One method of forecasting involves an analysis of rooms revenue from past years. Dollar and percent-

Exhibit 10.6   Sample 3-Day Forecast Form

Three Day Forecast

Date: _____

Day	Date

Starting Vacancies   _____

Final Check-out Count   _____

+ Chart %   _____

Computed Departure   _____

Total Available Rooms   _____

Estimated Total Room Arrival _____

Estimated Vacant Rooms   _____

Actual Reservation Count   _____
  % Last Day Canc.
  & No-show   _____

Net Reservations   _____

Estimated Last Day Additions
(Incl. Rooms Sold Over Counter) _____

Estimated Total Room Arrival   _____

_____
         Availability Status

Day	Date

Starting Vacancies   _____

2nd Back Count   _____
Estimated Final
Check-out Count   _____

+ Chart %   _____

Computed Departure   _____

Total Available Rooms   _____

Estimated Total Room Arrival _____

Estimated Vacant Rooms   _____

Book Count   _____
Est. Additional Reservations _____

Estimated Total Reservations _____
  % Last Day Canc.
  % No-show   _____

Net Reservations   _____

Estimated Last Day Additions
(Incl. Rooms Sold Over Counter) _____

Estimated Total Room Arrival   _____

_____
         Availability Status

Day	Date

Starting Vacancies   _____

1st Back Count   _____
Estimated Final
Check-out Count   _____

+ Chart %   _____

Computed Departure   _____

Total Available Rooms   _____

Estimated Rooms Arrival   _____

Estimated Vacant Rooms   _____

Book Count   _____
Est. Additional Reservations _____

Estimated Total Reservations _____
  % Last Day Canc.
  % No-show   _____

Net Reservations   _____

Estimated Last Day Additions
(Incl. Rooms Sold Over Counter) _____

Estimated Total Room Arrival   _____

_____
         Availability Status

_____
         Signature

---

age differences are noted and the amount of rooms revenue for the budget year is predicted.

For example, Exhibit 10.8 shows yearly increases in net rooms revenue for the Emily Hotel. For the years 19x1 to 19x4, the amount of rooms revenue increased from $1,000,000 to $1,331,000, reflecting a 10% yearly increase. Therefore, if future conditions appear to be similar to those of the past, the rooms revenue for 19x5 would be budgeted at $1,464,100, a 10% increase over the 19x4 amount.

Another approach to forecasting rooms revenue bases the revenue projection on past room sales and average daily room rates. Exhibit 10.9 presents rooms revenue statistics for the 120-room Holly Hotel from 19x1 to 19x4. An analysis of these statistics shows that occupancy percentage increased three percentage points from 19x1 to 19x2, one percentage point from 19x2 to 19x3, and one percentage point from 19x3 to 19x4.

Exhibit 10.7 Sample Daily Checklist for Accurate Room Counts

- Make counts of the rack and reservations. On tight days, a count should be made at 7:00 a.m., 12:00 p.m., 3:00 p.m., and 6:00 p.m. On normal days, a 7:00 a.m. and 6:00 p.m. count will suffice.

- Check room rack against the folio bucket to catch sleepers and skippers.

- Check housekeeping reports against the room rack to catch sleepers and skippers.

- Check for rooms that are due out, but still have balances on their folios, especially where credit cards are the indicated source of payment.

- Check reservations for any duplications.

- Call the reservations system to make sure all cancellations were transmitted.

- Check the switchboard, telephone rack, and/or alphabetical room rack to make sure that the guest is not already registered.

- Call the local airport for a report on cancelled flights.

- Check the weather reports for cities from which a number of guests are expected.

- Check reservations against convention blocks to catch duplications.

- Check with other hotels for duplicate reservations if a housing or convention bureau indicated the reservation was a second choice.

- Check arrival dates on all reservation forms to be sure none were misfiled.

- Check the rooms cancellation list.

- If a reservation was made through the reservations manager, sales manager, or someone in the executive office and the property is close to full, call that staff person. Often, such guests are personal friends and are willing to help out by staying somewhere else.

- Close to the property's cut-off time, consider placing a person-to-person phone call to any guest with a nonguaranteed reservation who hasn't arrived. If the person accepts the call, confirm whether or not he or she will arrive yet that night.

- After the property's cut-off time, if it becomes necessary, pull any reservations that were not guaranteed or prepaid.

- If any rooms are out-of-order or not presently in use, check to see if they can be made up. Let housekeeping know when a tight day is expected, so that all possible rooms are made up.

- Before leaving work, convey in writing all pertinent information to the oncoming staff. Good communication is essential.

Average daily room rates increased by $2, $2, and $3 respectively over the same periods. Therefore, if future conditions are assumed to be similar to those of the past, a rooms revenue forecast for 19x5 may be based on a 1% increase in occupancy percentage (to 76%) and a $3 increase in the average daily room rate (to $60). Given these projections, the following formula can be used to forecast net rooms revenue for the Holly Hotel:

$$
\begin{array}{llll}
\text{Forecasted} & \text{Rooms} & \text{Occupancy} & \text{Average} \\
\text{Rooms Revenue} & = \text{Available} \times & \text{Percentage} \times & \text{Daily Rate} \\
& = 43,800 \times & .76 \times & \$60 \\
& = \$1,997,280 &
\end{array}
$$

The number of rooms available is calculated by multiplying the 120 rooms of the Holly Hotel by the 365 days of the year. This calculation assumes

Exhibit 10.8   Rooms Revenue Summary—Emily Hotel

Year	Rooms Revenue	Increase Over Dollar	Prior Year Percentage
19x1	$1,000,000	—	—
19x2	1,100,000	$100,000	10%
19x3	1,210,000	110,000	10
19x4	1,331,000	121,000	10

Exhibit 10.9   Rooms Revenue Statistics—Holly Hotel

Year	Rooms Sold	Average Daily Rate	Net Rooms Revenue	Occupancy Percentage
19x1	30,660	$50	$1,533,000	70%
19x2	31,974	52	1,662,648	73
19x3	32,412	54	1,750,248	74
19x4	32,850	57	1,872,450	75

that all the rooms will be available for sale each day of the year. This will probably not be the case, but it is a useful starting point for projection.

This simplified approach to forecasting rooms revenue is meant only to illustrate the process. A more proper, detailed approach would consider the variety of different rates corresponding to types of rooms, types of guests, days of the week, and seasonality of business. These are just a few of the details affecting the forecasting of rooms revenue.

Estimating Expenses

Most expenses for front office operations vary proportionately in relation to changes in rooms revenue. Therefore, historical data can be used to calculate what percentage of net rooms revenue each expense item represents. These percentage figures can then be applied to the amount of rooms revenue forecasted, resulting in dollar estimates for each expense category for the budget year.

Typical rooms division expenses are payroll and related expenses; laundry, linen, and guest supplies; commissions and reservation expenses; and other expenses. Exhibit 10.10 presents expense category statistics of the Holly Hotel from 19x1 to 19x4, expressed as percentages of each year's rooms revenue. Based on this historical information and management's current objectives for the budget year 19x5, the percentage of rooms revenue for each expense category may be projected as follows: payroll and related expenses—17.6%; laundry, linen, and guest supplies—3.2%; commissions and reservation expenses—2.8%; and other expenses—4.7%.

Using these percentage figures and the expected rooms revenue calculated previously, expenses of the Holly Hotel's rooms division for the budgeted year are estimated as follows:

- Payroll and related expenses
  $1,997,280 \times .176 = \$351,521.28$

Exhibit 10.10   Expense Categories as Percentages of Rooms Revenue

Year	Payroll and Related Expenses	Laundry Linen and Guest Supplies	Commissions and Reservation Expenses	Other Expenses
19x1	16.5%	2.6%	2.3%	4.2%
19x2	16.9	2.8	2.5	4.5
19x3	17.2	3.0	2.6	4.5
19x4	17.4	3.1	2.7	4.6

- Laundry, linen, and guest supplies

    $1,997,280 \times .032 = $63,912.96

- Commissions and reservation expenses

    $1,997,280 \times .028 = $55,923.84

- Other expenses

    $1,997,280 \times .047 = $93,872.16

Since most front office expenses vary proportionately with rooms revenue (and therefore occupancy), another method of estimating these expenses is to estimate various costs per room sold and then multiply these costs by the number of rooms expected to be sold.

Refining Budget Plans

Departmental budget plans are commonly supported by detailed information gathered in the budget preparation process and recorded on worksheets and summary files. These documents should be saved to provide an explanation of the reasoning behind the decisions made while preparing departmental budget plans. Such records may answer questions which arise during budget review. These documents may also provide valuable assistance in the preparation of future plans.

Many hotels refine expected results of operations and revise operations budgets as they progress through the budget year. Re-forecasting is usually called for when actual results begin to vary significantly from the operations budget. Such variance may indicate that conditions have changed since the budget was first prepared.

Evaluating Front Office Operations

Evaluating the results of front office operations is an important management function. Without thoroughly evaluating the results of operations, managers will not know whether the front office is attaining planned goals. Successful front office managers evaluate the results of department activities on a daily, monthly, quarterly, and yearly basis. The following sections examine important tools with which front office managers can evaluate the success of front office operations. These tools include:

- Daily operations report

- Occupancy ratios

- Rooms revenue analysis

- The hotel's statement of income

- Rooms division income statement

- Rooms division budget reports

- Operating ratios and ratio standards

The Daily Operations Report

The **daily operations report,** also known as the **manager's report** or the **daily report,** contains a summary of the hotel's financial activities during a 24-hour period. The daily operations report provides a means of reconciling cash, bank accounts, revenues, and accounts receivable. The report also serves as a posting reference for various accounting journals and provides important data that must be input to link front and back office computer functions. Daily operations reports are uniquely structured to meet the needs of individual properties.

Exhibit 10.11 presents a sample daily operations report. Rooms statistics and occupancy ratios form an entire section of this sample daily operations report. Enriched by comments and observations from the accounting staff, statistics shown on the daily operations report may take on more meaning. For example, statistics about the number of guests in the hotel and valet sales (dry cleaning/laundry revenue) take on added significance when remarks indicate that valet sales are down while occupancy is up. This may imply to the manager that the front office staff is failing to inform guests of the valet services offered by the hotel.

The information provided by the report is not restricted to the general manager or to the front office manager. Copies of the daily operations report are generally distributed to all department and division managers in the hotel.

Occupancy Ratios

Occupancy ratios measure the success of the hotel in selling its primary product—rooms. The following rooms data must be gathered to calculate basic occupancy ratios:

- Number of rooms available for sale

- Number of rooms sold

- Number of rooms occupied by guests

- Number of guests

- Net rooms revenue

Generally, these data are found in the hotel's daily operations report. Occupancy ratios that can be computed from these data include occupancy percentage, average daily rate, multiple occupancy ratio, and average rate per guest. Computed occupancy percentage and average daily

Exhibit 10.11 Sample Daily Operations Report

DAILY OPERATIONS REPORT

Line	Summary of Revenue and Accounts Receivable		Today	Month To Date	Last Year
1	Room Revenue	+			
2	Meeting Room Rental	+			
3	Sales Tax	+			
4	Local Calls	+			
5	Long Distance	+			
6	Dry Cleaning - Laundry	+			
7	Guest Paid Outs	+			
8	Soda Machines	+			
9	Pool Tables	+			
10	Newspapers & Magazines	+			
11	Restaurant and Bar	+			
12	Commissions Earned	+			
13	Restaurant Rent	+			
14A	Taxable Misc. Sales	+			
14B	Nontaxable Misc. Sales	+			
15	Returned (List name & amount below Cks. in daily comments section)	+			
16A	Midway Money	+			
16B		+			
16C		+			
16D		+			
17	Misc. (List Below)	+			
18	TOTAL REVENUE	=			
19	Front Desk Paid	-			
20	City Ledger Paid	-			
21	Discounts (List Below)	-			
22	Yesterday's Outstanding Balance	+			
23	Today's Outstanding Balance	=			
24	Today's TL Balance	-			
25	Today's CL Balance	=			
26	Today's CL Transfers Total Line 27 through 34.				
27	American Express				
28	Bank Americard				
29	Carte Blanche				
30	Diners Club				
31	Exxon				
32	Master Charge				
33	Sohio				
33a					
34	Direct Billing				
35	CL Credits Today Total of Lines 20 & 21	+			
36	Yesterday's CL Balance	=			
37	Auditor's Signature				
37B	Mgr. Signature				

Approved as correct to the best of my knowledge & belief

Line	Room Statistics		Today	Month To Date	Last Year
55	Rooms Sold - 1 Person	+			
56	Rooms Sold - 2 Persons	+			
57	Rooms Sold - 3 or more	+			
58	Total Rooms Sold	=			
59	Complimentary Rooms	+			
60	Total Rooms Occupied	=			
61	Total Rooms Available				
62	PER CENT OCCUPANCY (Line 60 ÷ Line 61)		%	%	%
63	Average Rate Per Room Sold (Line 1 ÷ Line 58)				
64	Av. Rate Per Available Room Line 1 ÷ Line 61				
65	Total Guests				
66	No. Guests Per Occ. Room (Line 65 ÷ Line 60)				
67	List Comp. Rooms (Include Rm. No. & Name)				
68	List Number of Gtd. No Show Rooms Posted on tonights business (included in Line 1)				
69	List Special Groups In Lodge				
69a	Outside Temperature				
69b	General Weather				
69c	General Road Cond.				

PAID OUTS

Line	Account	Amount
38	Cleaning Supplies	
39	Laundry Supplies	
40	Room Supplies	
41	Office Supplies including postage	
42	Advertising	
43	Operations List Item	
44	Guest Transportation Including Van Expense	
45	Repair & Maint.	
46	Pool Supplies	
47	Guest DC&L	
48	Guest Paid Outs	
49	Papers & Mags.	
50	Mileage Expense	
51	Rest. & Bar	
52		
53		
54	TOTAL PAID OUTS	

DEPOSITS

Line	Cashier	Amount	+/-
70	Desk - 1st		
71	Desk - 2nd		
72	Desk - 3rd		
73	American Express		
74	Bank Americard		
75	Carte Blanche		
76	Diners Club		
77	Exxon		
78	Master Charge		
79	Sohio		
79a			
80	Direct Charge		
81	TOTAL DEPOSIT		

DEPOSIT PROOF

Line	Item		Amount
87	Yesterday's Outs. Bal	+ (22)	
88	Today's Revenue	+ (18)	
89	Today's Outs. Bal	- (23)	
90	Discounts	(21)	
91	Paid Outs	(54)	
92	Line 81a	+	
93		+ -	
94	TOTAL DEPOSIT	=	

Lodge
Day
Date

SUMMARY OF MISC. REVENUE [Line 17]

Line	Description	Amount
82		
83		
84		
85		
86	TOTAL MISC. REVENUE	

Daily Comments

Home Office Approval:

MML 4 Revised 4/77

CITY LEDGER PAYMENTS

Company Name	Gross	Credit Card Discounts	OTHER DEDUCTIONS *		Net
			Amount	Describe	

TOTAL (continue on back side if additional space needed)

* Only credit card charge backs; imprinter fees, tax exempt amount, travel agent commissions or District Mgr. adjustments can be entered here.

Source: Midway Motor Lodge, Lansing, Michigan.

rate may also appear on a property's daily operations report. These ratios typically are calculated on a daily, weekly, monthly, and yearly basis. Exhibit 10.12 shows annual occupancy percentages and annual average daily rates of cities within geographic regions of the United States.

The night auditor typically collects rooms division data and calculates occupancy ratios, while the front office manager analyzes the information to identify trends, patterns, or problems. When analyzing the information, the front office manager must consider how a particular condition may produce different effects in occupancy. For example, as multiple occupancy increases, the average daily room rate generally increases. This is because when a room is sold to more than one person, the room rate is greater than when the room is sold as a single. However, since the room rate for two people in a room is usually not twice the rate for one person, the average room rate *per guest* decreases.

The following sections examine how basic occupancy ratios are calculated for the Holly Hotel. Rooms data needed for the calculations are as follows:

- 117 rooms available for sale. (The Holly Hotel has 120 rooms, but 3 were out of order on this particular day.)

- 83 rooms sold.

- 85 rooms occupied by guests. (Rooms sold does not equal rooms occupied by guests because, on this particular day, single guests occupied two complimentary rooms which generated no rooms revenue.)

- 95 guests.

- $5,000 net rooms revenue.

Occupancy Percentage. The most commonly used occupancy ratio in front office operations is occupancy percentage. Occupancy percentage indicates the proportion of rooms sold to rooms available for sale during a specific period of time.

The occupancy percentage for the Holly Hotel is calculated as follows:

$$\text{Occupancy Percentage} = \frac{\text{Number of Rooms Sold}}{\text{Number of Rooms Available}}$$

$$= \frac{83}{117}$$

$$= .709 \text{ or } 70.9\%$$

Multiple Occupancy Ratios. Multiple occupancy ratios (frequently called **double occupancy ratios,** although this phrasing is not always strictly accurate) are used to forecast food and beverage revenue, to indicate clean linen requirements, and to analyze average daily room rates. Multi-

Exhibit 10.12 Annual Occupancy Percentages and Average Daily Rates

	Occupancy			Average Daily Rate		
	1986 Actual	1987 Estimated	1988 Projected	1986 Actual	1987 Estimated	1988 Projected
New England and Middle Atlantic Cities						
Boston, MA	73.0 %	73.0 %	75.0 %	$ 91.00	$ 105.00	$ 110.00
New York, NY	76.0	79.0	80.0	101.25	109.50	116.50
Philadelphia, PA	66.0	72.0	68.0	73.90	74.15	79.26
Subtotal	73.4 %	76.2 %	76.5 %	$ 94.08	$ 102.18	$ 108.70
North Central Cities						
Chicago, IL	69.1 %	69.9 %	68.5 %	$ 70.96	$ 75.35	$ 80.50
Cincinnati, OH	61.0	61.0	62.0	54.21	56.00	58.00
Cleveland, OH	60.2	61.0	61.0	50.84	52.00	53.00
Columbus, OH	54.6	54.0	55.0	47.70	48.00	49.00
Detroit, MI	72.0	66.0	64.0	61.50	64.00	65.50
Kansas City, MO	60.4	61.0	62.0	55.26	56.65	57.70
Minneapolis, MN	62.8	59.5	56.1	56.34	54.57	54.50
St. Louis, MO	62.0	63.0	64.0	55.00	56.60	58.50
St. Paul, MN	63.0	64.0	65.5	43.84	46.78	48.25
Subtotal	66.9 %	67.6 %	66.7 %	$ 66.81	$ 70.53	$ 74.67
South Atlantic Cities						
Atlanta, GA	63.4 %	63.0 %	67.0 %	$ 66.17	$ 66.00	$ 68.00
Daytona, FL	63.0	63.0	64.0	50.00	54.00	55.00
Fort Lauderdale, FL	62.0	60.0	60.0	68.00	69.00	70.00
Jacksonville, FL	63.0	60.0	60.0	49.00	52.00	54.00
Miami, FL	68.0	71.0	70.0	62.00	65.00	69.00
Naples/Ft. Meyers, FL	68.0	71.0	73.0	69.00	79.00	84.00
Orlando, FL area						
Disney/Kissimmee	79.0	82.0	83.0	50.00	53.00	56.00
International Drive	73.0	77.0	78.0	43.00	44.00	45.00
City of Orlando	48.0	56.0	58.0	43.00	45.00	47.00
Palm Beach, FL	68.0	66.0	66.0	61.00	66.00	68.00
Panhandle, FL	57.0	59.0	60.0	53.00	54.00	55.00
Tampa Bay, Fl	68.0	67.0	68.0	53.00	55.00	58.00
Washington, DC	67.4	67.0	68.0	85.00	88.00	92.00
Subtotal	65.7 %	66.7 %	68.3 %	$ 60.86	$ 62.50	$ 64.91
South Central Cities						
Chattanooga, TN	59.5 %	60.0 %	61.0 %	$ 33.93	$ 36.00	$ 38.00
Dallas/Ft. Worth, TX	56.7	57.0	59.0	59.25	63.00	66.00
Houston, TX	44.0	51.0	53.0	51.00	49.00	51.00
Knoxville, TN	58.4	60.0	61.0	39.35	41.00	43.00
Little Rock, AK	60.9	61.0	63.0	45.21	46.00	47.00
Memphis, TN	63.6	62.0	62.0	44.90	46.00	48.00
Nashville, TN	69.5	68.0	67.0	56.74	58.00	60.00
Subtotal	55.8 %	57.7 %	59.0 %	$ 51.84	$ 52.99	$ 55.26
Mountain and Pacific Cities						
Albuquerque, NM	62.3 %	61.5 %	62.5 %	$ 47.93	$ 48.00	$ 48.50
Boise, ID	57.0	59.0	60.0	36.00	38.00	39.00
Colorado Springs, CO	56.4	54.0	58.0	51.31	50.75	53.00
Denver, CO	55.7	55.0	57.0	55.93	56.00	57.00
Honolulu, HI	85.4	85.0	85.5	62.13	68.00	74.00
Los Angeles, CA	70.1	72.0	74.0	68.28	71.00	75.00
Orange County, CA	65.3	66.0	69.0	60.73	61.50	62.00
Phoenix, AZ	66.7	58.0	64.0	79.24	70.00	72.00
Portland, OR	57.0	59.0	60.0	56.00	57.00	58.00
San Diego County, CA	72.7	73.0	73.2	72.94	74.50	75.00
San Francisco, CA	72.3	74.0	71.0	88.08	92.50	96.50
Seattle, WA	66.0	68.0	68.0	67.00	68.00	70.00
Spokane, WA	65.0	65.0	65.0	45.00	45.00	46.00
Tucson, AZ	53.3	59.0	62.0	53.51	67.00	70.00
Subtotal	69.8 %	69.0 %	71.0 %	$ 66.54	$ 68.03	$ 71.00
Total Cities	67.0 %	67.6 %	69.0 %	$ 67.38	$ 70.98	$ 73.36

ple occupancy can be calculated by determining a multiple occupancy percentage or by determining the average number of guests per room sold. Either of these ratios may be used, as long as it is consistently applied.

The multiple occupancy percentage for the Holly Hotel is calculated as follows:

$$\text{Multiple Occupancy Percentage} = \frac{\text{Number of Guests} - \text{Number of Rooms Occupied}}{\text{Number of Rooms Occupied}}$$

$$= \frac{95 - 85}{85}$$

$$= .118 \text{ or } 11.8\%$$

The average guests per room sold for the Holly Hotel is calculated as follows:

$$\text{Average Guests per Room Sold} = \frac{\text{Number of Paid Guests}}{\text{Number of Rooms Sold}}$$

$$= \frac{93}{83}$$

$$= 1.12 \text{ Guests}$$

Average Daily Rate. Most front office managers calculate an average daily rate even though rates within a property vary significantly from single rooms to suites, from individual guests to groups and conventions, from weekdays to weekends, and from busy seasons to slack seasons.

The average daily rate for the Holly Hotel is calculated as follows:

$$\text{Average Daily Rate} = \frac{\text{Net Rooms Revenue}}{\text{Number of Rooms Sold}}$$

$$= \frac{\$5,000}{83}$$

$$= \$60.24$$

Average Rate per Guest. Resort hotels, in particular, are often interested in knowing the average room rate per guest. This rate is normally based on every guest in the hotel, including children.

The average rate per guest for the Holly Hotel is calculated as follows:

$$\text{Average Rate per Guest} = \frac{\text{Net Rooms Revenue}}{\text{Number of Guests}}$$

$$= \frac{\$5,000}{95}$$

$$= \$52.63$$

Rooms Revenue Analysis

Front office employees are expected to sell rooms at the rack (standard) rate unless a guest qualifies for an alternate room rate. A **room variance report** lists those rooms which have not been sold at rack rates. With this report, front office management can review the use of various special rates to determine whether staff have followed all appropriate front office policies and procedures. In a hotel with a computerized front office system, the computer can readily prepare a room variance report.

There are two other ways for front office managers to evaluate how effectively the front office staff is selling rooms:

- Analyzing actual rooms revenue as a percentage of potential rooms revenue

- Comparing the hotel's actual average rate to an ideal average rate

Actual to Potential Rooms Revenue. Potential rooms revenue is the greatest amount of rooms revenue that a hotel can reasonably generate on a given day, week, month, or year. The potential revenue for each room rate category is calculated by multiplying the number of rooms in that rate category by the rack rate at double occupancy. (Although many rooms may potentially hold more than two guests, the industry generally considers two guests per room to be the reasonable maximum when calculating potential rooms revenue.) The results are totaled to yield the total potential room revenue. For example, given specific room rates and occupancies, the potential rooms revenue for the Holly Hotel is calculated as follows:

50 double bed rooms at $60 double rate

                          Maximum Revenue = $3,000

60 double-double rooms at $70 double rate

                          Maximum Revenue = $4,200

10 suites at $95 double rate

                          Maximum Revenue = $ 950

Potential Rooms Revenue   = $8,150

The percentage of potential rooms revenue is calculated by dividing actual rooms revenue by the total potential rooms revenue. Assuming that actual rooms revenue for the day in question was $5,000, the percentage of potential rooms revenue for the Holly Hotel is calculated as follows:

$$\text{Percentage of Potential Rooms Revenue} = \frac{\text{Actual Rooms Revenue}}{\text{Potential Rooms Revenue}}$$

$$= \frac{\$5,000}{\$8,150}$$

$$= .6135 \text{ or } 61.35\%$$

This result reveals that, for the day in question, actual rooms revenue was 61.35% of the amount that could have been generated if all rooms were sold at double occupancy rack rates.

Ideal Average Rate. The ideal average rate is a rooms statistic developed by the accounting firm of Laventhol & Horwath.[3] The ideal average rate indicates the point at which rooms are sold at the best rate for the type of guests accommodated by a property. Using actual rooms statistics for a specific period (a month, season, or year), the ideal average rate indicates what the average room rate could have been for the property. The ideal average rate is based on the average of the revenue generated by selling the least expensive rooms first (from the bottom up) and from selling the most expensive rooms first (from the top down). Exhibit 10.13 shows the calculations involved in computing a property's ideal average rate.

The actual average rate collected by the hotel is compared with the ideal average rate as a measure of the efficiency of the front office staff in selling rooms within a rate structure. At least 95% of the ideal average rate should be consistently obtained. If it is not, then either the property's rates have not been established in accordance with demand, or the staff may be underselling rooms.

The probable effect of group and tour rates can be measured by selecting a day on which a number of groups in the hotel are paying special rates. The actual average rate for that day may be compared with the ideal average rate. The difference is likely to be the result of the special group and tour rates, not front office staff performance.

The Hotel's Statement of Income

The statement of income provides important financial information about the results of hotel operations for a given period of time. The period may be one month or longer, but cannot exceed one business year. Since a statement of income reveals the bottom line—the net income for a given period—it is one of the most important financial statements used by top management to evaluate the success of operations. Although the front office manager may never directly use the hotel's statement of income, this statement relies in part on detailed information—the rooms division income statement (discussed in the next section)—compiled and supplied by the front office.

The statement of income in Exhibit 10.14 is often called a consolidated statement because it presents a composite picture of all the financial operations of the hotel. Rooms division information appears on the first line, under the category of operated departments. The amount of income generated by the rooms division is determined by subtracting payroll and related expenses and other expenses from the amount of net revenue produced by the rooms division over the period covered by the income statement. Payroll expenses charged to the rooms division may include those associated with the front office manager, front desk agents, reservation agents, housekeepers, and uniformed service staff. Since the rooms division is not a merchandising facility, there is no cost of sales to subtract from the net revenue amount.

Recall that Exhibit 2.4 in Chapter 2 showed that the revenue generated by the rooms division is often the largest single amount produced by revenue centers within a hotel. Using the figures shown in Exhibit 10.14, the amount of income earned by the rooms division during the year was $1,414,843, or 84.1% of the total income of $1,682,209.

Exhibit 10.13   Sample Calculations for Ideal Average Rate

RATE STRUCTURE

Room Type	Number	Single	Double
Double Bed	150	$36	$44
Double-double	150	46	56
Suite	17	60	72

OCCUPANCY PERCENTAGE: 76% (240 occupied rooms)
DOUBLE OCCUPANCY: 1.36 (86 doubles)

PROCEDURE

STEP 1:   Least expensive rooms sold first at single occupancy.

150 double beds @ $ 36	= $5,400
90 double-doubles @ $ 46	= 4,140
	$ 9,540
Plus double occupancy	
86 double @ $8 =	688
	$10,228

Average daily rate ($10,228 ÷ 240) = $42.62

STEP 2:   Most expensive rooms sold first at single occupancy.

17 suites @ $60	= $1,020
150 double-doubles @ $46	= 6,900
73 doubles @ $36	= 2,628
	$10,548
Plus double occupancy	
17 suites @ $12	= $ 204
69 double-doubles @ $10	= 690
	894
	$11,442

Average daily rate (11,442 ÷ 240) = $47.68

STEP 3:   Average the high and the low.

$$\frac{42.62 + 47.68}{2} = \$45.15$$

Actual daily rate = $44.32

This procedure is used with the permission of Laventhol & Horwath.

The Rooms Division Income Statement

The hotel's statement of income shows only summary information. More detailed information is presented by the separate departmental income statements prepared by each revenue center. These departmental income statements are called **schedules** and are referenced on the hotel's statement of income.

Exhibit 10.14 references the rooms division schedule as *A1*. This rooms division income statement appears in Exhibit 10.15. The figures

Exhibit 10.14   Sample Consolidated Statement of Income

Holly Hotel
Statement of Income
For the year ended December 31, 19XX   **Schedule A**

	Schedule	Net Revenue	Cost of Sales	Payroll and Related Expenses	Other Expenses	Income (Loss)
Operated Departments						
Rooms	A1	$1,834,450		$292,495	$127,112	$1,414,843
Food and Beverage	A2	1,049,140	$356,620	408,360	109,406	174,754
Telephone	A3	102,280	120,088	34,264	3,174	(55,246)
Other Operated Departments	A4	126,000	20,694	66,552	13,462	25,292
Rental and Other Income	A5	122,566				122,566
Total Operated Departments		3,234,436	497,402	801,671	253,154	1,682,209
Undistributed Expenses						
Administrative and General	A6			195,264	133,098	328,362
Marketing	A7			71,650	64,086	135,736
Property Operation and Maintenance	A8			73,834	49,274	123,108
Energy Costs	A9				94,624	94,624
Total Undistributed Expenses				340,748	341,082	681,830
Income Before Fixed Charges		$3,234,436	$497,402	$1,142,419	$594,236	1,000,379
Fixed Charges						
Rent	A10					57,000
Property Taxes	A10					90,648
Insurance	A10					13,828
Interest	A10					384,306
Depreciation and Amortization	A10					292,000
Total Fixed Charges						837,782
Income Before Income Taxes and Gain on Sale of Property						162,597
Gain on Sale of Property						21,000
Income Before Income Taxes						183,597
Income Taxes						66,095
Net Income						$117,502

shown in Exhibit 10.15 for rooms division net revenue, payroll and related expenses, other expenses, and departmental income are the same amounts which appear on Exhibit 10.14 for the rooms division under the category of operated departments.

The rooms division schedule is prepared by the hotel accounting division, not by the front office accounting staff. The figures are derived from several sources, as follows:

Exhibit 10.15   Sample Rooms Division Income Statement

Holly Hotel Rooms Division Income Statement For the year ended December 31, 19XX		Schedule A1
Revenue		
Room Sales	$1,839,600	
Allowances	5,150	
Net Revenue		$1,834,450
Expenses		
Salaries and Wages	$245,218	
Employee Benefits	47,277	
Total Payroll and Related Expenses		292,495
Other Expenses		
Commissions	5,100	
Contract Cleaning	10,853	
Guest Transportation	20,653	
Laundry and Dry Cleaning	14,348	
Linen	22,443	
Operating Supplies	27,226	
Reservation Expenses	20,419	
Other Operating Expenses	6,070	
Total Other Expenses		127,112
Total Expenses		419,607
Departmental Income (Loss)		$1,414,843

Rooms Division Entry	Source Documents
Salaries and wages	Timecards, payroll records
Employee benefits	Payroll records
Commissions	Travel agency billings
Contract cleaning	Supplier invoices
Guest transportation	Invoices
Laundry and dry cleaning	Housekeeping and outside laundry/valet charges for employee uniforms
Linen	Supplier invoices
Operating supplies	Supplier invoices
Reservation expenses (if any)	Reservation system invoices
Other operating expenses	Supplier invoices (such as from equipment rentals, etc.)

Rooms Division Budget Reports

Generally, a hotel's accounting division also prepares monthly budget reports that compare actual revenue and expense figures to budgeted amounts. These reports provide timely information for evaluating front office operations. A front office manager's performance is often evaluated on how favorably the rooms division's monthly income and expense figures compare to budgeted amounts.

The budget report should show both monthly variances and year-to-date variances; however, the front office manager focuses on the monthly variances, because the year-to-date variances are essentially the summation of monthly variances. Exhibit 10.16 presents a rooms division budget report for the Holly Hotel for the month of January. This budget report does not show year-to-date figures, because January is the first month of the business year for this particular hotel.

Exhibit 10.16 shows both dollar and percentage variances. The dollar variances indicate the differences between actual results and budgeted amounts. Dollar variances are generally considered either favorable or unfavorable based on the following situations:

	Favorable Variance	**Unfavorable Variance**
Revenue	Actual exceeds budget	Budget exceeds actual
Expenses	Budget exceeds actual	Actual exceeds budget

For example, the actual amount of salaries and wages for rooms division personnel in the month of January was $20,826, while the budgeted amount for salaries and wages was $18,821, resulting in a variance of $2,005. The variance is bracketed to indicate an unfavorable variance. However, if the revenue variance is very favorable, an unfavorable variance in expenses (such as in payroll) is not necessarily negative. Rather, it may merely indicate the greater expense of serving more guests than were anticipated when the budget was created.

Percentage variances are determined by dividing the dollar variance by the budgeted amount. For example, the 7.61 percentage variance for net revenue shown in Exhibit 10.16 is the result of dividing the dollar variance figure of $11,023 by the budgeted net revenue amount of $144,780.

The budget report shows both dollar and percentage variances because dollar variances alone or percentage variances alone may not indicate the significance of the variances reported. For example, dollar variances fail to show the magnitude of the base. The monthly budget report for the front office of a large hotel may show that actual net revenue varied from the budgeted amount by $1,000. This may seem to be a significant variance, but if the $1,000 variance is based on a budgeted amount of $500,000, it represents a percentage difference of only 0.2%. Most front office managers would not consider this a significant variance. However, if the budget amount for the period was $10,000, a $1,000 dollar variance would represent a percentage variance of 10%, which most front office managers would consider significant.

Percentage variances alone can also be deceiving. For example, assume that the budgeted amount for an expense item is $10, and the actual expense was $12. The dollar variance of $2 represents a percentage variance of 20%. While this percentage difference appears significant, generally little (if any) of the front office manager's time should be spent investigating a $2 variance.

Virtually all actual results of front office operations will differ from budgeted amounts for revenue and expense items on a budget report. This is only to be expected because any budgeting process, no matter

Exhibit 10.16   Sample Monthly Rooms Division Budget Report

Holly Hotel
Budget Report—Rooms Division
For January 19XX

	Actual	Budget	Variances $	%
Revenue				
Room Sales	$156,240	$145,080	$11,160	7.69%
Allowances	437	300	(137)	(45.67)
Net Revenue	155,803	144,780	11,023	7.61
Expenses				
Salaries and Wages	20,826	18,821	(2,005)	(10.65)
Employee Benefits	4,015	5,791	1,776	30.67
Total Payroll and Related Expenses	24,841	24,612	(229)	(0.93)
Other Expenses				
Commissions	437	752	315	41.89
Contract Cleaning	921	873	(48)	(5.50)
Guest Transportation	1,750	1,200	(550)	(45.83)
Laundry and Dry Cleaning	1,218	975	(243)	(24.92)
Linen	1,906	1,875	(31)	(1.65)
Operating Supplies	1,937	1,348	(589)	(43.69)
Reservation Expenses	1,734	2,012	278	13.82
Uniforms	374	292	(82)	(28.08)
Other Operating Expenses	515	672	157	23.36
Total Other Expenses	10,792	9,999	(793)	(7.93)
Total Expenses	35,633	34,611	(1,022)	(2.95)
Departmental Income (Loss)	$120,170	$110,169	$10,001	9.08%

how sophisticated, is not perfect. Front office managers should not analyze every variance. Only significant variances require management analysis and action. The general manager and controller should provide the front office manager with criteria by which to determine which variances are significant.

Operating Ratios

Operating ratios assist managers in evaluating the success of front office operations. Exhibit 10.17 suggests over 20 ratios that may be useful to managers in evaluating the success of front office operations.

Labor tends to be the largest single expense item for the rooms division and for the entire hotel operation. For control purposes, labor costs are analyzed on a departmental basis. Dividing the payroll and related expenses of the rooms division by the division's net revenue yields one of the most frequently analyzed areas of front office operations—labor cost. Using figures from the consolidated income statement shown in Exhibit 10.14, the labor costs percentages of the major operating departments of the Holly Hotel for the year were:

Exhibit 10.17 Useful Rooms Division Operating Ratios

	Net Revenue	Payroll and Related Expenses	Other Expenses	Departmental Income
% of total hotel revenue	x			
% of departmental revenue		x	x	x
% of departmental total expenses		x	x	
% of total hotel payroll and related expenses		x		
% of change from prior period	x	x	x	x
% of change from budget	x	x	x	x
per available room	x	x	x	x
per occupied room	x	x	x	x

Department	Payroll and Related Expense	Net Revenue	Labor Cost Percentage
Rooms	$292,495	$1,834,450	15.94%
Food and Beverage	408,360	1,049,140	38.92
Telephone	34,264	102,280	33.50

The proper standards against which to compare these ratios are the budgeted percentages. Since labor costs are generally the largest expense, they must be tightly controlled. Any significant differences between actual and budgeted labor cost percentages must be carefully investigated.

One method for analyzing payroll costs involves a form similar to the one shown in Exhibit 10.18. Actual figures for the current period and previous period, as well as budgeted amounts, are itemized for comparative analysis. Any significant differences should be highlighted and explained in the remarks section. By conducting a payroll analysis, the front office manager demonstrates to hotel management that he or she attends to the most important controllable expense in the rooms division. Careful attention to staffing as the hotel's room counts fluctuate can guarantee that the percentage of payroll to revenue remains relatively constant from month to month.

Ratio Standards

Ratios are meaningful only when compared against useful criteria such as:

- Planned ratio goals

Exhibit 10.18   Sample Payroll Analysis Form

Front Office Payroll Analysis

Hotel: _____   Period Ending: _____

JOB CATEGORY	Amount Last Year	Amount This Year	Amount Budgeted
Front Office	_____	_____	_____
PBX	_____	_____	_____
Head Housekeeper	_____	_____	_____
Asst. Housekeeper, Housekeeping Staff	_____	_____	_____
"Housemen" & Porters	_____	_____	_____
Linen Staff	_____	_____	_____
Laundry Staff	_____	_____	_____
Reservations Staff	_____	_____	_____
Maintenance, Gardener & Asst. Maintenance	_____	_____	_____
Security, Life Guard, & Uniform Service Staff	_____	_____	_____

	(Last Year)	(This Year)
Payroll and Related Expenses	_____	_____
Net Revenue	_____	_____
Labor Cost Percentage	_____	_____
STATISTICS		
Rooms Rented	_____	_____
Rooms Cleaned	_____	_____
Housekeepers Hours Paid	_____	_____
Number of Rooms Per Housekeeper	_____	_____
Cost Per Room (Housekeepers)	_____	_____

REMARKS:

_____

_____

- Corresponding historical ratios

- Industry averages

Ratios are best compared against planned ratio goals. For example, to more effectively control labor costs a front office manager may project a goal for the current month's labor cost percentage that is slightly lower than the previous month's. The expectation of a lower labor cost percentage may reflect the front office manager's efforts to improve scheduling procedures and other factors related to the cost of labor. By comparing the actual labor cost percentage with the planned goal, the manager can assess how successful his or her efforts to control labor costs were.

Industry averages may provide a useful standard against which to compare ratios. These industry averages can be found in publications prepared by the national accounting firms serving the hospitality industry. Two important annual publications are *Trends in the Hotel Industry* (published by the accounting firm of Pannell Kerr Forster) and *U.S. Lodging Industry* (published by the accounting firm of Laventhol & Horwath).

Experienced front office managers realize that ratios are only indicators; they do not solve problems or necessarily reveal the source of a problem. At best, when ratios vary significantly from planned goals, previous results, or industry averages, they indicate that problems probably exist. Considerably more analysis and investigation may be necessary to determine the appropriate corrective actions.

Notes

1. For an extended illustration of how to use the Hubbart Formula to establish room rates, see Raymond S. Schmidgall, *Hospitality Industry Managerial Accounting* (East Lansing, Mich.: Educational Institute of the American Hotel & Motel Association, 1986), pp. 333-335.

2. Adapted from *Selling Out: A How-to Manual on Reservation Management* (East Lansing, Mich.: Educational Institute of the American Hotel & Motel Association, 1985).

3. The ideal average rate technique is used with the permission of Laventhol & Horwath.

Discussion Questions

1. How do the seven functions of management fit into the overall management process? How do these functions apply to the front office manager's position?

2. What kinds of special room rates might a hotel offer? What are two common methods of establishing room rates?

3. What information do front office managers require to develop room availability forecasts? Why are these forecasts important? How reliable are such forecasts?

4. What steps can front office employees take to control understays and unwanted overstays?

5. How do 10-day and 3-day forecasts help ensure efficiency in front office operations? What is the relationship between these forecasts?

6. What are the primary responsibilities of the front office manager in budget planning? How are they performed?

7. What occupancy ratios are commonly calculated by the front office? What is the significance of occupancy ratios?

8. What methods can a front office manager use to evaluate how effectively the front office is selling rooms?

9. How can front office managers use budget reports to analyze operations? Why is reporting of both dollar and percentage variances valuable?

10. Discuss useful standards against which front office managers should compare operating ratios. What is the significance of a variance from standards?

11 Managing Front Office Personnel

Many of the management functions discussed in Chapter 10 apply to managing front office personnel. The front office manager is often involved in recruiting and selecting employees, orienting new employees, developing performance standards for positions in the front office, training employees, and evaluating the performance of front office staff. In carrying out these responsibilities, front office managers must exercise skill in areas of planning, organizing, coordinating, staffing, and directing.

Recruiting and Selecting Employees

Employee recruitment is the process by which applicants are sought and screened as to their suitability for positions in the property. The process involves announcing job vacancies through proper sources and evaluating applicants to determine who should be considered for open positions.

The human resources division should provide the front office manager with whatever assistance is needed to help find the most qualified applicants for an open position. A small lodging operation probably will not have a human resources division. In these cases, the front office manager may be involved in such tasks as initial interviewing, contacting applicants' references, and related selection tasks. In all properties, the front office manager should personally interview top candidates for open front office positions.

The front office manager should always be involved in the selection of an applicant. Depending on the property, the front office manager may either hire the applicant or make a recommendation to the manager at the next higher organizational level.

Tools in the Selection Process

Important tools used in the selection process are job descriptions and job specifications. As pointed out in Chapter 2, a job description is a listing of all the tasks and related information which make up a work position. A job description may also outline reporting relationships, responsibilities, working conditions, equipment and material to be used, and other important information specific to the requirements of the property.

Job descriptions are helpful in recruiting and selecting employees because they clearly state the duties involved in a particular job. They may also explain how the position for which an applicant is applying relates to other positions in the front office operation. Formats and contents of job descriptions vary according to the needs of individual properties. Exhibits 11.1 through 11.4 present sample job descriptions for some typical front office positions.

Job specifications list the personal qualities, skills, and traits needed to successfully perform the tasks outlined by a job description. Although job specifications are specific to a particular position (based on the job description for the position), some general statements can be made about the skills, educational background, and personal qualities helpful in performing many front office tasks.

Successful performance in the front office usually requires certain skills that are acquired through education or experience. Applicants with practical skills, knowledge, and aptitude are likely to become valuable employees. Two specific skills frequently required in front office positions are mathematical aptitude (in order to understand the arithmetic involved in front office accounting) and typing skills (especially helpful for recordkeeping and for inputing data through computer terminals).

Since front office employees have a high degree of contact with guests, managers often look for certain personality traits in applicants— professional attitudes, performance, appearance, and demeanor, congenial personalities, flexibility, and so forth. Since evaluating applicants in terms of these personal qualities is potentially a very subjective process, experienced front office managers (perhaps with help from other front office staff) often use job specifications to list what each of these personal qualities encompasses.

For example, such a list might define an employee with a professional attitude as one who always reports to work on time. Professional performance might be marked by sensitivity to guests and their needs, a sense of humor, creativity, and good listening habits. A genial person may smile readily. A flexible employee might be defined as a team player willing to accept a different shift if necessary. An employee with a professional appearance is always neat and appropriately dressed.

After such a list is compiled, questions may still surface. For example, what is meant by "appropriately dressed"? In a resort, that might mean casual dress, while in a commercial hotel, it probably means business attire. Each description of a personal quality must be customized to fit the individual property.

Evaluating Applicants

Generally, front office managers evaluate job applicants by reviewing completed job application forms, checking applicant references, and interviewing selected applicants. In properties with a human resources division, applicants are initially screened on the basis of front office job descriptions and job specifications. In properties without a human resources division, the front office manager may be responsible for all aspects of evaluating applicants.

The completed job application form provides basic information to assess whether the applicant meets minimum job qualifications. Information contained on the completed form indicates how well the applicant

Exhibit 11.1   Front Desk Agent's Job Description

Position Title: Front Desk Agent   **Department:** Front Office

Immediate Supervisor: Front Desk Manager

Basic Function: To assist our guests efficiently, courteously and professionally in all front office related functions. To maintain a high standard of service and hospitality at all times.

Responsibilities and Job Duties:
1. Register guests and assign rooms, accommodate special requests whenever possible. Assist in pre-registration and blocking of reservations when necessary.

2. Stay up-to-date on room rates, packages, discounts, and how to handle each, as well as how each relates to other departments.

3. Possess a thorough knowledge of credit and check cashing policies and procedures and adhere to them.

4. Develop a thorough knowledge of the room rack, room locations, types of rooms, and room rack operations.

5. Develop detailed knowledge about the hotel's staff, services, and hours of operation.

6. Promptly notify housekeeping of all check-outs; also, inform housekeeping of late check-outs, early check-ins, special requests and part-day rooms.

7. Develop a working knowledge of the reservations department; take same day reservations and future reservations when necessary. Know cancellation procedures.

8. File room keys.

9. Develop a thorough knowledge of the posting machine.

10. Handle guest check-outs efficiently and in a friendly, professional manner.

11. Know cash handling procedures; file and post all charges to guest, master, and city ledger accounts.

12. Handle safe deposit boxes in accordance with the property's procedures.

13. Use proper telephone etiquette.

14. Understand and use proper mail, package, and message handling procedures.

15. Read and initial pass-on log and bulletin board daily to keep updated on all current information. Attend department meetings. Be aware of the daily activities and meetings taking place in the hotel.

16. Report any unusual occurrences and/or requests to a manager.

17. Know all safety and emergency procedures and how to act upon them. Be aware of accident prevention policies.

18. Maintain the cleanliness and neatness of the front desk area. Utilize free time cleaning and tidying work areas.

19. Understand that, at times, it may be necessary to move employees from their accustomed shifts to accommodate business demands.

20. Be aware that bending, stooping, and lifting items weighing 30 pounds or more may be required.

I have read and discussed the above with my manager and I fully understand the description of my job.

Signed by _____ Signed by _____
                        Employee   Supervisor

Exhibit 11.2   Front Office Cashier's Job Description

Position Title: Front Office Cashier

Basic Responsibility: Check guests out of the hotel

Immediate Supervisor: General Cashier

Functions/Duties:

- Operate electronic cash register
- Obtain housebank
- Obtain operating supplies
- Complete cashier pre-shift supply checklist
- Take a subtotal reading of all departments on the back of the cash report at the beginning of the shift
- Complete guest check-in procedures
- Post charges to guest accounts
- Handle paid-outs
- Transfer guest balances to other accounts
- Cash checks
- Complete guest check-out procedures
- Settle guest accounts
- Properly handle cash
- Properly handle traveler's checks
- Properly handle credit cards
- Properly handle direct billing requests
- Post city ledger payments
- Make adjustments
- Disperse records upon check-out
- Transfer folios paid by credit card to each credit card's master card
- Transfer folios charged to the city ledger to each company's master card
- Balance department totals
- Balance cash
- Prepare change request
- Handle safe deposit boxes
- Maintain the safe deposit

Exhibit 11.3   Reservations Agent's Job Description

Position Title: Reservations Agent   **Department:** Reservations

Immediate Supervisor: Front Office Manager

Major Responsibilities: To handle all future reservations, matching the needs of the guests with those of the hotel.

Job Duties:

1. Know the layout of the hotel including suites and parlors.
2. Follow all rules and regulations contained in the employee handbook.
3. Know the organization chart of the hotel as well as your own department.
4. Treat the guest with courtesy and respect; always refer to him or her by name.
5. Answer all phone calls promptly and in a courteous manner.
6. Follow strictly a policy of selective selling; weigh the value of each request before accepting it.
7. Secure all required information to ensure that the guest has a pleasant stay.
8. Be aware at all times of the selling status and rates of all package plans.
9. Know the credit policy of the hotel and how to credit code each reservation.
10. Have a complete understanding of our central reservations center and the procedures for operating the Teletype machine.
11. Process all transmissions of reservations, changes, and cancellations coming over the hotel's terminal, making sure to log every batch off the machine.
12. Understand the hotel's policy on guaranteed, no show, and assured reservations.
13. Process all convention "cards" coming from convention participants via mail.
14. Handle reservation requests from other departments and maintain a file of these requests.
15. Process rooming lists for sales groups; type up master accounts and reservations and indicate any special requests or billing instructions.
16. File all processed reservations, correspondence, etc.; make certain all files are current and in order.
17. Prepare all package plans, enclosing welcoming letters, complimentary orders, and coupons as needed.
18. Have a complete knowledge of our special rate clubs and know which benefits are included in each.
19. Understand the hotel's reservation cancellation procedure.
20. Process reservations and checks obtained through travel agents and keep a file on all commissions paid.
21. Process all advance deposits on reservations noting them in the deposit log and forwarding them to the desk for posting.
22. Know how to code suites, parlors, and sales groups in the coding book.
23. Handle daily correspondence; respond to inquiries and make reservations as needed.
24. Make sure that files are kept up-to-date and are rotated every three months.
25. Have a working knowledge of the sales and front desk areas and how they relate to reservations.
26. Maintain a clean and neat appearance at all times in your dress as well as your work area.
27. Promote good will by being courteous, friendly and helpful to our guests, managers, and fellow employees.
28. Be aware of, and adhere to strictly, all of the safety procedures set forth in the hotel manual.
29. Bending, stooping, lifting a weight of 30 pounds or more may be required.
30. Perform any reasonable request as directed by management.

_____   _____   _____   _____
Employee's Signature   Date   Manager's Signature   Date

Exhibit 11.4   Uniformed Service Job Description

Time to report to work (unless otherwise notified): _____

Days off (unless otherwise notified): _____

Policy on missing work or being late: _____

Meal arrangements (time, cost, place, etc.): _____

Paydays: _____

Clothes to wear to work: _____

Shoes to wear to work: _____

Special personal appearance requirements (hygiene, uniforms, cleanliness, etc.): _____

_____

_____

Specific Duties and Responsibilities:

1.   Maintain good personal appearance at all times. Wear the standard uniform including name tag.

2.   Transport hotel guests to and from the airport on request, obeying all traffic laws and forms of courtesy.

3.   Keep the limousines clean and in top running condition at all times. Immediately report to the general manager all items that require repair.

4.   Escort guests to their rooms, if requested. Deliver arriving baggage and remove departing baggage promptly, per guest request.

5.   Obtain guest laundry and dry cleaning from rooms and deliver it to the front office. Assist in distributing clean laundry and dry cleaning work after deliveries from the laundry.

6.   Work closely with the front office in carrying out all guest requests.

7.   Obtain telephone "leave-word messages" from the front desk and promptly deliver them to guestrooms.

8.   Keep the lobby directory posted and up-to-date.

9.   Watch for any unusual persons or activities and report them to management.

10.   Maintain an orderly, secure checkroom for the convenience of guests.

11.   Perform any other duties and responsibilities as requested.

Relationships:

1.   Report to: Assistant Manager

2.   Others: Work closely with front desk staff, room service department, and other staff members.

meets qualifications listed in job specifications. The form should be simple and should only require information that is important in considering how suitable the applicant is for the open position. Exhibit 11.5 presents a sample job application form.

References provided by applicants may be checked to verify that the applicants are who they say they are and have represented themselves correctly. Past employers may not provide any information other than the applicant's past job title, dates of employment, and salary verification. Former employers rarely reveal whether the person is eligible for rehire because it increases their potential liability in case the person charges

Exhibit 11.5   Sample Job Application Form

Clarion Hotel & Conference Center Lansing

6820 South Cedar Street   Lansing, Michigan 48911   517•694•8123

APPLICATION FOR EMPLOYMENT
(Please Print Plainly)

PERSONAL DATA   Date _____

NAME: _____
            LAST   FIRST   MIDDLE

ADDRESS: _____
            STREET   CITY   STATE   ZIP

SOCIAL SECURITY NUMBER: _____ PHONE: _____

IN CASE OF EMERGENCY CONTACT: _____
                            NAME   PHONE
_____
                                    ADDRESS

POSITION DESIRED: 1st Choice _____   2nd Choice _____

DATE AVAILABLE TO START WORK: _____ Are you 18 years of age or older? ☐ Yes ☐ No

SCHEDULE PREFERRED: Full Time ☐   Day ☐   For Summer Only ☐   Holidays O.K. ☐   Christmas Season Only ☐
                          Part Time ☐   Eve. ☐   School Term ☐   Weekends O.K. ☐   Full Year Round ☐

PART-TIME LIMITATIONS: If you are limited in the hours & days you can work, list here: _____

Do you have access to reliable transportation? ☐ Yes ☐ No

CITIZENSHIP: If you are not a citizen of the United States of America, do you have a permanent residence visa card or a letter or an I-94 form from the Immigration Service indicating that you are permitted to work in this country? YES ☐   NO ☐

POLICE RECORD: Have you ever been convicted of other than minor traffic violations? If yes, give date, place, offense, and outcome of each violation. YES ☐   NO ☐

EDUCATIONAL DATA

	NAME AND LOCATION OF SCHOOL	List Diploma or Degree	Circle Last Year Completed	Grade Average	MAJOR OR PRINCIPLE COURSES STUDIED
HIGH SCHOOL			1 2 3 4		
COLLEGE			1 2 3 4		
TRADE, BUSINESS, CORRESPONDENCE, MILITARY OR NIGHT SCHOOL			1 2 3 4		
SCHOLASTIC HONORS, EXTRACURRICULAR ACTIVITIES:					

PERSONAL ACHIEVEMENTS AND INTERESTS: List any activities, honors or interests that would be helpful on the job or which show leadership ability. Do not list the name of an organization if it is indicative of race, religion, creed, color, sex or national origin of its members.

_____

Have you ever been employed by Longs/Clarion Hotel-Lansing. If yes explain. _____

Position Held: _____ Date Hired: _____ Date Left: _____

LIST ANY OTHER EXPERIENCES, SKILLS OR QUALIFICATIONS WHICH ARE APPLICABLE TO THE JOB YOU ARE SEEKING.
_____

MILITARY DATA

HAVE YOU EVER SERVED IN THE U.S. ARMED FORCES? _____ IF YES, WHAT BRANCH? _____

DATE _____ RANK _____ SPECIAL TRAINING _____

(continued)

Exhibit 11.5 (*continued*)

EMPLOYMENT DATA - Attach additional sheets if necessary

1. NAME, ADDRESS & PHONE OF MOST RECENT EMPLOYER	TELEPHONE NO.

COMPANY NAME:

ADDRESS:

CITY: STATE: ZIP:

IMMEDIATE SUPERVISOR (NAME & POSITION)	DATE HIRED	STARTING RATE
YOUR JOB TITLE & DUTIES	DATE LEFT	LAST RATE

REASON FOR LEAVING   MAY WE CONTACT THIS EMPLOYER?   YES ☐   NO ☐

2. NAME, ADDRESS & PHONE OF PREVIOUS EMPLOYER	TELEPHONE NO.

COMPANY NAME:

ADDRESS:

CITY: STATE: ZIP:

IMMEDIATE SUPERVISOR (NAME & POSITION)	DATE HIRED	STARTING RATE
YOUR JOB TITLE & DUTIES	DATE LEFT	LAST RATE

REASON FOR LEAVING   MAY WE CONTACT THIS EMPLOYER?   YES ☐   NO ☐

3. NAME, ADDRESS & PHONE OF PREVIOUS EMPLOYER	TELEPHONE NO.

COMPANY NAME:

ADDRESS:

CITY: STATE: ZIP:

IMMEDIATE SUPERVISOR (NAME & POSITION)	DATE HIRED	STARTING RATE
YOUR JOB TITLE & DUTIES	DATE LEFT	LAST RATE

REASON FOR LEAVING   MAY WE CONTACT THIS EMPLOYER?   YES ☐   NO ☐

REFERENCES

LIST THREE PERSONS WHO ARE QUALIFIED TO EVALUATE YOUR CAPABILITIES (OTHER THAN RELATIVES)

	NAME	ADDRESS	PHONE	OCCUPATION
1				
2				
3				

I certify the information supplied by me in this application is true and correct and I authorize investigation of all statements including former employers and references. I hereby release from all liability or responsibility all persons, companies or corporations furnishing such information. I understand that any misrepresentation or omission of facts by me in this application is cause for my discharge in the event I am hired. The employment relationship with Clarion Hotel-Lansing is based on the mutual consent of the employee and the employer. The relationship can be terminated at will at any time. Affirmative Action E.E.O.

SIGNATURE   DATE

Courtesy of Clarion Hotel & Conference Center, Lansing, Michigan.

libel, slander, or defamation of character. (Front office managers must be familiar with their own property's policy regarding how to handle callers inquiring about the work record of current or past employees.)

Care must be taken in structuring questions included in application forms because there are federal, state, and some local laws that prohibit discriminatory hiring practices. Exhibit 11.6 is a guide that lists employment questions which may be discriminatory and ways of avoiding the problem. Such a guide may also be helpful in developing questions used in interviewing applicants. Since laws and their interpretations vary from state to state, an attorney should review the property's application forms, related personnel forms, and interview procedures to ensure that they do not violate current antidiscrimination laws.

The sample interview evaluation form presented in Exhibit 11.7 lists some key traits for employees in the hospitality industry. Portions of this form should be structured by job specifications specific to the front office. The front office manager can use such a form to evaluate an applicant's strengths and weaknesses. After interviewing an applicant, the front office manager completes the form by scoring the applicant according to the following criteria:

- Score zero if the applicant meets an acceptable level of skill in a given area, or if the skill is not needed.

- Score plus one, two, or three according to the degree to which the applicant surpasses the acceptable level of skill in a given area.

- Score minus one, two, or three according to the degree to which the applicant fails to meet the acceptable level of skill in a given area.

Every applicant has both strengths and weaknesses. An interview evaluation form helps ensure that a shortcoming in one area does not unduly lower an applicant's chances for further consideration. With this interview evaluation form, the applicant with the highest point total will probably make the best employee.

After evaluating all of the applicants, the best applicant for the position should be selected and hired. Other applicants who were interviewed for the position should be informed. If there are other positions for which these persons may be qualified, they should be encouraged to apply for them.

The Orientation Process

New employees should be given an orientation when they arrive for work on their first day. A well-planned and organized orientation helps a new employee get off to a good start in the new job. The first days on a new job are usually filled with anxiety. The employee feels like a stranger in an unfamiliar environment. The front office manager should take full responsibility for orienting new front office employees.

Exhibit 11.6 Pre-Employment Inquiry Guide

SUBJECT	LAWFUL PRE-EMPLOYMENT INQUIRIES	UNLAWFUL PRE-EMPLOYMENT INQUIRIES
NAME:	Applicant's full name. Have you ever worked for this company under a different name? Is any additional information relative to a different name necessary to check work record? If yes, explain.	Original name of an applicant whose name has been changed by court order or otherwise. Applicant's maiden name.
ADDRESS OR DURATION OF RESIDENCE:	How long a resident of this state or city?	
BIRTHPLACE:		Birthplace of applicant. Birthplace of applicant's parents, spouse or other close relatives. Requirement that applicant submit birth certificate, naturalization or baptismal record.
AGE:	*Are you 18 years old or older?	How old are you? What is your date of birth?
RELIGION OR CREED:		Inquiry into an applicant's religious denomination, religious affiliations, church, parish, pastor, or religious holidays observed. An applicant may not be told "This is a Catholic (Protestant or Jewish) organization."
RACE OR COLOR:		Complexion or color of skin.
PHOTOGRAPH:		Requirement that an applicant for employment affix a photograph to an employment application form. Request an applicant, at his or her option, to submit a photograph. Requirement for photograph after interview but before hiring.
HEIGHT:		Inquiry regarding applicant's height.
WEIGHT:		Inquiry regarding applicant's weight.
MARITAL STATUS:		Requirement that an applicant provide any information regarding marital status or children. Are you single or married? Do you have any children? Is your spouse employed? What is your spouse's name?
SEX:		Mr., Miss or Mrs. or an inquiry regarding sex. Inquiry as to the ability to reproduce or advocacy of any form of birth control.
HEALTH:	Do you have any impairments, physical, mental, or medical which would interfere with your ability to do the job for which you have applied? Inquiry into contagious or communicable diseases which may endanger others. If there are any positions for which you should not be considered or job duties you cannot perform because of a physical or mental handicap, please explain.	Inquiries regarding an individual's physical or mental condition which are not directly related to the requirements of a specific job and which are used as a factor in making employment decisions in a way which is contrary to the provisions or purposes of the Michigan Handicappers' Civil Rights Act. Requirement that women be given pelvic examinations.
CITIZENSHIP:	Are you a citizen of the United States? If not a citizen of the United States, does applicant intend to become a citizen of the United States? If you are not a United States citizen, have you the legal right to remain permanently in the United States? Do you intend to remain permanently in the United States?	Of what country are you a citizen? Whether an applicant is naturalized or a native-born citizen; the date when the applicant acquired citizenship. Requirement that an applicant produce naturalization papers or first papers. Whether applicant's parents or spouse are naturalized or native born citizens of the United States; the date when such parent or spouse acquired citizenship.
NATIONAL ORIGIN:	Inquiry into languages applicant speaks and writes fluently.	Inquiry into applicant's (a) lineage; (b) ancestry; (c) national origin; (d) descent; (e) parentage, or nationality. Nationality of applicant's parents or spouse. What is your mother tongue? Inquiry into how applicant acquired ability to read, write or speak a foreign language.
EDUCATION:	Inquiry into the academic vocational or professional education of an applicant and the public and private schools attended.	
EXPERIENCE:	Inquiry into work experience. Inquiry into countries applicant has visited.	
ARRESTS:	Have you ever been convicted of a crime? If so, when, where and nature of offense? Are there any felony charges pending against you?	Inquiry regarding arrests.
RELATIVES:	Names of applicant's relatives, other than a spouse, already employed by this company.	Address of any relative of applicant, other than address (within the United States) of applicant's father and mother, husband or wife and minor dependent children.
NOTICE IN CASE OF EMERGENCY:	Name and address of person to be notified in case of accident or emergency.	Name and address of nearest relative to be notified in case of accident or emergency.
MILITARY EXPERIENCE:	Inquiry into an applicant's military experience in the Armed Forces of the United States or in a State Militia. Inquiry into applicant's service in particular branch of United States Army, Navy, etc.	Inquiry into an applicant's general military experience.
ORGANIZATIONS:	Inquiry into the organizations of which an applicant is a member excluding organizations, the name or character of which indicates the race, color, religion, national origin or ancestry of its members.	List all clubs, societies and lodges to which you belong.
REFERENCES:	Who suggested that you apply for a position here?	

*This question may be asked only for the purpose of determining whether applicants are of legal age for employment.

Source: Michigan Department of Civil Rights

Exhibit 11.7   Sample Interview Evaluation Form

INTERVIEW EVALUATION FORM

Applicant
Name_____

Position
Evaluated_____   Date_____

	Poor Match	Acceptable	Strong Match
	−3 −2 −1	0 +1	+2 +3

JOB RELATEDNESS
General background   _____
Work experience   _____
Similar companies   _____
Interest in job   _____
Salary requirements   _____
Attendance   _____
Leadership   _____

EDUCATION AND INTELLECTUAL ABILITIES
Formal schooling   _____
Intellectual ability   _____
Additional training   _____
Social skills   _____
Speaking and listening skills _____
Writing skills   _____

PHYSICAL
General health   _____
Physical ability   _____
Cleanliness, dress, and posture _____
Energy level   _____

PERSONAL TRAITS
First impression   _____
Interpersonal skills   _____
Personality   _____
Teamwork   _____
Motivation   _____
Outlook, humor, and optimism _____
Values   _____
Creativity   _____
Stress tolerance   _____
Service attitude   _____
Independence   _____
Maturity   _____
Decisiveness   _____
Insight into self   _____
Flexibility   _____

                    TOTAL POINTS _____

The plan should be to make the employee's transition into the new job as smooth as possible. At the least, the orientation should include information about the following areas:

- The hotel—its history, reputation for service, names of key management personnel, plans for growth, and company policies

- The benefits—wages, insurance, employee discounts, vacations, paid holidays, and uniforms

- The working conditions—applicable training schedules, work schedules, breaks, meal periods, overtime, safety, security, and social activities

- The job—the set of tasks the new employee will perform, how the job fits into the organization of the front office, how the front office fits into the total organization of the hotel, performance standards, and what is expected from the employee

- The front office team—introductions to fellow employees, explanation of key responsibilities of each employee, and who reports to whom in the front office

- The rules and regulations—regarding, for example, smoking, entry and exit, disciplinary action, parking, and so on

Much of this information should be contained in the property's employee manual or handbook. Time should be set aside during an employee's first day of work to complete all tax withholding, insurance, and similar forms. If uniforms and/or lockers are to be provided, they should be available. A tour of the entire facility, especially of the different types of guestrooms, is also in order.

Training

One of the most important responsibilities of a front office manager is to ensure that department employees receive proper training. This does not mean that the front office manager must assume the duties and responsibilities of a trainer. The actual training functions may be delegated to supervisors or even to talented employees. However, the front office manager should be responsible for ongoing training programs in the department.[1]

Job Lists and Job Breakdowns

Job lists and job breakdowns for each front office position are the basic tools with which to build an effective skills training program as well as an efficient system for evaluating employee performance. A **job list** for a skilled front office position is a list of tasks that must be performed. The tasks on the job list should reflect the total job responsibility of the employee. However, the list should not be a detailed breakdown of the steps that make up each task. The job list should simply state what the employee must do in performing the job.

Exhibit 11.8 presents a sample job list for an afternoon shift front desk agent. Note that each line on the sample job list begins with a verb typed in capital letters. This format stresses action and clearly indicates to an employee what he or she will be responsible for doing. Whenever possible, tasks should be listed in an order that reflects the logical sequence of daily responsibilities.

Job breakdowns specify how each task on a job list should be performed. The format of job breakdowns can vary to suit the needs and

Exhibit 11.8   Sample Job List: Front Desk Agent

Date Prepared   xx/xx/xx

JOB LIST

Position: Front Desk Agent (afternoon shift)

Tasks: Employee must be able to:

1. PARK in designated area.
2. WEAR proper uniform.
3. PUNCH in.
4. COMMUNICATE with afternoon supervisor.
5. COUNT bank.
6. GREET guests.
7. DETERMINE guests' needs.
8. CHECK IN guests.
9. POST all charges.
10. COORDINATE room moves.
11. CONTROL safety deposit boxes.
12. PROVIDE directions for guests.
13. HANDLE messages/packages for guests.
14. ANSWER telephone.
15. CHECK OUT guests.
16. COLLECT guests' outgoing mail.
17. COMPLETE maintenance log sheet.
18. COMMUNICATE with security personnel.
19. REDEEM guest gift certificates and promotional coupons.
20. VERIFY gift shop charges.
21. CONTROL outlet banks and keys.
22. RUN outlet reports on computer.
23. COMMUNICATE with housekeeping personnel.
24. TAKE room reservations.
25. INVENTORY room keys.
26. COUNT bank.
27. BALANCE daily work.
28. MAKE log book entries.
29. RUN shift reports on computer.
30. PUNCH out.

requirements of individual properties. Exhibit 11.9 presents a sample job breakdown which is designed to serve not only as a training guide for a newly hired front desk agent, but also as a tool for evaluating the performance of all front desk agents on the afternoon shift.

The first column in Exhibit 11.9 shows tasks from the job list presented in Exhibit 11.8. The second column breaks down each task by identifying the specific, observable, measurable steps that an employee must take in order to accomplish the task shown in the first column. These steps are written as **performance standards.**

The third column presents additional information. Generally, this information explains why each step of the task is performed according to the standards listed in the second column. Note that the additional information column contains content information, while the steps and procedures in the first two columns are the process elements of the job. The additional information column can also be used to stress the hospitality

Exhibit 11.9   Sample Job Breakdown as Performance Standard

JOB LIST	PERFORMANCE STANDARD	ADDITIONAL INFORMATION	1st Qtr. Yes/No		2nd Qtr. Yes/No		3rd Qtr. Yes/No		4th Qtr. Yes/No	
8. CHECK IN guests.	A. SMILE pleasantly.	To make the guest feel welcome and at ease. Guests are often tired when they check in. They may have been traveling and/or working all day.								
	B. IDENTIFY the name of the reservation.	Reservations may be under the guest's name, a company name, or the name of the person who made the reservation. Check each name in the above order until you locate the reservation.								
	C. SECURE complete folio information.	Complete information is important for identifying the guest. This information may be used to locate the guest, mail the bill, return lost and found items, or forward mail and packages.								
	D. SECURE credit information.	Company policy and state laws require positive guest identification. A charge card is sufficient. If a charge card is not available, a driver's license or passport is acceptable.								
	E. ASSIGN room.	If possible, the room should be in accordance with the guest's request.								
	F. PAGE bell staff.	The guest service agent who has established goodwill and has the guest in a good mood can pass that feeling on to the bell staff. He/she should introduce the guest and say something pleasant as the guest follows the bell person to the room.								

aspects of the job, such as desired attitudes. Additional information may also include pointers which may help the employee to perform a task according to the property's standards.

The fourth column is set up as a checklist which is used to record quarterly performance evaluations. A performance evaluation identifies an employee's strengths and weaknesses. The weaknesses indicate specific training needs.

It is important for employees to know the standards that will be used to measure their job performance. Therefore, it is important to break down the tasks and document those standards. In order to serve as a performance standard, each item in the second column of the job breakdown must be observable and measurable. The front office manager conducting a quarterly performance evaluation should be able to simply check the "Yes" or "No" column: "Yes, the employee performed the task correctly," or "No, the employee failed to conform to the performance standard."

Job breakdowns become useless when performance standards cannot be observed or measured. For example, a performance standard such as "BE happy" is useless when it comes to evaluating a front office employee's performance. One manager may think that an employee looks happy; another manager may think differently. However, a performance standard can state that an employee should "SMILE." A smile is an observable behavior; an employee is either smiling or not smiling, regardless of who is doing the observing.

Developing Job Breakdowns

If one person in the front office is assigned the responsibility of writing every job breakdown, the job may never get done, unless the operation is very small with a limited number of tasks. The best job breakdowns are written by those who actually perform the tasks. Therefore, job breakdowns should be written by a standards group set up within the front office. Members of this group should include the front office manager and several experienced front office employees.

Most hospitality organizations have a policy and procedures manual. Although this manual rarely contains the detail necessary to set up effective training and evaluation programs, portions of it may be helpful to members of a front office standards group as they write job breakdowns for each position within their department. For example, if the procedure sections of the manual include job descriptions and job specifications, they may help a standards group in writing job lists and performance standards. The policy sections may be helpful sources of additional information which can be included in the job breakdowns.

The job breakdowns for tasks which involve the use of equipment may already be written in the operating manuals supplied by vendors. For example, a front office standards group should not have to write performance standards for operating computers at the front desk. Instead, the standards group may simply refer to (or even attach) appropriate pages from the operating manual supplied by the vendor for in-house training.

Developing job breakdowns involves breaking down each task on each front office job list by writing the performance standards which state the specific, observable, measurable steps that an employee must take in order to accomplish the task. The front office manager should assist the group in writing performance standards for at least two or three positions within the front office. While assisting the group in writing performance standards, the manager should stress that each performance standard must be observable and measurable. The value of each performance standard can be tested by asking whether or not the manager or supervisor can evaluate an employee's performance by simply checking a "Yes" or "No" in the quarterly performance review column.

After the standards group has written job breakdowns for two or three tasks, the writing of job breakdowns for the other tasks in the front office should be assigned to individual members of the group. Within two weeks, they should submit their work to the front office supervisor, who then assembles the breakdowns, has them typed in a single format, perhaps similar to that shown in Exhibit 11.9, and provides copies to all of the group's members. A final meeting can then be held, with the group carefully analyzing the breakdowns, simplifying procedures, and reaching consensus on the job breakdowns for each position within the front office. After the job breakdowns have been finalized, they should be used immediately to train the department's staff.

Training to Standards

Job breakdowns can be used to train new employees and retrain experienced employees to perform tasks according to established standards. The front office manager can use performance evaluations based on job breakdowns to identify the training needs of experienced employees. Because of their detail, job breakdowns are also very useful in training newly hired employees who have little or no experience in hospitality jobs. A comprehensive training plan can be developed from the job lists of the positions that the new employees will occupy. The lesson plans of specific training sessions can be based on the job breakdowns.

For example, Exhibit 11.10 shows a sample five-day training plan developed from the sample job list in Exhibit 11.8. The front desk agent masters one group of related tasks at a time and must completely conform to performance standards before progressing to the next group of related tasks listed on the training plan. It is not always possible (or desirable) to teach tasks to employees in the same sequence in which the tasks are actually performed on the job.

A five-step training method can be used to train both newly hired employees and experienced employees. The five steps are:

1. Prepare to train

2. Conduct the training

3. Coach trial performances

4. Reverse roles (trainee trains the trainer)

5. Follow through

Exhibit 11.10   Sample Five-Day Training Plan

```
                                                    Date Prepared:   xx/xx/xx

    Position:   Front Desk Agent, afternoon shift

    Employee: _____


                                           100% Conformity
                     Tasks                  to Standards
    Day 1

         1.    PARK in designated area.
         2.    WEAR proper uniform.
         3.    PUNCH in.
         4.    COMMUNICATE with afternoon supervisor.
         5.    COUNT bank.
        13.    HANDLE messages/packages for guests.
        21.    CONTROL outlet banks and keys.
        25.    INVENTORY room keys.
        26.    COUNT bank.
        30.    PUNCH out.


    Day 2

         6.    GREET guests.
         7.    DETERMINE guests' needs.
         8.    CHECK IN guests.
         9.    POST all charges.
        24.    TAKE room reservations.


    Day 3

        10.    COORDINATE room moves.
        11.    CONTROL safety deposit boxes.
        12.    PROVIDE directions for guests.
        14.    ANSWER telephone.
        18.    COMMUNICATE with security personnel.


    Day 4

        15.    CHECK OUT guests.
        16.    COLLECT guests' outgoing mail.
        17.    COMPLETE maintenance log sheet.
        19.    REDEEM guest gift certificates and promotional coupons.
        20.    VERIFY gift shop charges.


    Day 5

        22.    RUN outlet reports on computer.
        23.    COMMUNICATE with housekeeping personnel.
        27.    BALANCE daily work.
        28.    MAKE log book entries.
        29.    RUN shift reports on computer.
```

This training method can be adapted to meet the special needs and requirements of almost any front office operation. The method can be used for either individualized instruction or for group training programs.

The following sections briefly describe each step of the training method. Exhibit 11.11 summarizes the five-step training method as a job list for those conducting the training.

Prepare to Train

Some front office managers think they know the skills required of employees so well that they can teach them to others without any thought or preparation. However, it is easy to forget important details. Trainers need a written format to guide them while conducting training sessions. The following sections point out how trainers should prepare for training.

Write training objectives. Training objectives describe the tasks which the trainee will be expected to demonstrate at the end of the training session. These tasks should already be listed in the first column of the job breakdown. In addition, training objectives should clearly state that the only acceptable performance is 100% conformity to standards. The employee should be told the training objectives at the start of the training session.

Develop lesson plans. Write step-by-step lesson plans for demonstrating the tasks which the employee is expected to learn. It should be easy to develop lesson plans directly from the performance standards shown in the second column of the job breakdown for tasks which the employee is scheduled to learn.

Decide on training methods. When planning the training session, determine which teaching methods will be most appropriate for accomplishing the training objectives. Exhibit 11.12 presents several popular group training methods.

Establish a timetable. Establish a timetable for instruction. Decide how long the training session will take. Then, determine when the volume of business will be such that training can be conducted without interruption or distraction.

Select the training location. Job-related training should be conducted at the work station(s) where the work will be performed. Determine when the training can best occur without interfering with daily front office functions. Make sure that the employee's position at the training location will provide an uninterrupted view of the tasks which will be demonstrated. Also, the employee should be able to see the demonstration from the actual position from which he or she will be performing the task(s). If an employee is observing across the table from the trainer, then every movement will appear to be the reverse of the way it is to be actually performed. This may seem like a minor point, but it can become so frustrating that an employee may develop resistance to learning the task(s).

Assemble training materials/equipment. Gather copies of the appropriate job list and job breakdowns. These are the most important materials needed for the training session. The job breakdown should indicate other materials and/or equipment that will be needed for teaching a particular task. All these materials and the necessary equipment should be set up in the area where the training is to take place.

Set up the work station. If a work station will be used as the training location, lay it out exactly the way it is usually stocked. Each piece of

Exhibit 11.11　Five-Step Training Method: A Job List for Trainers

STEP 1:	**PREPARE TO TRAIN**	
	WRITE	training objectives.
	DEVELOP	lesson plans.
	DECIDE	on training methods.
	ESTABLISH	a timetable.
	SELECT	the training location.
	ASSEMBLE	training materials/equipment.
	SET UP	the work station.
STEP 2:	**CONDUCT THE TRAINING**	
	PREPARE	the trainee.
	BEGIN	the training session.
	DEMONSTRATE	the procedures.
	AVOID	jargon.
	TAKE	adequate time.
	REPEAT	the sequence.
STEP 3:	**COACH TRIAL PERFORMANCES**	
	ALLOW	the trainee to practice.
	COACH	the trainee.
STEP 4:	**REVERSE ROLES (TRAINEE TRAINS THE TRAINER)**	
	BE TRAINED	by the trainee.
	BE EVALUATED	by the trainee.
STEP 5:	**FOLLOW THROUGH**	
	CONTINUE	positive reinforcement.
	PROVIDE	constant feedback.
	COACH	a few tasks each day.
	EVALUATE	the trainee's progress.

equipment should be positioned in the same way that the employee is expected to operate and/or maintain it.

Conduct the Training

After the trainer has prepared for the training, the actual training session can begin. The following sections suggest guidelines for how to present the training.

Prepare the employee. Present an overview of the training session and help the employee become motivated to learn. Explain the training objectives for the session and let the employee know exactly what will be expected. Tell the employee why the training is important, how it relates to the job, and how the employee will benefit from it. Help the employee understand how the objectives relate to the total responsibilities of that particular position in the front office operation. Emphasize how the employee can make immediate use of the skills that will be learned.

Begin the training session. Use the job breakdowns as a training guide. Encourage the employee to study the job breakdowns so that he or she will know the standards by which performance will be evaluated. Follow the sequence of each step in the performance standards column of

Exhibit 11.12   Group Training Methods

GROUP TRAINING: WHAT'S IT ALL ABOUT?			
I. Consider Training in Groups When: • several employees need training in the same task • a large amount of information must be dispensed to several or more employees • individualized training methods are not practical			
II. Popular Group Training Methods			
Method	**Overview of Procedures**	**Advantages**	**Disadvantages**
1. Lecture	Least effective method. One person does all the talking, may use hand-outs, visual aids, question/answer to supplement lecture.	Less time needed for trainer preparation than other methods; provides a lot of information quickly when retention of details is not important.	Does not actively involve trainees in training process; trainees forget much information when it is only presented orally.
2. Demonstration	Very effective for basic skills training. Trainer shows trainees how to do something; can include opportunity for trainees to also perform the task(s) being demonstrated.	Emphasizes trainee involvement; several senses (seeing, hearing, feeling) can be involved.	Requires a great deal of trainer preparation and planning.
3. Seminar	Good for experienced employees. Can use several group methods (lectures, discussions, conference) which require group participation.	Group members are involved in the training; can use many group methods (role playing, case study, etc.) as part of the seminar activity.	Planning is time-consuming; trainer(s) must have skill in conducting a seminar; much time is required for training experience.
4. Conference	Good problem-solving approach. Group approach to considering a specific problem or issue—and reaching agreement on statements or solution.	Much trainee participation; obtains trainee consensus; can use several methods (lecture, panel, seminar) to keep sessions interesting.	Group may be hard to control; group opinions generated at the conference may differ from manager's ideas conflict can result.
5. Panel	Good when using outside resource people. Provides several points of view on topic in order to seek alternatives to the situation. Panel members may have differing views but also must have objective concerns for the purpose of the training.	Interesting to hear different points of view; process invites employees' opinions; employees are challenged to consider alternatives.	Requires a great deal of preparation; results of the method can be difficult to evaluate.

Exhibit 11.12 (*continued*)

Method	Overview of Procedures	Advantages	Disadvantages
6. Role Playing	Good for guest relations training. Trainees pretend to be selected people in specific situations and have an opportunity to experiment with different approaches for dealing with the situation.	Trainees can learn possible results of certain behaviors in a classroom situation; skills in dealing with people can be practiced; alternative approaches can be analyzed and considered.	Much time is spent getting points across; trainers must be skillful and creative in helping the class learn from the situation.
7. Case Studies	Good for teaching situational analysis. The case study is a description of a real or imagined situation which contains information that trainees can use to analyze what has occurred and why.	Can present a real-life situation which enables trainees to consider what they would do; can be used to teach a wide variety of skills in which application of information is important	Cases are difficult to write and time-consuming to discuss; the trainer must be creative and skillful in leading discussions, making points, and keeping trainees on the track.
8. Simulations	Good for skill development. Trainees imitate actions required on the job (such as repeating the steps in a demonstration after it is presented).	Training becomes "real," trainees are actively involved in the learning process; training has direct applicability to jobs to be performed after training.	Simulations are time-consuming; they require a skillful and creative trainer.
9. Projects	Good for experienced employees. Projects require the trainees to do something on the job which improves the operation as well as helps them learn about the topic of the training.	Projects can be selected which help resolve problems or otherwise improve the operation; trainees get first-hand experience in the topic of the training; little time is needed up front of the training experience.	Without proper introduction to the project and its purpose, trainees may think they are doing somebody else's work. Also, if they do not have an interest in the project—for example, there is no immediate impact on their own jobs—it will be difficult to obtain and maintain their interest.

Source: Lewis C. Forrest, Jr., *Training for the Hospitality Industry* (East Lansing, Mich.: Educational Institute of the American Hotel & Motel Association, 1983), pp. 148-149.

the job breakdowns. Tell the employee how to do each step and explain why each step is important.

Demonstrate the procedures. As each step is reviewed, demonstrate how to do it. The employee will understand and retain more by seeing a demonstration than by listening to a lecture. Encourage the employee to ask questions at any point where he or she does not fully understand the demonstration or the explanation.

Avoid jargon. Use words that the new employee can understand. Jargon and technical terms that may be familiar to other employees may seem like a foreign language to a person new to the job.

Take adequate time. Proceed slowly. Remember that the new employee is seeing and hearing many things for the first time. Carefully show and explain everything the employee should know about the step. It is often difficult for many trainers to slow the pace of their instruction and maintain it at a level appropriate for the employee. Try not to become frustrated if the employee does not understand each step as well or as soon as expected.

Repeat the sequence. Go through the entire sequence once and then a second time to ensure that the employee knows the process thoroughly. When going through the process for the second time, ask the employee questions to check on his or her comprehension. Follow the job breakdowns and repeat the steps as often as necessary until the employee knows the procedure.

Coach Trial Performances

After the trainer and the employee agree that the employee is familiar with the job and able to complete the steps in an acceptable manner, the employee should try to perform the tasks alone.

After properly demonstrating and explaining new skills, allow the employee to practice. Immediate practice results in good work habits. Have the employee demonstrate each step of the task presented during the training session. Then have the employee explain each step while performing it. This will help check for comprehension.

Coaching will help the employee gain the skill and confidence necessary to perform the job. As a coach, compliment the employee immediately after correct performance; correct the employee immediately when problems are observed. If bad habits form at this stage of the training process, they may be very difficult to break in the future. Be sure that the employee understands not only how to perform each step, but also the purpose for the step.

Reverse Roles

This step in the training method reverses the roles of the trainer and trainee: the trainee acts as a trainer and presents the training to the trainer. After the employee has mastered the responsibilities of the job (as specified in the performance standards of the job breakdowns), he or she should be given the opportunity to train the trainer. Most teachers will admit that they mastered their subject not when they were students learning the material, but when they actually taught the material to others. Training the trainer enables new employees to feel this same sense of mastery. Reversing roles also gives the trainer an opportunity to show confidence in the employee's performance and to demonstrate respect for the employee's abilities.

Follow Through

Once the employee has been coached in trial performances of the job, he or she is ready to try it alone. However, the trainer's coaching responsibilities remain the same. The trainer must observe the new employee's work to ensure conformity to performance standards.

The trainer should gradually reduce coaching as the employee learns to perform according to standards set by the job breakdowns. However, the trainer should periodically check on the employee and follow through.

Continue positive reinforcement. Reinforcement reminds the employee of what he or she has learned. It is important to recognize the difference between positive and negative reinforcement. Positive reinforcement acknowledges correct performance; negative reinforcement corrects incorrect performance. Reinforcement may take the form of verbal feedback during or after training.

When an employee is on the job and strays from performance standards set by the job breakdowns, first compliment the person for performing some of the tasks correctly and then guide the employee back to the correct procedures. This technique will improve employee performance and help the employee develop a positive attitude toward training.

Provide constant feedback. Feedback occurs when the trainer tells the employee how he or she is performing throughout the training. The trainer should tell the employee what is correct as well as what is incorrect about his or her performance. The amount of feedback given to a employee is determined by the trainer's own judgment.

An employee usually has questions about new tasks which have been learned. The trainer should always encourage questions and discuss ways of improving performance and efficiency. A new employee also needs to know where to go for help when the trainer is not available.

Coach a few tasks each day. A new employee can retain only a limited amount of information at one time before becoming tired and frustrated. In one training session, teach what the employee can reasonably be expected to master and allow time for practice. Then, teach more material in later sessions until all of the job responsibilities are covered.

Evaluate the employee's progress. Evaluation is the guideline that is most often forgotten in training. Training efforts should be evaluated in terms of whether the trainee accomplished the training objectives. Did the employee actually demonstrate the behavior that the trainer specified before training began? If not, the trainer should provide additional guidance and practice. Evaluation should take place before, during, and at the completion of training, as well as periodically after training.

The last procedure in the training program is for the employee to evaluate the trainer. This important feedback can identify the trainer's strengths and weaknesses. The evaluation should be viewed as a tool by which a trainer can capitalize on current strengths, eliminate weaknesses, and become better at teaching and coaching.

Notes

1. A complete discussion of the training function is beyond the scope of this book. For a detailed treatment of this topic, see Lewis C. Forrest, Jr., *Training for the Hospitality Industry* (East Lansing, Mich.: Educational Institute of the American Hotel & Motel Association, 1983).

Discussion Questions

1. How are job descriptions and job specifications used in the selection process?

2. How are application forms and interview evaluation forms useful? What cautions apply to their use?

3. What points should be covered in an employee orientation?

4. How does a job breakdown expand on the information contained in a job list?

5. What steps are involved in developing job breakdowns?

6. Why is preparation for training important? How can trainers prepare for training?

7. What guidelines can help trainers effectively train?

8. What is the purpose of having an employee perform trial performances of the trained tasks? How can the trainer coach the employee?

9. Why should the trainer and the trainee reverse roles after the employee has learned the responsibilities of the job?

10. How should the trainer follow through on training?

Conclusion:
The Challenge Ahead

Hotels can be fascinating places to work. Few businesses can match the challenge and stimulation of hotel work. The front office, in particular, offers abundant opportunities for promotions and for transfers to other departments. Hotel managers and supervisors often begin their careers at the front desk and work their way up the hospitality career ladder.

Reduced to its most basic element, a hotel's business is providing overnight accommodations for travelers. However, the methods of attracting guests, providing them with rooms and amenities, taking care of them while they are at the property, and encouraging return visits are constantly changing. A chief element of the appeal of the lodging industry is the rapid pace of innovation and change.

Technological advances frequently affect the hospitality field. The major change currently taking place is the computerization of hotel operations, and front office computerization is leading the way. Front office staff members are able to work closely with central reservation computers and computerized property management systems, boosting their career potential as properties become more and more computerized in the future.

Hotels of the Future

Discussion of technological advances leads to the question: What does the future hold for the lodging industry? In the coming years, hotels will probably offer the same service levels available today—economy, mid-range, and world-class.

Economy hotels will have fewer staff due to far greater automation. Although it contradicts our current notions of hospitality, there could even be hotels with no staff at all. They might function in the following manner:

- At a national reservation center, a voice-activated computer takes and confirms a reservation.

- At the hotel, a self-registration terminal establishes registration and credit on the basis of the guest's credit card, and a rooming slip is issued.

Careers at a Glance

"The front office of a hotel is the perfect place to start a career in the hospitality industry. The training and overall picture of the business that a person receives in the front office is by far the best stepping stone into management.

My career in the hospitality industry started at the Hilton Reservations Service Center in Chicago, Illinois. Selling rooms in properties all over the world gave me excellent training in sales techniques and in dealing with travel agencies, tour operators, and other businesses. I also developed the skills necessary to move into handling convention reservations at a large Chicago property.

In 1975, I relocated to Phoenix, working in the front office of the Mountain Shadows Resort, first under the Del Webb banner and then under the Marriott sign. During this time, I was promoted from Reservations Manager to Assistant Front Office Manager, and then to Front Office Manager. After starting on a manual system, we updated to several types of computerized systems, including Lodgistix and Hotel Information Systems. From my experience, I would recommend that a new employee start on a manual system to get a feel for the overall operation before moving to a computerized system. The manual system was invaluable in helping me understand the "big picture" of rooms management.

During my employment at Mountain Shadows, I had the opportunity to be in-volved with other departments of the hotel, especially while I was Manager on Duty. This provided me another way to view all aspects of hotel management.

In 1984, I opened an independent all-suite property as Rooms Division Manager. Although this position required a lot of long hours and hard work, I thoroughly enjoyed the hotel opening phase. It allowed me to experience hotel operations from the initial establishment phases right up to full-time operation. The pre-opening duties of personnel and construction management further enhanced my career potential.

I am presently Manager of Training and Development Services for Ramada Management Institute in Phoenix, where I started as a Management Trainer in 1985. Ramada is progressive in its training division, offering workshops, teletraining, and other training tools and guides to help its hotels run smoothly.

My expertise in the front office area certainly helped establish my career in the hospitality industry, and has helped me to achieve my goals with Ramada. Within only a year and a half at Ramada, I had attained the qualifications for a General Manager position.

And it all started with "Reservations, this is Kathy, how may I help you?"

Kathy Friend
Manager, Training and Development Service
Ramada Inc.

- Moving sidewalks take the guest to the guestroom, where the guest's credit card unlocks the door to the room.

- In the room, electricity, water, and other facilities are controlled by sensors. Food and beverage dispensers in or near the room are controlled by use of the credit card.

- Beds are recessed into the wall, and appear as needed at the touch of a button.

- For cleaning, fully automated vacuum devices remove everything from the room except the furniture. Containers in the room hold the guest's belongings.

- Access to the guestroom is restricted at check-out time. No services are available to the stayover guest until he or she has registered again.

- The account is settled by credit card.

If this seems sterile and impersonal—it is. While many industries automate wherever possible, the human element is the determining element in the hospitality industry. Automation cannot ultimately provide truly personal service.

The world-class hotels of the future will probably be even more service-oriented than they are today. Floor concierges, butlers, and valets may be assigned to each guest checking in. Amenities may include deluxe snacks, in-room computers, teleconferencing, and videophones. Theme hotels—antique, super-modern, farm, underwater, airborne, casino, health-oriented, and so on—will become popular among the extremely affluent. Pampering will be the goal of these hotels, even more than it is today.

Mid-range hotels will offer much more automation and will try out innovative operating methods. The computerization of some services, which we already see today, will continue. Theme hotels (though less elaborate than world-class theme hotels) that use costuming, service, and special facilities to create a unique hospitality experience may become more common.

Future Opportunities

Where will employees fit into the lodging industry of the future? Entrepreneurial, innovative people will find the future as promising in hospitality as in any other industry.

Even a completely automated hotel will need programmers, designers, and others to develop and implement systems which will be acceptable to the public. Mid-range properties will probably require the same number of staff as today. Maximizing the hotel's profitability will continue to be a concern, and bright, creative people will still be in great demand. World-class hotels will require even more staff, probably with greater qualifications. Bilingual and better educated staff will be common, and diversified job skills will probably be required.

Front Office Employment

For people interested in front office employment, the process of breaking into the field is often a mystery. A few sound suggestions can help guide newcomers to the lodging industry.

Careers at a Glance

"Never in a million years did I see myself in the hospitality industry.

I had always wanted to be in a medical profession. After spending five years going to several different schools, I decided to get some help. I wanted to find a career with opportunity, challenge, and variety. After attending the UCLA Extension Service's Career Counseling Program, I decided to try the hospitality industry.

I had absolutely no experience in this kind of work and thought it would be difficult to find a job. I applied at the Los Angeles Airport Hilton & Towers, but did not even specify what position. They hired me as a desk clerk. I had never worked on a computer before, and was a little intimidated. I came to find it was not difficult at all.

I worked hard as a registration clerk and after a month and a half my supervisors decided to train me as a cashier. I had worked as a cashier for another month and a half when we needed someone to work the night shift. Although leery at first, I decided it would be great experience for me. It was!

I worked as a cashier and also learned the rooms audit. This gave me insight into things that were done during the day. It made everything come together. After working at night for three months, I went back to working days and was promoted to chief clerk. I learned how to do a housekeeping report and to run other reports off the computer. I had been chief clerk for about three months when I moved to Scottsdale, Arizona. I had also gained experience in reservations while working at the Hilton, so I applied for a job as a Reservations Supervisor at Camelview—A Radisson Resort.

It was a whole new world at the Radisson. I had worked in an airport property with 1,283 rooms, corporate clientele, and full computerization. I walked into a completely manual property of only 200 rooms. Most of our guests were leisure travelers. It was a challenge for me, but I learned so much! After working as a Reservations Supervisor for nine months, I was promoted to Front Office Manager. Within only two years, I had gone from a desk clerk to a front office manager.

I have had many opportunities to learn new things and be challenged by new goals. I have always wanted to work with people and this has been a perfect career for that. Anyone who wants to work with people—and who wants a challenge—should try the hospitality industry. Not only has it been fun, it has also met my needs for diversity, opportunity, and challenge. I still have much to learn and other areas to try. This is truly a business you can grow with!"

Sally Barrett
Front Office Manager
Camelview—A Radisson Resort

Preparing for Hotel Employment

Perhaps the most important recommendation for novices is to get as much formal education as possible. It is essential to complete high school before going to work full-time in a hotel. If possible, you should also consider attending a trade school, college, or university that offers a hotel, restaurant, and institutional management program. In recent years, there has been a significant increase in the number of colleges and universities offering programs in hospitality management. With the demand for trained personnel remaining strong in most areas of the industry, graduates of these programs find ready placement.

Not all of the education for industry positions takes place in formal classrooms. For students who may be unable to attend college, another option is to take courses offered by the Educational Institute of the American Hotel & Motel Association. This non-profit educational foundation has developed courses in all areas of the hospitality industry. They are offered in independent learning (home study) and team learning formats.

However, before you commit yourself to a career in the lodging industry, it is important to actually work in a hotel for at least a few months. While many people view the hospitality industry as one of great opportunity, it is not for everyone. It is clearly preferable to find out as early as possible if such a career is for you. High school and college students can gain this experience during the summer months, or may be able to work part-time in a hotel during the school year.

Education and experience are also advised if you are considering switching careers, or have graduated from college in an unrelated area and have decided to enter the hospitality field.

Preparing for Advancement

Much the same advice applies to people already in the lodging industry who want to advance to supervisory or management level positions. In most cases, managers spend several years learning the hotel business. No one becomes a manager without experience and training. Experience in most of the departments and functional areas of a hotel is usually necessary to advance to the managerial level.

Further education can also be extremely helpful in preparing for career advancement. Industry courses at university summer schools, corporate training programs, and short courses or seminars can all be helpful in reviewing skills or in learning new material. In addition, the Educational Institute offers planned educational programs leading to industry-recognized certification for department heads and general managers. These programs are an excellent way to prepare for the increased responsibility of supervisory and managerial positions.

Preparation is the key to success in the hospitality field for experienced professionals and novices alike. Hospitality is a great industry with a variety of jobs, interesting people, and beautiful places to work. While an entry-level position won't pay an executive-level salary, it can help you determine whether hospitality is right for you. Background training and education improve your chances for higher income and increased responsibility.

Starting the Search

The process of finding work in a hotel front office can be approached from a number of different angles. One straightforward method is to call the personnel offices of the hotels and motels listed in the yellow pages of the local telephone book. Asking whether there are any openings at the front desk or telephone switchboard or in uniformed service might result in an opportunity to fill out an application or in an interview.

Perhaps an even more successful approach is to go in person to a hotel's personnel office or directly to the front desk to fill out an application for a front office job. Approaching the front office manager directly about a job opening shows initiative, which can be a big advantage in actually getting a job interview and a job offer.

Classified advertisements in local newspapers can sometimes be a source of hotel front office job leads. A number of organizations may also be able to provide information about job openings and advice about the job search process:

- The local hotel association often has an employment service listing openings at member properties.

- Large cities often have a union hall for hotel employees. The union placement office may be able to provide referrals and registration for placement as openings occur.

- Some employment agencies specialize in hotel, restaurant, and lounge placements. They often advertise, and are listed in the phone book. Check to see whether fees are paid by you or the hotel.

Probably the best source of job information, however, is the advice of friends, relatives, and acquaintances who already work in hotels. They usually know before anyone else about openings in their own hotels or nearby properties.

If initial job hunting efforts are unsuccessful, do not get discouraged. In a seasonal area, jobs won't open up until tourists return, but at that time hotels may start to frantically look for employees. Avoid becoming a nuisance, but follow up weekly with a telephone call after putting in an application. It reminds the hotel of your interest and may result in a job offer.

A well-prepared resume is also strongly recommended. Resume preparation styles vary, and there are "resume shops" which can help answer questions. Most libraries also have sources to guide the resume writer. In general, a resume should list all positions you have held, your educational background, your strengths and major assets, and any other points which may make you attractive to potential employers. Any experience or education which seems to apply directly to the job you are applying for should be included, and perhaps even stressed. If a resume has not been requested earlier, you should attach it to the application form and give it to the person doing the initial screening.

Career Paths for Front Office Employees

Front office positions are high-profile jobs. Entry level jobs efficiently performed can lead to early promotions. A career starting at the front office can progress in a number of different ways. One possible career path is presented in Exhibit 1.

There are, of course, many other routes to the top. The timing of such career steps cannot be accurately predicted because of the variables involved. Many hotel employees prepare themselves for career oppor-

Exhibit 1   Hotel Career Path

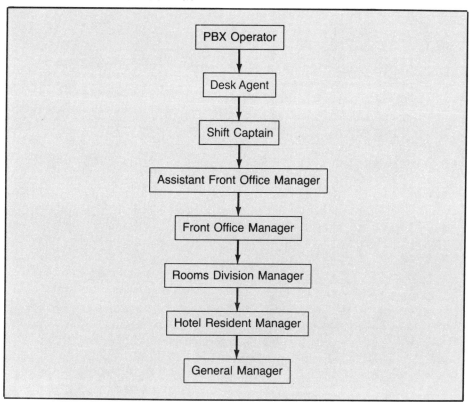

tunities as they arise. There is a lot to be said for planning ahead, setting goals, and working hard to achieve them.

Hotel employment provides the opportunity to apply for a number of positions within the system. Once you build a solid employment record in one area of the hotel, the potential is good for moves to other departments and for promotions. Sales and marketing, accounting, and management staff often started their careers at the front desk. In the early years of your hotel career, the more experience you gain in different departments and functional areas, the greater your value becomes to the hotel. In order to properly perform the duties of general manager, for instance, you will need experience in maintenance, finance, food and beverage, sales and marketing, housekeeping, and human resources—in addition to the front office.

To get a firsthand account of the process of career advancement in the hotel industry, talk to a general manager or department head about his or her employment experiences. He or she will probably have occupied a number of different positions in several types of properties and may be able to give you valuable advice. Also, consider the variety of experiences in the career narratives from hospitality industry professionals throughout this chapter. The path you take may resemble theirs or be completely different.

Careers at a Glance

"The hospitality industry and I were meant for each other—only I didn't know it at first.

My involvement in the hospitality industry began at age 16 when I went to work as a bellboy at a local conference resort in Minneapolis, Minnesota, back in 1972. I worked my way up to captain of the desk clerks before leaving in 1974. After graduating from high school, I went to work in Aspen, Colorado, as a desk clerk/housekeeper in a condominium complex. I gained an understanding of the day-to-day servicing of the guests' needs and the importance of the "much-abused maid."

From there I moved to Phoenix, Arizona, where I worked as an apartment manager and learned basic maintenance and repairs. In 1977, realizing that I missed the hotel business—it really gets into your blood!—I went to work as a desk clerk for the Ramada Safari Resort in Scottsdale, Arizona. I spent the next year learning the night audit.

My next move was one of the most important in my career. I opened the Radisson Resort Scottsdale in 1978 as head night auditor. Computers had still not entered the workplace and all work was being performed manually, from the reservation board to the NCR 250 posting machines. I then entered the Radisson Hotel Corporation's Management Training Program. After one year as an auditor, I was sent to Minneapolis on an intensive six-week training program. The major emphasis was in food and beverage operations—specifically, the steward department. Radisson then sent me back to Scottsdale where I struggled with "dishpan hands" for the next nine months.

The corporation next sent me to Shreveport, Louisiana, in July of 1980 as Director of Purchasing for Le Bossier Hotel and Night Club. I was responsible for all initial purchasing. This was a classic example of on-the-job training. I was again sent back to Scottsdale, this time as Director of Purchasing.

Soon after, I decided to return to my first love, front office management. When I opened the Camelhead Granada Royale in Phoenix, Arizona, I was responsible for setting up an entire front office. During this stage of my career I learned a lot about the "big picture"—how all the departments work together in an effort to produce the highest possible return on the investment, while providing constantly better service to their customers.

From 1983 to 1984, I was back at the Ramada Hotel Corporation. During this period, they were installing computers and satellite dishes at various test properties and I was able to work in an advisory capacity, holding the position of Assistant General Manager at the same time.

Having opened four hotels in various positions, I was excited when the Hilton Pavilion broke ground in Mesa, Arizona, in 1984. I was hired as Resident Manager with responsibilities including front office organization, computer and satellite dish installation, and the planning and physical layout of the rooms, front office, and administrative offices.

In 1986, based on the organizational and management skills I had acquired, I was given the opportunity by Coury Development, Inc., the owners of the Hilton Pavilion, to become either the General Manager of the hotel or the General Manager of the development company. Although my goal was to become a first-class hotel general manager, I saw an unlimited potential for growth in development while staying involved in hotel operations. Since that time I have been promoted to Vice President of the corporation.

The hospitality industry is a fast-paced and hard-driving business that involves you in a world of excitement and constant change. I will love it forever!"

Craig C. Johnson
Vice President/General Manager
Coury Development, Inc.

Professional Enrichment

After finding a job and becoming a member of the lodging industry, it is essential to stay on top of new developments and changes in the hospitality field. There are several ways to do this.

An excellent way to stay abreast of new developments is to read hospitality industry trade and professional journals. Most hotels receive these periodicals daily; they often contain tips and suggestions on improving hotel, restaurant, or lounge operations.

Many hotels have educational refund programs to encourage further formal schooling for their employees. As suggested earlier, more schooling won't guarantee you a better job, but it will increase your chances for advancement.

On-the-job training is also an excellent way to gain experience. For example, a month of working under the direction of a master chef can instill more food preparation knowledge than can years of reading books.

Whether through self-study, formal education, or on-the-job training, gaining additional knowledge in the specifics of all areas of hotel operations is essential to developing a successful career in the hotel industry.

Personal Satisfaction

Perhaps more than anyone else on the entire staff, a front office employee understands how satisfying hotel work can be. Helping people all day long can be a rewarding experience. A hotel is a constantly changing, often vibrant place to work. When it becomes boring and commonplace, the guests sense it and go elsewhere. The name of the game is to keep them coming back with excitement and expectation. Every person who works in the hotel is responsible for seeing that this occurs.

Hospitality is a service industry. As Ellsworth Statler has said, "Life is service. The one who progresses is the one who gives his fellow human beings a little more, a little better service." Service, he states, "means the limit of courteous, efficient attention from each particular employee to each particular guest."[1] Providing that service can make for a fulfilling, satisfying life. The opportunity for achievement in the front office—indeed, in the hotel industry as a whole—is limited only by your individual goals.

Notes

1. Floyd M. Miller, *Statler—America's Extraordinary Hotelman* (New York: Statler Foundation, 1968), p. 140.

Appendix

Anatomy of Computer Systems

by Michael L. Kasavana

Every business collects and analyzes data about its operations. While all businesses use some type of information system, a computerized system enables management to achieve its goals much more easily. A computer system can streamline the process of collecting and recording data and expand the ways in which information is organized and reported. In addition, a computer system enables management to speed up the process by which useful information is made available to decision-makers.

How much does a manager need to know about a computer to operate one? About as much as a motorist needs to know about auto mechanics to drive a car.

In order to use an automobile as an effective means of transportation, a motorist does not need to master the mechanical wonders of the internal combustion engine. He or she only needs to know how to turn the ignition key, push the gas pedal, apply the brake, and so on. Sparks jump, pistons pump, and gears turn, regardless of the driver's knowledge of mechanical engineering. However, if a motorist has some understanding of auto mechanics as well as basic auto maintenance skills, the car should perform even better and meet his or her transportation needs for a longer period of time.

Similarly, in order to use a computer as an effective means of operating an information system, a manager does not need to learn the intricacies of electronic circuitry etched on silicon chips. The manager simply needs to learn the

Adapted from Michael L. Kasavana and John J. Cahill, *Managing Computers in the Hospitality Industry* (East Lansing, Mich.: Educational Institute of the American Hotel & Motel Association, 1987), Chapters 3 and 4.

commands by which to instruct the computer to carry out the desired functions. However, if a manager also has some basic knowledge about the essential operations of a computer system, he or she will be better equipped to use a computer as an effective tool in managing information needs.

Data Processing

Data processing involves transforming raw facts and isolated figures into timely, accurate, and useful information. Every day, hospitality managers are bombarded with facts and figures about the results of operations. However, these individual pieces of data are relatively meaningless until they undergo a process that organizes or manipulates them into useful information.

Data processing is not unique to the world of business; it is an important function that occurs in everyday life as well. Everyone processes data. For example, consider what may happen on a typical payday.

After receiving a paycheck, a person may consider all of the items he or she would like to purchase, the cost of those items, and the difference between the amount of the paycheck and the total amount of the planned purchases. If the amount of the paycheck is greater than the amount of planned purchases, the person may decide to place the surplus amount in a savings account. If, on the other hand, the total amount of planned purchases is greater than the amount of the paycheck, the person may reconsider the purchase options or, perhaps, consider taking out a loan.

In this example of data processing, a collection of data (the amount of the paycheck and the purchase options) is processed (totaled and compared) and, thus, transformed into information (surplus or deficit) useful in making decisions (what to buy).

The conversion of data into information is accomplished through a cycle of events identified as **input, process,** and **output.** Using the terms of our previous example of data processing in everyday life, the paycheck and the purchase options are inputs; totaling the planned purchases and comparing that total with the amount of the paycheck is the processing; and the resulting surplus or deficit is the output. The sequence of input, process, and output is the basic **data processing cycle** as illustrated in Exhibit 1.

During input, data are collected and organized to simplify subsequent processing functions. During processing, input data are mathematically manipulated or logically arranged to generate meaningful output. The output can be reported for immediate use or saved for future reference.

Electronic Data Processing

The speed, accuracy, and efficiency required for an effective information system are often best achieved through electronic data processing. The difference between data processing (DP) and electronic data processing (EDP) lies in the automation of the process and the addition of a memory unit. Exhibit 2 illustrates the electronic data processing cycle.

Electronic data processing employs a computer system. The automation of input, process, and output events within the basic data processing cycle results in faster and more efficient operation. Also, the addition of a memory unit allows for the storage of data and/or instructions for more reliable and thorough processing.

A **bit** is the smallest unit of electronic data. The term bit is short for a *BI*nary digi*T* (which is either zero or one). All characters (letters, numbers, and symbols) are represented by a special sequence of binary digits. For example, the characters "A," "B," and "C" may be converted into binary code as follows:

$$A = 01000001$$
$$B = 01000010$$
$$C = 01000011$$

Exhibit 1   The Data Processing Cycle

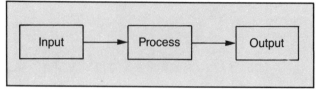

A special sequence of bits representing a single character is called a **byte.** A byte is a group of adjacent bits which work, or are operated on, as a unit. Theoretically, a byte may be any length, but the most common length for a byte is eight bits, with some computers using seven.

Bytes take up memory space and are typically measured as **kilobytes.** A kilobyte represents approximately one thousand bytes (1,024 bytes, to be exact). Kilobyte is often abbreviated as *K* or *KB* and is used to describe computer memory capacity. A **megabyte** (*M* or *MB*) represents approximately one million bytes.

Advantages of Electronic Data Processing

The primary function of all information systems, including computerized ones, is to transform data into timely, accurate, and useful information. Electronic data processing achieves this objective by:

- Reducing turnaround time
- Streamlining output
- Minimizing the handling of data

Turnaround time refers to the time which elapses between data input and information output. An efficiently designed data processing system provides managers with rapid access to the information they need in order to make timely and effective decisions. Computer systems are able to minimize turnaround time for almost all data processing tasks.

A frequent criticism of electronic data processing is that computer systems produce large volumes of irrelevant information. This criticism is misdirected. If a computer system overwhelms management with reams of useless information, it is not the fault of the computer—it is the fault of the computer system design. An

Exhibit 2 The Electronic Data Processing Cycle

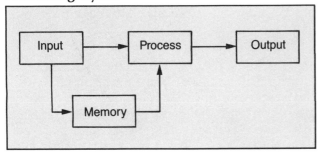

efficiently designed electronic data processing system streamlines output. Streamlining the output of a computer means generating only those reports which are requested by those who will actually use the information.

Reducing the number of times that data must be handled enhances both the speed and the accuracy of data processing tasks. Consider the difference between a manual accounting system and a computerized one.

In a manual accounting system, the amounts of invoices which are received must first be recorded in a journal. The amounts are carried over to a ledger. Amounts recorded in the ledger are then used to prepare financial statements. During each of these steps, it is possible for a bookkeeper to make any number of mistakes, such as recording the wrong number, writing a number's digits in the wrong order (transposing them), calculating a total incorrectly, and so on. The greater the number of times data must be handled, the greater the possibility for error.

In a computerized data processing system, the invoice amount is entered only once. The amount can then be accessed by the programs which prepare the journal, ledger, and financial statements. Therefore, when the amount of the invoice is entered correctly, all of the subsequent financial statements will be mathematically correct. If the amount is entered incorrectly, but the mistake identified and corrected, the correction automatically flows from the journal through to the financial statements. With electronic data processing, there are fewer opportunities for error because it is not necessary to rehandle the same data at each step in the accounting process.

Types of Computers

A computer is a managerial tool capable of processing large quantities of data much more quickly and accurately than any other data processing method. Computers can perform arithmetic operations such as addition, subtraction, multiplication, and division, and they can perform logical functions as well, such as ranking, sorting, and assembling operations. In addition, computers are capable of storing and retrieving tremendous amounts of information and thereby allow managers to exercise control over procedures which might otherwise be overlooked.

Advances in computer technology have made it difficult to classify computers in terms of variables other than memory capacity. In the past, computers were relatively easy to classify in relation to such variables as:

- Speed of operation
- Size of components
- Number of peripheral devices supported
- Number of simultaneous users
- Extent of software library
- Complexity of operation
- Cost

However, recent advancements in computer design and technology have made it increasingly difficult to differentiate computers by any single variable. Given this situation, it is best to discuss the different types of computers from a historical perspective and define mainframe computers, minicomputers, and microcomputers in terms of their places in the evolution of computer technology.

Mainframe Computers

The term **mainframe computer** was originally used to describe the *main frame*work of the central processor within a computer system. The first mainframe business computers appeared in the early 1950s and were made up of vacuum tubes for electronic circuitry. Punched cards were the main source of input, and magnetic drums were used for internal storage. First generation computers were slow, bulky, and generated extraordinary amounts of heat.

A second generation of mainframe computers evolved in the early 1960s as transistors and diodes became the main circuit components. Transistors were smaller, faster, and more reliable than the vacuum tubes which they replaced. Magnetic cores replaced magnetic drums as main storage, and magnetic tape and disks became available for external data storage.

In the mid-1960s, transistor technology was replaced by solid-state logic in the form of silicon chips with integrated circuitry. Silicon chips are pieces of semiconductor material onto which electronic circuitry is etched. These chips are no larger than one's fingernail and can hold as much information as did hundreds of electronic tubes connected to the original mainframe computers. Along with the installation of silicon chips, computer storage shifted from magnetic cores to integrated circuit boards that provided expandable storage.

The use of silicon chips produced gains in efficiency and also reduced the size and cost of computers. Many businesses soon found that their data processing needs could be met by a minicomputer.

Minicomputers

The third generation of computers (early 1970s) produced the **minicomputer**—a slower, less powerful, but smaller and cheaper alternative to the mainframe computer. The exploitation of the computer's commercial potential began with the appearance of the minicomputer. These systems possess the same components as larger mainframe computers, but typically have reduced memory capability and slower processing abilities. Minicomputers also allow fewer users to simultaneously interact, and support fewer peripheral devices (such as printers and display screens). Although the minicomputer is less powerful than a mainframe computer, it is generally more powerful than a microcomputer.

Microcomputers

The fourth generation of computers (mid 1970s) introduced the **microcomputer,** or "personal computer." This term is used for the smallest computers on the market. Despite their small size, they contain the same types of components as the larger machines and may also have additional options such as hard disks, color monitors, graphics capability, and others. Many hospitality businesses find that their data processing needs can be met by microcomputers.

A microcomputer is so compact that its **central processing unit (CPU)** is contained on a single silicon chip that is less than one quarter of an inch square and uses less energy than a 100-watt light bulb. The CPU of a microcomputer is also known as a **microprocessor.** The microprocessor is an integrated circuit package containing a complete electronic circuit or group of circuits. Its circuits make up a central processing unit which controls the computer, carries out calculations, directs the flow of data, and performs many other functions as well.

Businesses that in the past used mainframes and minicomputers exclusively are currently using powerful microcomputers. Some microcomputers are designed to be portable and small enough for executives to use while traveling.

Regardless of type, every computer must have each of these three hardware components: an input/output unit, a central processing unit, and an external storage device.

Computer Hardware

The physical equipment of a computer system is called **hardware.** Computer hardware is visible, movable, and easy to identify. In order to have a computer system, three hardware components are required: an input/output unit, a central processing unit (CPU), and an external storage device. Exhibit 3 shows how these three components are related.

An **input/output (I/O) unit** allows the user to interact with the computer system. The user can input data through a keyboard and receive output on a display screen and/or on paper through a printer.

The central processing unit is the control center of the computer system. Inside are the circuits and mechanisms that process and store information and send instructions to the other components of the system. The computer is said to **read** when it takes data in for processing and to **write** when it sends processed data out as

Exhibit 3   Computer Hardware Components

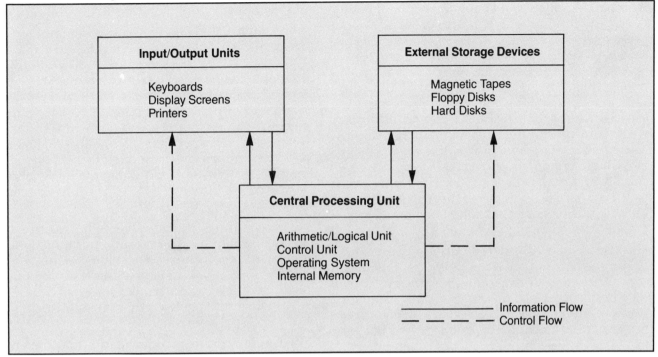

information. All input entering the computer system from any input device is processed by the CPU before it is sent to the internal memory or to an output device. Similarly, all output (sent to a display screen, printer, or other device) has first been processed by the CPU. There is no direct link between input and output devices. Whenever information is to be moved within the computer system, it must pass through the CPU.

An **external storage device** is a piece of equipment that retains data and/or programs that can be accessed by the CPU. Data and programs can be permanently stored on such external devices as magnetic tapes, floppy disks, and hard disks.

The following sections discuss each of the three hardware components in greater detail.

Input/Output Units

Input/output units include keyboards, display monitors, and printers. For most data processing, the computer system needs a keyboard for input and a display screen for output. If a paper record of the processed data is desired, a printer is also needed.

Keyboards are the most common input devices. The number, positioning, and function of the keys on any particular keyboard will depend on the type of computer system used and the needs of the individual user as well.

The type of display screen (also called a monitor or simply a screen) will also depend on the type of computer system used and the needs of the individual user. Most display screens for microcomputer systems are capable of displaying both text and graphics (e.g., graphs, pie charts, etc.). Many are equipped with controls for adjusting brightness and contrast, and some units can be tilted for optimal viewing position. Display screens may be purchased as monochrome or color units. Those with color capability can produce impressive graphic displays. Also, these output units may be programmed to various foreground and background color combinations while operating many software applications.

Some computer manufacturers have developed terminals that enable the user to move the cursor without having to type a command from a keyboard. One such device is the **touch-screen terminal.** A touch-screen terminal is a cathode ray tube with a grid of tiny beams of light over its glass screen. When the screen is touched in a sensitized area, the light beam is broken. This causes a signal to be transmitted to the computer, which then selects from memory the relevant information. The touch-screen terminal is especially appealing to those who cannot type well, or to those interested in simplified input procedures. Since touch-sensitive screens can move large quantities of data easily, they are especially effective as order entry devices in food service operations and are useful for many graphic business applications (such as charts, graphs, and so on).

Printers are considered output devices and part of the hardware of a computer system. They can be classified in relation to how they actually go about printing processed data. Impact printers, such as dot matrix and daisywheel printers, print character by character and line by line. Non-impact printers include thermal, ink jet, and laser printers.

Impact printers depend on the movement of a print head or paper feeding mechanisms to place data on the page. The simplest printers place characters in a row, then return the carrier to the left margin as the paper is moved up to another line. A line-printing terminal (LPT) is an impact printer that prints one line of type at a time.

All impact printers rely on the durability of their mechanical parts for accurate print positioning, and all are in some degree limited as to the type of data they can print and their ability to move around the page. Non-impact printers, on the other hand, achieve accurate print positioning electronically, and have the capability of using a greater range of type styles more quickly and efficiently than impact printers.

Common I/O Units in the Hospitality Industry

The most common I/O unit at work in the hospitality industry is the **CRT (cathode ray tube).** The CRT unit is composed of a television-like video screen and a keyboard which is similar to a typewriter keyboard. Data entered through the keyboard can be displayed on the screen.

The CRT operator can edit and verify the on-screen input prior to sending it for processing.

A unit that used to be more common in the hospitality industry is the teletype terminal (TTY). The TTY is less expensive than the CRT unit, but does not include a video display component. Instead, input is entered through a keyboard and printed out on a roll of paper. As the operator enters data into the system, a printed report can be made at the TTY console. The entered data is then communicated to a remote unit for processing. After processing, the information is relayed back to the TTY and printed out on paper.

For example, the housekeeping department of a hotel could use TTYs to communicate up-to-date data regarding room status to the front desk. The TTY would enable the housekeeping department to retain a printed record of the messages which pass between room attendants and front desk personnel.

Communicating room status may not require all the capabilities of the CRT unit which is used at the front desk. Therefore, the cost of a CRT unit for the housekeeping department may not be justified. However, this kind of upper-management decision may involve a preference for consistency of equipment.

Other types of I/O equipment common in the hospitality industry include keyboard and operator display units such as electronic cash registers and line-printing terminals. An electronic cash register (ECR) is a computer-based unit which is designed to record cash (and related) transactions and monitor cash balances. A hotel's food and beverage operation may use ECRs to communicate with the front desk. In a computerized hotel system, restaurant charges can be entered into a point-of-sale unit in the restaurant and transmitted to the front office where guest folios are automatically updated with the charges.

One important difference among I/O units is the type of output they produce. A CRT unit displays output on a monitor for the user to examine; this type of output is referred to as **soft copy** because it cannot be handled by the operator or removed from the computer. Printers, however, generate a paper copy of the output which is called a **hard copy.** Many systems are designed so that they can produce both types of output. For example, a computer at a hotel's front desk might have a CRT unit which the clerk can use to view a soft copy of guest folios during check-in and check-out. When the guest checks out, a hard copy of the folio will be generated from a printer so that the guest can keep a copy. Obviously, output displayed on a screen is much more temporary and its use more restricted than output printed on paper. Generally, hospitality managers obtain essential reports in hard copy form, allowing storage outside the computer and providing a base for information backup.

The Central Processing Unit

The central processing unit (CPU) is the most important and most expensive hardware component found within a computer system. It is the "brain" of the system and is responsible for controlling all other system components. As shown in Exhibit 3, the CPU is composed of four subunits.

The first subunit is the **arithmetic and logical unit (ALU),** which performs all the mathematical, sorting, and processing functions.

The second subunit is the **control unit,** which is responsible for determining which units in the computer system can be accessed by the CPU. If a unit is capable of interacting directly with the CPU, it is said to be **on-line; off-line** refers to the condition in which there is no established connection between a system unit and the CPU. It is important to realize that although computer units may be switched on (powered-up), they are not necessarily on-line. For example, when a printer is connected to a CPU and its power switch is turned on, the operator can switch the printer to either on-line or off-line status. The printer will respond to commands from the CPU only when it is on-line.

The third subunit of the CPU houses a portion of the **operating system.** The operating system is responsible for orchestrating the hardware and the software within the computer system. It establishes the system's priorities and directs its resources to effectively accomplish desired tasks.

The final subunit of the CPU is the system's **internal memory,** which is housed in a set of specialized circuits. One part of internal memory, called **read only memory (ROM),** holds a permanent record of information that the computer needs to use each time it is turned on. ROM stores a permanent control program entered by the computer manufacturer and may also house the computer's operating system. The control program contains specific sets of commands and instructions which guide the most fundamental routines carried out by the computer system. For example, the control program contains instructions for the conversion of keyboard entries into binary codes for processing by the CPU.

Another part of internal memory, called **random access memory (RAM),** holds a temporary version of the programs and/or data which users are processing. All data which a user enters into the system are temporarily stored in the random access memory area of the computer's internal memory. Since data stored in RAM can be accessed and/or altered by the user, RAM is often described as **read/write memory:** the user can both "read" from RAM (retrieve data) and "write" to RAM (store data).

When the computer loses electrical power, or is turned off, all user data stored in RAM is lost forever. For this reason, RAM is referred to as **volatile memory.** In order to save data stored in RAM for future use, the user must instruct the computer to save it on some type of external storage device.

External Storage Devices

An external storage device is the hardware component of a computer system that retains data and/or programs that can be accessed by the CPU. Data and programs can be permanently saved on a variety of external storage devices.

An important factor in selecting the kind of external storage device for a particular computer system is the kind of access which users wish to have to the stored data. User access to stored data will be addressed in the following sections, which discuss some of the more common external storage devices: magnetic tapes (cassette and reel-to-reel), floppy disks, and hard disks.

Magnetic Tapes

Magnetic tapes are external storage devices that are made from a polyester base material coated with an oxide compound. It is this compound which gives the tape its durability and electromagnetic properties. Magnetic tapes (cassette and reel to reel) are referred to as a **sequential access medium** because they store data in linear sequence.

User access to data stored on magnetic tape is similar to the way in which anyone searches for a portion of a recording stored on a cassette tape recorder—the user must wind and rewind the tape until the desired portion of data is found. Because this can be a cumbersome process, magnetic tape is not a feasible storage device for the everyday computer needs of many hospitality operations. However, using magnetic tapes to store some kinds of data may be a great deal less expensive than using disks. Therefore, in some situations, magnetic tapes could serve as an ideal backup system on which to store data which are not required on a regular basis.

Floppy Disks

Floppy disks (also called **diskettes**) are popular external storage devices and are frequently used for shipping data and programs from one location to another. They are made of thin, flexible plastic protected by a cardboard jacket. The plastic is coated with a magnetized oxide compound designed to hold electronic information. The size of the floppy disk depends upon the type of computer system used.

When a user instructs the computer to store information on a floppy disk, the information is stored in an area of unused disk space. A user can also instruct the computer to write over information that is already stored on the disk. This can be convenient for updating inventory records, personnel files, and so on. However, if information is written over old information, the old information is erased and cannot be retrieved again.

Floppy disks are referred to as a **random access medium** because data can be stored in any available location on the disk. Since the tracks and sectors of the disk are numbered, the computer system allows a user to access stored data quickly and easily.

Hard Disks

Hard disks (also called **fixed** or **rigid disks**) are external storage devices that are much faster to use and store far greater amounts of information than floppy disks. Hard disks are permanently on-line to the computer system. Since hard disks hold so much more data than floppies, copying their contents may require numerous floppy disks and can be very time-consuming. It is for these reasons that **tape streamers** have become popular. Tape streamers are magnetic tape cartridges containing seven-track tape and a large storage capacity. They permit rapid copying of all data stored on even the largest hard disk formats. Removable hard disks are also gaining in popularity and becoming a convenient backup storage method. Technological advancements are making laser discs a feasible medium for permanent storage of information. Eventually, laser discs will become less expensive, more readily available, and reusable.

Hardware Configurations

Hardware configuration refers to the design and layout of the hardware components of a computer system. The size of a hospitality operation and the number of departments needing access to the computer system are significant factors in selecting the appropriate configuration of hardware components.

A very small hospitality operation may find that a single microcomputer work station is sufficient to meet the needs of its limited number of users. This work station would be a complete system with input/output units, a single CPU, and external storage capability.

Other hospitality operations may have a number of user groups from different departments that need access to the computer system. These properties can avoid spending unnecessary funds on computer equipment by selecting the particular configuration of hardware components which best meets the needs of their operations. In many cases, it is possible for users to share output devices (such as printers and external storage facilities) and/or the internal memory and processing capability of a central processing unit.

The advantages and disadvantages of each configuration should be considered before purchasing a computer system. The major differences among the various configurations are speed and cost. The CPU is the most expensive component in a computer system; therefore, the more CPUs a configuration requires, the greater its cost will be. The tradeoff in configuring a number of CPUs, however, is that the closer the CPU is to the I/O devices, and the fewer I/O devices making demands on the CPU, the faster the computer system will seem to operate.

The following sections discuss four basic configurations of hardware components: stand-alone configuration, distributed configuration, integrated configuration, and combined configuration.

Stand-Alone Configuration

A **stand-alone configuration** creates self-sufficient work stations, each with a complete set of the same hardware components. The presence of many individual computers at different locations limits communication to sharing data by exchanging external storage media (disks). The duplication of hardware components makes this a relatively expensive hardware configuration.

Distributed Configuration

The **distributed configuration** is an improvement over the stand-alone configuration. Each work station possesses a complete computer system. The presence of an I/O device, CPU, and external storage device at each location provides a multiprocessor environment.

What distinguishes this configuration from the stand-alone configuration is that the work stations are cabled together. The cabling serves as a hardware interface which creates a **local area network (LAN)** of individual work stations. A local area network enables users to share data, programs, and output devices (such as printers). Data sharing facilitates system-wide communications, and program sharing enables users who are not in possession of a particular software program to benefit from its operation. From an economic perspective, device sharing is perhaps the most important benefit derived from networking. Expensive peripheral devices, such as high capacity storage devices and laser printers, can become available to all work stations cabled within the network.

Since each user group has its own computer, there is also more specialized application capability (use and storage). An additional benefit

Exhibit 4   Distributed Hardware Configuration

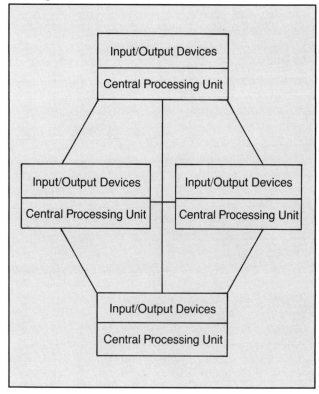

is that an individual system encountering operational problems does not affect the operation of the other systems in the network. Exhibit 4 diagrams a distributed hardware configuration.

Integrated Configuration

An **integrated configuration** creates a number of work stations, all of which are dependent upon a single central processing unit and external storage device. While the I/O units may be distributed throughout the hospitality establishment, both the CPU and the external storage device are centrally located. Exhibit 5 diagrams one possible integrated configuration. Each I/O unit communicates with the CPU, and the CPU and external storage device work closely together. Since the integrated configuration is dependent on a single CPU and centralized storage device, power failures or system failures can render the entire computer system inoperable and/or result in a permanent loss of stored data.

Exhibit 5   Integrated Hardware Configuration

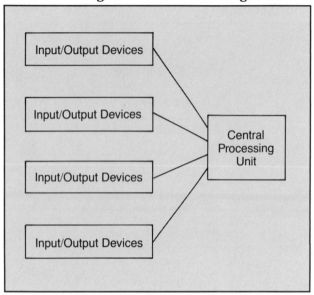

Combined Configuration

A particular variation of a distributed configuration is a **combined configuration** which interfaces a microcomputer to an already established integrated configuration. While the microcomputer is stand-alone in nature (it possesses its own I/O unit, CPU, and external memory device), its connection to the integrated configuration allows for significant application flexibility not otherwise available. For example, the transfer of data files from the external storage device of the integrated configuration to the microcomputer allows detailed analysis of those files without affecting the ongoing workings of the integrated design.

The combined configuration is an important arrangement used in the hospitality industry. Assume that the integrated configuration depicted in Exhibit 5 is a hotel's electronic cash register system with a centralized processing unit and storage device. Connecting a microcomputer to this system enables a user to transfer a day's sales and produce analytical reports without interfering with the ongoing work of the hotel's cash register system. Exhibit 6 illustrates a combined hardware configuration.

Computer Software

The hardware of a computer system does nothing by itself. In order for hardware compo-

nents to operate, there must be a set of instructions to follow. Instructions that command a computer system to perform useful tasks are called **computer programs.** A set of programs that instructs or controls the operation of the hardware components of a computer system is called **software.** Software programs tell the computer what to do, how to do it, and when to do it.

Many people's first exposure to the power of computers is through **applications software** such as word processing packages, electronic spreadsheet programs, or database management systems. This appendix provides a brief overview of these applications and describes how they operate in conjunction with the hardware components of a computer system.

Experienced computer users are familiar with **systems software** which must be present for applications software to establish a connection with computer hardware components. The discussion of systems software in this appendix focuses primarily on operating systems, with particular emphasis given to the disk operating systems of microcomputers.

Applications Software

Applications software is a term for sets of computer programs designed for specific uses such as word processing, electronic spreadsheet analysis, and database management. Many of these types of applications are purchased separately from the hardware components of a computer system and are usually available at retail computer outlets or from vendors of hospitality computer systems.

When a business plans to computerize its information system, the choice of applications software is always a decision which must be made before selecting computer hardware components. Management must determine what functions or tasks the computerized information system will be required to perform and then identify which applications software will best meet those needs. Only after these decisions have been made is management in a position to decide which kind of computer hardware components are needed to run the required software programs. Not all applications software is available for every computer brand, and the com-

Exhibit 6   Combined Hardware Configuration

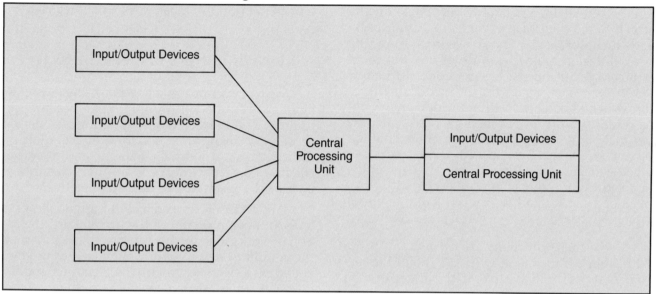

patibility of software programs and hardware components is a critical factor in purchase decisions. By focusing first on which applications software will best meet the needs of the hospitality operation, managers can ensure that the computer system which is eventually purchased will be able to accomplish all of the desired tasks.

Some software programs are very application-specific, while others can be used to perform a variety of different tasks. For example, a restaurant manager can purchase a software package designed specifically to perform menu engineering. This type of software performs all of the necessary calculations involved in menu engineering and prints a graph displaying the results. Because this software has one specific purpose, it is designed so that it requires no direct intervention by the user. The user simply inputs the appropriate data and the program does the rest.

Other types of applications software are less task-specific. For example, a spreadsheet program can be used for a number of different applications, although the user must be able to create the various spreadsheets which will accomplish the appropriate tasks.

The following sections provide a brief overview of typical applications software such as word processing packages, electronic spreadsheet programs, and database management systems.

Word Processing Software

Word processing is an electronic means of writing, editing, storing, and printing textual material. A user inputs characters (letters, numbers, or symbols) from the keyboard of the computer system. The characters are then processed by the CPU, retained in the CPU's temporary memory (RAM), and appear immediately as output on the user's display screen. The flashing cursor on the display screen indicates where characters entered at the keyboard will appear.

The arrow keys found on the keyboard allow the user to move anywhere within the text appearing on the display screen. This makes it easy for the user to add, delete, correct, combine, and perform other basic editing tasks. Changes that are input at the keyboard are immediately made to the textual material which appears on the display screen. This edited version of the textual material replaces the original version in the CPU's temporary memory (RAM).

Special function keys and special combinations of keys permit the user to move words, phrases, paragraphs, pages, or even entire chapters of textual material from one point on the screen to another. Many word processing packages include special features which allow the user to design the appearance of the document to meet specific needs. For example, with a few keystrokes, margins for the entire document, or for particular passages within the document, can be reset; columns of numbers can be aligned by decimal point; single-spaced textual material can be converted to double-spaced, triple-spaced, or whatever the user desires. These changes in the appearance of a document are executed in fractions of a second and are reflected in the output which appears on the user's display screen.

Since these functions are carried out in the CPU's temporary memory (RAM), all of the textual material will be lost if the computer is turned off, or if it loses power. In order to save the current version of textual material, the user must transfer it to an external storage device, such as a disk. Word processing systems contain specific instructions for saving processed material. Once saved on an external storage device, the textual material can be retrieved at any time for reprinting, updating, editing, or any further processing. Once material is stored to a disk, additional backup is recommended as insurance against a disk being damaged, lost, or simply wearing out. Therefore, it is extremely important to make at least one extra copy of every disk that is used.

Some printers will not be able to carry out all of the special word processing features offered by a sophisticated word processing package. Other printers may be able to carry out many of these options, but only at the expense of additional printer hardware (such as print wheels or font cartridges) which is typically purchased separately from the basic printer components. The user's manual provided by the software manufacturer generally identifies the types and models of printers which can support application features. The degree to which a particular printer supports the special printing features of a word processing package is an important consideration when selecting printers.

Many word processing systems are also able to carry out mathematical functions, proofread with spelling and grammar checkers, create useful business forms, and "personalize" mailings by merging names and textual material.

Electronic Spreadsheet Software

With a computerized accounting system, figures are entered only once into the accounting records. These entered amounts can then be accessed by programs which prepare mathematically correct journals, ledgers, and financial statements. This feature and others are made possible by electronic spreadsheet software.

An electronic spreadsheet program allows a user to input a model of the accountant's traditional worksheet in the temporary memory of the computer system and view it as output generated on a display screen. The electronic model is essentially a blank page of a worksheet which is divided into **rows** (usually numbered from top to bottom) and **columns** (usually lettered from left to right). The rows and columns intersect to form **cells.** The coordinates of a cell (the particular column letter and row number) identify what is typically called the **address** of a cell.

Cells can hold different types of data: alpha data, such as labels for the columns and rows; numeric data, such as dollar amounts; and formulas, which instruct the computer to carry out specific calculations, such as adding all numbers in a certain range of cells. The cells in which formulas are entered will display the results of the calculations. If any of the amounts entered in the range of cells changes, a formula is able to immediately recalculate the amounts and place the new total in the same designated cell.

Electronic spreadsheet software is not limited to bookkeeping functions; it is capable of performing many different kinds of tasks which may be extremely useful to managers in the hospitality industry. The recalculation feature of electronic spreadsheet programs offers managers opportunities to explore "what if" possibilities. For example, an electronic spreadsheet could be created to indicate the effects that different room occupancy levels may have on a hotel's food and beverage operation, telephone revenue, gift shop sales, and other revenue-producing centers. Information which could take hours to calculate manually takes only seconds when calculated electronically.

The speed with which electronic spreadsheet software can generate information is an important factor that increases a manager's ability to make decisions. A manager is less likely to request certain kinds of information or reports when he or she knows that valuable personnel will be tied up for hours. With electronic spreadsheet software, a manager has all kinds of information and reports at his or her fingertips—and in a matter of seconds.

Most electronic spreadsheet software packages have **graphics capability.** That is, the programs are able to generate graphs (bar charts, line graphs, pie charts, etc.) from data entered in worksheets. This can be a valuable management tool for communicating information. However, in order for users to view the graphic designs which they are able to create, their display screens must have graphics capability. This is an important consideration when selecting computer hardware. Printers may have limited graphics capability as well. Just because a particular bar chart appears as soft copy on a display screen does not mean that the printer can produce hard copy of the chart. When selecting hardware components for a computer system, users must take care that the components fully support the capabilities of the software applications which they plan to run on the system.

Since an electronic spreadsheet program creates a worksheet in the temporary memory (RAM) of the computer system, if a user turns off the computer or exits from the program without saving the worksheet, all the work that went into creating the worksheet will be completely lost. To make a permanent record of a worksheet, the user must save it on some type of external storage device such as a disk. Once a worksheet has been properly stored, it can be retrieved at any time and brought into the computer's temporary memory for updating and additional processing. Many programs permit users to save material to external storage devices while they are still in the process of creating their worksheets. Once material is stored to a disk, additional backup is recommended as insurance against a disk being damaged, lost, or simply wearing out. Therefore, it is extremely important to make at least one extra copy of every disk that is used.

Database Management Software

Database management software is a term for programs which allow users to catalog and store information about their businesses for future use. A **database** is a collection of related facts and figures designed to serve a specific purpose. The structure of the database provides a means of organizing related facts and figures and arranging them in ways that facilitate searching for data, updating data, and generating accurate, timely, and useful reports for management. Database management refers to the design and organization of databases as well as to the means by which data are handled within the computer system.

There is nothing mysterious about the function of a database management system. It is simply a computer program that permits the organization and storage of information in a central location. Since a database stores information like any other storage device, its overall function is similar to that of standard office filing systems.

Think of a database as a filing cabinet. The way information is organized within a filing cabinet will depend on the kind of information which is stored and the particular needs of the user. File cabinets have separate file drawers. Each file drawer contains separate file folders. The folders within each drawer contain similar records of related information. Each record within a folder contains specific facts and/or figures.

In the language of database management software, the file cabinet is the database, the drawers of the cabinet are called **files,** the folders within the drawers are called **records,** and the detailed facts and/or figures in the records are called **fields.**

For example, an inventory database might be set up for inventory control. Assume that this database is made up of a single file. The file would contain one record for each inventory item, and each record would contain a number of fields, such as the item's name, number, cost, quantity on hand, re-order point, and so on. Different users of the computer system can access this database to perform any number of desired functions, such as:

- Generating inventory checklists to assist managers and supervisors in taking physical inventory

- Performing variance analyses on the differences between actual quantities of items on hand and the quantities projected (perpetual inventory) by the computer system

- Calculating the total value of items in inventory

The value of a database management system can be enormous. Not only does a database management system save storage space, but, more important, it limits the number of times that data must be handled and ensures that all applications using the database are working with the same information.

Currently, there are databases for all types of users. Many database packages involve a complex set of commands used to define fields and establish records, but an experienced (or patient) user can learn to efficiently organize large amounts of information.

Applications Software and User Concerns

After identifying the type of applications software that will meet the specific information needs of the hospitality operation, managers must research available software packages and eventually make a purchase decision. There are some general criteria which may guide managers in making purchase decisions. These criteria focus on fundamental user concerns. The following sections describe three basic concerns that users generally have in operating any type of applications software:

- User friendliness

- Integration of the software system

- Completeness and usefulness of program output

User-Friendly Software

Some applications software packages are easier for new users to operate than others. Soft-

ware that is **menu-driven** or designed with **interactive programs** is generally more user-friendly than packages without these features.

In order to operate many of the more sophisticated software packages, users must be familiar with dozens of keystrokes which are required to carry out specific operations. Menu-driven software packages provide on-screen information explaining which keystrokes are required to carry out commonly used program commands. Users are generally able to access this on-screen information at any time while operating within the software program.

Many software packages provide users with a keyboard **template** which identifies common keystrokes. This template is usually placed directly on the keyboard and guides users as they operate the computer system.

Some user-friendly software packages provide interactive programs, which help users carry out specific operations by prompting them to respond to a predetermined sequence of inquiries. After the user responds to one prompt, the next inquiry in the series is presented. Interactive software is very popular among hospitality operations because it is easy to use and helps ensure that all required information is collected and entered into the computer system. When front desk employees are required by the computer system to answer a series of prompts regarding guests at the time of check-in, the property is able to generate complete and useful guest history information. Interactive systems are usually able to generate reports at any time during computer operation. This provides an effective means of ensuring that data is processed and timely information is made available to decision-makers.

Batch programs are non-interactive computer operations. These programs do not provide the user with prompts or on-screen instructions on how to input data or keystroke commands. These programs assume the user is already well-informed about input procedures. Batch program execution is generally faster than interactive software because there is no time spent prompting the user in how to input data or carry out various operations. However, batch programs may often prevent on-line editing and may not have the ability to generate reports in as timely a fashion as interactive programs.

Integrated Software

Integrated software allows several programs to use the same database. For example, data about the menu sales mix is essential to calculating both food service revenues and standard food costs. An electronic cash register (ECR) which has the ability to calculate and store menu counts can capture this data at the time of a sale. Since menu item prices are also normally stored in an ECR, a revenue report can be generated without any further data entry by the user. Similarly, an ECR with a recipe costing module can use the identical menu sales mix data to produce standard food cost reports.

If the restaurant does not have such a system, menu sales mix data must be collected from an analysis of guest checks and then entered into an adding machine, or non-integrated computer program, to produce revenue information. Similarly, in order to calculate standard or ideal food costs without an ECR with the capabilities described previously, the standard recipe cost for each menu item must first be determined and then menu sales mix data entered for a second time into the adding machine or non-integrated computer program.

The advantages of integrated software over non-integrated software include speed and data integrity. Since pieces of data are handled only once, it is possible to update data for all applications at the same time.

Program Output

Screen and report formats are important concerns to the users of an application program. While the issues of interactive versus non-interactive and integrated versus non-integrated software are important, the true value of a program lies in the completeness and usefulness of its output. Screen displays must allow for easy reading and eye comfort. Cluttered, jumbled, or unclear screens are more difficult to use than those with good spacing and legible information. In addition, display screens with color capabilities are often very helpful to inexperienced users whose eyes can readily follow the color differences.

Systems Software

Hardware refers to the equipment within a computer system. Software refers to the instructions that direct the operations of the hardware. How do the hardware and software work together? How are priorities established within the system? Answers to these and related questions are explained by the functions performed by **systems software.**

The primary purpose of systems software is to control the interactions between hardware components of a computer system and software application programs. Although applications software instructs the computer how to manipulate data to yield desired results, each set of these programs depends on systems software for its instructions to be carried out correctly.

The read only memory (ROM) of the central processing unit stores a permanent control program installed by the computer manufacturer which enables the computer to read commands and instructions that program fundamental operations of the computer system. This control program is part of systems software; it instructs the computer how to interpret information received through a keyboard and other input devices, and how to output information to a display screen and other output devices.

Other portions of systems software, typically installed by the computer manufacturer, consist of programs which assist in the start-up process of the computer. The computer manufacturer may also provide diagnostic routines which are programs used to test the correct functioning of various hardware components. Some diagnostic routines are initiated by the user and are explained in the user's manual provided by the computer manufacturer. These routines should be carried out whenever a faulty hardware component is suspected.

The Operating System

Another portion of systems software is called the **operating system.** Like other types of systems software, the operating system controls interactions between hardware components of a computer system and applications software programs. An operating system is necessary for a computer system to be able to carry out instructions generated by applications software programs. The operating system manages routine computer functions while maintaining system priorities.

A computer system must have a control mechanism if it is to run applications software programs without constant intervention from the user. For example, when a user instructs a computer to save a program or data to an external storage device, something must happen within the computer system so that the entered command successfully initiates the proper sequence of operations for storing the program or data. The management of such routine functions is handled by the computer's operating system.

In simplest terms, the operating system is the program that controls the execution of other programs. Think of the operating system as the traffic controller of a busy metropolis, directing the flow of traffic by controlling the signals at every street corner. Like the traffic controller, the operating system is at the center of computer activity, directing the flow of data and instructions from applications software programs to the various hardware components of the computer system.

Disk Operating System (DOS)

There are a variety of operating systems for different types and brands of computers, and there are different types of operating systems which can run on the same type of computer. Most of the operating systems for microcomputers can be purchased at retail computer outlets. These operating systems are called **disk operating systems** and contain systems software programs.

Some of these systems software programs operate without user intervention. For example, DOS monitors application programs during their execution, making sure that any operation that is attempted is possible. If the computer system is attempting to print, DOS checks to see that there is a printer on-line with the system. If there is not, DOS signals the user that a problem exists.

Other systems software programs within DOS can be easily commanded by the user to prepare, manipulate, or locate information stored on disks. The user simply inputs the appropriate DOS command, and DOS tells the computer what to do, step by step. Some of the most useful DOS commands include operations such as the following:

- Formatting new disks
- Finding out what files are stored on a particular disk
- Copying files from one disk to another, or copying the entire contents of a disk to another disk
- Comparing the contents of files or entire disks to verify that they are identical
- Erasing files

The user manuals produced by the manufacturers of operating system software give detailed instructions on how to carry out these commands. Users must enter the commands *exactly* as their manuals instruct. Key substitutions that may work on typewriters (such as typing the numerals 1 and 0 by using the lower case "L" or the upper case "o" letter keys) will not be processed to produce the desired results.

Information Backup Procedures

Backup procedures should not be left to emergency situations. Information backup should be a standard operating procedure to ensure that data is not lost at any time. Four ways to back up information are:

- Redundant copy
- Duplicate copy
- Hard copy
- Fault-tolerant processing

While many computer manufacturers advocate using more than just a single backup procedure, management must ensure that at least one procedure is used regularly. The following sections describe each of these information backup procedures.

Redundant Copy

Redundant copy may not be a very popular backup technique in the hospitality industry because it requires two storage devices working simultaneously. Exhibit 7 illustrates that as transactions occur, they are saved to two external storage devices. Assuming that a food service system employs a disk drive as a base for one external storage device, a second disk drive is required. As data is input, it is sent to both drives for storage on their respective disks. This can be an expensive hardware configuration and requires more attention than other backup methods. It is analogous to recording a theatrical performance on two tape recorders simultaneously. Many people feel it is more efficient to concentrate on producing one superior recording and duplicating it at a later time. Two recordings are still obtained, but through duplication, not redundancy.

Duplicate Copy

Duplicate copy is the most popular and efficient means to accomplish information backup. This backup strategy is illustrated in Exhibit 8. The computer system writes to only one storage device, so a second disk drive is not needed. A copy of the data on the single drive can be made later. It can be duplicated on the same device with a blank disk or can be placed on magnetic tape. Because magnetic tape is comparatively inexpensive, but not as efficient as a workable storage device (due to its sequential access characteristics), some operators use it as duplicate copy. At the end of the day, the disk is duplicated onto magnetic tape for backup purposes. Since the backup tape is stored and used only in case of a disk error or failure, its sequential access method does not severely reduce the operation's ability to maintain efficient computer operations.

Hard Copy

Exhibit 9 illustrates the hard copy backup strategy. Hard copy (printouts from disk files) should only be used as a backup technique in conjunction with redundant or duplicate copy procedures. The user who relies solely on hard copy information backup will encounter an avalanche of work should data files need to be reconstructed. In this case, all information stored on hard copy must be manually re-entered to recreate the system's database. When used to supplement one of the other two approaches,

Exhibit 7 Redundant Copy

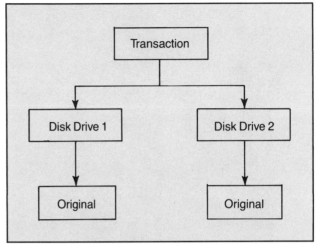

Exhibit 8 Duplicate Copy

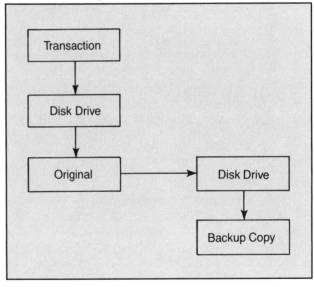

hard copy backup provides a means for troubleshooting any missing or incorrect transactional recordings. Should a mishap occur that affects only a small section of a disk, that area of the disk can be compared with the most current hard copy to recover any information that may have been lost.

Fault-Tolerant Processing

A more recently adopted on-line verification procedure is termed fault-tolerant processing. A fault-tolerant procedure is capable of adjusting

Exhibit 9   Hard Copy

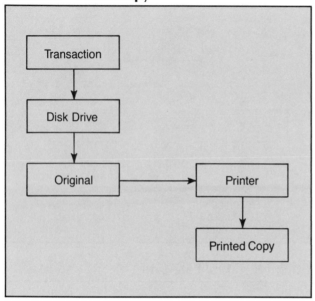

(or at least continuing) operations after one or more of its components has stopped functioning. In essence, the system disregards the device which, for whatever reason, becomes out of synchronization. In comparison to a redundant system, which requires the user to purchase two disk drives that operate simultaneously, fault-tolerant designs employ a variety of devices in unique on-line configurations.

One approach to fault-tolerant processing is termed **switched backup.** In a switched backup design, there are two central processors; one is used for processing data while the second is activated upon the failure of the first. Obviously, in this case, one processor sits idle until a failure occurs. It is for this reason that switched backup is usually perceived as an inefficient backup procedure.

Triple modular redundancy is an alternative approach that involves triplicate hardware components. For most hospitality operations, this fault-tolerant processing design is not cost justifiable.

Perhaps the best current fault-tolerant approach for the hospitality industry is **comparison logic,** which is illustrated in Exhibit 10. In a comparison logic design, there are two paired processors actively working at all times. Data processed by the first pair of processors (A and B) are compared with the data processed by the second pair of processors (C and D). If data processed by the first pair of processors match the output from the second pair, processed data go forward as information output. A failure of any one of the paired processing units presents no problem to the system, since its work is a duplicate of the other three.

Human Factors

Although it is the last concept presented in this appendix, human factors are perhaps the most critical in ensuring successful computer use. None of the advantages afforded by computers materialize unless the people using the system are properly trained. In addition to training, there should be current, accurate system documentation. In effect, the overall performance of the entire computer system hinges on the human engineering aspect of computer use.

Training is an ongoing process which prepares both new and present employees to use the system. Whether during conversion to a new computer system or during new employee orientation, hands-on training is the most successful teaching method. There is no better way to become familiar with computer operations than through experience using the system. Training, however, does not have to take place at the hospitality establishment where it may impede daily operations. Many computer vendors have test sites available where employees can be trained to operate computers. However, they should be avoided when vendor trainers use different equipment from that purchased by the hospitality operation. Training personnel on different equipment from that used in their actual positions could cause them to become confused, disoriented, and less confident in their abilities to use the on-site system.

Documentation is a complete record of the software the operation will use. It is an important part of the human factor of computing because it facilitates the training process, explains the operation of the computer, and details the procedures required by applications software. Good documentation provides flow charts of how the programs work and interact with each other. If the documentation includes an accurate listing of the program code, the software may be

Exhibit 10 Fault-Tolerant Processing—Comparison Logic

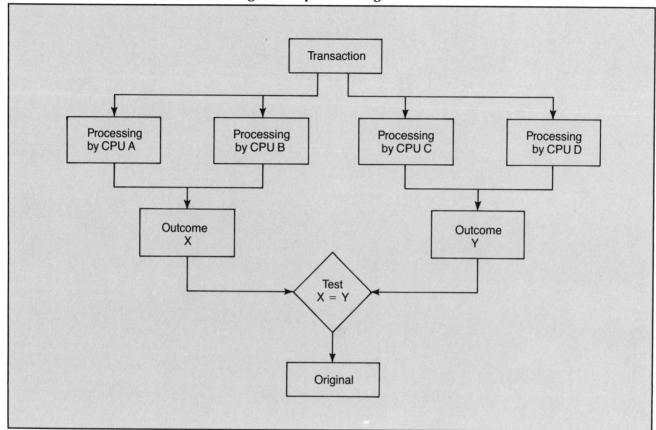

customized to better fit the operation's needs, and future modifications may be made more easily. In addition, the documentation should include complete operation instructions to ensure not only that the programs are used correctly, but also that infrequently used options are not forgotten over time. Finally, the documentation should include users' manuals which highlight all of the features of a specific applications software program, including input specifications, processing routines, and output format options. These manuals are available from software vendors when requested.

One strategy for converting to a computerized system is to transfer all applications to the computer simultaneously—to go "cold turkey." However, the most successful approach to implementing a new system appears to be through **parallel conversion.** In parallel conversion, functions are transferred to the computer system on an application-by-application basis. As new ap-

plications software is purchased for the system and as employees are trained in its use, more and more operational functions can be computerized. For example, a hotel might convert the accounting functions first. Later, the front desk could be computerized, and finally the food and beverage operations. This allows each department to train its employees, test the software, and verify results independently. Parallel conversions should provide a comfort level for everyone involved.

Finally, perhaps the most important human factor in computerization concerns the ways in which computerized data processing and computer-generated reports are used by managers in their decision-making processes. Remember that the computer is a managerial tool. It cannot do everything. It can only take user-specified input and generate output according to the dictates of its programmed procedures.

Glossary

A

ACCOUNT

A form in which financial data are accumulated and summarized.

ACCOUNT AGING

A method for tracking past due accounts according to the date the charges originated.

ACCOUNT ALLOWANCE

Either a decrease in a folio balance as compensation for unsatisfactory service or as a rebate for a coupon discount; or a correction of a posting error detected after the close of business.

ACCOUNT BALANCE

A summary of an account in terms of its resulting monetary amount; specifically, the difference between the total debits and the total credits to an account.

ACCOUNT POSTING MACHINE

An electro-mechanical or electronic device used in semi-automated hotels. An account posting machine is used to post, monitor, and balance charges and credits to front office accounts.

ACCOUNT RECEIVABLE

An amount owed to the hotel.

ACCOUNT RECEIVABLE VOUCHER

See **Charge Purchase Voucher.**

ACCOUNTS PAYABLE MODULE

A back office computer application which tracks the hotel's purchases and helps the hotel maintain sufficient cash flow to satisfy its debts.

ACCOUNTS RECEIVABLE LEDGER

A grouping of accounts receivable, including the guest ledger and the city ledger.

ACCOUNTS RECEIVABLE MODULE

A back office computer application which monitors guest accounts and account billing and collection when integrated with the front office guest accounting module.

ADJACENT ROOMS

Rooms close to each other, perhaps across the hall.

ADJOINING ROOMS

Rooms with a common wall but no connecting door.

ADVANCE DEPOSIT GUARANTEE

A type of reservation guarantee which requires the guest to furnish a specified amount of money in advance of arrival.

ADVANCE RESERVATION RACK

See **Reservation Racks.**

AFFILIATE RESERVATION NETWORK

A hotel chain's reservation system in which all participating properties are contractually related.

AIRPORT HOTEL

A hotel located near a public airport. Airport hotels vary widely in size and service level.

ALLOWANCE VOUCHER

A voucher used to support an account allowance.

AMERICAN PLAN (AP or FAP)

A billing arrangement under which room charges include the guestroom and three meals. Also called the full

American plan. See also **Modified American Plan, European Plan.**

ARRIVAL DATE

The date a guest plans to register at the hotel.

AUDITING

The process of verifying front office accounting records for accuracy and completeness.

AUDIT TRAIL

An organized flow of source documents detailing each step in the processing of a transaction.

AUDIT WORK TIME

The period from the end of day until the completion of the audit.

AUTHORIZATION CODE

A code generated by an on-line credit card verification service, indicating that the requested transaction has been approved.

AVAILABILITY REPORT

A report which contains expected arrival and departure information for the next several days, typically prepared as part of the night audit.

AVERAGE DAILY RATE

An occupancy ratio derived by dividing net rooms revenue by the number of rooms sold.

AVERAGE RATE PER GUEST

An occupancy ratio derived by dividing net rooms revenue by the number of guests.

B

BACK OFFICE APPLICATIONS

Computer software designed for specific back office uses. Typical back office applications include accounts receivable, accounts payable, payroll accounting, and financial reporting modules.

BACK OF THE HOUSE

The functional areas of a hotel in which personnel have little or no direct guest contact, such as engineering, accounting, and personnel.

BANK

See **Cash Bank.**

BED AND BREAKFAST (B&B)

A small lodging operation whose owner usually lives on the premises and serves a breakfast for guests.

BLOCK

An agreed-upon number of rooms set aside for members of a group planning to stay at a hotel.

BOOK

To sell or reserve rooms ahead of time.

C

CALL ACCOUNTING SYSTEM

A device linked to the hotel telephone system which accurately accounts for guest telephone calls by identifying each phone number dialed from guestroom telephones and tracking charges.

CANCELLATION

A reservation voided at the request of the guest.

CANCELLATION HOUR

The hour after which a property may release for sale all unclaimed non-guaranteed reservations, according to property policy.

CANCELLATION NUMBER

A number issued to a guest properly canceling a reservation, proving that a cancellation was received.

CASH ADVANCE VOUCHER

A voucher used to support cash flow out of the hotel, either directly to or on behalf of a guest.

CASH BANK

An amount of money given to a cashier at the start of each workshift so that he or she can handle the various transactions that occur. The cashier becomes responsible for this cash bank and for all cash, checks, and other negotiable instruments received during the workshift.

CASH VOUCHER

A voucher used to support a cash payment transaction at the front desk.

CASINO HOTEL

A hotel with gambling facilities.

CENTRAL PROCESSING UNIT (CPU)

The control center of a computer system.

CENTRALIZED ELECTRONIC LOCKING SYSTEM

An electronic locking system which operates through a master control console at the front desk which is wired to every guestroom door.

CENTRAL RESERVATION SYSTEM

A network for communicating reservations in which each property is represented in a computer system database and is required to provide room availability data to the reservations center on a timely basis. See also **Affiliate Reservation Network, Non-affiliate Reservation Network,** and **Intersell Agency.**

CHARGE VOUCHER

A voucher used to support a charge purchase transaction which takes place somewhere other than the front desk. Also referred to as an account receivable voucher.

CHECK-OUT

The procedures involved in the departure of a guest from a property, including settlement of the guest's account. Also, a room status term indicating that the guest has settled his or her account, returned the room keys, and left the hotel.

CHECK-OUT TIME

The hour by which departing guests must check out of a property.

CITY ACCOUNT

See **Non-guest Account.**

CITY LEDGER

The collection of all non-guest accounts, including house accounts and unsettled departed guest accounts.

CLOSED

The status of a date for which a reservation system will not accept additional reservations.

COMMERCIAL HOTEL

A property, usually located in a downtown or business district, that caters primarily to business clients. Also called a transient hotel.

COMMERCIAL RATE

A special room rate agreed upon by a company and a hotel for frequent guests. Also called a corporate rate.

COMMISSION AGENT REPORT

A summary of reservation transactions for which commissions are owed to travel agents.

COMPLIMENTARY (COMP)

A room status term indicating that the room is occupied, but the guest is assessed no charge for its use.

COMPRESSED WORK SCHEDULE

A method of working full-time hours in fewer than the traditional five days—for instance, four 10-hour days.

CONCIERGE

An employee whose basic task is to serve as the guest's liaison with both hotel and non-hotel attractions, facilities, services, and activities.

CONDOMINIUM HOTEL

See **Time-share Hotel.**

CONFERENCE CENTER

A property specifically designed to handle group meetings. Conference centers are often located outside metropolitan areas and may provide extensive leisure facilities; most offer overnight accommodations.

CONFIRMATION

See **Reservation Confirmation.**

CONNECTING ROOMS

Rooms with individual entrance doors from the outside and a connecting door between. Guests can move between rooms without going through the hallway.

CONTINENTAL BREAKFAST

A small meal which usually includes a beverage, rolls, butter, and jam or marmalade.

CONTROL FOLIO

An accounting document used internally by a front office computer to support all account postings by department during a system update routine.

CORPORATE GUARANTEE

A type of reservation guarantee in which a corporation signs a contractual agreement with the hotel to accept financial responsibility for any no-show business travelers it sponsors.

CORPORATE RATE

See **Commercial Rate.**

CORRECTION VOUCHER

A voucher used to support the correction of a posting error which is rectified before the close of business on the day it was made.

CREDIT (CR)

An entry on the right side of an account.

CREDIT CARD GUARANTEE

A type of reservation guarantee supported by credit card companies, who guarantee participating properties payment for reserved rooms that remain unoccupied.

CREDIT CARD IMPRINTER

A device used to press a credit card invoice against a credit card, recording card information for use in billing and collection procedures.

CREDIT CARD INVOICE

The form designated by a credit card company to be used for imprinting a credit card and recording the amount charged. Also called a credit card voucher.

CRT (CATHODE RAY TUBE)

See **Display Screen.**

CURRENT RESERVATION RACK

See **Reservation Racks.**

CUT-OFF DATE

The date agreed upon between a group and a property after which all unreserved rooms in the group's block will be released.

D

DAILY OPERATIONS REPORT

A report, typically prepared by the night auditor, which summarizes the hotel's financial activities during a 24-hour period and provides insight into revenues, receivables, operating statistics, and cash transactions related to the front office. Also known as the manager's report.

DAILY TRANSCRIPT

A detailed report of all guest accounts that indicates each charge transaction that affected a guest account that day, used as a worksheet to detect posting errors.

DATABASE

A computerized collection of related facts and figures designed to serve a specific purpose.

DATA PROCESSING

The transformation of raw data into timely, accurate, and useful information.

DAY RATE

A special room rate for less than an overnight stay.

DAY SHIFT

A hotel workshift, generally 7:00 a.m. to 3:00 p.m.

DAY USE

A room status term indicating that the room will be used for less than an overnight stay.

D CARD

An auditor's report used in semi-automated front office accounting systems.

DEBIT (DR)

An entry on the left side of an account.

DENIAL CODE

A code generated by an on-line credit card verification service, indicating that the requested transaction has not been approved.

DIRECT BILLING

A credit arrangement, normally established through correspondence between a guest or a company and the hotel, in which the hotel agrees to bill the guest or the company for charges incurred.

DISK DRIVE

A piece of computer hardware which writes data to and reads data from a floppy disk or a hard disk.

DISPLAY SCREEN

An output device of a computer system which is usually capable of displaying both text and graphics. Also called a monitor, a CRT, or simply a screen.

DNCO (DID NOT CHECK OUT)

A room status term indicating that the guest made arrangements to settle his or her account (and thus is not a skipper), but has left without informing the front office.

DOUBLE

A room assigned to two people; may have one or more beds.

DOUBLE BED

A bed approximately 54 inches by 75 inches.

DOUBLE-DOUBLE

A room with two double (or perhaps queen) beds; may be occupied by one or more people. Also called a twin-double.

DOUBLE-ENTRY BOOKKEEPING

A system for recording financial transactions in which every transaction creates entries that affect at least two accounts.

DOUBLE OCCUPANCY RATIOS

See **Multiple Occupancy Statistics.**

DUE BACK

A situation that occurs when a cashier pays out more than he or she receives; the difference is due back to the cashier's cash bank. In the front office, due backs usually occur when a cashier accepts many checks and large bills during a shift, such that he or she cannot restore the initial bank at the end of the shift without using the checks or large bills.

DUE OUT

A room status term indicating that the room is expected to become vacant after the following day's check-out time.

E

EARLY ARRIVAL

A guest who arrives at a property before the date of his or her reservation.

ECONOMY/LIMITED SERVICE

A level of service emphasizing clean, comfortable, inexpensive rooms and meeting the most basic needs of guests. Economy hotels appeal primarily to budget-minded travelers.

ELECTRONIC LOCKING SYSTEM

A locking system which replaces traditional mechanical locks with sophisticated computer-based guestroom access devices. See also **Centralized Electronic Locking System** and **Micro-fitted Electronic Locking System.**

EMERGENCY KEY

A key which opens all guestroom doors, even when they are double-locked.

EMPLOYEE FOLIO

A folio used to chart transactions on an account assigned to an employee with charge purchase privileges.

END OF DAY

An arbitrary stopping point for the business day, established so that the audit can be considered complete through that time.

EUROPEAN PLAN

A billing arrangement under which meals are priced separately from rooms. See also **American Plan, Modified American Plan.**

EVENING SHIFT

A hotel workshift, generally 3:00 p.m. to 11:00 p.m.

EXECUTIVE FLOOR

A floor of a hotel which offers world-class service. Also called the tower concept.

EXPECTED ARRIVALS LIST

A daily report showing the number and names of guests expected to arrive.

EXPECTED DEPARTURES LIST

A daily report showing the number and names of guests expected to depart as well as the number of stayovers.

EXPRESS CHECK-OUT

A pre-departure activity which involves the production and early morning distribution of guest folios for guests expected to check out that morning.

EXTERNAL STORAGE DEVICE

A piece of computer hardware that retains data and/or programs that can be accessed by the central processing unit. See also **Floppy Disk, Hard Disk,** and **Magnetic Tape.**

F

FAMILY RATE

A special room rate for parents and children in the same room.

FAP

See **American Plan.**

FAX (FACSIMILE) MACHINE

A copier-like machine which transmits full-page documents over telephone lines.

FINANCIAL REPORTING MODULE

A back office computer application which helps the hotel develop a chart of accounts in order to produce balance sheets, income statements, and transactional analysis reports.

FIT (FREE INDEPENDENT TRAVELER)

A guest coming to the hotel as an individual and not part of a group.

FLEXTIME

A program of flexible work hours which allows employees to vary their times of starting and ending work.

FLOOR LIMIT

A limit assigned to hotels by credit card companies indicating the maximum amount in credit card charges the hotel is permitted to accept from a card member without special authorization.

FLOPPY DISK

An external storage medium for a computer. Also called a diskette.

FOLIO

A statement of all transactions affecting the balance of a single account.

FOLIO TRAY

A bin used to store guest folios. In non-automated and semi-automated properties, folios remain in the tray throughout occupancy, except when they are used in posting transactions. Also called a folio bucket.

FRANCHISING

A method of distribution whereby one entity that has developed a particular pattern or format for doing business—the *franchisor*—grants to other entities—*franchisees*—the right to conduct such a business provided they follow the established pattern.

FRONT DESK

The focal point of activity within the front office, usually prominently located in the hotel lobby. Guests are registered, assigned rooms, and checked out at the front desk.

FRONT DESK AGENT

A front office employee whose responsibilities center on the registration process, but also typically include pre-registration activities, room status coordination, and mail, message, and information requests.

FRONT OFFICE

A department of the rooms division which is the most visible department in a hotel, with the greatest amount of guest contact. Traditional front office functions include reservations, registration, room and rate assignment, room status, maintenance and settlement of guest accounts, and creation of guest history records. Also, the physical location at which front-of-the-house activities are coordinated.

FRONT OFFICE ACCOUNTING FORMULA

The formula used in posting transactions to front office accounts: Previous Balance + Debits − Credits = Net Outstanding Balance.

FRONT OFFICE APPLICATIONS

Computer software designed for specific front office uses. Typical front office applications include reservations, rooms management, guest accounting, and general management modules.

FRONT OFFICE AUDIT

See **Night Audit.**

FRONT OFFICE CASHIER

A front office employee whose responsibilities center on the guest accounting cycle.

FRONT OFFICE CASH SHEET

A form completed by front office cashiers which lists each receipt or disbursement of cash during a workshift. It is used to reconcile actual cash on hand with the transactions which occurred during the shift.

FRONT OFFICE LEDGER

See **Guest Ledger.**

FRONT OF THE HOUSE

The functional areas of the hotel in which employees have extensive guest contact, such as food and beverage facilities and the front office.

FULLY AUTOMATED

A computer-based system of front office recordkeeping which eliminates the need for many handwritten and machine-produced forms common in non- and semi-automated systems.

G

GENERAL MANAGEMENT MODULE

A front office computer application, usually a report-generating package which depends on data collected through reservations, rooms management, and guest accounting modules.

GOAL

A definition of the purpose of a department or division, which directs the actions of employees and the functions of the department or division toward the hotel's mission.

GOVERNMENT RATE

A special room rate available at some hotels for government employees.

GROUP RATE

A special room rate for a number of affiliated guests.

GUARANTEED RESERVATION

A reservation which assures the guest that a room will be held until check-out time of the day following the day of arrival. The guest guarantees payment for the room, even if it is not used, unless the reservation is properly canceled. Types of guaranteed reservations include prepayment, credit card, advance deposit, travel agent, and corporate.

GUEST ACCOUNT

A record of financial transactions which occur between a guest and the hotel.

GUEST ACCOUNTING MODULE

A front office computer application which maintains guest accounts electronically, eliminating the need for folio cards, folio trays, and posting machines.

GUEST CYCLE

A division of the flow of business through a hotel which identifies the physical contacts and financial exchanges between guests and hotel employees.

GUEST FOLIO

A folio used to chart transactions on an account assigned to an individual person or guestroom.

GUEST HISTORY FILE

A collection of guest history records, constructed from expired registration cards or created through sophisticated computer-based systems which automatically direct information about departing guests into a guest history database.

GUEST HISTORY RECORD

A record of personal and financial information about hotel guests which is relevant to marketing, sales, and servicing the guest's return. State law may require retention of certain guest data for some period of time.

GUEST LEDGER

The set of accounts for all guests currently registered in the hotel. Also called the front office ledger, transient ledger, or rooms ledger.

GUEST LEDGER REPORT

A report which carries the current account balances of all registered guests, typically prepared as part of the night audit.

GUESTROOM KEY

A key which opens a single guestroom door if it is not double-locked.

GUEST SERVICE REPRESENTATIVE

See **Front Desk Agent.**

H

HANDICAP ROOM

A room with special features designed for handicapped guests.

HARD COPY

A printed paper copy of information, as opposed to information on a display screen. Also, the last page in a set of folio copies which is the hotel's copy of the folio.

HARD DISK

An external storage medium that is much faster to use and can store much more information than a floppy disk. It is permanently on line to the computer system.

HARDWARE

The physical equipment of a computer system. Computer hardware is visible, movable, and easy to identify.

HIGH BALANCE ACCOUNT

A front office account which is at or approaching its credit limit. Also called a high risk account.

HIGH BALANCE REPORT

A report which identifies guests who are approaching an account credit limit, typically prepared by the night auditor.

HORIZON

The future time frame for which a property accepts reservations.

HOUSE ACCOUNT

See **Non-guest Account.**

HOUSEKEEPING

The department within the rooms division which inspects rooms for sale, cleans occupied and vacated rooms, and coordinates room status with the front office. In some hotels, the housekeeping function is considered an independent hotel division.

HOUSEKEEPING STATUS

See **Room Status.**

HOUSEKEEPING STATUS REPORT

A report prepared by the housekeeping department which indicates the current housekeeping status of each room, based on a physical check.

HOUSE LIMIT

A credit limit established by the hotel.

HOUSE USE

A room status term indicating that the room is being used by someone on the hotel staff at no charge.

HOUSING/CONVENTION BUREAU

A reservations office which coordinates room requirements at several hotels for large conventions.

I

IDEAL AVERAGE RATE

A rooms statistic which indicates the point at which rooms are sold at the best rate for the type of guests accommodated by a property.

IN BALANCE

A term used to describe the state when the totals of debit amounts and credit amounts for a set of accounts are equal.

INCENTIVE RATE

A special room rate for guests in affiliated travel and tourism organizations because of the potential referral business they can generate for the hotel.

INCENTIVE TRAVEL

Travel financed by a business as an employee incentive.

INCOME STATEMENT

See **Statement of Income.**

INDEPENDENT HOTEL

A hotel with no ownership or management affiliation with other properties.

INFORMATION BOOK

A collection of information kept at the front desk for front desk agents to use in responding to guest requests, including simplified maps of the area, taxi and airline company telephone numbers, bank, theater, church, and store locations, and special event schedules.

INFORMATION RACK

An alphabetical index of registered guests, used in routing telephone calls, mail, messages, and visitor inquiries. The information rack normally consists of aluminum slots designed to hold information rack slips.

INFORMATION RACK SLIP

A slip containing a guest's name, room number, room rate, and departure date.

INPUT/OUTPUT UNIT

A piece of computer hardware which allows a user to interact with the computer system. Input/output units include keyboards, display screens, and printers.

IN-ROOM BEVERAGE SERVICE SYSTEM

A system which dispenses beverages within a guestroom, monitors sales transactions, and determines inventory replenishment quantities. Two popular systems are non-automated honor bars and microprocessor-based vending machines.

IN-ROOM FOLIO REVIEW AND CHECK-OUT

A system which allows guests to use in-room computers to access guest folio data and approve and settle their accounts.

IN-ROOM MOVIE SYSTEM

A system which provides guestroom entertainment through a dedicated television pay channel. Automatic posting of charges to the appropriate guest folio may be possible.

INTEGRATED SOFTWARE

Software which allows several programs to use the same database.

INTERFACE APPLICATIONS

Stand-alone computer software packages which may be linked to a front office management system, including point-of-sale systems, call accounting systems, and electronic locking systems.

INTERNAL CONTROL

The policies, procedures, and equipment used in a business to safeguard its assets and promote operational efficiency.

INTERSELL AGENCY

A central reservation system that handles reservations for more than one product line, such as airline companies, car rental companies, and hotel properties.

INTERVIEW EVALUATION FORM

A form used by the front office manager to evaluate an applicant's strengths and weaknesses.

J

JOB BREAKDOWN

A specification of how each task on a job list should be performed.

JOB DESCRIPTION

A listing of all the tasks and related information which make up a work position. A job description may also outline reporting relationships, responsibilities, working conditions, equipment and material to be used, and other important information specific to the requirements of the property.

JOB LIST

A list of tasks that must be performed for a front office position.

JOB SHARING

An arrangement by which two or more part-time employees share the responsibilities of one full-time position.

JOB SPECIFICATION

A list of the personal qualities, skills, and traits needed to successfully perform the tasks outlined by a job description.

JOURNAL FORM

An account recording format in which each entry includes a description of the affected account, the charge or payment entry, and the resulting account balance. Journal form is typically used for front office accounting documents.

JUNIOR SUITE

See **Mini-suite.**

K

KEY RACK

An array of numbered compartments used to maintain guestroom keys.

KING

A room with a king-size bed; may be occupied by one or more people.

KING BED

A bed approximately 78 inches by 80 inches.

L

LATE ARRIVAL

A guest with a reservation who expects to arrive after the hotel's designated cancellation hour and so notifies the hotel.

LATE CHARGE

A transaction requiring posting to a guest account that does not reach the front office until the guest has checked out and left the hotel.

LATE CHECK-OUT

A room status term indicating that the guest is being allowed to check out later than the hotel's standard check-out time.

LATE CHECK-OUT FEE

A charge imposed by some hotels on guests who do not check out by the established check-out time.

LEAST-COST ROUTING

A feature of an active call accounting system that directs calls over the least costly available line, regardless of carrier.

LEDGER

A grouping of accounts.

LETTER OF CONFIRMATION

A letter sent to a guest to verify that a reservation has been made and that its specifications are accurate.

LIMITED SERVICE

See **Economy/Limited Service.**

LOCK-OUT

A room status term indicating that the room has been locked so that the guest cannot re-enter until he or she is cleared by a hotel official.

LOG BOOK

A journal in which important front office events and decisions are recorded for reference during subsequent shifts.

M

MAGNETIC STRIP READER

A device which reads data magnetically encoded and stored on the magnetic tape strip on the back of a credit card and transmits these data to a credit card verification service.

MAGNETIC TAPE

An external storage medium for a computer which is used much like a standard cassette tape.

MAIL AND INFORMATION CLERK

A once-common front office position, responsible for distributing mail and messages to guests and answering requests for information.

MAIL, MESSAGE, AND KEY RACK

An array of numbered compartments used to maintain guestroom keys and to store messages and mail being held for guests.

MANAGEMENT CONTRACT

An agreement between the owner/developer of a property and a professional hotel management company. The owner/developer usually retains the financial and legal responsibility for the property, and the management company receives an agreed-upon fee for operating the hotel.

MAP

See **Modified American Plan.**

MASTER FOLIO

A folio used to chart transactions on an account assigned to more than one person or guestroom, usually reserved for group accounts. A master folio collects charges not appropriately posted elsewhere.

MASTER KEY

A key which opens all guestroom doors which are not double-locked.

MICROCOMPUTER

The smallest type of computer available, which meets the data processing needs of many hospitality businesses. Also called a personal computer.

MICRO-FITTED ELECTRONIC LOCKING SYSTEM

An electronic locking system which operates as individual units. Each door has its own microprocessor which contains a predetermined sequence of codes; a master console at the front desk stores code sequences for each door.

MID-RANGE SERVICE

A modest but sufficient level of service which appeals to the largest segment of the traveling public. A mid-range property may offer uniformed service, airport limousine service, and food and beverage room service; a specialty restaurant, coffee shop, and lounge; and special rates for certain guests.

MINI-SUITE

A single room with a bed and a sitting area. The sleeping area may be in a bedroom separate from the parlor or living room. Also called a junior suite.

MISSION

The unique purpose that sets a hotel apart from other hotels. A mission expresses the underlying philosophy that gives meaning and direction to the hotel's actions, and addresses the interests of guests, management, and employees.

MODIFIED AMERICAN PLAN (MAP)

A billing arrangement under which the daily rate includes charges for the guestroom and two meals—typically breakfast and dinner. See also **American Plan, European Plan.**

MOTEL

A lodging facility that caters primarily to guests arriving by automobile.

MULTIPLE OCCUPANCY STATISTICS

Occupancy ratios, indicating either a multiple occupancy percentage or the average number of guests per room sold, used to forecast food and beverage ratios, indicate clean linen requirements, and analyze average daily room rates.

N

NET CASH RECEIPTS

The amount of cash and checks in the cashier's drawer, minus the amount of the initial cash bank.

NIGHT AUDIT

A daily review of guest accounts (and non-guest accounts having activity) against revenue center transaction information which helps guarantee accuracy in front office accounting.

NIGHT AUDITOR

An employee who checks the accuracy of front office accounting records and compiles a daily summary of hotel financial data as part of a night audit. In many hotels, the night auditor is actually an employee of the accounting division.

NIGHT SHIFT

A hotel workshift, generally 11:00 p.m. to 7:00 a.m.

NON-AFFILIATE RESERVATION NETWORK

A central reservation system which connects independent (non-chain) properties.

NON-AUTOMATED

A system of front office recordkeeping characterized by the exclusive use of handwritten forms. The elements of non-automated systems have determined the structure of many front office processes in even the most advanced automated facilities.

NON-GUARANTEED RESERVATION

A reservation arrangement where the hotel agrees to hold a room for the guest until a stated reservation cancellation hour on the day of arrival. The property is not guaranteed payment in the case of no-shows.

NON-GUEST ACCOUNT

An account created to track the financial transactions of a local business or agency with charge privileges at the hotel, a group sponsoring a meeting at the hotel, or a former guest whose account was not satisfactorily settled at the time of departure.

NON-GUEST FOLIO

A folio used to chart transactions on an account assigned to a non-guest business or agency with hotel charge purchase privileges.

NON-GUEST LEDGER

See **City Ledger.**

NO-POST STATUS

A term used to indicate a guest who is not allowed to charge purchases to his or her room account.

NO-SHOW

A guest who made a room reservation but did not register or cancel.

O

OBJECTIVE

A measurable end which an organization must achieve in order to effectively carry out its mission.

OCCUPANCY PERCENTAGE

An occupancy ratio which indicates the proportion of rooms sold to rooms available for sale during a specific period of time.

OCCUPANCY RATIO

A measurement of the success of the hotel in selling rooms. Typical occupancy ratios include average daily rate, average rate per guest, multiple occupancy statistics, and occupancy percentage.

OCCUPANCY REPORT

A report prepared each night by a front desk agent which lists rooms occupied that night and indicates those guests expected to check out the following day.

OCCUPIED

A room status term indicating that a guest is currently registered to the room.

ON-CHANGE

A room status term indicating that the guest has departed, but the room has not yet been cleaned and readied for resale.

ON-LINE

A condition in which a piece of hardware is capable of interacting directly with the central processing unit.

OPEN

The status of a date for which a reservation system can still accept reservations.

ORGANIZATION CHART

A schematic representation of the relationships between positions within an organization, showing where each position fits into the overall organization and illustrating the divisions of responsibility and lines of authority.

OUT OF BALANCE

A term used to describe the state when the totals of debit amounts and credit amounts for a set of accounts are not equal.

OUT-OF-ORDER

A room status term indicating that the room cannot be assigned to a guest. A room may be out-of-order for maintenance, refurbishing, extensive cleaning, or other reasons.

OVERAGE

An imbalance that occurs when the total of cash and checks in a cash register drawer is greater than the initial bank plus net cash receipts.

OVERBOOKING

Accepting reservations that outnumber available rooms.

OVERFLOW FACILITY

A property selected to receive central system reservation requests after room availabilities in chain properties within a geographic region have been exhausted.

OVERSTAY

A guest who stays after his or her stated departure date.

P

PACKAGE PLAN RATE

A special room rate for a room as part of a combination of events or activities.

PAID-OUT

Cash disbursed by the hotel on behalf of a guest and charged to the guest's account as a cash advance.

PARENT COMPANY HOTEL

A property which is owned and operated by a multiple-unit company. Parent company hotels often carry the same name, and their managers report to a central or corporate headquarters. The parent company typically establishes standard operating procedures.

PAYROLL ACCOUNTING MODULE

A back office computer application which processes such data as time and attendance records, pay distribution, and tax withholdings.

PBX (PRIVATE BRANCH EXCHANGE)

A hotel's telephone switchboard equipment. Also, the telephone switchboard department or function.

PIA (PAID IN ADVANCE)

A guest who pays his or her room charges in cash during registration. PIA guests are often denied in-house credit.

PICK-UP ERROR

An error on a posting machine which occurs when the user enters an incorrect previous balance in the process of posting.

POINT OF SALE

The location at which goods or services are purchased. Any hotel department that collects revenues for its goods or services is considered a revenue center and thus a point of sale.

POINT-OF-SALE (POS) SYSTEM

A computer network which allows electronic cash registers at the hotel's points of sale to communicate directly with a front office guest accounting module.

POSTING

The process of recording transactions on a guest folio.

POSTING MACHINE

See **Account Posting Machine.**

PREPAYMENT GUARANTEE

A type of reservation guarantee which requires a payment in full made before the day of arrival.

PRE-REGISTRATION

A process by which sections of a registration card or its equivalent are completed for guests arriving with reservations. Room and rate assignment, creation of a guest folio, and other functions may also be part of pre-registration activity.

PRINTER

An output device of a computer system that produces hard-copy output on paper.

PROGRAM

A set of instructions that command a computer system to perform useful tasks.

PROMOTIONAL RATE

A special room rate offered to promote future business.

PROPERTY DIRECT

A method of communicating reservation requests directly to a hotel, by telephone, mail, property-to-property link, telex, cable, or another method.

PROPERTY MANAGEMENT SYSTEM (PMS)

A computer software package which supports a variety of applications related to front office and back office activities. See also **Front Office Applications.**

Q

QUAD

A room assigned to four people; may have two or more beds.

QUALITY ASSURANCE

An approach to ensuring the consistent delivery of services.

QUEEN

A room with a queen-size bed; may be occupied by one or more people.

QUEEN BED

A bed approximately 60 inches by 80 inches.

R

RACK RATE

The standard rate established by the property for a particular category of rooms.

RATIO ANALYSIS

The analysis of financial statements and operating results using ratios.

READ

In reference to computers, to take data in for processing.

REFERRAL GROUP

A group of independent hotels which have banded together for the common good. Hotels within the group refer their guests to other affiliated properties.

REFUSAL REPORT

See **Turnaway Report.**

REGISTRATION

The procedure by which an incoming guest signifies his or her intent to stay at a property by completing and signing a registration card.

REGISTRATION CARD

A printed form for a registration record. In most states, the guest's signature on a registration card is required by law.

REGISTRATION RECORD

A collection of important guest information created by the front desk agent following the guest's arrival. The registration record includes the guest's name, address, telephone number, and company affiliation; method of payment; and date of departure.

RESERVATION

An agreement between the hotel and a guest that the hotel will hold a specific type of room for a particular date and length of stay.

RESERVATION CONFIRMATION

An oral or written verification of the information contained in a reservation record. See also **Letter of Confirmation.**

RESERVATION CONFIRMATION NUMBER

A code which provides a unique reference to a reservation record and assures the guest that the reservation record exists.

RESERVATION FILE

A computer-based collection of reservation records.

RESERVATION INQUIRY

A formulation of a reservation request which collects the proposed date of arrival, date of departure, type and number of rooms, room rate code, and number of persons in party.

RESERVATION RACKS

Racks which store lists of anticipated arrivals. In an advance reservation rack, reservation rack slips are arranged by the guests' scheduled dates of arrival and, within each day's grouping, alphabetically by the guests' or groups' names. A current reservation rack is a portable subset of the advance reservation rack used by front desk agents during registration.

RESERVATION RACK SLIP

A slip used in a reservation rack.

RESERVATION RECORD

A collection of data that identifies a guest and his or her anticipated occupancy needs before arrival at the property, and enables the hotel to personalize guest service and appropriately schedule needed staff.

RESERVATIONS AGENT

An employee, either in the front office or in a separate department within the rooms division, who is responsible for all aspects of reservations processing.

RESERVATIONS CONTROL BOOK

A binder with a tally page for each day of the year, used in non-computerized hotels to track reservations.

RESERVATIONS HISTORY

A collection of statistics on all aspects of the reservations process, including the number of guests, occupied rooms, reservations by source, no-shows, walk-ins, overstays, and understays.

RESERVATIONS MODULE

A front office computer application which enables a hotel to rapidly process room requests and generate timely and accurate rooms, revenue, and forecasting reports.

RESERVATION STATUS

An indicator of a room's long-term availability for assignment.

RESERVATIONS WALL CHART

A specially designed chart which displays hotel rooms vertically and days of the month horizontally. When accommodations are available, the reservations agent can assign a specific room by taping over the line that represents that room. Also called a reservations density chart.

RESERVATION TRANSACTIONS REPORT

A summary of daily reservations activity in terms of record creation, modification, and cancellation.

RESIDENTIAL HOTEL

A hotel whose guest quarters generally include a sitting room, bedroom, and kitchenette for permanent or semi-permanent guests. Many other types of hotels also offer residential accommodations, and residential hotels may offer short-term accommodations.

RESORT HOTEL

A hotel which provides scenery and activities unavailable at most other properties, and whose guests are typically vacationers. Resort hotels are the planned destination of their guests.

REVENUE CENTER

An operating division or department which sells goods or services to guests and thereby generates revenue for the hotel. The front office, food and beverage outlets, room service, and retail stores are typical hotel revenue centers.

REVENUE FORECAST REPORT

A projection of future revenue calculated by multiplying predicted occupancies by current room rates.

ROOM ASSIGNMENT

The identification and allocation to a guest of an available room in a specific room category, finalized as part of the registration process.

ROOMING

The procedures involved in greeting a guest, assigning a room, and escorting or directing the guest to the room.

ROOM NIGHT

One room occupied for one night.

ROOM RACK

An array of metal file pockets designed to hold room rack slips arranged by room number. The room rack summarizes the current status of all rooms in the hotel.

ROOM RACK SLIP

A form which contains the guest's name and other relevant information, completed during the registration process and placed in the room rack slot corresponding to the room number assigned to the guest.

ROOM RATE

The price a hotel charges for overnight accommodations.

ROOM RATE RANGE

The range of values between the limits dictated by the cost structure of the hotel.

ROOM REVENUE AND COUNT REPORT

A report which shows the rack rate for each room and the actual rate at which the room was sold, providing an opportunity to analyze room revenues.

ROOMS DIVISION

The division of a hotel which includes the front office, reservations, telephone switchboard, housekeeping, and uniformed service departments and functions. The rooms division plays an essential role in providing the services guests expect during a hotel stay.

ROOMS LEDGER

See **Guest Ledger.**

ROOMS MANAGEMENT MODULE

A front office computer application which maintains current information on the status of rooms, assists in the assignment of rooms during registration, and helps coordinate guest services.

ROOM STATUS

A code or description indicating the occupancy and housekeeping status of a room. Common room status terms include occupied, on-change, out-of-order, and check-out.

ROOM STATUS DISCREPANCY

A situation in which the housekeeping department's description of a room's status differs from the room status information which guides front desk employees in assigning rooms to guests.

ROOM STATUS REPORT

A report which allows front desk agents to identify vacant and ready rooms, typically prepared as part of the night audit.

ROOM VARIANCE REPORT

A report listing any discrepancies between front desk and housekeeping room statuses, as well as rooms which have not been sold at rack rates.

S

SCHEDULE

A departmental income statement referenced on the hotel's statement of income.

SECOND-PARTY CHECK

A check made out to the person presenting the check.

SECURITY MONITOR

A closed-circuit television monitor which allows front office employees to monitor security and safety throughout the hotel from a central location.

SELF CHECK-OUT

A computerized system, usually located in the hotel lobby, which allows the guest to review his or her folio and settle the account to the credit card used at check-in.

SELF-REGISTRATION

A computerized system which automatically registers a guest and dispenses a key, based on the guest's reservation and credit card information.

SELF REGISTRATION/CHECK-OUT TERMINAL

A piece of computer hardware typically located in the lobby of a fully automated hotel. Some resemble automated bank teller machines, while others are unique in design and may posses both video and audio capability.

SEMI-AUTOMATED

A system of front office recordkeeping characterized by the use of both handwritten and machine-produced forms and electro-mechanical equipment such as posting machines.

SEMI-PERMANENT FOLIO

See **Non-guest Folio.**

SERVICE BUREAU

A data processing business which enables properties to enjoy the benefits of automation without having to support in-house computer systems.

SETTLEMENT

The collection of payment for an outstanding account balance, bringing the balance to zero. A guest can settle an account by paying cash, charging the balance to a credit card, deferring payment to a direct billing, or using some combination of these payment methods.

SHORTAGE

An imbalance that occurs when the total of cash and checks in a cash register drawer is less than the initial bank plus net cash receipts.

SINGLE

A room assigned to one person; may have one or more beds.

SINGLE BED

A bed approximately 36 inches by 75 inches.

SKIPPER

A room status term indicating that the guest has left the hotel without making arrangements to settle his or her account.

SLEEPER

A room status term indicating that the guest has settled his or her account and left the hotel, but the front office staff has failed to properly update the room's status. The room is vacant, but is believed to be occupied.

SLEEP-OUT

A room status term indicating that a guest is registered to the room, but the bed has not been used.

SOFT COPY

Output on a display screen which cannot be handled by the operator or removed from the computer.

SOFTWARE

A set of programs that controls the operation of the hardware components of a computer system. Software tells the computer what to do, how to do it, and when to do it.

SPLIT FOLIO

An arrangement whereby a guest's charges are separated into two or more folios.

STATEMENT OF INCOME

A financial statement which provides important information about the results of hotel operations for a given period of time.

STAYOVER

A room status term indicating that the guest is not checking out today and will remain at least one more night.

STRATEGY

A method by which a department or division plans to achieve its goals.

STUDIO

A room with a studio bed—a couch which can be converted into a bed; may also have an additional bed.

SUITE

A parlor or living room connected to one or more bedrooms.

SUITE HOTEL

A hotel whose guestrooms have separate bedroom and living room or parlor areas, and perhaps a kitchenette.

SUPPLEMENTAL TRANSCRIPT

A detailed report of all non-guest accounts that indicates each charge transaction that affected a non-guest account that day, used as a worksheet to detect posting errors.

SUPPORT CENTER

An operating division or department which does not generate direct revenue, but plays a supporting role to the hotel's revenue centers. Support centers include the housekeeping, accounting, engineering and maintenance, and personnel functions.

SWITCHBOARD OPERATOR

An employee, in either the front office or a separate telephone department within the rooms division, who handles calls coming into the hotel and takes and distributes messages for guests.

SYSTEM UPDATE

A fully automated audit routine which accomplishes many of the same functions as a non-computerized night audit routine and more. Daily system updates enable file reorganization, system maintenance, and report production, and provide an end-of-day time frame.

T

T-ACCOUNT

A two-column account recording format (resembling the letter T) in which charges are posted to the left side and payments to the right side.

TELEWRITER

A device which transmits handwritten messages using a specially designed writing surface.

TELEX

An international communication network often used to communicate reservation requests. Telex communication is faster than the postal service and more reliable than the telephone since the hotel receives a written message.

TERMINAL

An input/output device of a computer system composed of a keyboard and a display screen or a printer.

THIRD-PARTY CHECK

A check made out to someone who has then signed the check over to the person presenting the check.

TIME-SHARE HOTEL

A group of condominium units whose owners associate and hire a management company to operate their units as a hotel. The condominium units normally contain bedrooms, living room, dining area, and kitchen.

TIME STAMP

A device to record the current time and date on folios, mail, and other front office paperwork.

TOUR GROUP

A group of people who have had their accommodations, transportation, and related activities arranged for them.

TOWER CONCEPT

See **Executive Floor.**

TRAINING OBJECTIVE

A description of a task which a trainee will be expected to demonstrate at the end of a training session.

TRANSACTION

The exchange of merchandise, property, or services for cash or a promise to pay.

TRANSACTIONAL ACCOUNTING SYSTEM

An accounting system in which the occurrence of a transaction initiates activity.

TRANSACTIONAL DOCUMENTATION

Paperwork which identifies the nature and amount of a transaction, and is the basis for data input to a front office accounting system.

TRANSFER VOUCHER

A voucher used to support a reduction in balance on one folio and an equal increase in balance on another. Transfer vouchers are used for transfers between guest accounts and for transfers from guest accounts to non-guest accounts when they are settled by the use of credit cards.

TRANSIENT HOTEL

See **Commercial Hotel.**

TRANSIENT LEDGER

See **Guest Ledger.**

TRAVEL AGENT GUARANTEE

A type of reservation guarantee under which the hotel generally bills the travel agency after a guaranteed reservation has been classified a no-show.

TRAVEL AND TOURISM INDUSTRY

A group of businesses which provide necessary or desired products and services to the traveler, comprising lodging operations, transportation services, food and beverage operations, retail stores, and activities.

TRAVELER'S CHECK

A prepaid check sold by banks and other financial institutions which is considered equivalent to cash.

TRIPLE

A room assigned to three people; may have two or more beds.

TURNAROUND TIME

The time which elapses between data input and information output in the data processing cycle.

TURNAWAY REPORT

A report which tracks the number of guests refused because rooms were not available as requested. Also called a refusal report.

TWIN

A room with two twin beds; may be occupied by one or more people.

TWIN BED

A bed approximately 39 inches by 75 inches.

TWIN-DOUBLE

See **Double-double.**

U

UNDERSTAY

A guest who checks out before his or her stated departure date.

UNIFORMED SERVICE

A department within the rooms division including parking attendants, door attendants, porters, limousine drivers, and bellpersons.

V

VACANT AND READY

A room status term indicating that the room has been cleaned and inspected, and is ready for an arriving guest.

VOUCHER

A document detailing a transaction to be posted to a front office account, used to communicate information from a point of sale to the front office. Common vouchers include cash, charge, transfer, allowance, and paid-out vouchers. Also, a form provided by travel agents to their clients as a receipt for advance registration payments. See also **Credit Card Voucher.**

VOUCHER RACK

A container for storing vouchers for future reference and verification during the night audit.

W

WAKE-UP DEVICE

A specially designed clock which allows multiple alarm settings to remind front desk agents or telephone operators to place wake-up calls.

WALK

To turn away a guest due to a lack of rooms.

WALK-IN

A person who arrives at a property without a reservation and requests a room.

WORLD-CLASS SERVICE

A level of service which stresses the personal attention given to guests. Hotels offering world-class service provide upscale restaurants and lounges, exquisite decor, concierge service, opulent rooms, and abundant amenities.

WRITE

In reference to computers, to send processed data out as information.

Z

ZERO OUT

To settle in full the balance of a folio account as the guest checks out.

Index

A

Access control, 143-144
  devices, 141
Account
  aging, 197
  allowance, see Allowance
  balance, 154
  correction, see Correction
  integrity, 172-173
  payable module, 71
  posting machine, see Posting, machine
  receivable, 156
  receivable ledger, 156
  receivable module, 71
  receivable voucher, 162
  transfer, 162-163
Accounting division, 32-33, 41, 42, 52, 144,
      153, 155, 157, 172, 189, 215, 228
Accounting transfer system, 82
Activity report, 185
  exhibit, 186
Actual to potential rooms revenue, 225
Adding machines, 53
Adjacent rooms, 48, 100
Adjoining rooms, 48
Advance deposit guaranteed reservation,
      78-79, 89
  cancelling, 93-94
Advertising, 18, 19-20, 82, 200, 264
Affiliate reservation network, 81-82
Aged accounts receivable report, 198
Airline companies, 82
Airport hotels, 6-7
Airport pick-up, 6, 13
Alarms
  silent, 149
  fire, 150
Allowance, 162
  voucher, 56, 156, 162
  voucher exhibit, 163
Ambience, 3, 11
Amenities, 5-6, 10, 12, 14, 46, 107, 261
American Hotel & Motel Association, 263
American plan, 110
Annual average daily rates, 223
Annual occupancy percentages, 223
Annual operations budget, 215
Appearance, 236
Application forms, 236-242, 264
Applications software, 280-286
Architecture, 3
Arrival stage, 46-50
Assistant manager, 34

B

B&Bs, 8
Back office interface, 70-71
Back of the house, 30
Back-up procedures, 286-288
Bail-out factor, 209
Balance sheets, 71
Bank, see Cash, bank
Banquets, 19, 32
Bars
  honor, 72
  in-room, 66
Batch programs, 284-285
Bed and breakfast hotels, 8
Bellpersons, 31, 141
Bell service, 117
Benefits, 33, 246
Beverages, in-room systems, 72, 156
Bilingual staff, 261
Billing
  and collection, 194-197
  cycle, 195
  policy, 195
  scheduling chart, 196
Binary digit, 272
Bit, 272
Block, 84, 111-112
Bookkeeping, 153
Bottom line, 226
Brand loyalty, 21-22
Budgeting, 215-219
Budget reports, 229-231
Business travel, 18
Butlers, 261
Buying influences, 19-22
Byte, 272

Audiovisual equipment, 10, 135
Audit
  posting formula, 173
  recapitulation sheets, 174, 176
  trail, 63, 176, 178
  work time, 172
Auditing, 50, 164
Authorization code, 115
Automation, lodging industry (exhibit), 55
Average daily room rate, 125, 216-218, 222,
      224
Average rate per guest, 224

C

Cable television, 5, 15
Call accounting systems, 66, 71, 177, 180, 194
Campgrounds, 11
Cancellation, 41, 86, 90-91, 92-94, 184, 212-213
  bulletin, 89-115
  hour, 78, 79, 89, 91, 92, 122
  number, 91, 92, 93
  number log (exhibit), 93
Career paths, 259, 264-265
Car rental, 5-6, 82-83
Carrier services, 66
Case studies, 255
Cash, 113, 114, 164, 171, 184
  advance, 163-164
  advance voucher, 163
  bank, 65, 144, 166
  deposit envelope, 166
  payment, 162, 190
  report, 177
  sheet, 164-166, 174, 177
  voucher, 57, 156, 162, 164
Cashier's checks, 113
Cash register, 53, 64-65, 144, 149, 276
  audit, 144
  electronic, 42, 70, 276
Casino hotels, 9, 34
Catering, 27, 32
Cathode ray tube, 276
Centralized electronic locking systems,
      142-143
Central processing unit, 274, 277
Central reservation systems, 40, 54, 68-69,
      79, 81-82, 83, 91, 100
Certified public accountants, 167
Chain hotels, 15-18
  management contract, 16-17
  parent company, 15-16
Charge
  privileges, 106, 158-160, 190
  purchase, 162
  vouchers, 42, 56, 156, 162
Charter flights, 9
Check guarantee services, 114-115
Check-out, 189-194
  notices, 193
  time, 212
Checks, 113-115
Choice of doors, 125-126
City accounts, 155
City ledger, 156, 157, 158, 169, 190, 191
  typical accounts, 195
Civic clubs, 3

Closed-circuit television, 67, 144
Coaching, 256
Collection, 158
  schedule, 196
Colleges, 262
Combined configuration, 280
Comment cards, 138
Commercial hotels, 5-6
Commercial rate, 111, 206
Commission agent report, 94
Communications, 129-133, 149
  equipment, 82
Compensation, 33
  for poor service, 162
Complaints, 33, 43, 50, 57, 123, 129, 136-140
Complimentary rate, 111, 206
Compressed work schedule, 37
Computers, 54, 57, 62, 64, 82, 95, 112, 135,
    177-178, 184-185, 259
  applications, 68-72
  in-room, 71, 192, 261
  mainframe, 273-274
  software, 280-286
  systems, 87-88, 271-289
Concierge, 12, 13, 40, 42-43, 50, 58, 104, 133,
    136, 261
Condominium hotel, 8-9
Conference, 5, 14
  centers, 9-10
  rooms, 6-7
  training, 254
Confirmation, 52, 70
  as binding, 96
  letter, 41, 54, 55, 90, 121
  letter exhibit, 91
  number, 89, 91, 92
Confirmed reservations, 90-92, 99
Connecting rooms, 48, 100
Control
  book, 84-86, 94, 215
  folio, 187
  key, 145
Controller, 231
Controlling, 204
Convention bureaus, *see* Housing/conven-
    tion bureaus
Conventions, 14, 19, 98, 99, 118, 123, 214-215
Coordinating, 204
Corporate guaranteed reservation, 79
Corporate rate, 206
Correction, 162
  voucher, 162
  voucher exhibit, 163
Cost of sales, 226
Coupons, 42, 117, 162, 197
Courtesy vehicles, 6, 104, 142
CPU, *see* Central processing unit
CR, 154
Credit, 154
  check, 39, 50, 113
  denial, 117, 118
  limits, 70, 160, 171, 173
Credit card, 41, 42, 89, 115-116, 155, 158-159,
    189
  check-cashing guarantee, 113-114
  companies, 184
  fraud, 115
  guaranteed reservation, 78
  guaranteed reservation, cancelling, 93

imprinter, 67
invalid, 115
invoice, 57
on-line authorization, 54, 67, 115
late charges, 195
transfer, 190-191
verification service, 89
voucher, 51, 116, 190
Credits, 158
CRT, *see* Cathode ray tube

D

Daily arrival and departure report, 87-88
Daily operations report, 220
  exhibit, 221
Daily report, 177, 184, 187, 220
Daily transaction report (exhibit), 179
Daily transcript, 174
  exhibit, 175
Daisywheel printers, 276
Dallet Jones, 86
Database, 190
  management software, 283-284
Data processing, 271-273
Day rate, 111
Day shift, 37
D card, 177
Death on premises, 149
Debit, 154, 158
Defamation of character, 240-243
Demonstration training, 254
Denial code, 115
Dentist lists, 149
Departmental activity reports, 171
Department detail and summary reports, 184
Departure
  date, 104, 210, 211
  stage, 51
Destination information center, 82
Direct billing, 41, 51, 54, 56, 57, 116, 155,
    158-159, 189
  transfer, 191
Directing, 204
Direct mail, 20
Direct reservations, 81, 83-84
Disabled access, *see* Handicapped guests
Discounts, 42
Discretionary income, 19
Discrimination, 120, 243-244
Disk operating systems, 286
Distributed configuration, 279
DNCO, 48
Door attendants, 31, 141
Door in the face, 125-126
Dot matrix printers, 276
Double-double, 48, 49
Double-entry bookkeeping, 154-155
Double occupancy, 225
  ratios, 222
DR, 154
Drunk/disorderly behavior, 120
Dry cleaning revenue, 220
Due back, 166, 184

E

Economy hotels, 14-15, 259-261
ECR, 40, 72, 276
Education, 262-263
Educational Institute of AH&MA, 263
Electro-mechanical systems, 53
Electronic cash registers, 42, 70, 276
Electronic locking systems, 62, 71, 119,
    142-143
Elevators, observation of, 144
Embezzlement, 173
Emergencies, 50, 148-150
Emergency key, 141-142
Employee
  folio, 156
  handbooks, 26, 246
  manual, 246
  part-time, 37
  relations, 33
  theft, 143
Employment agencies, 264
End of day, 172, 184
Engineering and maintenance, 33, 40, 131-132
Entertainment, 9, 14
Entrances, observation of, 144
Equipment, 52-54, 135
Escalators, observation of, 144
European plan, 110
Evaluating, 205, 219-234, 246-249, 257
Evening shift, 37
Executive floors, 12-13
Executive housekeeper, 31, 108-109
Expected arrival and departure lists, 94-95,
    187
Expected arrival lists, 41, 54, 69
Expenses, 218-219, 231
Expiration date, 115, 116
Express check-out, 191-192
  form (exhibit), 192

F

Facsimiles, *see* Fax machines
Fair Credit Billing Act, 196
False imprisonment, 116
Family rate, 111, 206
Fax machines, 66, 67, 130
Federal Fair Debt Collection Practices Act, 196
Financial reporting module, 71
Financial statements, 32
Fire, 150
First aid, 150
FIT, 80
Fixed disks, 278
Flextime, 37
Floor limit, 116, 160, 173
Floor plan, 47
  exhibits, 49, 112
Floor shows, 9
Floppy disks, 275, 278
Folios, 42, 46, 53, 54, 56, 57, 103, 106, 107,
    135-136, 155-156, 158, 176, 192
  bucket, 62, 175
  electronic, 54, 64, 155, 158, 177
  exhibit, 159

in-room review, 71
tray, 62, 63, 106, 158
Food and beverage division, 31-32
leased, 27
Foot in the door, 125-127
Forecasting
committee, 213
forms, 213-215
formula, 212-213
occupancy, 41, 47, 54
revenue, 41, 54
room availability, 208-215
Franchising, 17-18
Free independent traveler, 80
Front desk, 50, 57-58
as emergency command center, 149
design, 57-58
Front desk agent, 35-36, 39-40, 125, 141
job description, 237
Front office
accounting, 42, 113, 153-200
accounting formula, 160
agents, 39
audit, 51
cashier, 30, 32-33, 35-36, 41-42, 53, 64, 144,
149, 166
cashier job description, 238
cash sheet, 164-166
computer applications, 68-72
computer system, 64
equipment, 52-54, 58-67
forms, 55-57
goals, 36
ledger, 156, 157
manager, 222
manager job description, 205
operations, 35-39
organization, 35-36
systems, 52-54
update, 51
Front of the house, 30
Fully automated recordkeeping systems, 54
Future hotels, 259-261
Future room availability schedules, 56

G

Gambling, 9, 34
General management module, 70
General manager, 34, 231, 265
Goals, 26-27, 203
front office, 36
Government checks, 113
Graphics, 275, 283
Grounds, 33, 34
Groups, 84, 214-215
meetings, 9-10
rate, 111, 226
reservations, 84, 98-99, 100
reservations form (exhibit), 85
training methods, 254-255
Guaranteed reservation, 78-79, 89, 121,
122-123
Guest
account folio, *see* Folios
accounts, 35, 41, 50, 77, 155, 171
cycle, 45-54, 55-57, 88, 153

folios, *see* Folios
ledger, 156-157, 169, 190
ledger audit, 177
ledger report, 185
ledger report exhibit, 186
lists, 184-185
mail and messages, 40, 83-84, 129-130, 166,
191
relations, 50, 122, 136-140
service representative, 39
services, 35, 50, 51, 133-136, 199
signature, 104
valuables, 104, 141
Guest accounting, 32-33, 51, 135
cycle, 41, 47-50
module, 70
Guest history
database, 190
file, 51, 53, 77
record, 35, 47, 54, 57, 106, 107, 189, 190,
198-200
record software, 199
Guestroom key, 142

H

Handicapped guests, 58, 135
Hard copy, 276
Hard disks, 275, 278
Hard sell tactics, 40, 125
Hardware, 274-280
High balance account, 160, 173, 184
exhibit, 185
High risk accounts, 160
Hiring practices, discriminatory, 243-244
Honor bars, 72
Horizon, 52, 88
Hotel
airport, 6-7
bed and breakfast, 8
casino, 9
chains, 15-18
classifications, 4-18
commercial, 5-6
condominium, 8-9
conference center, 9-10
franchising, 17-18
independents, 15, 17
local association, 264
management programs, 262-263
referral groups, 17-18
residential, 8
resort, 8
suite, 7
theme, 261
transient, 5
House accounts, 155, 157, 160
Housekeeping, 31, 39, 51, 130-131, 190, 213
schedule, 107
status, 47, 53, 60, 107-108
status report, 109, 181
status report exhibit, 110
House limits, 160, 173
Housing/convention bureaus, 84, 98
Hubbart formula, 207-208, 234
Human resources, 33, 235, 236

I

Ideal average rate, 226, 227
Illness, 149
Image, 11, 15
Impact printers, 276
In balance, 181
Incentive
awards, 117
rates, 206
travel, 19
Income statement, 71
hotel, 226, 228
rooms division, 226-229
Independent certified public accounts, 167
Independent hotels, 15, 17
Information
book, 134-135
rack, 53, 56, 62, 104, 107
slips, 53
Ink jet printers, 276
Input/output units, 274-277
In-room bars, 66
In-room folio review, 71, 192
Insurance
companies, 16-17
forms, 246
Integrated configuration, 279
Integrated software, 285
Interactive programs, 284
Internal auditors, 167-169
Internal control, 164-169, 172-173, 187-188
inspection checklist, 167-169
Internal memory, 277
Intersell agency, 79, 81, 82-83
Interviewing, 235, 236, 243
evaluation form, 243, 245
Invoices, 187
Ironing boards, 135

J

Jargon, 99-100, 255
Job breakdowns, 246-250, 252, 255, 256
Job descriptions, 26, 35, 37-38, 235-236
front desk agent, 237
front office cashier, 238
front office manager, 205
reservations agent, 239
uniformed service, 240
Job lists, 246, 249, 250
Job sharing, 37
Job specifications, 35, 38-39, 235-243
Journal form, 154
Junior suite, 47-49

K

Key
control, 33, 40, 50, 141-143
deposit, 142, 194
rack, 60
return boxes, 142
Kilobyte, 272

L

Labor
  cost percentage, 232
  costs, 231, 232
  relations, 33
  schedules, 213, 215
Landscaping, 33, 34
Laser discs, 278
Laser printers, 276
Late charges, 51-52, 72, 156, 193-194, 194-195
Late check-out fees, 193
Laundry, 4
  revenue, 220
Laventhol & Horwath, 4, 226, 234
Least-cost routing, 66
Lecture training, 254
Ledgers, 156-157, 178
Lesson plans, 252
Liability, 144-145, 240
  notice (exhibit), 146
Libel, 240-243
Limited service hotels, 14-15
Limousine drivers, 31
Linen closet, 135
Lobby, 57, 144
Lockers, 246
Lock-out, 48
Locks, 119
Log book, 129, 131, 137, 138, 140
Long-distance service, 66, 130
Long-term leases, 16
Loss report form (exhibit), 148
Lost and found, 50, 147-148
Luggage, 118, 141

M

Magnetic strip reader, 67, 68, 115
Magnetic tape, 185, 277-278
Mail, 40, 83-84, 129-130, 166, 191
Mail and information clerk, 35-36, 40
Mail and message rack, 60, 62, 130
Mailing lists, 199
Mail, message, and key rack, 58, 60-61
Mainframe computers, 273-274
Maintenance, 33, 40
Management
  company, 8
  contracts, 16-17
  functions, 34-35
  process, 203-206
  reports, 94
Manager-on-duty, 34-35
Manager's report, 220
Managing personnel, 235-258
Marketing, 18, 32, 51, 125, 132-133, 190, 197
Master folio, 136, 155
Master key, 142
Mathematical aptitude, 38-39, 236
Medical emergencies, 149
Meeting planners, 84
Meeting rooms, 19
Megabyte, 272
Menu-driven, 284
Message lights, 61, 130
Messages, 40, 41, 191

Method of payment, 39, 47, 50, 104, 113-117
Microcomputers, 274
Micro-fitted electronic locking systems, 142
Minicomputers, 274
Mini-suite, 48, 49
Mission, 25-26, 27
  statement, 25-26
Mobile home parks, 11
Modified American plan, 110
Money orders, 113
Movie system, in-room, 71-72, 156
Multiple occupancy, 222-224
  ratios, 222-224
  statistics, 86

N

Net cash receipts, 166
Net income, 226
Net revenue, 226
Newsletters, 132-133
Night audit, 42, 51, 53, 56, 64, 70, 155, 160, 161, 171-188
  sequence, 178-185
Night auditor, 42, 54, 160, 164, 171-172, 197, 222
Night auditor's report, 177
Night shift, 37
Non-affiliate network, 81-82
Non-automated recordkeeping systems, 52-53
Non-guaranteed reservations, 79, 122
  cancel or change, 92, 93
Non-guest accounts, 155, 171
Non-guest folio, 155
Non-guest ledger, 157
No-post status, 106, 159
No-shows, 78, 91, 95, 170, 184
  billings, 93
  percentage of, 209-210, 214

O

Objectives, 26, 203
Occupancy
  data, 209
  forecast, 41, 54, 95, 208, 213
  history, 209
  percentage, 42, 172, 222
  ratios, 220-224
  report, 108-109
  stage, 50-51
  status, 109
Occupational Safety and Health Administration, 150
Off-line, 277
On-change, 48, 108, 190
On-line, 277
On-line verification, 115
Operating manuals, 249
Operating ratios, 232-234
Operational analysis, 52
Operational reports, 171
Order-takers, 119, 125

Organization charts, 27-30, 35
  samples, 36, 28, 29
Organizing, 203
Orientation, 243-246
OSHA, 150
Out of balance, 181
Outside contracting, 33
Overage, 166, 184
Overbooking, 84, 209
Overflow facilities, 81
Overstays, 95, 212
  percentage of, 210-211, 214

P

Package plan rate, 111, 206
Paid-in-advance lists, 113, 159
Paid-outs, 163, 166
  vouchers, 56, 156
Panel training, 254
Pannell Kerr Forster, 234
Parent company hotels, 15-16, 17
Parking, 4
Parking attendants, 31, 141
Part-time employees, 37
Passwords, 143
Payment method, *see* Method of payment
Payroll, 32, 213, 226
  accounting module, 71
  analysis, 232
  analysis form, 233
  checks, 113
  costs, 232
PBX, 30, 41
Performance evaluations, 249, 250
Performance standards, *see* Standards, performance
Personal checks, 113-115
Personal computers, 54, 274
Personality, 236
Personnel, 33. *See also* Human resources
Physician lists, 149
PIA, *see* Paid-in-advance
Pick-up error, 175
Planning, 203-219
Pleasure travel, 19
PMS, *see* Property management systems
Pneumatic tubes, 194
Point(s) of sale, *see* POS
Police, 150
Policy and procedures manual, 249
Poor service, compensation for, 162
Porters, 31
POS
  charge status, 107
  devices, 175
  equipment, 177
  registers, 42
  system, 71, 156
  terminals, 159
Positive reinforcement, 257
Post-dated checks, 114
Posting, 42, 50, 62, 155, 180, 181
  error, 162
  machine, 53, 62-64, 158, 175
Potential rooms revenue, 225
Pre-arrival stage, 45-46

Pre-departure folio, 191
Pre-employment inquiry guide, 244
Prepayment guaranteed reservation, 78, 89
Pre-registration, 39, 41, 46, 47, 53, 54, 69, 95, 103-104
Preventive maintenance, 137
Preview channel, 72
Printers, 71, 275, 276, 282
Private branch exchange, 30
Procedural requests, 135-136
Profit plan, 215
Project training, 255
Promotional
   materials, 197-198
   programs, 42, 259
   rates, 206
Property management systems, 68, 71
Public relations, 40, 132-133

Q

Quality assurance, 11-12, 33
Quality control, 12
Questionnaires, 18, 51, 138
   exhibit, 139

R

Rack rate, 109-110, 125, 182, 206
Random access memory, 277
Range check, 178
Rate schedules, seasonal, 110
Rates, special, 14
Ratios, as standards, 232-234
Read only memory, 277
Read/write memory, 277
Recordkeeping systems, 158
Recreation, 8, 33, 34
Recreational vehicle parks, 11
Recruiting, 204, 235-243
References, applicant, 235, 236, 240-243
Referral groups, 17-18
Referral network, 40
Re-forecasting, 219
Refusal report, 94
Refusing accommodations, 120-121
Register tapes, 172
Registration, 35, 39, 46-47, 103-127, 192
   book, 52
   card, 39, 51, 52, 53, 55, 103, 104-106, 114, 198
   card exhibits, 105, 106
   preprinted, 95
   process, 103-117
   record, 47, 104-106, 158
Research questionnaire, 18, 51, 138, 139
Reservation, 20, 30, 35, 68-69, 77-102, 122-123, 208
   agent, 35-36, 40-41, 46, 125
   agent job description, 239
   as contract, 96
   availability, 84-88
   cancellation, 41, 86, 92-94
   cancellation number, 91, 92
   card, 130
   centers, 82

changes, 41, 86
computer systems, 87-88
confirmation, 90-92, 187
confirmation number, 89, 91, 92
control book, 84-86, 94
density chart, 87
file, 55
form, 84
form (exhibit), 80
group, 84
histories, 95
horizon, *see* Horizon
inquiry, 79-84
maintenance, 92-94
mix, 77, 78
module, 54, 68-69
network, 53
problems, 99-101
rack, 55, 94, 184
rack, advance, 62, 69
rack, current, 62
record, 46, 55, 88-90, 93, 99, 103, 158
reports, 94-95
screen (exhibit), 81
status, 18, 39, 47, 107
systems, central, 40, 54, 68-69, 79, 81-82, 83, 91, 100-101
transactions report, 94
wall chart, 86, 94
Reserving credit, 116
Residential hotels, 8
Resident manager, 34
Resort hotels, 8, 42, 110
   guest histories and, 198
Resources, 203
Resumes, 264
Retail outlets, 34
Revenue
   centers, 28-30, 31, 42, 56, 132, 156, 171, 172
   center summaries, 187
   forecast report, 94
   forecasts, 54, 215-218
   report (exhibit), 180
Robbery, 149-150
   description form, 149
Role playing, 139, 255
Roll-away beds, 135
Room
   and key rack, 59
   availability forecasting, 208-215
   count checklist, 217
   count planning, 215
   diagrams, 49
   forecast formula, 212-213
   inspection, 190
   rack, 52-53, 59-61, 106, 108-109, 111, 172
   rack card, 53
   rack slip, 56, 107, 108
   revenue analysis, 225
   revenue and count report, 182-183
   revenue forecasts, 41
   revenue reports, 56
   revenues, 32, 42, 125, 172, 219
   service, 32, 66
   statistics, 220
   status, 35, 39, 47, 51, 66, 107-109, 130, 189-190
   status, computerized, 109
   status, definitions, 48

status discrepancies, 107-108, 171, 181, 187
status report, 185
types, 48
variance report, 187, 225
Room and rate assignment, 35, 46, 47, 52-53, 70, 77, 103, 106-113, 119
Room rates, 39, 90, 104, 107, 109-111, 182, 206-208
   and tax report, 184
   average daily, 216-218, 222
   Hubbart formula, 207-208, 234
   range, 109
   rule-of-thumb approach, 207
   schedule, 206
   special, 206
Rooms
   division, 30-31
   income statement, 226-229
   ledger, 157
   management module, 69-70
Rule-of-thumb approach, 207

S

Safe deposit boxes, 40, 42, 50, 144-147
Safes, 144
Safety, 33
Sales, 32
   and marketing, 32, 40
   journal, 172
   presentation, 119
   receipts, 64-65
Schedules, 227
Scheduling, 204
Second-party checks, 113, 114
Secretarial service, 12, 43
Security, 33, 50, 115-116, 117, 140-151
Self check-out, 192-193
Self-registration, 119, 120
Self-registration/check-out terminals, 67
Semi-automated recordkeeping system, 53
Seminars, 254, 263
Semi-permanent folio, 155
Separation of duties, 172-173
Service
   bureau, 32, 54
   directory, 40
   importance of, 20-21
   intangibility of, 11
   levels, 4, 11-15, 25-26, 259-261
   mid-range, 13-14
   world-class, 12-13
Settlement, 51, 55, 155, 164, 166, 169-170, 171, 189-200
Shortage, 166, 184
Simulation training, 255
Skipper, 48
Slander, 116, 240-243
Sleeper, 48, 108, 122
Sleep-out, 48
Smoke detectors, 150
Social directors, 8
Soft copy, 276
Software, 280-286
Sound equipment, 10
Source documents, 229
Special rates, 14, 206

Split folios, 135-136
Spreadsheet software, 282-283
Staffing, 38, 204, 208, 213
Stairways, observation of, 144
Stand-alone configuration, 279
Standard operating procedures, 16
Standards, 12, 15-16, 17, 215, 232-234, 250-258
    group, 249
    performance, 26, 235, 247-258
Statler, Ellsworth, 3, 267
Stayover, 48, 211
Stockholders meetings, 19
Storage of valuables, 55
Strategic marketing, 190, 199
Strategies, 26-27, 203
    front office, 36
Studio, 48
Suite hotels, 7, 18, 47-49
Summary files, 219
Supplemental transcript, 174
Supplies, 135
Support centers, 28-30
Supporting documents, 172
Surveillance, 50, 143-144
    equipment, 33
Switchboard, 30-31, 185
    operator, 35-36, 40, 41, 53, 56-57
System back-up, 184-185
Systems software, 285
System update, 171, 178, 185-188

T

T-account, 154
Tally sheet (exhibit), 86
Tape streamers, 278
Target market, 4
Tax withholding forms, 246
Teamwork, 43
Teleconferencing, 261
Telegrams, 166
Telephone
    equipment, 65-67
    services, 130
    room status systems, 66
Teletype terminal, 276
Television
    cable, 15
    closed-circuit, 67
    satellite, 15
Telewriter, 67, 108
Telex, 40, 67, 84
Tenants, 8

Ten-day forecast, 213-215
Theme hotels, 261
Thermal printers, 276
Third-party checks, 113, 114
Three-day forecast, 215
Ticket office service, 12
Time-share hotels, 8-9
Time stamp, 67, 130
Touch-screen terminal, 276
Tour
    groups, 5, 14, 98-99, 118, 123
    operators, 84, 98
    rates, 226
Tower concept, 12
Trade associations, 19
Trade schools, 262
Training, 33, 38, 204, 235, 246-258, 288
    five-day plan, 251
    five-step method, 250-258
    group methods, 254-255
    manuals, 26
    methods, 252
    objectives, 252
Transactional accounting system, 161-164
Transactional analysis reports, 71
Transactional documentation, 172, 178
Transaction tapes, 64-65
Transfer voucher, 56, 57, 156, 163
Transient hotels, 5
Transient ledger, 157
Travel
    agent, 18, 20, 40, 79, 84, 89, 98, 122, 184
    agent guaranteed reservation, 79
    agent guaranteed reservation, cancelling, 94
    and tourism, 3-4
    business, 18
    groups and conventions, 19
    pleasure, 19
    purpose for, 18-22
Traveler's checks, 113
Trial balances, 54
Turnaway report, 94
Turnaround time, 272
Turn-down service, 12
Typing skills, 38-39, 236

U

Uncollectible accounts, 196-197
Undated checks, 114
Understays, 95
    percentage of, 211-212

Uniformed service, 4, 31, 50, 53
    job description, 240
Uniforms, 246
Union contracts, 36
Union placement office, 264
United States Postal Service, 129-130
Upselling, 119-120, 125-127

V

Valuables, 141, 144-147
Variances from budget, 230-231
Videophones, 261
VIP list, 123
Volatile memory, 277
Volume purchase discounts, 16
Vouchers, 53, 56, 117, 156, 160, 161, 172, 176, 181
    allowance, 56, 162
    allowance exhibit, 163
    cash, 57, 164
    charge, 56
    correction, 162
    correction exhibit, 163
    credit card, 51, 116, 190
    paid-out, 56
    rack, 63, 64
    transfer, 56, 57, 163

W

Wage and hour laws, 36
Waiting lists, 96
Wake-up calls, 31, 37, 41, 66, 67, 130
Walking the guest, 122
Walk-ins, 47, 53, 54, 95, 121-122, 214
    percentage of, 210
Wall chart, 86-87, 94
Wet bar, 7
Word processing software, 281-282
Work orders, 132, 137
    exhibit, 133
Work schedules, 246
Worksheets, 219
Workshifts, 36-37

Z

Zero out, 190

Richard C. Nelson, CHA
Regional Vice President,
 Managing Director
Grand Hyatt Washington
Washington, D.C.

Jerome J. Vallen, CHA
Professor
William F. Harrah College of Hotel
 Administration
University of Nevada, Las Vegas
Las Vegas, Nevada

John A. Norlander, CHA
President
Radisson Hotel Corporation
Minneapolis, Minnesota

Peter E. Van Kleek, CHA
Dean, School of Hotel/
 Restaurant Management
Northern Arizona University
Flagstaff, Arizona

Thomas W. Staed, CHA
President
Oceans Eleven Resorts, Inc.
Daytona Beach Shores, Florida

Jack J. Vaughn, CHA
General Manager, Opryland Hotel/
Senior Vice President, Opryland
 USA, Inc.
Nashville, Tennessee

William R. Tiefel
President
Marriott Hotels & Resorts
Washington, D.C.

Larry K. Walker, CHA
President
Cypress Hotel Management
 Company
Orlando, Florida

Educational Institute Fellows

Stephen W. Brener, CHA
President
Stephen W. Brener Associates, Inc.
New York, New York

Patrick J. Gorman
Chairman & Chief Executive Officer
Encore Marketing International, Inc.
Lanham, Maryland

Richard W. Brown, CHA
Vice President & Assistant
   to the Chairman
Banfi Vintners
Old Brookville, New York

Arnold J. Hewes
Executive Vice President
Minnesota Hotel Assn.
St. Paul, Minnesota

Melinda Bush, CHA
Publisher, Hotel & Travel Index/
Executive Vice President, Hotel
   Directories
Reed Travel Group
Secaucus, New Jersey

H. Steven Norton, CHA
Executive Vice President
Resorts International, Inc.
Atlantic City, New Jersey

Peter C. Crafts, CHA
Coordinator, Hotel & Lodging
   Program
Fanning School of Health &
   Technical Occupations
Worchester, Massachusetts

W. Kirk Smith, CHA
Chairman & Chief Executive
   Officer
Southern Host Hotels, Inc.
Norcross, Georgia

Richard L. Erb, CHA
Chief Operating Officer
Grand Traverse Resort
Acme, Michigan